Generalist Practice

SECOND EDITION

Generalist Practice

A TASK-CENTERED APPROACH

Eleanor Reardon Tolson • William J. Reid • Charles D. Garvin

Columbia University Press   New York

Columbia University Press
Publishers Since 1893
New York   Chichester, West Sussex

Library of Congress Cataloging-in-Publication Data
Tolson, Eleanor Reardon, 1942–
    Generalist practice : a task-centered approach / Eleanor Reardon Tolson,
    William J. Reid, Charles D. Garvin—2nd ed.
        p.   cm.
    Includes bibliographical references and indexes.
    ISBN 0–231–12182–2 (cloth : alk paper)

    1. Social case work.   2. Social group work.   3. Family social work.
    4. Task-centered social work.   I. Reid, William James, 1928–
    II. Garvin, Charles D.   III. Title.

HV43.T6 2003
361.3'2—dc21

                                                            2002067616

Columbia University Press books are printed on permanent
and durable acid-free paper.
Printed in the United States of America
c 10 9 8 7 6 5 4 3 2 1

To Fred, Ricky, and Janet

CONTENTS

AUTHORS AND CONTRIBUTORS

Charles D. Garvin, Ph.D., is professor emeritus at the School of Social Work, University of Michigan. He has taught in both masters and doctoral programs and is a past director of the Joint Doctoral Program in Social Work and Social Science. Many of his numerous articles concern small groups, and his books include three editions of *Contemporary Group Work*, two editions of *Interpersonal Practice in Social Work*, and two editions of *Social Work in Contemporary Society*, all published by Allyn & Bacon. He is the co-editor of *Direct Practice*, published by Sage, and of the journal *Small Group Research*.

Bageshwari Parihar, Ph.D., is a partner and CEO of Therapeutic Interventions, Inc., a substance-abuse treatment center, and director of the Rolling Meadows Counseling Services, which provides counseling and consultation services, in Rolling Meadows, Illinois. He has also been Deputy Director of Programs at Englewood Community Mental Health Organization and an administrator at Martha Washington Hospital Alcoholism Treatment Center. He has taught social work at Louisiana State University and at Kashi Vidyapith in India. He has written *Task-Centered Management in Human Services*, as well as a number of articles in the areas of management and alcoholism.

Gregory L. Pettys, Ph.D., is an assistant professor at the School of Social Work, Brigham Young University, where he teaches research, human behavior, and cultural diversity. He has also taught at Washburn University at Topeka. His research interests include international and cross-cultural social work. He has published articles about Asian Indian immigrants and identity, media stereotypes of the elderly, and international field placements.

Kollengode R. Ramakrishnan, Ph.D., is a professor of social work at West Texas A&M. His scholarly interests and publications center on community development, especially in developing countries; population control; and teenage pregnancy. He has worked as a community organizer for the Economic Opportunity Agency, Little Rock, Arkansas.

Blanca M. Ramos, Ph.D., is an assistant professor at the School of Social Welfare and the Department of Latin American and Caribbean Studies, State University of New York at Albany. She teaches practice and social work with culturally diverse clients. Her scholarly interests focus on cross-cultural social work. She has extensive experience as a clinical social worker and community organizer with vulnerable populations.

William J. Reid, D.S.W., is a Distinguished Professor at the School of Social Work, State University of New York at Albany, where he teaches research methods and clinical practice. His most recent books are *Science and Social Work: A Critical Appraisal* (with Stuart Kirk) and *The Task Planner,* both published by Columbia University Press.

Eleanor Reardon Tolson, Ph.D., is associate professor emerita at the Jane Addams College of Social Work, University of Illinois at Chicago, where she taught practice, research, and human behavior. She has also taught at the Universities of Chicago and Washington. Her authored and edited books include *The Metamodel and Clinical Social Work, Perspectives on Direct Practice Evaluation,* and *Models of Family Treatment.*

PREFACE

Generalist Practice: A Task-Centered Approach is intended to be used in practice classes for undergraduate and entry-level graduate students. The first edition of this volume was prompted by the accreditation standards of the Council on Social Work Education which require that generalist practice methods be taught to these students. The accreditation standards present a challenge to practice instructors who must now teach students to work with a variety of systems without sacrificing skill mastery. It was hoped that by explicating the task-centered approach with individuals, families, groups, organizations, and communities in one volume, and with a numbering system that permits content to be studied by topic as well as by system, the challenge would be more easily met.

The book has now been used to teach thousands of students, and it appears that a task-centered approach can be applied successfully across systems and that teaching one method enhances students' skills. The integration of task-centered and generalist practice provides a practice model with specific, tested treatment directives and is responsive to environmental contexts.

In this, the second edition of *Generalist Practice: A Task-Centered Approach*, we have updated the literature, included more case examples, and modestly expanded content about systems and ecological theory as well as other approaches to practice. Most important, we have added chapter 16, which describes the use of task-centered practice with culturally diverse clients.

As noted, a numbering system is employed so that the content can be studied by topic and repetition is minimized. The numbering system is explained at the end of chapter 1. We have found that once readers understand this system, they appreciate its benefits.

Many colleagues and students have contributed to the task-centered approach. Although they are too numerous to name, we are grateful to each and every one of them. We are particularly grateful to those whose work with clients appears in this book: Monica Glaser, Denise Kane, Susie Merrihew, Nick Natale, and Ed Nieminen. Ronald H. Rooney provided case material, the group recording guides, and the task review schedule. We are in his debt. We also acknowledge the support and technical contributions of staff members at Columbia University Press for both editions of this book: John Michel (editor), Gioia Stevens, Anne McCoy, and Rita Bernhard.

Generalist Practice

I

INTRODUCTION: TASK-CENTERED AND GENERALIST PRACTICE

The hallmark of generalist practice is the ability to work with multiple systems including the individual, family, small group, organization, and community. The necessity for developing this capacity rests on five observations. First, the difficulties people confront are usually multidetermined. This means that there are multiple causes for problems. For example, a learning disability, a disorganized family, and an inadequate school system might all contribute to the problem of truancy. The effective resolution of the problem would require work with the child, the family, and the school. Second, systems of all sizes experience challenges and turn to social workers for help. Third, people and their social and physical environments are inextricably interconnected and, as a result, social workers must be prepared to work with client systems, their environments, and the interactions between them (Miley, O'Melia, and DuBois 2001). Fourth, it is often more efficient to include work with larger systems when the same problem is experienced by a number of people or families. Fifth, prevention and reform efforts usually require work with multiple systems.

The challenge is to acquire the skills necessary to work effectively with a variety of systems, problems, populations, and settings in a relatively short period of time. This challenge has been accentuated by the Council of Social Work Education (CSWE) which, by means of its acreditation standards, requires a generalist orientation to be taught at the undergraduate level and at the entry level of graduate programs

(Sheafor and Landon 1987). We believe that mastering one practice approach, task-centered (TC), that has been applied across systems and with a large array of clients and problems produces competent generalist practitioners. TC has two additional advantages as the core approach for generalist practice. It has been rigorously tested and found effective, and it is an open framework, which means that it can accommodate interventions drawn from other approaches.

1.1.0 THE GENERALIST PERSPECTIVE

A useful description of the generalist worker is as follows: "The generalist social worker [has] the tools to work in various settings with a variety of client groups, addressing a range of personal and social problems and using skills to intervene at practice levels ranging from the individual to the community" (Schatz, Jenkins, and Sheafor 1990:219). Some definitional confusion pertains to the distinction between generalist practice and generic knowledge. Generic knowledge is that which is common to all social workers. For example, all social workers share knowledge about values and human behavior. Although we touch on issues that are part of our generic knowledge base, like values and human development, the topic of this book is generalist practice.

The roots of the generalist perspective have been traced to the inception of social work with the Charity Organization Society (COS) in the late 1800s (Sheafor and Landon 1987). The COS workers, as well as the settlement house workers who followed, were concerned not only with the plight of individuals but with the social conditions that produced those plights. In other words, both groups were concerned about the individual in the environment and the transactions between the two. Others (Schatz, Jenkins, and Sheafor 1990) trace the generalist perspective to the Milford Conferences, which occurred during the 1920s. By that time a number of specialized social services had evolved and the conferences were established to identify the generic elements within social casework. The need to identify generic content for the purpose of establishing a professional identity was made more urgent by the merger of several social work professions into the National Association of Social Workers in 1958.

Although these phenomena and others foreshadowed the development of a generalist orientation, it was not until the seventies that scholarly attempts to develop holistic practice approaches emerged. The first of them was Bartlett's *Common Base of Social Work Practice* (1970). Volumes by Meyer (1970), Pincus and Minahan (1973), Goldstein (1973), Siporin (1975), Morales and Sheafor (1977), Germain and Gitterman (1980), and Hartman and Laird (1983) followed. These efforts were particularly notable for developing two themes. One is the common knowledge or skill necessary for a "goal oriented planned change process" (Pincus and Minahan 1973:xiii) across the traditional specializations (casework, group work, and community organization) or the various system levels. A second theme is the relationship between systems and their environments. Both the literature and the movement toward generalist practice continued into the 1980s culminating in the curriculum policy statements of CSWE.

In spite of many efforts, the generalist orientation has not been uniformly defined or developed. In fact, there is disagreement about whether it is a model for practice or a perspective for practice. Sheafor, Horejsi, and Horejsi (2000) define a perspective as a way of viewing or thinking about practice: "The generalist perspective focuses a worker's attention on the importance of considering . . . various levels of intervention (51)." A model (or an approach) for practice is, in contrast, a set of procedures that tell the practitioner what to do. Models for practice are specific and often the result of research, whereas perspectives are general and testing their effect is very difficult, if not impossible. In spite of the definitional debate, a number of principles for generalist approaches have been articulated:

1. Incorporation of the generic foundation for social work and use of multilevel problem-solving methodology.
2. A multiple, theoretical orientation, including an ecological systems model that recognizes an interrelatedness of human problems, life situations, and social conditions.
3. A knowledge, value, and skill base that is transferable between and among diverse contexts, locations, and problems.
4. An open assessment unconstricted by any particular theoretical or interventive approach.

5. Selection of strategies or roles for intervention that are made on the basis of the problem, goals, and situation of attention and the size of the systems involved.
(Group for the Study of Generalist and Advanced Generalist, as cited in Schatz, Jenkins, and Sheafor 1990:223)

The relationship between these principles and TC will be described in the following section.

1.2.0 THE TASK-CENTERED APPROACH

TC was developed in the early 1970s by Reid and Epstein (1972). It falls within the category of approaches referred to as "problem solving." Problem solving, as an approach to social work practice, was first articulated by Helen Harris Perlman (1957). TC has the following characteristics:

1. As noted, it is a problem-solving method of intervention.
2. It is highly structured, which means that the procedures for implementing the model are specific.
3. It focuses on solving problems as clients perceive them.
4. It is time-limited.
5. It is theoretically open and thus can be used with many theoretical orientations.
6. Change occurs through the use of tasks, which are activities designed to ameliorate the identified problems. Tasks can be developed from an array of practice approaches, as well as from problem-solving activities with clients.
7. It is present-oriented.
8. It is an empirical approach to practice in that it (a) was developed from research findings about practice; (b) was constructed with concepts that are researchable; (c) has been tested and found effective; and (d) contains within its procedures activities necessary to evaluate case outcomes.
9. It is appropriate for use with culturally diverse clients, as discussed in chapter 16.

Like the rationale for learning to be a generalist, the rationale for employing TC is based on several factors. First, it is in concert with many of the principles of generalist practice, including its problem-solving focus; openness to multiple theoretical orientations; and procedures that are transferable among a variety of systems, problems, populations, and settings. Second, TC has been tested and found effective with individuals and families. It is one of very few approaches to social work practice that can make this claim. Research findings will be detailed in the following chapters. Third, TC has been applied to work with all systems—individual, family, group, organization, and community. Fourth, it is relatively easy to incorporate interventions from other approaches into the TC framework. Examples of this will be provided in the following chapters. Finally, TC is consistent with the orientation that survey research has found to be most frequently used: "Thus, it appears that action-oriented and task-centered methods are increasingly being used to teach social work practice" (LeCroy and Goodwin 1988:47).

Although TC has many advantages, we are not suggesting it is a magic bullet (were there a magic bullet, social workers would not be needed). Indeed, in some cases, the desired goals will not be reached; in others, no progress may be made at all. Rather, our argument is that, in most cases, TC should be the approach of first choice. The rationale for this position rests on (1) the advantages described in the preceding paragraph; (2) the literature on dropouts; and (3) the relative ease of moving from TC to other approaches, rather than vice versa.

The literature on dropouts indicates that a substantial percentage of clients leave treatment prematurely, that the suspected cause in a number of these cases is the lack of congruence between worker and client with respect to the focus of treatment or target problem, and that the drop-out rate might be lower in time-limited modalities. Since TC mandates congruence on target problems and is time-limited, relying on it as the approach of first choice should enable us to engage more clients whom we might otherwise lose.

With respect to movement away from TC, our experience has been that, when TC has been insufficiently effective, clients are generally amenable to trying other, more complicated, and more time-consuming approaches. We think this occurs because they have experienced for themselves that a parsimonious and straightforward approach is not adequate.

1.3.0 GENERALIST PRACTICE, THE TASK-CENTERED APPROACH, AND THE ECOSYSTEMS PERSPECTIVE

The development of generalist practitioners is obviously a highly desirable goal. The practical problem in accomplishing this goal is that an enormous amount of time would be required if students had to learn a unique approach to practice for each system and each situation. It is our hypothesis that educating students to use TC with systems ranging from the individual to the community will produce competent beginning-level generalists within a reasonable period of time. The openness of both TC and the generalist perspective also provide a sound base for incorporating other theories and intervention procedures as skill levels mature. In addition to the practical problem involved in educating generalist practitioners, there is a conceptual problem. This problem concerns helping practitioners to recognize the possibility and necessity of working with systems other than the most immediate ones—those that present themselves or those to which others refer us. A solution to this problem lies in the ecosystems perspective, which enables us to see people and problems in their environmental contexts and about which a large, robust literature exists. However, since the ecosystems perspective continues to evolve, there is no one description of it on which everyone agrees. Since space limits us here to only a brief description of this perspective, the reader is encouraged to consult additional sources (see, for example, Germain and Gitterman 1996; Kemp, Whittaker, and Tracy 1997; Meyer and Mattaini 1995; and Norlin and Chess 1997).

The ecosystems perspective is a collage of two bodies of theory: ecological theory and general systems theory. It is called a "perspective" because it provides a way of thinking about people and their environments rather than offering domain-specific content or a methodology for practice (Meyer 1983; Kemp, Whittaker, and Tracy 1997). Ecological theory has been borrowed from zoology, and the word *ecology* refers to the relationship between an animal and its environment. The fundamental proposition in this perspective is that human systems and environments are in constant interaction and in a continual process of adaptation and accommodation that is mutually influencing. For our purpose, the most useful concept from this perspective is the ecomap, one version of which is illustrated in Figure 1.1. Other important concepts are habitat (the physical and social environment), niche (the place the system occupies), goodness-of-fit (the extent to which there is a harmony between the system and the environment), stress (result of a misfit), and coping (strategies to ameliorate stress).

Systems theory combines ideas from a number of fields including information theory and biology. Like ecological theory, it stresses the importance of the relationship between people and their environments. For our purposes, its most salient contributions are the definition of a system and the concept of boundaries. A system is defined as a complex of elements that form an organized, interrelated whole. Two of the concepts that capture some of the organization of systems are hierarchy and subsystems. Using a family system as an example, it is apparent that the family members are the elements that, taken together, form the whole or the unit. Boundaries are evident because we can define who is part of the system and who is not. Families exhibit a clear hierarchy, with parents expected to have more power than children. It is also apparent that the work of the family is carried out by subsystems, such as the marital, parental, and sibling subsystems. The division of power and labor and the number of subsystems are more complex in larger systems like organizations. The concept of boundaries is used to examine the amount of information exchanged between systems or subsystems. When boundaries are rigid, little information is exchanged. When they are open, adequate amounts of information are exchanged. When they are porous, too much information is exchanged and one system can be overwhelmed by another. Other useful concepts include steady state and homeostasis (the tendency of systems to maintain a dynamic equilibrium and the mechanisms for doing so) and equi- and multifinality (the relationship between means and ends).

The fundamental contribution of an ecosystems perspective to task-centered generalist practice is that it expands our ability to recognize the possibilities and necessity to work with a variety of systems. The ecomap in Figure 1.1 is derived from ecological theory and can be used to analyze human situations within this perspective. Typically, however,

FIGURE 1   *Systems and Target Problems*

the individual, rather than the problem, is nested in the center of the concentric circles. We have placed the problem at the center, because it is the target of change in this approach to practice.

Examination of the various systems within the concentric circles enables us to consider how each contributes to the existence of the problem. The example of a child failing academically has already been used to illustrate this kind of examination. Consider another example: child abuse or neglect.

Individual: the child might be "hard-to-manage."

Family: the parent(s) might be deficient in resources, problem-solving skills, or impulse control.

Organization: child welfare workers might be overloaded and parent education nonexistent.

Community: the community might be transient and without the capacity to provide social support.

Society: this society tends to regard children as property.

(Garbarino 1982)

Ecological theory thus provides a useful road map for examining problems in context. Each of the systems should also be considered with respect to the way the problem affects the system. For example, a serious illness can have a debilitating effect on family members, as well as on the individual patient. A serious illness that affects many people, like autoimmune deficiency syndrome (AIDS), has a devastating effect on individuals, families, organizations that serve the patients, the communities in which they reside, and the society as it struggles to protect individual rights in the face of a feared epidemic.

Finally, the likely impact of each system for solving or alleviating the problem needs to be considered. Which system is most likely to resolve the particular problem of academic failure, child abuse, or physical illness?

Thus, for each problem we are asked to address, we must consider each of the systems identified—individual, family, community, organization, and society—with three questions in mind. First, what is the role of this system in causing or maintaining the problem? Second, what is the impact of the problem on each of the systems? Third, what is each system likely to contribute to solving the problem? Finally, we can consider the context as a whole and with respect to the concept of "goodness of fit," that is, the extent to which the context promotes the growth of the primary systems.

In addition to helping us analyze the involvement of each system, the ecosystems perspective, through the concept of boundaries, enhances our ability to examine the interactions among systems. For example, an eight-year-old child, Oliver Wilson, was referred for behavioral problems in school. The teacher and principal cared about the child and were using appropriate means to modify his behavior but with little success. During a home visit, the social worker met a nurturing and concerned mother who reported that her son was well behaved at home. The clue to the problem came at the very end of the visit. When the social worker asked Ms. Wilson if she had any questions, the mother replied, "There's one thing that I don't understand. When Oliver acts up at home, I don't call the school. I don't understand why they call me." This question indicated that the problem resulted from rigid boundaries between the systems, with little information exchange.

When communication in the form of home report cards was established, the problem was resolved.

1.4.0 SELECTING THE SYSTEM FOR WORK

Consideration of the questions identified in section 1.3.0 will identify the possibilities for work with the various systems. The next step is to choose that system with which we will conduct most of our work in our attempt to resolve target problems. The chosen system will be referred to as the primary system. This does not mean that other systems will be ignored. Our decisions, at this point in our knowledge development, will have to be based on our best judgments and practice wisdom since no empirical literature exists to guide us.

Actual system selection probably entails consideration of four variables: problem identifier, problem location, location of necessary changes, and problem-solver location. First, the system that identifies the problem is important, because, in many cases, identifying a problem indicates both motivation and accessibility for working toward solving it.

Second, the system in which the problem is located indicates where the impact must be made. Sometimes different people will identify different locations for the same problem. For example, teachers often locate problems of children in the child, whereas the child often locates the problem in the teacher. Thus the teacher is saying that the child is bad, and the child is saying that the teacher is mean. Someone else might say that the school system is inadequate. Yet another person might say that the problem is located in our society, which tolerates poverty. These locations are determined by explanations about the *causes* of problems. When we refer to the location of a problem, we are not referring to the location of the cause of the problem. Rather, we are referring to where change will be seen. If, then, a child is truant, the desired change—school attendance—will be seen in the child's behavior. Thus the child is the location of the problem to be changed.

Third, the system in which changes must occur to achieve problem alleviation must be determined. This brings us to the consideration of the problems' causes, as identified above. Continuing the truancy example, the child might be truant because of conditions in the family, the school, or the neighborhood. Exploration of the truancy problem will reveal which systems are interfering with the child's school attendance.

Finally, the system best able to make the necessary changes must be considered. In the case of truancy, the problem location is the child. The system in which changes must occur to solve the problem might be the family. But the family conditions might be sufficiently chaotic that homemaker services are necessary. Thus the system best able to make the changes becomes the social welfare agency, which must be persuaded to provide a homemaker.

Some examples are in order. A married couple seeks help for marital communication problems. In this case, the problem identifier and location of the problem, necessary changes, and problem solvers are all the same: the couple. The couple, then, becomes the primary system for work.

A child is referred for truancy. On exploration, the social worker learns that the mother is keeping the child at home to provide care for younger children because the mother is temporarily incapacitated. The mother agrees to allow the social worker to help her find other alternatives. In this case, the problem (truancy) is located in the child but changes must occur in another system (family) for the problem to be solved. It is likely the problem can be solved by the combined efforts of the family and the social worker. The primary system becomes the family.

A woman complains that she cannot allow her children to play outside because the neighborhood is too dangerous. This problem cannot be solved by the woman and the social worker alone. If community groups exist that are willing to take on the problem, then the problem location, location for change, and problem solving are all located in the same system: the community. The community groups become the primary system.

A community group has become concerned about the physical deterioration of the neighborhood. It learns that residents cannot borrow money for home repairs because of an illegal banking practice called "red-lining." The group gathers evidence to bring this practice to the authorities' attention. Here the problem is located in one system, the community, but the solution is in the hands of another system, an organization (banks), and the organization is unwilling to change. Thus another organization (banking regulators) becomes involved to enforce the law and solve the problem. The primary system for work is the community group.

As these examples illustrate, only one firm rule exists for choosing the primary system, namely, its willingness to accept help. In some cases, the primary system will be the one in which the problem is located. In other cases it will be the system that must change in order for the problem to be alleviated. In still other cases, it will be the problem-solving system. Decisions are easiest when all three are the same.

The primary system will usually reflect one of the three following conditions:

1. The system has an internal problem that is capable of being resolved internally and either requests or agrees to accept help to resolve it;
2. The system has an external problem, either requests or agrees to accept help to resolve it, and alleviation of the problem is expected to be possible through the combined resources of the system and social worker; and
3. Change in the system is necessary to solve the problem of another system, and the system agrees to help.

One system is not covered by these guidelines for selecting a primary system. That system is the small group when the group is not a natural one. In these circumstances, the small group is constructed by the social worker for the purpose of solving the problems of another system—usually the individual. Group treatment is offered because it seems the most likely and efficient avenue to achieving the desired changes. When the group is a natural one, like a group of tenants, the guidelines can be applied. The issue of deciding to use group treatment will be covered in part 4. In fact, the issue of selecting systems will be covered in each of the sections that follow.

Two final comments about choosing appropriate systems are in order. First, although one primary system will usually exist, often we will need to work with other systems to some extent. Second, we will, at times, err in selecting primary systems. The mistake will manifest itself through our inability to resolve targeted problems. The remedy is, of course, to try to engage the system that is needed to resolve the problems successfully.

1.5.0 COLLATERALS AND REPRESENTATIVES OF OTHER SYSTEMS

Collaterals are people involved with the primary system. They might be personally or professionally related to the primary system. For example, when the primary system is an individual, collaterals might include family members and schoolteachers or physicians. Work with collaterals has always been a component of TC. We do not hesitate to involve them on the client's behalf *provided* they are important to problem resolution and the client has granted permission. Clients are always fully informed about our contacts with collaterals.

Although, in this chapter, we have used the generalist phrase "work with other systems," in fact we rarely work with other entire systems. More often we work with representatives of other systems like individual family members or friends, teachers, physicians, or public assistance workers. In other words, we work with collaterals.

Thus it may appear that the TC approach is no different than the generalist approach with respect to the inclusion of others. In fact, however, recognizing the similarity and difference between the two is enriching. The similarity suggests that work with others (by whatever name) is an important bridging concept between the two approaches. The differences strengthen each of the concepts. TC contributes specificity to the generalist idea. Collaterals and procedures for working with them can be identified. Ultimately their contributions to problem resolution can be determined. The generalist perspective expands our thinking about collaterals in two ways. First, it directs us to consider other systems systematically. Second, it illuminates the fact that collaterals are representatives of other systems and that potential conflicts may exist. As representatives of other systems, collaterals are accountable to others, and they must operate within the rules and procedures of other systems. The recognition that collaterals are involved in more than one system should enable us to work with them more effectively.

Furthermore, uniting the two concepts, "work with collaterals" and "work with other systems (or representatives of other systems)" should foster some social work roles that are vitally important but often receive insufficient attention. These roles include broker, mediator, and advocate (Compton and Galaway 1989; Middleman and Wood 1989). We act as brokers when we take on tasks that involve linking the client to resources. We act as mediators when we take on tasks designed to resolve disputes between the clients and other people. We act as advocates when we argue for the client. All these roles entail work with others.

1.6.0 NEW APPLICATIONS

Since the appearance of the first edition of this volume (1994), there have been a number of additions to the task-centered model. These developments have occurred across several dimensions. Task planners evolved to assist in generating task alternatives and thus further explicate this aspect of the model. Treatment protocols have been developed for particular populations like at-risk elementary school children and for case management in the schools and in the community. TC supervision represents a new application of the model. These additions to TC are described below and referred to in the text.

Task planners. Task planners consist of descriptions of problems and task menus that can be used in problem resolution. Task planners for more than one hundred clinical problems (e.g., substance abuse, child maltreatment, anxiety, depression, child behavior disorder, couple conflict) have been published (Reid 2000). Also available are task planners for the frail elderly (Reid 2000) and for Temporary Assistance for Needy Families (TANF) (Reid and Kenaley 2000). Task planners are not viewed as prescribing tasks for particular problems but rather as a resource to provide both practitioners and clients with an array of action possibilities to consider along with links to relevant literature and research. They are intended to facilitate rather than supplement basic principles and methods of task planning.

A task-centered social worker in the classroom. Social Worker–Teacher Classroom Collaboration (SWTCC) is a model of intervention for at-risk elementary school children that places a social worker and a teacher in a classroom together (Viggiani, Bailey-Dempsey, and Reid, in press). The model is particularly useful for classrooms that have a high number of children with academic, behavioral, or attendance difficulties and in circumstances in which student social workers can serve as practitioners. Using task-centered methods, social workers intervene with behavioral and attendance issues, which permits teachers to focus their efforts on teaching. Weekly collaborative meetings facilitate ongoing communication between the teachers and the social workers. SWTCC was tested using social work interns in two classrooms in an urban elementary school in Albany, New York. A quasi-experimental design that included the use of comparison classrooms indicated that SWTCC fostered appropriate classroom behavior, such as following rules, and had a positive effect on attendance problems. Social worker, teacher, student, and parent questionnaires revealed that the intervention was perceived positively.

Task-centered case management in the schools. This variation, mentioned briefly in the first edition, has been designed primarily to help children at risk of school failure with specific focus on problems of grades, attendance, and classroom behavior. In consultation with the family, the social worker forms a case management team that includes the worker as leader, the student, one or two of the student's teachers or other school personnel, and the parents. Depending on the case, the team might also include such other members as a student peer, a member of the extended family, or a community agency representative. Considerable weight is given to the student's input in team member selection, especially the teacher(s) to be invited. In addition, the social worker sees the child and his or her parents in individual and family sessions.

The main purpose of the case management team is to identify and work on school-related problems. All team members are involved in developing and carrying out tasks to solve the problems. For example, students might undertake tasks of completing homework assignments, making up detention time, and attending classes; parents' tasks might include facilitating and monitoring homework and providing reinforcers for successful school performance; teachers' tasks might include providing students extra help and obtaining information about school resources or policies that might affect the student, as well as coordinating activities of team members; and social workers assume tasks to secure resources such as tutors and Big Sisters. The case management teams meet every other week to review the status of problems and the progress on tasks, to resolve obstacles to task completion, and to plan new tasks. Meetings with children and their families, which usually take place on alternate weeks, focus on problem-related tasks and obstacles. Median service length (in various trials of the model) has been sixteen weeks.

Since its original conception (Bailey-Dempsey 1991), the case management model has undergone an extensive research and development process (Bailey-Dempsey and Reid 1996). The primary experimental trial is reviewed in section 6.1.0. Applications have been incorporated in part 2, "Families." A complete protocol for the model is available from the second author of the present text.

Task-centered case management with the frail elderly in the community. In this adaptation, practitioners work with elderly clients, caregivers, and service providers to meet the needs of the elderly in the community (Naleppa and Reid 1998, 2000, in press; Huh 2000). Since most elderly want to "age in place," a major purpose of the approach is to provide the help necessary to maintain clients in their own homes. In the sessions, which usually take place in the client's home, the older person is involved in identifying the problem and the needs, and in task planning and implementation. Such involvement (as opposed to having caregivers and practitioners develop and carry out tasks) is viewed as empowering the older client. To protect client autonomy, guidelines have been developed that emphasize the client's right to make decisions, even when others have to implement them. Other guidelines, such as handling client reminiscences in focused interviewing, provide additional adaptations of basic task-centered procedures to work with an elderly population. The approach also makes use of intervention "modules" (Liberman 1988). Most modules take the form of task planners, as described earlier. Additional modulees—e.g., ways of helping clients with grief and loss issues—have been devised to supplement task-centered methods. A field test of the model suggested that elderly clients were, in general, active participants in all steps of the model, from identifying problems to suggesting and implementing tasks (Naleppa and Reid 1998). The approach appeared to be instrumental in helping clients remain in the community. A controlled trial of the model is now in progress. The application is discussed further in part 2, "Families."

Task-centered supervision. In task-centered supervision (TCS), the basic structure and methods of task-centered practice are applied to educational supervision, including field instruction (Caspi and Reid 1998, in press). TCS outlines a series of activities to be carried out during and between supervision meetings. In short, during each supervisory session the supervisee and supervisor engage in a process of selecting practice and learning objectives for immediate, targeted work. These objectives are considered, mutually evaluated, prioritized in order of perceived importance, and formulated as "target goals." Up to three target goals are selected for work at each supervision meeting. Actions, or tasks, for attaining target goals are then developed. For each target goal, up to three tasks are selected. These tasks are usually implemented by supervisees between supervision meetings in their work with clients. Tasks may take a variety of forms, such as learning new skills ("Observe processes of triangulation in the B family") or using a particular intervention ("Confront Mr. C regarding his denial of a drinking problem"). Before finalizing the selection of tasks, potential obstacles to task implementation are considered, as in the basic practice model. Similarly other steps of the basic model, such as procedures for planning and rehearsing tasks, task review, and recording task progress are adapted for purposes of supervision. Supplementary components provide opportunities for didactic teaching, for dealing with the supervisee's feelings, and for handling other issues likely to arise in supervision.

Other applications since the first edition include task-centered mediation with post-divorce couples (Donahue 1996), group treatment of single parents in a college setting (Raushi 1994), group treatment of sex offenders (Kilgore 1995), psycho-educational and task-centered group intervention for family members of people with AIDS (Pomeroy, Rubin, and Walker 1995) and a task-centered approach with Vietnamese families (Nguyen 1999). Additional applications and current projects, in this country and abroad, as well as examples of task planners, a task-centered tutorial, and a comprehensive bibliography of task-centered methods, can be found at the task-centered web site, http://www.task-centered.com.

1.7.0 OTHER APPROACHES, CONCEPTS, AND PERSPECTIVES

There are many approaches and perspectives for social work practice (for succinct descriptions of other approaches, see Sheafor, Horejsi, and Horejsi 2000 or, for more extended descriptions within a generalist perspective, see Lehmann and Coady 2001). Most of those that have existed for some time have been considered in one way or another within this volume. However, we do want to mention a few here. They are managed care, empowerment, the strengths perspective, and the solution-focused approach. Managed care is included because it is having a pervasive effect on the delivery of service. Empowerment is a philosophy that, we believe, should influence all approaches to practice including TC. The strengths perspective and solution-focused work are included because they have increased in popularity since the first edition of this book and because of the way they deal with the concept of problem, a concept that is central to the social work profession and to TC.

Managed care is an orientation to the delivery of service (Chambliss 2000). It emphasizes cost-effectiveness and efficiency. Supporters claim that it also enhances quality of care, but this is a matter of debate. Regardless of the merits (or demerits) of managed care, it currently shapes the environment for practice by determining the amount and type of service offered. Task-centered generalist practice is particularly valuable in this environment. It is a time-limited approach, which means that it fits the constraints of managed care. The fact that its effectiveness has been demonstrated means that it offers a valuable tool for providing service that does not jeopardize quality in the pursuit of cost reductions.

Empowerment is a vital philosophical concept for social work practice. The mission of social work is to aid and abet those who are disadvantaged and disenfranchised, and many of our clients are among those who possess the least power. Solomon (1976) defines the powerless as "anyone who is haunted by severe limitations of their self-determination and an inevitable sense of dependency" (12). Gutierrez (1990) has examined the empowerment literature and culled several techniques common to empowerment approaches. These are (1) "accepting the client's definition of the problem"; (2) "identifying and building on existing strengths"; (3) "engaging in a power analysis of the client's situation"; (4) "teaching specific skills"; and (5) "mobilizing resources and advocating for clients" (151–52). The first technique, accepting the client's definition of the problem, is clearly consistent with TC. The second, fourth, and fifth techniques—identifying and building on strengths, teaching specific skills, and mobilizing resources and advocating—are often incorporated in TC through the development of client tasks, practitioner tasks, and work with collaterals. The one aspect of empowerment practice not systematically included in TC is a power analysis. However, there is nothing about the structure or philosophy of TC that would preclude incorporating a power analysis.

The strengths perspective has become popular within social work education during the past decade. The basic principles in this approach are as follows:

1. Every human system has strengths;
2. Traumas and struggles may be injurious but they may also be sources of challenge and opportunity;
3. The upper limits of the capacity to grow and change are unknown and client aspirations should be taken seriously;
4. Client systems are best served by collaborating with them;
5. Every environment has resources.

(Saleebey 1997:12–15)

The focus in the strengths perspective is the client's vision for the future, and assessment emphasizes the identification and articulation of strengths in the client system and the environment. Intervention consists of implementing collaboratively developed strategies that build on strengths and resources (Early and Glenmaye 2000).

A considerable amount of overlap exists between the strengths perspective and TC. Both stress collaboration. Both focus on what clients want to achieve. Both are eclectic in that they use other interventions as appropriate (see the case example in Early and Glenmaye 2000). Both also build on client strengths and resources, albeit in different ways. The strengths perspective emphasizes the articulation of these strengths and resources, whereas, in TC, they are assumed in the development of tasks (tasks based on client weaknesses would be futile).

A major difference between the two approaches seems to result mainly from the fact that the strengths perspective developed as a re-action against traditional problem-solving approaches in which prob-lems were often located in the client and solidified with a diagnostic label. In fact, TC, which is a problem-solving model, also eschews fo-cusing on client pathology. Unfortunately many advocates of the strengths perspective fail to differentiate between problems that are at-tributed to clients by professionals and those problems-in-living that clients identify themselves. Some of the more radical adherents of this perspective even reject the use of the word *problem*. This is dangerous because denigrating client-identified concerns is disempowering. Al-though Saleebey (1997) acknowledges that this is "a very serious criti-cism" and contends that "there is nothing, however, in the strengths approach that mandates the discounting of the problems of life that people bring to us" (238), not all adherents share this point of view, and the possibility of ignoring client concerns for the sake of adhering to any particular philosophy is risky, to say the least.

As Blundo (2001) has put it: "To learn the strengths perspective one must seriously challenge the basic foundations of practice knowledge, the 80 years of variations on a basic theme of disease and expertise as it is taught and practiced today" (301). However, the strengths perspective will need to come to grips with a central dilemma: how to reconcile its radical vision of working with clients with the many demonstrably ef-fective models that focus on client problems as "pathologies"— cogni-tive, cognitive-behavioral, and interpersonal interventions for depres-sion; exposure therapies for phobias, obsessive-compulsive disorder, and post-traumatic stress syndrome; psycho-educational treatment of fami-lies with schizophrenic members; problem-solving skills training with ag-gressive children—to name but a few. In TC, most such interventions can be adapted for use within the structure of the model. It is not at all ap-parent how the strengths perspective can achieve such an integration.

The solution-focused model is a time-limited approach that evolved from work with families (De Jong and Berg 1998). The focus of this approach is on helping clients achieve solutions to their problems as they define them. Positive, specific goals are carefully developed. The emphasis on solutions and goals creates optimistic expectations and stresses clients' strengths. Careful attention is given to the "exceptions," the times when problems do not occur. The emphasis on solutions and goals creates optimistic expectations and stresses clients' strengths. There are differing opinions about the extent to which problems are focused on. Some suggest that discussion of problems is minimal, whereas others contend that a thorough understanding of problems is necessary to the development of solutions and relapse plans (Christensen, Todahl, and Barrett 1999).

There are many similarities between solution-focused work and TC. Most evident are brevity and a focus on client-determined concerns. Both emphasize collaboratively solving problems, an emphasis that communicates optimism. Both make use of client problem-solving actions (tasks) in the real world. There are, however, a number of differences. In its current form, the solution-focused model is guided by a postmodern, constructionist epistemology, whereas the task-centered approach is modernist and realist in its philosophy. How these contrasting viewpoints (which we shall not discuss here) affect actual practice is not completely clear, but we shall comment on a few differences at the practice level.

Much of the divergence between the two models is concerned with the client's problem. In the solution-focused approach, as it is customarily presented, it is not assumed that there has to be a connection between the problem and the intervention (de Shazer 1988). The problem serves largely as a motivator for new behavior, and it is the latter (the solution) that receives attention—hence the name. In the task-centered approach it is assumed that a collaborative effort by the client and practitioner to understand the problem as the client perceives it, as well as contextual factors, can provide useful information about how best to resolve it. Also, in TC, collecting baseline data on problem occurrence is seen as an important ingredient in helping both client and practitioner assess progress. Thus the task-centered model has a formal, although brief, assessment phase. The solution-focused approach usually does not. As Peller and Walter (1995:77) observe, "The word assessment does not fit into a solution-focused orientation." (However, as noted earlier, there is variation within the solution-focused school on the importance to attach to the problem.)

In addition, the task-centered model makes use of structured sequences of activities, such as the Task Planning and Implementation Sequence. The solution-focused method is much more fluid. In TC, provisional time limits are set at the beginning of contact, whereas the solution-focused model has no preset time limits, although most cases turn out to be brief.

1.8.0 STRUCTURE AND CONTENT OF THIS BOOK

This book contains four major parts, as well as the introductory and concluding chapters and the chapter on diversity. The major parts describe work with individuals, families, groups, and larger systems. The first three pertain to individuals, families, and groups and are composed of four chapters each. The chapters describe pretreatment considerations, the initial phase of treatment, the middle phase of treatment, and termination. The fourth part, "Larger Systems," is composed of two chapters only—work with organizations and work with communities—because we have less experience in applying TC to work with them. We are grateful to authors Bageshwari Parihar (organizations) and Gregory L. Pettys and Kollengode R. Ramakrishnan (communities) for sharing their expertise in these chapters. Only one chapter, chapter 16, is devoted to work with culturally diverse clients because it is necessary to describe only modifications to TC. Blanca M. Ramos has generously contributed her special knowledge to writing this chapter.

A numbering system is used to identify the content in each chapter. This numbering system is consistent for the first three parts. For example, the topic "Theoretical Base" is covered in 2.2.0 ("Individuals"); 6.2.0 ("Families"); and 10.2.0 ("Groups"). To locate related content in parts 1, 2, and 3, change chapter numbers as shown in Table 1.1.

The numbers used to identify topics in chapters 14, 15, and 16 are the same as those used in part 1 except that they are preceded by the appropriate chapter number, that is, 14, 15, or 16. Thus section 14.3.0.0 deals with the same topic as that in section 3.0.0, 7.0.0, and 11.0.0. The numbering system enables the reader to cover the content in two ways. The book may be read in the ordinary fashion—from

TABLE 1.1 *Locating Related Content in Parts 1, 2, and 3*

	Part 1 Individual	Part 2 Families	Part 3 Groups
Chapters	2	6	10
	3	7	11
	4	8	12
	5	9	13

front to back—or it can be read by topic; for example, content about the theoretical base for working with all systems can be examined together. The numbering system also allows the reader to refer back to the discussion of a topic in earlier sections. For example, the discussion of values begins in 2.4.0 and is elaborated in 6.4.0, 10.4.0, 14.2.4.0, and 15.2.4.0. This is important, because we have avoided repeating content as much as possible.

Checklists, questions for consideration, and practice exercises have also been included so readers can monitor their own understanding and skill development. Finally, description of work with each system concludes with an extended case illustration.

PART ONE *Individuals*

2

PRETREATMENT CONSIDERATIONS

2.0.0 INTRODUCTION

Some general issues must be considered before practicing or learning an approach to social work practice. First, one must know whether the approach is effective and the kinds of clients and problems it is likely to impact. Second, the theoretical assumptions that underlie the approach must be examined. Third, the approach must be studied within the context of social work practice. It must be consistent with both the mission and values of the social work profession. Fourth, basic skills that are prerequisites to the effective implementation of the approach must be acknowledged and acquired. Finally, the decision to apply the approach in a particular case must be made.

Each of these issues is briefly addressed in this chapter under the following headings: "Effectiveness and Replicability," "Theoretical Base," "Mission and Purpose," "Social Work Values," "Relationship," and "The Appropriate System for Work." The content provided about these topics is necessarily brief. Entire books have been written about most of them, and the reader is encouraged to pursue additional readings.

2.1.0 EFFECTIVENESS AND REPLICABILITY

One of the most important attributes of an approach to helping people is its effectiveness. In other words, when considering the use of a particular approach, the first question to ask is, "Does it work?" The answer to this question, for TC with individuals, is a resounding yes.

The second question that should be asked is, "What is the evidence that it works?" Many kinds of evidence exist. Most scholars believe that the most desirable evidence is that which is derived from scientific experiments. TC has been the subject of more than thirty-five published studies and doctoral dissertations, and the findings have been consistently positive (Reid 1992, 1997). Many of the studies have been controlled group experiments, which are the most rigorous tests of effectiveness (Gibbons, Bow, and Butler 1985; Gibbons et al. 1979; Larsen and Mitchell 1980; Newcome 1985; Reid 1975, 1978; Reid and Bailey-Dempsey 1995; Reid et al. 1980). Recently a relatively new kind of study, called meta-analysis, has been conducted (Gorey, Thyer, and Pawluck 1998). In this kind of investigation the impact, called the "effect size," of a number of interventions are compared. The effect size for TC was found to be among the largest and notably larger than that for other generalist approaches.

To demonstrate the importance of controlled group studies for determining effectiveness, one of the experiments will be described briefly here (Reid 1978). Approximately forty social work students worked with two clients each. One of the clients was randomly assigned to the experimental condition; that is, one client received task-centered treatment. The other client was assigned to the control condition; in this study, that meant that the client received supportive attention. Supportive attention was a placebo treatment in which clients could, for example, discuss concerns, explore historical material, or, with children, engage in play activities. No tasks or other task-centered activities were used with clients in the control or supportive attention condition. The problems experienced by all the clients were measured before they received either TC or supportive attention and after they received one of these conditions. The problems experienced by the clients who received TC showed significantly more improvement than those experienced by the clients who received supportive attention.

The study described is considered to be a rigorous one because many alternative explanations for the changes in the problems can be eliminated. Because so many social workers were used, changes cannot be attributed to the special talents of one worker, for example. Because many different problems were treated across the eighty-seven clients, changes cannot be attributed to the type of problem. Because many different clients were randomly assigned to the conditions, changes cannot be attributed to special client characteristics like motivation. Thus changes are probably the result of the treatment procedure employed, namely, TC.

After the social worker has determined that the approach he or she is considering is effective, the social worker will want to consider whether that approach is likely to work with a particular problem-client-setting configuration. Fortunately TC has been used with many different clients, many different problems, and in many settings.

Client characteristics include age, gender, race or ethnicity, socioeconomic class, and education. TC has been used with a diverse array of clients on the dimensions of age, gender, and race. Clients have ranged in socioeconomic class from the very poor to the upper middle class and, in education, from the illiterate to those with doctoral degrees. TC has been used in the United Kingdom and in some developing countries, as well as in the United States. Books describing TC practice have been translated into five different languages.

TC has been used with an enormous array of psychosocial problems. These problems have been categorized in a problem typology. The original typology included the following groupings: interpersonal conflict, dissatisfaction in social relations, problems with formal organizations, difficulties in role performance, problems of social transition, reactive emotional distress, and inadequate resources (Reid and Epstein 1972). Experience with the model suggested two more categories of problems (Reid 1978): (1) decision-making problems; and (2) psychological or behavioral problems not classified elsewhere. The last category was added because the model was found useful with a variety of phenomena like phobic reactions and self-image problems.

Settings in which the task-centered approach has been used include mental health services, family services, schools, hospitals, industry, corrections services, child welfare, public assistance, and nursing homes. Thus TC is likely to be an effective approach to helping a wide variety of clients, with a large array of problems, in most social work settings. The approach does have limitations, however. It is not used with people who do not identify a problem they want help with. Like other "talking therapies," it cannot cure chronic mental illness, although it has been used to supplement chemotherapies with good results. It is not useful with clients who seek self-understanding for its own sake or for those simply seeking support. Such clients are rare, however, since most who desire self-understanding and support expect that it will change something.

The second consideration concerns replicability. For a treatment approach to be used by others, it must be specific. The procedures that comprise the task-centered approach are specific, a reason why it has been so widely used.

Another consideration that involves replicability concerns resources. The social worker must consider whether she and the client have the resources necessary to implement the approach. For example, various forms of token economies (reward systems) have been shown to be effective with child behavior problems. However, in order to implement the token economies, someone must be present, willing, and able to provide the child with appropriate rewards when the desired behavior occurs. Such a person is not always available. Other approaches to treatment require years of contact. Many clients cannot afford the time or expense.

Fortunately, with the task-centered approach, only two resources are necessary. The first is a social worker who knows how to use the approach. The second is a client who has a problem that he or she wants help with.

The following checklist is the first of many that readers will encounter in this volume. Their purpose is to provide the reader with a succinct summary of the content and to enable the reader to critique his or her own work.

2.1.1 CHECKLIST FOR EFFECTIVENESS AND REPLICABILITY

___ 1. Is the treatment approach effective?
___ 2. Is the treatment approach likely to be effective with this particular client-problem situation?
___ 3. Do I know enough about the approach to be able to replicate it?
___ 4. Are resources required to implement the approach available?

2.1.2 QUESTIONS TO CONSIDER

1. A teacher or social worker you admire describes an intervention that he or she used successfully with a particular client. Does this mean the intervention is effective? Why?

2. You attend a conference and learn that many professionals are enthusiastically reporting good results about a particular form of treatment? Does this mean the treatment is effective? Why?

3. You meet a person who has had his or her particular problem cured with a particular treatment approach? Does this mean the intervention is effective? Why?

2.2.0 THEORETICAL BASE ⊤·∪

Theories are sets of concepts, constructs, and propositions that describe and explain natural phenomena—in our case, the functioning of individuals. TC is not a theory. It is a practice approach. Practice approaches consist of directives that tell the social worker how to proceed. Before describing how theory is used in task-centered practice, we need to explain what theory is and what it does. We shall also describe the assumptions about people, problems, motivation, and change that are embedded in TC. Finally, we will identify some important dimensions of human functioning.

Behavioral or personality theory is used to answer the question, "Why?" When we ask questions like, "Why is Johnny misbehaving in class?" or "Why is Mr. Johnson unable to hold a job?" we are seeking explanations. Explanations have primarily two sources. The first is conventional reasoning. Conventional reasoning might suggest that Johnny is misbehaving in school because he does not know what behaviors are expected or because he is bored. It might suggest that Mr. Johnson cannot hold a job because he does not have the necessary skills or because jobs in the unskilled labor market, of which he is a member, are temporary ones.

The second source for explanations is theory. This becomes somewhat complicated because many different theories of human behavior or personality exist. The theory you choose to apply will determine the explanation. Thus, in the case of Mr. Johnson, if you use cognitive theory, you might decide that Mr. Johnson fails because he believes he will fail. If you use ego psychological theory, you might decide that Mr. Johnson fails because he has an ego deficit. If you use interpersonal problem-solving theory, you might decide that Mr. Johnson fails because he is deficient in consequential thinking.

A distinguishing characteristic of TC is that it is a practice model that is not attached to a particular theory of behavior. This means that, when an explanation is required, we turn first to explanations based on reasoning. When a theoretical explanation is needed, we are free to apply the theory or combination of theories that best explains the problem encountered rather than relying consistently on only one theory to explain all problems. TC can draw from a variety of behavioral theories for the purpose of understanding problems, especially those that provide a good fit with the model and have research support. Included are social learning, cognitive, systems, and ecological theories, as well as theories pertaining to families, groups, organizations, and communities. However, unlike approaches that are tied to a theory of behavior, we never use theory to determine the target problem or focus of treatment.

In short, TC is an empirical and eclectic model of practice. We begin by intervening with problems rather than by employing theoretical explanations to determine the cause of the problems. The model is based on data or facts about factors that seem to produce good outcomes rather than hypotheses about causes or explanations, unless the hypotheses are supported by evidence. Instances do arise, of course, when theory is necessary to clarify problems and to identify obstacles.

The freedom from a particular behavioral theory, probably more than any other of its characteristics, makes TC an ideal base for generalist practice. It also makes it an ideal base for eclectic practice. Eclectic practice borrows the best elements of many different approaches. The use of TC as a base for eclectic practice will be discussed more extensively in section 4.7.0.

Although TC is formally free of behavioral theory, work by and with people can probably never entirely escape theory or, at least, explanations. This is because we all —and this includes social workers and their clients—have our favorite explanations for what befalls people. Psychologists have labeled these favorite explanations as "naive" or "implicit" personality theories. Naive theories might be as simple as thinking the events of one's life are based on luck or bad blood.

It is important, for several reasons, to be aware of the naive behavioral theories that you and your clients hold. First, pejorative notions that lead to discriminatory behavior often hide out in these theories. Naive, pejorative theories about minorities or women, for example, might produce treatment goals that are unnecessarily modest. Second, the tendency to use a particular explanation might lead you to ignore other sources of explanation. For example, the social worker who automatically attributes problems to deficits in the individual will overlook factors like depriving environments. Third, if your clients hold naive theories that are incongruent with yours, this will likely produce an impasse in treatment or even cause the client to drop out. The client, for example, might believe that his or her failure in school or at work is the result of an incompetent teacher or boss. You might believe that failures in school or at work are usually the result of lazy students and workers. Obviously the client and worker in this situation would be working at cross-purposes. The client would feel misunderstood. The social worker would think the client is resistant and uncooperative.

TC is based on a modest set of assumptions about people and problems, and the source of motivation and change (Tolson 2001). People are seen as active problem solvers who are capable of making choices about their wants and needs and participating in change efforts. They become clients when their independent problem-solving efforts are blocked or insufficient. Problems are believed to be inevitable and the result of unmet wants. Wants are shaped by belief systems, which include values, expectations, and appraisals. For example, parents who value higher education and expect their children to attend college are likely to appraise a B grade-point average as a problem. Parents without such values or expectations are unlikely to evaluate the same grade-point average as a problem. Because unmet wants provide the motivation for change, it is imperative that clients determine the target problems if this motivation is to be captured. Action, particularly client action, is believed to be the most efficient route to change and, frequently, a necessary precursor to attitudinal or emotional change. We believe that most problems can be alleviated through client tasks, which are actions developed collaboratively by practitioners and clients during the treatment sessions and implemented between sessions. Furthermore, action and the feedback that ensues are important influences on self-efficacy, which determines the amount and persistence of effort that the client is likely to expend in the future (Bandura 1986). A few specific research findings about change also influenced the development of TC. They are as follows: (1) intervention in a client system tends to produce most of its possible results quickly; (2) time limits generally accentuate practitioners' and clients' problem-solving efforts; and (3) change in problems resulting from short-term intervention tends to be as durable as change resulting from long-term intervention (Reid 1992, 1997).

(As stated previously, theories of human behavior abound, and thus so do descriptions and explanations of how and why people behave as they do.) We believe that, when explanations are needed, more than one source should be considered. This is because behavior is usually multi-determined, and accepting one reason will often overlook other important causes. Ten dimensions of human functioning useful to understanding individuals are described below. The first three (health, and physical and intellectual functioning; information and knowledge; and resources) are actually derived from practice wisdom. The remaining seven (stage of development; roles; cognition; self-concept; skills; stress; and social support) are derived from theories of behavior. The descriptions of the dimensions are, by necessity, brief. We encourage additional reading about them.

Health, and Physical and Intellectual Functioning   These are characteristics that the client brings to the helping endeavor and that are not directly modifiable by the social worker. They are, however, important to consider. On occasion psychotherapy has been used in an attempt to cure conditions that were the result of brain tumors, lead poisoning, chronic fatigue syndrome, even menopause. Clients should be referred to appropriate physicians when the problems they are experiencing might be related to physical illness or when the client's physical health has been neglected. In addition to causing some of the problems that are brought to our attention, illness also affects the individual's ability to cope with other problems. The parent with constant pain, fatigue, or insomnia will have difficulty dealing with a child's behavioral problems.

Physical and intellectual disabilities must, of course, be considered when planning treatment. Clients with limited mobility cannot be expected to carry out tasks that require a great deal of physical activity. Clients with intellectual deficits or severe mental health problems may not even be able to identify their troubles. Sometimes disabilities are not visible. It is good practice to ask each client whether he or she has any disabilities or illnesses.

Information and Knowledge   Often people are unable to deal with their problems adequately, because they simply do not have the requisite information. Sometimes the missing information is concrete and specific, such as where to secure certain kinds of services. Sometimes it is more comprehensive, such as knowledge of child development for new mothers. Sometimes the missing information is specific but subtle, as in the following example. A patient was hostile and uncooperative with medical staff. It turned out that his hostility emerged because no one responded when he used his call button. Further investigation revealed that the button was inoperative. In another case, a young girl—much to the anxiety of her family—was setting fires. Examining how the child used matches revealed that, because she was left-handed, the flame of the match burned her hand, whereupon she dropped the lit match and started a fire. Supplying or discovering pertinent information is probably one of the most overlooked but important functions we provide.

Resources   Many people, even those with full-time employment, do not have sufficient income. Time, too, has become a scarce resource, as securing adequate income has, for many, become an all-consuming struggle. Lack of transportation or child care limits opportunities. Dilapidated housing and dangerous neighborhoods affect the quality of life in the present, as well as hope for the future. Problems of all types are magnified when they must be confronted with a paucity of resources. Furthermore, the incidence of many problems increases with economic hardship. It is our responsibility to help clients secure all available resources. In many situations, needed resources are not immediately available. It is then our job to create them.

Stage of Development   Staged-based theories of development examine changes in the physical, cognitive, or social and emotional domains as they occur over the life span (Berk 1998). There are many such theories, and they can be grouped into four theoretical orientations: cognitive, humanistic, social learning, and psychoanalytic. Recognizing a client's stage of development will suggest some of the issues in a client's life and provide context. The concept of a "social clock" captures the notion that there are age-graded expectations for life events, such as getting married or beginning a career (Neugarten 1979). Since people make social comparisons to evaluate themselves and their accomplishments, being on or off time can significantly impact feelings of self-worth. Havighurst's "Developmental Tasks" delineate expected accomplishments across six life stages. For purposes of illustration, a few tasks in each stage are listed below. It should be recalled, however, that society's age-based expectations are becoming increasingly fluid and that there are distinct differences in these expectations between college and noncollege populations. For example, those who attend college are expected to marry later, enter careers later, and begin families later.

Infancy and Early Childhood
Learning to talk
Learning to walk
Learning sex differences and sexual modesty

Middle Childhood
Learning to get along with age-mates
Developing fundamental skills in reading, writing, and calculating

Adolescence
Achieving emotional independence of parents and other adults
Preparing for an economic career

Early Adulthood
Selecting a mate
Starting a family
Getting started in an occupation

Middle Age
Assisting teenage children to become responsible and happy adults
Adjusting to aging parents

Late Maturity
Adjusting to decreasing physical strength and health
Adjusting to retirement and reduced income

(Havighurst 1972)

Perhaps the most popular stage-based theory among social workers is Erikson's "Psychosocial Stages" (1950). Each stage focuses on the ego qualities that are expected to develop at particular ages. They are as follows: zero to two years, trust versus mistrust; two to three years, autonomy versus shame and doubt; three to six years, initiative versus guilt; six to twelve years, industry versus inferiority; twelve to eighteen years, identity versus role confusion; eighteen to thirty-five years, intimacy versus isolation; thirty-five to sixty years, generative capacity versus stagnation; over sixty, ego integrity versus despair. In this schema the ego qualities are thought of as a continuum, with the ideal solutions near the midpoint of the range. For example, neither absolute trust nor absolute mistrust would produce very functional behavior. It is useful to consider the impact of the environment on the development of these qualities. For example, the problem of poverty experienced in infancy and early childhood may impact the baby's experience of developing trust that the environment and significant others will meet his or her needs. The same problem experienced during adolescence, along with a lack of opportunity for employment, might foreclose or limit the role of worker as part of one's identity.

Roles   Roles are particular positions or statuses in society that have prescribed expectations for behavior (Davis 1996). They include parent, child, spouse, man or women, and teenager, as well as occupational positions such as nurse, physician, teacher, and so on. Some of the problems related to role behavior include insufficient training, ambiguity, role conflict, and overload. Parenting is frequently used as an example of a role for which our society provides insufficient training.

The role of employee is often difficult for young people from deprived environments who have not been exposed to role models. Ambiguity occurs when the behavioral expectations for a role are unclear. Role conflict occurs when a person occupies two roles with opposite expectations. This has been used to explain the difficulty some women experience in raising families (Rossi 1975). It is thought that the executive capacities necessary to run a household and rear children conflict with the traditional socialization of women as nurturers. Role overload occurs when a person has more roles than he or she can manage.

Cognition   Cognition can refer to a number of bodies of knowledge. First, it can refer to logical reasoning and the acquisition of knowledge. Second, it can refer to cognitive therapies. Third, it can refer to social cognition theory. Cognition, as it pertains to logical reasoning and cognitive therapies, is described in this section. Social cognition is described in the following section, "Self-Concept."

Piaget (1952) developed a stage-based description of cognitive development. The four stages he identified are sensorimotor (birth to twenty-four months); preoperational (two to seven years); concrete operational (seven to twelve years); and formal operational (over twelve). During the sensorimotor stage, children learn to coordinate simple behaviors and become aware of the permanence of objects. During the preoperational phase, they learn to use language and pretend play as well as acquire basic knowledge about cause, number, and spatial relationships. During the concrete operational stage, they acquire the ability to use logic, but its application is limited to concrete events. Once formal operations have been acquired, logic and reasoning can be applied to abstract concepts.

Although it is not usually necessary for social workers to become expert in the development of logical thought, some knowledge about it is necessary for assessing client functioning. Obviously it is important in working with children. Too often children are assumed to have capacities that they simply do not have. For example, many people expect young children to follow rules when playing games, but this ability does not usually occur until about age seven. With adults, too, we sometimes expect too much. Since not everyone reaches formal operations, it should not be assumed that all adult clients are capable of logical and abstract thinking. Furthermore, heightened emotions and stress often interfere with the ability to think clearly.

(In cognitive therapies, the goal is to modify aspects of cognition that are thought to be causally related to a client's emotions and behavior.) This is based on the premise that emotion is not the direct result of our experiences but, rather, the result of our experiences as we interpret them. Accessible aspects of cognitions pertain to content and process (Granvold 1995). Cognitive content refers to actual thoughts that can be identified by standardized instruments or by asking clients to complete logues. Cognitive process refers to perception and information processing, and focuses on identifying errors in reasoning such as overgeneralization ("since my husband was abusive, all men are abusive"). Process is revealed during interviews and is more difficult to assess than content. There are an ever increasing number of cognitive therapies. Beck (1976) emphasizes distortions in thinking, such as focusing on failure rather than success. Ellis (1962) identifies irrational beliefs like "I must be perfect" or "Everyone must love me" that impact emotions. Meichenbaum (1977) focuses on automatic but faulty self-instructions as a cause of undesirable behaviors. Others (e.g., D'Zurilla 1988) identify deficient problem-solving skills, such as an inability to generate alternative solutions or to recognize consequences as a cause of dysfunctional behavior.

Suspected dysfunctional cognitions should be carefully assessed usually by asking the client to keep a logue of their thoughts. Once the specific dysfunctions are identified, the procedures for cognitive restructuring can be incorporated in TC by designing tasks that implement them.

Self-Concept   This concept refers to perceptions of the self. Interest in this variable probably can be traced to Socrates' dictum, "Know thyself." Self-esteem refers to self-evaluation or self-regard. Self-concept is illuminated by social cognition theory, which is the "study of how people interpret, analyze, remember, and use information about themselves and the social world" (Nurius and Berlin 1995:513). This theory has contributed at least two important observations about self-concept. First, self-concept is situationally responsive. This means that we hold many notions (called schemas) about ourselves, and those that are operating at any given time depend on the environmental circumstances. Self-esteem will vary in association with self-concept. Second, people have multiple self-concepts. Among them are our actual selves, our possible selves, and our "ought" selves. Possible selves refer to how we see ourselves in the future. The number of possible selves decline as we age. "Ought" selves consist of expectations about how we should be. Discrepancies between our actual and "ought" concepts can cause considerable distress.

One of the concepts that integrates self-concept and cognitive content, as described in the preceding section, is expectancies. Expectancies are an aspect of self-concept, and they refer to our beliefs about our ability to influence or control our personal world. Three well-known types of expectancies are locus of control, self-efficacy, and learned helplessness (Granvold 1995). Locus of control refers to where a person attributes causation. Those who attribute causation to themselves have an internal locus of control. Those who attribute causation to outside forces have an external locus of control. An internal locus of control has been found to be associated with enhanced functioning in many areas. Self-efficacy is the belief that we can, through our behavior, have the impact or outcome that we desire. Learned helplessness is the belief that nothing we do will make a difference.

There are behavioral procedures, like positive self-statements, for directly enhancing self-esteem (for other strategies, see Reid 2000:231–33). These procedures can be incorporated into TC through the use of tasks and have proven useful when the target problem is self-esteem. The utility of the concept of expectancies, however, is not limited to a particular target problem. Expectancies will affect the degree to which clients are hopeful about solving any problem, and therefore affect the extent of effort they will expend to resolve them. Thus it is useful to consider expectancies with all clients and to provide extra support for clients who are pessimistic.

Environmental Contingencies   It has been repeatedly demonstrated that the antecedents and consequences to behavior not only affect the acquisition of behavior (learning it) but also the frequency with which the behavior is performed (Behaviorists suggest the dictum, "Know thy contingencies"). Respondent or classical conditioning emphasizes the stimuli for behavior. Pavlov's dog was taught to salivate at the sound of a bell. Some of us pick up a cigarette when the telephone rings. Operant conditioning emphasizes the consequences to behavior. A behavior can elicit five possible types of consequences. Two of the consequences are reinforcing, which means that they make the behavior more likely to occur in the future. A behavior is positively reinforced when something desirable ensues (we get a cookie). A behavior is negatively reinforced when something undesirable is taken away (we do not have to wash the dishes). Two of the consequences to a behavior are punishing, which means that they make the behavior less likely to occur in the future. A behavior is punished by application when something undesirable is administered after the behavior occurs (a spanking). A behavior is punished by removal when something desirable is taken away (we lose car privileges). The fifth possible consequence is that the behavior is ignored. This process is called *extinction* and, like punishment, reduces the likelihood of the behavior occurring in the future. Consequences can be concrete as in the examples above, or they can be social like praise or derision.

When target problems concern desirable behavior that occurs infrequently or undesirable behavior that occurs frequently, a close examination of the environment for the purpose of discovering the contingencies to the behavior is in order. The contingencies are then altered for the purpose of changing the frequency of the behavior. Incentives have been incorporated in TC since its inception, and changing contingencies is often part of our work with collaterals.

Skills   We all have differing skills, and they operate at differing levels of proficiency. It is important to differentiate between behaviors that are occurring infrequently because of inappropriate contingencies, as described in the preceding section, and behaviors that are not occurring because the skill is not in the person's repertoire. If the skill has not been attained, no amount of reinforcement will increase the frequency with which it is performed. Some of the skills that have been examined and are relevant to psychosocial functioning include assertiveness, coping, negotiating, communicating, problem solving, social skills, and stress management. Behaviorists have developed procedures for teaching skills, and the procedures can be incorporated in

TC through tasks. The *Task Planner* (Reid 2000) includes several of these skills.

Stress   Stress occurs when people are overtaxed in some way. Stress is not the same as stimulation. In fact, being understimulated is sometimes stressful. Furthermore, everyone does not experience the same event or situation as stressful, because the individual's perception of the extent of the challenge in relation to his or her ability to cope with it will influence the amount of stress he or she experiences (Lazarus 1966). One approach to measuring stress, the "Social Readjustment Rating Scale," rates forty-three life events in terms of how stressful they are (Holmes and Rahe 1967). Included on the scale are death of a spouse, divorce, marital separation, vacation, and change of eating habits. Other ways of measuring stress focus on the number of chronic or routine stressors. Regardless of how stress is measured, it has been found to be associated with physical and psychological illness. Clients who are experiencing excessive stress can be helped to eliminate some of its sources or to cope with it through stress management (Lehrer and Woolfolk 1993).

Social Support   Social support includes the emotional support, advice, and guidance, as well as the tangible services, that people obtain from their social relationships (Eli 1984). A deficit of social connections "has been shown to be an important risk factor in psychological well-being, illness, and even death . . . [whereas] support enhances immunity to illness, influences health-related behaviors, and maximizes adaptation and recovery from illness" (133). Significant supportive relationships are usually characterized by geographical proximity, frequent interaction, trust, and reciprocity. When social support is lacking, we can help clients develop supportive relationships or locate appropriate support groups.

Spirituality   Spirituality was not included in the first edition of this book because it had received little attention in the professional literature, especially in social work. However, some recent studies have found it to be related to well-being (Hodge 2001). Currently knowledge is insufficient to suggest how or whether spirituality might be incorporated in practice. However, we can recognize that spirituality is an asset for many clients and respect its influence on them.

2.2.1 CHECKLIST FOR THEORETICAL BASE

___ 1. Am I operating on an explanation for the target problems in this case?

___ 2. If so, what is it?

___ 3. Is this explanation necessary?

___ 4. What alternative explanations might apply? (Consider the dimensions of functioning described in this section.)

___ 5. Does the client have an explanation in mind?

___ 6. If so, what is it?

___ 7. Do the client's explanations conflict with mine?

2.2.2 QUESTIONS TO CONSIDER

1. For the following statements, identify those that are practice directives and those that are explanatory.

    a. Establish a contract with your clients.

    b. Inappropriate behavior is the result of the person's learning history.

    c. Use time limits whenever possible.

    d. Many child abusers have themselves been abused as children.

2. Why does the fact that TC is free of behavioral theory on the formal level make it an ideal base for generalist and eclectic practice?

3. For the following problems or situations, write down the first explanation that comes into your head. Do it privately so that you will be more likely to be honest.

    a. a young, African-American teenager has become pregnant

    b. a young, white teenager has become pregnant

    c. a middle-aged man has been demoted

    d. a middle-aged woman has been demoted

    e. depression

    f. failure

    g. stealing

Now examine your responses to see if any patterns emerge. Are your explanations different for African-Americans than for whites? Are your explanations about men different than those about women? Do you tend to attribute most problems to one arena, such as the individual, the family, or society?

4. What are the dangers of relying on only one theory?
5. What are the differences between behavioral theory, change theory, and a practice model?

2.3.0 MISSION AND PURPOSE

Another prerequisite to becoming a professional social worker entails understanding and commitment to the mission and purpose of the profession. *Mission* refers to our collective humanitarian cause, our raison d'être. It has been described as the "persistent and deliberate effort to improve the living or working conditions in the community or to relieve, diminish, or prevent distress" (Flexner 1915:584). This includes the identification and eradication of "new evils" (Lee 1929). Currently our mission is captured by the phrase "social justice," which is the quest for "an ideal condition in which all members of a society have the same rights, protection, opportunities, obligations, and social benefits" (Barker 1995:354). The number and severity of problems that reflect social injustice is extensive: poverty, racism and sexism, toleration of domestic abuse and crime-ridden neighborhoods, discrimination of the disabled, illiteracy and ineffective educational systems, and inequitable distribution of wealth and resources. It can be argued that our most pressing problem is poverty. Poverty is correlated with almost all other social problems. The poor are disproportionately represented among those who are mentally ill, who abuse children, and who are deprived of resources for health care, legal assistance, education, and so on. Furthermore, no other profession is committed to serving the disadvantaged and disenfranchised.

The nature of our mission is, perhaps, the best argument for generalist practice. Social justice cannot be attained by using only one modality of practice. We must be equipped to aid individuals and to impact the communities and organizations that affect the quality of their lives.

Purpose, as used here, is more circumscribed than *mission*. The general purpose of social work is to provide service. Purpose is more specifically defined by individual workers or agencies. The purpose of social workers in family service agencies is generally to improve individual or family functioning. The purpose of social workers in child-protective agencies is to prevent the abuse and neglect of children. The purpose of social workers in secondary settings like schools and hospitals is to alter the social or psychological factors that prevent the client from using the primary services.

It is apparent that an unlimited number of specific purposes exist within social work. Briar (1977) observed: "The unavoidable vagueness inherent in the breadth of goals [purposes], together with the resulting wide variation in what social workers actually do, has given rise to serious doubts among some segments of the profession about the identity of social work" (1530). However, many diverse purposes are necessary if we are to accomplish the mission defined above.

2.3.1 CHECKLIST FOR MISSION AND PURPOSE

___ 1. What is my purpose in this agency?
___ 2. Is the purpose of the agency consistent with the mission of social work?
___ 3. What are my goals with each of my clients?
___ 4. Are these goals consistent with the purpose of the agency?

2.3.2 QUESTIONS TO CONSIDER

1. Try to identify case goals that would be inconsistent with agency purposes, and agency purposes that would be inconsistent with the mission of social work.

2. You probably have an expectation about the kind of social work you will practice. How will this kind of practice further the mission of social work? What aspects of our mission will your practice not advance? What can you do about these omissions?

3. Which is more important to social work: reform or rehabilitation? Is it proper to help individuals adjust to depriving or demeaning environments?

4. How is capitalism related to the mission of social work? Can our objectives be achieved within a capitalistic society?

5. How might the purposes of TC differ from the purposes of other approaches?

2.4.0 SOCIAL WORK VALUES

The *NASW Code of Ethics* (National Association of Social Workers 1996) delineates six values that are central to the profession of social work. They are service, social justice, dignity and worth of the person, importance of human relationships, integrity, and competence. Service and social justice have been discussed in the preceding section, "Mission and Purpose." The value of competence is reflected in our concern for effectiveness, which was also described in a preceding section. However, it is worth emphasizing that effectiveness is not only a technical issue but also an ethical one: Clients have a right to effective treatment (Myers and Thyer 1997). The importance of human relationships pertains to our belief that relationships are central to human development, well-being, and the provision of service. Integrity refers to our trustworthiness and honesty. These characteristics are particularly important, because we work with vulnerable people and sometimes with people who have no choice about receiving our services. Concern for the dignity and worth of the person has a long history in social work and requires elaboration.

Respect for persons is central to the philosophy of social work. Some have argued that, in fact, respect for persons is a presupposition of all morality or moral systems (Plant 1970). It is certainly our moral imperative: "There is a particular value so emphasized by caseworkers and so involved in caseworkers' thinking that it is impossible to understand casework treatment without reference to it. 'Respect for persons' is more than anything the value which gives casework its particular character" (Moffett 1968:27). This value means that human beings are entitled to respect as persons regardless of their roles, stature, behavior, or even their character. Furthermore, it means that human beings are to be treated with equal respect. Thus the essential dignity of the mentally ill, criminals, the poor, and minorities is no different than that of those who are admired and accomplished. Social workers are not respecters of particular persons but impartial respecters of the dignity of all people.

There are two indicators of the extent to which we respect people. They are individualization and self-determination. Individualization refers to recognizing and treating each person as unique. Stereotyping is the reverse of individualization. When we stereotype, we apply a fixed idea to an individual. Stereotypes are most commonly applied to the disadvantaged and disenfranchised. Unfortunately diagnostic labels are often used to stereotype. Terms such as *schizophrenic, adult child of an alcoholic,* and *abuser* can be used to see a person as an assemblage of generalized characteristics rather than as an individual.

Respect for the right to self-determination might be thought of as the operational definition of respect for the dignity of human beings. Our ability to allow clients to make their own decisions is a measure of the extent to which we respect their dignity as individuals.

The reader will discover that TC fully implements the value of respect for the client's right to self-determination. The client has the final word in determining the target problems and the strategies or tasks selected to ameliorate them. The conversion of this value to a treatment procedure was anticipated by Briar and Miller (1971) with the suggestion that clients might make more progress when offered maximum opportunities for self-determination.

The incorporation of procedures that assure that self-determination will be respected does not, of course, eliminate all value dilemmas. In fact, genuine value conflicts are inherent in living. The rights of the abused child and the abusing parent will always be in conflict. The right to obtain an abortion will raise ethical dilemmas for some social workers. Conflicts will exist with other professionals. Disruptive children might interfere with the ability of teachers to educate all children in the classroom, but disruptive children also have the right to an education.

2.4.1 CHECKLIST FOR SOCIAL WORK VALUES

___ 1. Am I permitting my clients to determine the direction of our efforts?
___ 2. If I am not, why not?
___ 3. What does this tell me about my own values?
___ 4. What corrective actions are necessary?

2.4.2 QUESTIONS TO CONSIDER

1. Your client confides that he or she intends to commit suicide. What do you do? Why? Identify the value(s) being considered and the nature of the value conflict.
2. Your agency has conducted a study to examine its effectiveness. The results are disappointing. The director has decided to "bury" the findings because publication might result in a loss of funding with concomitant reductions in services to clients. What is your position on the matter? Why?
3. Your client wishes to regain custody of her children who have been removed from the home because they were neglected. You doubt her capacity to care for them. What do you do? Why?

2.5.0 RELATIONSHIP

Implementing any approach to practice effectively requires the ability to relate to people. Relationship has been an important concept in social work and psychotherapy since the inception of these professions. At one time it was believed that a good professional relationship between the practitioner and client would, in itself, cause the desired changes (Rogers 1957). Virtually hundreds of research projects about some aspect of relationship were conducted based on this belief, and we now know that, although the relationship is associated with outcome, it is not sufficient to cause change by itself (Greenberg, Elliott, and Lietaer 1994). Rather, it is recognized as a nonspecific factor that is thought to act as a mediating variable. This means that it is important in all approaches to practice, because it influences the impact of other variables. For example, the client will be more willing and able to share information when a good relationship exists, and this information will, in turn, enable the social worker to be more helpful. Or the client might be more willing to follow the social worker's suggestions when the relationship is a good one.

The discovery that relationship is not, in itself, curative has produced some changes in the professional literature. Many recent conceptualizations of relationship refer to it as the "therapeutic alliance," which is intended to capture the idea that clients also make a contribution to the quality of the relationship. Although an association between alliance and outcome has been found in a number of studies, there is unfortunately no clear consensus on the definition of alliance and little is known about the behaviors or characteristics that are likely to produce effective alliances (Henry et al. 1994). As a result, our description of the components of effective relationships must largely rely on work done from about 1950 to 1980.

It should be noted that the term *professional* has been used to describe the relationship. This means that the client-worker relationship differs from nonprofessional relationships. The professional relationship has a purpose other than simple pleasure. It is formed in order to get work accomplished. The professional relationship is not reciprocal; the client does not have the obligation to return behaviors in kind. The professional relationship is governed by the ethical canons of the profession, which are articulated in the NASW Code of Ethics.

2.5.1 COMPONENTS OF EFFECTIVE PROFESSIONAL RELATIONSHIPS

The three aspects of relationship that have received the most attention are warmth, empathy, and genuineness (Nugent 1992; Beutler, Machado, and Neufeldt 1994). They are sometimes referred to as the "core conditions" or the "facilitative conditions." They were the core of the client-centered approach to psychotherapy (Rogers 1957) and have been the focus of much research over the years. Warmth, empathy, and genuineness are conveyed through words, paralanguage, and body language. Some specific behaviors that convey these conditions to the client include:

1. verbal statements that express interest, concern, and involvement (Caracena and Vicory 1969; Tepper 1973);
2. clarity of verbal expressions (Caracena and Vicory 1969);
3. concerned facial expressions, eye contact, head nods, and a posture that leans toward the client (Tepper 1973; D'Augelli 1974);
4. relaxed body posture (Mehrabian 1973; Tepper 1973);
5. frequent, brief responses by the therapist (Feitel 1968); and
6. vocal tone (Pope 1979).

The combination of eye contact, forward trunk lean, closer distance, and positive verbal message has been found to convey the highest degree of empathy (Haase and Tepper 1972). Movements of the body, head, and hands, and smiling, convey warmth (Bayes 1972). In general, the facilitative practitioner is "keenly attentive . . . having a manner that patients experience as natural or unstudied, saying or doing nothing that decreases the client's self-respect, at times giving direct reassurance . . . and leaving no doubt about his 'real' feelings" (Strupp, Fox, and Lesser 1969:80).

Conveying empathy, one of the most important interviewing skills, entails verbalizing the client's feelings. It requires an accurate recognition of them. Ideally social workers are continuously aware of the feelings their clients are experiencing. This is not easy, because in this society we are conditioned to conceal our emotions. This means that clients will often not recognize or acknowledge their emotions. It also means that we might be inclined to pretend not to notice them. In other words, we have to overcome the standard rules of polite behavior and help clients to recognize and articulate feelings that are often painful and sometimes embarrassing. Doing so requires that we attend to the subtle clues clients provide. These include facial expression, body language, and tone of voice. Unless the client's emotions are crystal clear, it is wise to make empathic statements with a questioning tone of voice: "You seem very disappointed by your mother's reaction?" This allows the client to correct us if we are wrong about the emotion identified. Often a client's emotions are obscure, and we will want to inquire about them directly: "What are you feeling as you talk about your mother?" With experience, social workers develop large affective vocabularies that allow them to articulate empathy with precision. They also become skilled at identifying positive emotions as well as painful ones.

In addition to the behaviors that convey warmth, empathy, and genuineness, other behaviors have been identified that convey a deficit of the core conditions. These include inactive interviewers, frequent interruptions, verbose responses, and frequent silences (Hargrove 1974; Pierce 1971; Pierce and Mosher 1967; Pope et al. 1974; Staples and Sloane 1976; Strupp and Wallach 1965; Truax 1970; Truax and Carkhuff 1967).

The social worker must also master other basic interviewing skills (Ivey and Authier 1978). The most important of these skills, namely, exploration, is the ability to acquire information through questioning. Questions can be closed or open. Closed questions can be answered with a few words; for example, "Where do you live?" Open questions allow the client more room to choose how to respond; for example, "Can you tell me more about your relationship with your daughter." Other interviewing skills include using minimal encouraging phrases ("Uh huh"), paraphrasing, and summarizing.

Effective social workers are able to convey warmth, empathy, and genuineness and keep work progressing. This requires another interviewing skill: directiveness. Directiveness refers to the extent to which the practitioner structures intervention by controlling the topic of discussion.

Other important skills include advising (Fortune 1981), confrontation (Johnson 1971), self-disclosure (Hackney and Cormier 1994; Mann and Murphy 1975), and reinforcing (Sloane et al. 1975). A word of caution is necessary with respect to confrontation and worker self-disclosure. Confrontation with a cold or domineering therapist can lead to deterioration (Tovian 1977). It is most effective when directed at client strengths rather than pathology. Self-disclosure occurs when workers share information about themselves. Self-disclosing has been shown to help clients to share information. However, it should be used judiciously and infrequently, and it probably should be avoided with severely mentally ill clients.

The expertness or credibility and attractiveness of the social worker are also likely to influence the course of work. These characteristics, along with trustworthiness, are believed to determine the worker's persuasive power and have been found to be associated with outcome in a few clinical studies (Beutler, Machado, and Neufeldt 1994). Credibility is conveyed by one or more of the following attributes: credentials, opinion of others, reliability, warmth and friendliness, and energy (Johnson and Matross 1977). Attractiveness has been defined in many different ways. Among them are cooperativeness and goal facilitation, physical appearance, likability, similarity, competence, warmth, and familiarity (Tolson 1988).

Articulating client strengths has become a popular skill. It is reasonable to believe that doing so is useful because it might enhance client self-efficacy and the relationship between client and worker. As yet there appear to be no empirical studies of its impact, however.

Social workers not only need a large repertoire of relationship skills, but they must be able to select the skills that are likely to be influential with a particular client. This is especially challenging in multicultural contacts (for a more detailed discussion, see chapter 16, section 16.2.5.0). Potential barriers to communication in these contacts include language and the interpretation of nonverbal communication (Lum 2000). Particular skills might be interpreted differently. For example, it was found that the use of self-disclosure reduced the perception of trustworthiness for Mexican undergraduate students (Cherbosque 1987), whereas it enhanced rapport with Asian-Americans (Tsui and Schultz 1985). We still know little about which skills are likely to be most effective with particular clients. It does appear, however, that disadvantaged clients are more likely to remain in treatment if the worker is warm and does not allow long silences during the interview (Jacobs et al. 1972).

Relationship is an important aspect of all our professional contacts. Good relationships with other professionals, such as the schoolteachers of our child-clients and the physicians and nurses of our ill ones, are imperative if we are to secure their cooperation. Relationships with those to whom we refer clients or from whom we receive referrals are similarly important.

2.5.2 RELATIONSHIP IN TASK-CENTERED WORK WITH INDIVIDUALS

Relating to clients when using TC requires all the skills identified in section 2.5.1. Social workers explore thoroughly, listen attentively, and demonstrate warmth, empathy, and genuineness. They advise, confront, disclose, reinforce, and assume the responsibility for directing work.

The assumption about relationship in TC is consistent with the research concerning relationship: Relationship is important as a mediating variable rather than a curative one. In fact, some TC practitioners prefer to use the term *rapport* rather than *relationship* to emphasize this theoretical distinction.

We have occasionally encountered clients who appear to need a longer term, *supportive relationship*. It seems that some female teenagers are among this group. We have only impressionistic information to support this observation. However, the possibility that teenagers—at least some female ones—might need longer-term relationships is in accord with the developmental issue of this life stage: the search for identity. We suggest that another approach to practice be employed when the relationship is likely to be a curative variable for a particular client. When you are in doubt about the importance of the relationship for a particular client, it is usually preferable to try TC first. The reasons for beginning with TC are (1) you will quickly learn if TC is not going to work; and (2) it is easier to switch from short-term work to long-term work than vice versa.

The second distinguishing characteristic of the TC relationship is its highly collaborative nature. Tapes of TC interviews reveal a great deal of mutuality between the contributions of workers and clients. In fact, they often sound like partners. Both parties are engaged in problem solving, and they are engaged as equals.

2.5.3 CHECKLIST FOR RELATIONSHIP

(If tapes of interviews are unavailable, see section 3.1.2 on role plays to practice these skills.)

___ 1. Paralanguage. Is my voice relaxed? My pitch low?

___ 2. Body language. Is my posture relaxed? Do I lean slightly toward the client? Do I use head nods and smiles?

___ 3. Verbal behavior. Do I use minimal encouraging phrases? Do I speak at length? Do I allow long silences? Do I express empathy and collaborative intentions? Do I use a mixture of open and closed questions?

___ 4. Directiveness. Do I keep the interview(s) focused?

___ 5. Do I reinforce client behavior? How?

___ 6. Which skills need improvement? What other skills would I like to add to my repertoire?

___ 7. How am I going to improve or add skills?

2.5.4 QUESTIONS TO CONSIDER

1. You are a school social worker, and a teacher wants one of your clients expelled. What relationship skills might you use in attempting to prevent this?

2. A client continuously repeats his or her "story" to the point that it interferes with attempts to change the situation. What might this indicate? What might you try to do to lessen this behavior?

3. You have a nonverbal client. What might you do to increase his or her verbal participation?

2.6.0 THE APPROPRIATE SYSTEM FOR WORK

The parameters for deciding on the primary system were discussed in chapter 1. At this point—pretreatment—the decision to work with an individual should be treated as highly tentative. Confirmation or revision of the decision will be made after the location of the problems, necessary changes, and problem-solvers are identified.

The initial decision to begin working with an individual is usually based on the problem identifier. The problem identifier can be a person seeking service for themselves, a person seeking service for someone else, or another professional making a referral. The nurse who mentions that a patient is having difficulty, the teacher who refers an underachieving child, or a social worker who refers a client from another agency are all problem identifiers.

In the pretreatment stage, our decision to work with an individual is based on someone else thinking that an individual is experiencing a problem. Sometimes we learn, after contact, that the problems are marital ones, for example, and our decision about the primary system must be revised. Sometimes we learn that the problem cannot be solved by the client and social worker alone. Often this will lead us to identify another primary, natural system. On other occasions we might want to consider using case management. In this approach, a new or artificial system is created that consists of the client, practitioner, and important collaterals. This group meets and works together as a management team. This approach will be developed in the family chapters, and, of course, much of the content in the group chapters will also be applicable.

The accuracy of our decisions about the primary system should be reviewed throughout treatment. The decision will be reconsidered during assessment in the initial stages of treatment and as part of revising assessments during the middle phase of treatment.

2.6.1 QUESTIONS TO CONSIDER

1. Why have I decided to work with an individual client?
2. What other systems might be involved?
3. Am I open to revising this decision?

3

THE INITIAL PHASE OF TREATMENT

3.0.0 COMPONENTS OF THE INITIAL PHASE

The most meaningful definition of a phase of treatment is based on the practitioner's purpose. The purpose of the initial phase is to prepare to intervene. The purpose of the middle phase is to intervene. And the purpose of the final or termination phase is to wrap up the work. However, phases can also be approximately defined by the number of sessions. The initial phase of task-centered treatment with individuals can consume any amount of time from a fraction of one session to four sessions. The middle phase usually lasts about six to eight sessions, and the termination phase one session. The actual length of a phase will depend, to some extent, on the complexity of the work to be done.

The initial phase is comprised of the following activities: explanation of role, purpose, and treatment procedures; obtaining necessary facts; targeting problems and determining problem priorities; exploring the target problem; developing a problem specification and a goal statement; setting time limits; contracting; and making assessments. Each of these activities are described in detail below.

Before proceeding, the reader is advised to become familiar with the work conducted with two clients, Mrs. Carter and Ronnie Paige, which is described at the end of chapter 5. We refer to this work in this and the following two chapters to illustrate treatment procedures.

3.1.0 Explanations of Role, Purpose, and Treatment Procedures

Often, when clients come to us, they know little about what to expect. Sometimes their expectations are quite erroneous. When they are sent to us or we are sent to them by schoolteachers, medical doctors, and the like, they are in even greater need for information about why they are there and what the experience will be like. Explanations about role, purpose, and procedures have two functions. First, they partially alleviate the client's fear of the unknown. Second, they help the client to participate in the treatment endeavor.

Explanation of role and purpose includes several items of information. First, and most obvious, the client needs to know your name, title, and the name of the institution for which you are working: "I am Ms. Jones and I am a social worker here at St. Joseph's Hospital." It is often helpful to give the client your name and telephone number in writing. The way you introduce yourself indicates how you want to be addressed. If the setting is an informal one, you might want to say, "I am Sandy Jones. You may call me Sandy."

The client also needs to know something about what you do as a social worker. Misconceptions about social workers abound. At least two dimensions exist on which past experience might impact current expectations. The first concerns the type and purpose of treatment. The second concerns the client's satisfaction with the experience. To learn about both, Ms. Jones might inquire, "Have you ever worked with a social worker before?" Clients who have had previous experience should be asked to describe the experience. This allows the social worker to correct any preconceived ideas about how she and the client will work together. Depending on the client's description, Ms. Jones might say, "I'm glad you had a good experience working with Mr. Henry during your last hospitalization. I know and like/respect Mr. Henry, too" (Tip: Always "ride the coattails" of a positive connection during early contacts). "You and I will be doing similar things together." Or, "It sounds like you've had a terrible time with your public assistance worker. But social workers here at the hospital operate differently." In the latter example, the worker would identify how the work will differ.

When the client has no information about social workers, you will have to start from scratch. "Social workers here at St. Joseph's work with clients to help them get ready to leave the hospital." We have found that examples are usually helpful: "Sometimes clients need special equipment like wheelchairs. Sometimes stress at home or work makes people sick in the first place, so we help patients figure out how to deal with those stresses." Sometimes clients are unfamiliar with the agency the social worker represents. This is often the case when a child welfare worker investigates a complaint. In these cases, the social worker will have to ascertain what the client knows about the agency and provide information or correct misinformation.

Clients who are referred need additional information. They need to know who referred them and why: "Your teacher, Ms. Smith, asked me to meet with you, because she thinks you are having some problems with your schoolwork." Usually the reason for referral can be stated in general terms. Of course, it should always be stated tactfully: "Ms. Smith said you are the laziest kid she's ever met," is clearly inappropriate.

Be sensitive to the client's reaction to referral information. Sometimes clients are hurt by such information. For example, a child might be strongly attached to a teacher and might interpret the referral to mean that the attachment is not reciprocated. When this occurs, it is important to address the effect and clarify the meaning of the referral. For example:

SOCIAL WORKER: You seem upset that Ms. Smith asked me to see you.

CHILD: Ms. Smith doesn't like me anymore.

SOCIAL WORKER: I think she likes you very much and wants to see you do well in school.

Clients might respond to referrals for suspected child abuse with anger, and to referrals from physicians with fear. Any negative reaction needs to be discussed.

With respect to the timing of this activity, it should obviously occur early in the contact with a new client. Reading about this activity actually takes longer than doing it. With self-referred clients, it will take about two or three minutes. With clients referred by others, it will usually take no more than five minutes.

We explain treatment procedures for the purpose of (1) making the experience less mysterious (and fearful) for the client; and (2) enabling the client to participate in treatment productively. The actual treatment procedures to be explained will probably make more sense once the reader has finished part 1 of this book and thus understands TC. The procedures are briefly identified here and described in detail in the following chapter. We have found that explaining several aspects of the approach to the client is essential. In fact, the importance of client preparation has been validated by several research studies (Zwick and Attkisson 1984; Sloane et al. 1970; Acosta et al. 1983).

The first procedure to be explained refers to target problems and is twofold. It concerns the facts that (1) you and the client will work on a few specific areas; and (2) the client will select the areas or problems that he or she wants help with. This is important because it conveys respect for the client's right to self-determination and empowers the client.

The second characteristic of the model that must be explained is that it is time-limited. The explanation of this is important for several reasons. First, time limits probably help to keep some people in treatment who would otherwise drop out (Tolson and Brown 1981). Second, when the practitioner intends to use time-limited treatment, clients have a right to know the duration of treatment. A surprise ending might be interpreted as rejection. Finally, setting time limits conveys hope and thus is likely to support the client's motivation.

Finally, in any approach to treatment the client must be informed about confidentiality and any limits to it. For example, if the client is mandated to receive treatment by the court, the worker would describe the kind of information that would have to be reported in any judicial proceedings.

Following the explanation of procedures, the worker should confirm the client's understanding of them and solicit/observe the client's reaction to the procedures. Any confusion or negative reaction should be discussed. A social work student followed her explanation of procedures to a very young boy with the question, "What would you like us to work on together?" His confusion was obvious in his response,

"How about a puzzle?" An occasional client is troubled by the time limits. Usually we try to postpone this concern for reasons that will be made clear in the section on time limits (section 3.2.0). Some clients who are accustomed to being told what to do will be surprised to learn that they will determine the target problems. They may have to be helped to identify areas of concern, as described in section 3.4.0.

The explanation of procedures should occur no later than the end of the first session or contact. With clients who are not experiencing any internal pressure to tell their story, it will probably occur early in the interview after the explanation of role and purpose. Explanations of purpose and procedures are brief, but they often require repeating. If treatment begins to drift or if the client's efforts begin to wane, the first intervention attempted should be to repeat aspects of these explanations: "As I understand it, you want very much to ___ and we only have ___ more sessions left, so perhaps we'd better focus on getting ___ accomplished." Often this is sufficient to remobilize efforts.

3.1.1 CHECKLIST FOR EXPLANATION OF ROLE, PURPOSE, AND TREATMENT PROCEDURES

___ 1. Does the client know:
    ___ a. my name
    ___ b. my title
    ___ c. the name of the agency
    ___ d. the purpose of the agency
    ___ e. my purpose within the agency
    ___ f. who referred him or her
    ___ g. the reason for referral

___ 2. Does the client understand that together we will work toward changing specific aspects of his or her situation?

___ 3. Does the client realize that he or she will choose these aspects or targets of treatment?

___ 4. Has the client been told that we will work together for a specific number of sessions?

___ 5. Does the client understand confidentiality and any limits to it?

3.1.2 EXERCISES: GENERAL INSTRUCTIONS

All the exercises in this part, task-centered treatment with individuals, can be completed by forming groups of two or three people. In groups of two people, one plays the role of the client and the other, the social worker. In groups of three people, the third person acts as the observer. The observer uses the checklist to determine that all skills are used and provides qualitative feedback about the use of the skills. (Whether you use an observer depends on the amount of time available. Role plays will take twice as long if an observer is used because an additional person must have the opportunity to enact the role of social worker.) Whether the groups are composed of two or three people, the person enacting the role of client should also provide feedback to the social worker. Roles should be exchanged so that everyone has a chance to play each role. The exercises can be used either during class sessions or outside class.

Feedback is most useful when it balances positives and negatives, and when it is behaviorally specific. This means that the strengths of the person enacting the role of social worker, as well as areas that need improvement, should be noted. It also means that suggestions should be made in a way that can be acted on. For example, "You did not seem very warm" is not as helpful as "You seldom made eye contact."

Feedback is, of course, only meaningful if it is received. Receiving negative feedback is sometimes difficult because social work skills seem so closely related to who we are. It is helpful to think of acquiring social work skills as similar to learning to play the piano, tennis, or bridge. All these activities require practice, and the degree of skill that can be acquired is unlimited. This means that we should all expect to need practice to master these skills and that even the most talented can expand their behavioral repertoires.

It is often useful for the recipient of feedback to make notes concerning the comments. This not only serves as a memory aid but enables the individual to consider the feedback at a time when he or she is less defensive.

Some suggestions concerning the role of client are also in order. Unless otherwise noted, these exercises are most effective when the person playing this role assumes a somewhat neutral position. This means that you do not behave like either the most or least cooperative client imaginable. Also, it is helpful to assume the behavior of a client or another person you have known.

Several considerations affect the number of exercises you choose to use and the order in which you use them. These include the experience of the learner, the opportunity to practice in the field, and the time available. The most essential exercises in chapter 3 are those provided for identifying and prioritizing target problems, exploration, and problem specification. Furthermore, the exercises can be combined if desired. For example, the three most essential ones can be combined if one long block of time is available. Similarly, explaining role, purpose, and procedures (including time limits) and contracting can be combined.

If the exercises are performed in class, instructors can circulate in the room, eavesdropping on each group briefly as role plays are progressing. This provides an opportunity to reinforce effective interviewing skills, provide corrective feedback on deficient ones, and resolve difficulties in using TC. Following the role plays, it is helpful to reconvene as a class for the purpose of discussing any difficulties encountered.

3.1.3 EXERCISE FOR EXPLAINING ROLE, PURPOSE, AND PROCEDURES

Following the general instructions provided in section 3.1.2, practice explaining role, purpose, and procedure. This can be done with a voluntary and nonvoluntary client. Notice how the "client" status alters the way you use these skills. For example, you might enact the role of a school social worker with a student who has sought your help for academic problems and then with a student who has been referred by a teacher. If desired, practicing these skills can be combined with practicing the explanation of time limits.

3.2.0 TIME LIMITS

Numerous studies have been conducted on the effect of time limits on treatment (Johnson and Gelso 1980; Koss and Shiang 1994). The conclusion from these studies is that short-term treatment is at least as effective as treatment of indefinite lengths and is probably more effective. In addition to the relationship between time limits and effectiveness, fewer clients seem to drop out of time-limited treatment (Tolson and Brown 1981). Finally, surveys have revealed that the median length of treatment in the helping professions is between five and eight sessions (Garfield 1994).

The time limit in task-centered work is usually between six and twelve interviews. Sometimes two time limits are established: one for the initial phase and one for the remainder of treatment. For example, you might tell a client: "It should not take more than four sessions for you to help me understand your situation. I think we should be able to accomplish most of your goals in an additional six sessions." The number of sessions will depend on the worker's "best guess" as to how much time is needed. The initial phase in our experience has never taken longer than four sessions, however, and the work to be done during that phase often can be accomplished in just one or two sessions.

Time limits and TC can be used in long-term monitoring situations if the client has problems for which he or she wants our help. Work with such cases can be conceptualized as successive short-term contracts. Thus a contract might be established to work on helping the client monitor the school performance of his or her children for six sessions. This contract might be followed by one that concerns improving housing conditions, and so on. As with other clients, usually no more than three problems should be targeted at one time. Time limits can also help to provide quality service even when the social worker has a large caseload and many clients who require monitoring. A few clients can be receiving task-centered interventions for six to twelve weeks while others are simply monitored. As treatment contracts with these clients are completed, other clients can be moved to "the front burner" while the original active clients are returned to the monitoring status.

Time limits are generally set near the end of the first session. This gives the social worker an opportunity to get a sense of the scope and magnitude of the problems. Sometimes problems are so clearly and completely presented that the initial-phase work is accomplished without any need to set a separate time limit.

Social workers are often reluctant to use time limits. Several factors might account for this. First, our profession has had a historic reverence for long-term treatment. Second, social workers are usually generous people and limiting the amount of service seems to strike some of them as ungiving. Third, some social workers are afraid they will not be able to reach the desired goals within a short period of time.

Remember that you may be offering less contact but, according to research findings, you are offering better-quality service when you use time limits. Remember that your clients really do not want to see you for the rest of their lives any more than you want to see your physician or attorney regularly. Rather, clients want the most relief possible in the shortest period of time—just like the rest of us. Remember that time limits can always be extended. In fact, moving from time-limited treatment to long-term treatment is much simpler than the reverse. Time-limits imposed on long-term clients are often experienced as rejection. Finally, think about how automatically you use time limits when you need to be productive. For example, do you give yourself time limits to write term papers or complete assignments?

Reluctance to use time limits is often expressed by being vague about them or disqualifying them even as they are set: "We'll meet for six to ten sessions but, if that is not enough, we can always meet longer." Sometimes reluctance is expressed by setting too many sessions—twelve sessions instead of six. Our best advice about time limits is this: "Try them. You'll like them." Be sure, however, to give them a fair test. This means that you should (1) set a specific number of sessions; (2) set a realistic number of sessions without padding; and (3) avoid indicating that more sessions can be added, unless the client is absolutely adamant about needing this reassurance.

Time limits are, in fact, frequently altered, and this will be discussed in the next chapter. If our flexibility about them is made clear too quickly, however, time limits lose their power to enhance the productivity of our work with clients. A final suggestion about time limits concerns work with young children. Often they do not have a good sense of time. As a result, we have found it useful to provide them with some concrete indicator. A calendar can be used so that the child can color in the day of each session and count the remaining, uncolored sessions.

3.2.1 CHECKLIST FOR TIME LIMITS

> — 1. Have I set a specific number of interviews with the client?
> — 2. If the client is a child, have I provided a concrete indicator of the number of sessions?

3.2.2 EXERCISE FOR TIME LIMITS

Practice explaining time limits along with explaining other treatment procedures as described in section 3.1.2.

3.3.0 OBTAINING NECESSARY INFORMATION

Since task-centered treatment is focused and specific, beginning social workers sometimes fail to obtain the basic, minimal information to understand the context of the clients' lives. Some of this information is often referred to as "face sheet data." It includes address, phone number, age, race or ethnicity, gender, religion, marital status, referral source, the reason for referral, and family constellation.

Even this basic information allows the social worker to develop some anticipatory empathy. The address reveals the kind of neighborhood the client lives in. Is it dangerous? Are many services available in that locale? Will it be difficult for the client to get to your location? Age and gender will tell you something about the common struggles and concerns that your client might be experiencing. Age, gender, race, and ethnicity might alert you to the extent to which the client must confront injustice and bigotry. (Necessary information specific to cultural diversity is described in chapter 16, section 16.3.3.0.) Referral information will provide the broad outlines of the problem situation that the client is struggling with.

In addition, information should be obtained about all members of the family and the household. The social worker should not assume that these two groups are the same. For each member of both groups the social worker should know the age, gender, relationship to the client, occupation, place of employment, and grade in school or highest grade achieved. The whereabouts of family members not living in the household is also important. Source and amount of household income should also be determined. All this information will give the social worker some ideas about the stresses (including economic ones), stability, aspirations, and available support within the family. Some words of caution are in order for securing even this minimal information. First, if the information you seek does not seem pertinent to solving the problem the client presented, your questions might strike the client as impertinent or intrusive. Certain questions might even be threatening or embarrassing for some clients. An unwed, pregnant teenager might be reluctant to reveal the whereabouts of the father of her child. A woman might be embarrassed to tell the worker that her husband is in prison. Employment might not be admitted if the client is also receiving public assistance. Thus even questions that seem innocuous must be asked sensitively. In order not to appear intrusive, you need to explain why you are asking the questions: "I need to know something about your family situation in order to determine which agency or program will best fit your needs." This kind of statement is a form of "meta-communication" or communication about communication. Experienced practitioners use it frequently. It is also important to let clients know how you will use the information, that is, to inform them of the limits, if any, to confidentiality.

A second precaution concerns your interpretation of the data. While it is useful to know general characteristics of minority groups or women or forty year olds and to consider your client's status on these and other dimensions, you also need to avoid stereotyping. For example, many African-Americans do have extended family networks, but not all African-Americans have them. Many single-parent households are impoverished, but not all single-parent households fall into that category. Women experience discrimination, but not all of them are willing or able to acknowledge it. Thus you need to use your knowledge of human behavior to understand clients and their situations, but, at the same time, you need to individualize the particular client.

If the agency has an intake process, some of this information will be obtained before you see the client. If not, some of it—like address and phone number—will probably be obtained during the first few minutes of the first contact. Social workers have a choice about the manner in which they obtain information about the remaining areas identified. They can inquire about all these areas in a structured fashion at the beginning of contact, or they can wait until the clients volunteer information as they tell their stories and then follow up in a structured fashion to fill in the gaps. The choice depends on the client. Clients who are eager to tell their stories should be allowed to do so. With those who are hesitant, asking simple, factual questions might "break the ice." (Some hesitant clients are concerned about confidentiality, and it might be necessary to repeat explanations of confidentiality for them.)

3.3.1 CHECKLIST FOR OBTAINING NECESSARY INFORMATION

Do I have the following information about the client?

__ Address
__ Phone number
__ Age
__ Race and ethnicity
__ Gender
__ Sexual orientation
__ Religion
__ Marital status
__ Parental status
__ Occupation
__ Education
__ Place of employment
__ Source of income
__ Amount of Income
__ Health
__ Referral source
__ Reason for referral
__ Members of family constellation
__ Members of household constellation

Do I have the following information about family and household members?

> _ Relationship to client
> _ Age
> _ Gender
> _ Race or ethnicity
> _ Occupation or grade in school
> _ Source of income
> _ Health
> _ Whereabouts

3.3.2 EXERCISE FOR OBTAINING IDENTIFYING INFORMATION

It is generally not necessary to practice this skill individually, because the activities involved are similar to those required for exploration (see section 3.5.2). If you have not obtained some of the information identified above, however, you should consider the obstacles. Are you uncomfortable inquiring into some aspects of your clients' lives? If so, what are they and how can you become comfortable? Do the clients seem uncomfortable about sharing certain basic information? If so, how can you increase their comfort?

3.4.0 TARGETING PROBLEMS AND DETERMINING PROBLEM PRIORITIES

Target problems are feelings, behaviors, or circumstances that the client wants to change. Identifying them is the most critical activity in task-centered practice. One of the fundamental tenets of task-centered practice is that it is the client who determines the target problems. Clients are explicitly asked what they would like to be different in their lives. Social workers are expected to suggest problems that they or others have noticed. The client, however, has the ultimate right and responsibility to select the target problems.

The rationale for client-determined target problems is twofold: (1) the client's right to self-determination is respected; and (2) work is likely to be more effective when the target is something the client wants to change because client-determined problems capture the client's motivation.

The process of identifying target problems begins with making a list of potential target problems. Clients are asked what circumstances they would like to change. Most clients readily identify aspects of their lives that are troubling. Some clients need a little help. With them, we engage in a problem search that consists of inquiring about various aspects of their lives, including work or school, home life, friends, and so on. A small number of clients deny the need for assistance. Targeting problems with this group will be discussed in detail in the following section.

Before continuing to describe the process of targeting problems, a warning about the use of the word *problem* is in order. For some clients the word, itself, is problematic. Acknowledging "problems" suggests to some people that they have personal deficits. Often, over time, however, clients, who initially deny the existence of problems in their lives, begin to use the word themselves. With these clients, we use whatever word they prefer. Some are more comfortable referring to goals or challenges, for example.

When clients are referred by others, the problems identified by the referral source are usually described in general terms before the client is asked to identify potential target problems. This procedure is used because referred clients are often puzzled about why they are seeing a social worker.

Clients are encouraged to list as many problems as they can think of. "What else would you like to change?" is often asked. Problems identified by the referral source and the social worker are added to the list. Clients should be helped to state each problem in one succinct sentence. Examples of target problems are as follows: "My mother/father nag me"; "I feel depressed/anxious/angry"; "I am about to be fired, and I have no other sources of income"; or "We are going to be evicted, and I have no place to live."

Note that problem statements refer to undesirable behaviors, feelings, events, or circumstances. Although we use the word *goals* at this point if clients are uncomfortable with the word *problem*, the social worker should avoid conceptual confusion between problems and goals at this early stage of treatment. The reason, a somewhat subtle one, is that clients frequently present goals, and accepting the goal statement at face value sometimes hides the actual problem. For example, Mrs. Bartolo stated that she needed to find a job. This was a goal, but the social worker accepted it as the problem statement. The client negated all efforts to help her locate employment by failing to implement tasks even though she expressed willingness. When the social worker finally reexplored the problem situation, he learned that Mrs. Bartolo's husband had a health problem that neither of them understood. Physicians had left them with the impression, however, that it was serious and that Mrs. Bartolo would have to become the breadwinner. Once the problem was redefined as, "Mr. and Mrs. Bartolo do not understand Mr. Bartolo's medical problem," work proceeded smoothly.

The point is that the same goal can be an attempt to solve different problems. Employment can be used to solve boredom, loneliness, and lack of self-esteem, as well as providing financial resources. Only by knowing the condition that the client is trying to alter can the social worker help the client to evaluate a range of possible solutions.

Once the list of potential problem statements is developed, the social worker asks the client to prioritize the problems: "Which is the most important issue? Which is next most important?" This procedure is repeated until all the potential problems are ranked in order of importance to the client. Frequently it is necessary to repeat the list several times during the course of prioritizing.

The social worker reviews the priorities to determine if urgent ones are low on the list. If so, the social worker identifies the consequences of ignoring urgent problems and asks the client to reconsider the priorities. Sometimes clients, especially children, will place a higher priority on problems that others identified than on those they identified themselves. This, too, is questioned. In either situation, the client makes the final decision.

The problems that receive priority ratings of 1, 2, or 3 generally become the target problems. We have found that it is usually difficult to focus on more than three problems at a time. Focusing on three target problems is just a rule of thumb, however. The actual number will depend on the complexity of the problems and the capacity of the participants. A warning about targeting problems is in order. Sometimes social workers, especially inexperienced ones, feel helpless to change one or more of the problems the client mentions, and they react to their feelings of helplessness by ignoring or dismissing these problems. This is a critical mistake. All problem areas the client identifies, no matter how intransigent they seem, must be acknowledged and prioritized. It is acceptable to admit to the client that, at the moment, you are not sure how to change a particular area but that you will think about it seriously during the coming week. The professional behavior is then to seek information from others or at the library.

A social worker can legitimately reject a client-identified problem in one circumstance: when ethics are in question. One client presented his problem as needing to become a more successful pimp. The social worker quite properly refused to help him with this problem. Similarly a paranoid client said that she needed to kill her neighbors who were sending poisonous gas into her apartment. Again, help with this target problem was properly denied. Notice that both these clients identified their problems in the form of goals. Had the social workers inquired about how becoming a better pimp or killing the neighbors would be likely to change the clients' lives, they might have identified legitimate target problems.

3.4.1 TARGETING PROBLEMS IN SPECIAL CIRCUMSTANCES

The process of targeting problems seems quite easy, and, in many cases, it is. However, great skill is required when clients prefer to avoid all contact with a social worker or when contact is mandated. The challenge is to find some area in which the client has at least a minimal amount of interest in change. Perhaps the client wants the social workers or the agency "off his back." We then treat the fact that the agency/social worker is "on his back" as the target problem and go to work. Sometimes it is a matter of connecting the demands of a social institution to something a client really wants. For example, Mrs. Carter wanted her children returned to her care. The court determined that in order to achieve this she would have to correct certain problems, including excessive drinking and inadequate housing. Mrs. Carter willingly and successfully worked to meet these conditions because she wanted her children to be returned to her care. Note that, in this case, the target problem was defined as the fact that the client did not have custody of her children. If it had been defined as drinking or inadequate housing, it is unlikely she would have been willing to alter these conditions.

Some clients choose to work on problems that seem relatively unimportant to others. An example of this occurred when Mrs. Goldman, who was paralyzed as a result of a spinal cord injury incurred in an automobile accident, refused to participate in her rehabilitation. On receiving the referral, the social worker learned that Mrs. Goldman was concerned about how her children and husband were managing at home without her. Respecting the client's definition of her problem, the social worker arranged a family conference. During the conference all the details of family life were reviewed until Mrs. Goldman was satisfied that her family was managing. She then participated fully in her rehabilitation program. As this case illustrates, we have found that it is best to respect the client's choice. The seemingly less important problems may simply be more important to the client than others realize. Often the seemingly more serious problems will be targeted later.

Sometimes the importance of a problem becomes apparent to the client as that problem becomes an obstacle to solving the targeted problems. Finally, some clients apparently have to test us by targeting a relatively minor issue in order to determine our trustworthiness.

The critical skill is to be able to identify some area in which the client desires change. Nonverbal clues are sometimes provided: facial expressions or topics avoided. Sometimes repetitive themes are suggestive: the client who is always uncooperative with the nursing home staff after visits from certain family members. These clues can be used to suggest potential target problems to the client. As always, the client has the right to reject our suggestions, and we have the obligation to respect the client's decision.

With some clients, all our skill and effort will not produce a target problem. These clients are either uninterested in addressing any problem areas or uninterested in addressing them with us. We respect their right to refuse services and, if possible, terminate treatment with them. Termination should, of course, be handled so that the client will feel comfortable returning if the need or desire for service arises in the future. Sometimes termination is not possible because of legal or social mandates: The abusing parent and the parolee must be monitored. Social workers in these circumstances must continue contact. In our opinion, this kind of contact should be seen as social control rather than treatment. It is certainly not task-centered practice. Furthermore, the workers should be honest with the clients about their role. Actually it is inappropriate to refer to people whose behavior is being monitored as clients, since the word *client* connotes a person who has voluntarily engaged the services of another.

3.4.2 CHECKLIST FOR TARGETING AND PRIORITIZING PROBLEMS

> — 1. Have I located at least one problem that the client wants help with?
> — 2. Are any of the problem statements actually goals?
> — 3. Have all potential problem areas been prioritized?
> — 4. Should the priority given any of the problems be challenged?

3.4.3 EXERCISE FOR TARGETING AND PRIORITIZING PROBLEMS

Using the general instructions for role plays provided in section 3.1.2, practice targeting and prioritizing. In this exercise, however, those playing the role of client should assume one of the following roles:

1. You have a fairly large number of problems;
2. You are feeling badly but have difficulty identifying the specific, troubling phenomena; or
3. You are a nonvoluntary client who has problems, but initially you do not want to see a social worker.

In other words, you want to present a somewhat challenging situation for practicing the skills of targeting and prioritizing. However, do not confuse a challenging situation with an impossible one.

3.5.0 EXPLORING TARGET PROBLEMS

Some information about the target problems will be acquired during the process of identifying and prioritizing them. Usually this information will not be sufficient to plan intervention strategies, however. The following questions would provide the minimal information that must be secured for each target problem:

1. What occurs that is troubling?
2. Where does it occur?
3. When does it occur?
4. Who else is present when it occurs?
5. How often does it occur?
6. What is the duration of the phenomena?
7. How severe is the problem?
8. What has the client or others done to try to solve the problem?
9. What has been the result of previous problem-solving efforts?
10. What are the client's expectations about what will solve the problem?
11. What is the cognitive meaning of the problem to the client?
12. What is the client's affective reaction to the problem?
13. What are the antecedents or stimuli to the occurrence of the problem?
14. What are the consequences or responses to the occurrence of the problem?
15. What other contextual factors bear on the problem?
16. What is the impact of other systems on the problem?
17. What is the impact of the problem on other systems?

The first nine questions are intended to acquire a good description of the problem and potential solutions. Some of them are described in greater detail in section 3.6.0 ("Developing the Problem Specification").

The remaining questions are intended to understand the context of the problem. Every problem is embedded in a context of biopsychosocial and historical factors, including potential obstacles and resources that may be relevant to the problem. Contextual factors that help you to understand the problem or that have a direct bearing on its course should be explored. Questions 10 through 15 pertain to the dimensions of functioning described in section 2.2.0. Specifically questions 10, 11, and 12 pertain to cognitions and related affect. Questions 13 and 14 pertain to environmental contingencies. Question 15 directs us to consider other dimensions of functioning, such as skills, stress, and so on. The last two questions focus our attention on the interaction between the problem and systems other than the individual.

The problems of Mrs. Dale, an eighty-three-year-old woman who lives alone in a third-story walk-up, illustrate the necessity of contextual exploration. Her arthritis is making it increasingly difficult for her to climb the stairs. Her depression, a long-term problem, has recently become worse. She presents the social worker with some hard questions. Should she stay or move? What supports does she need to be able to stay? If she moves, what are her options? Exploration of contextual factors might include her health and physical functioning, her depression, and her social network, as well as the availability of community resources.

The list of questions given above will provide the minimal amount of information needed. Workers should not hesitate to gather whatever information seems necessary. Sometimes this will require that the worker ask questions that may be embarrassing or seem intrusive to the client. In these instances, it is helpful to explain to the client why you are asking the question(s).

At this point in treatment, the worker should be able to develop a succinct, one-sentence description of each target problem. This description should identify the problem as a behavior, situation, or feeling that is unwanted by the client. It should not be stated as a goal at this point. Ideally the problem will be stated in the client's own words.

The following two case illustrations might help to clarify some of the variations that occur in the process of targeting and exploring problems. Work with the first client, Sammy, demonstrates that clients who are resistant to treatment can sometimes be engaged through a problem search. Work with the second client, Mrs. Bradford, illustrates that target problems sometimes become redefined through the process of exploration.

The foster parents of Sammy, a fifteen-year-old Caucasian male, sought help from a child welfare agency because Sammy was noncompliant and uncooperative at home and at school. Although they stated that they would not be able to keep him in the home if his behavior did not change, they were also reluctant "to give up on him" because his life had been so unstable. At first contact, the worker shared the referral information with Sammy, who denied the validity of all complaints. Either the adults had the wrong information or the problems were someone else's fault. He said that he did not need to see a social worker and that it was okay if he had to live somewhere else. The social worker assured him that he did not have to see her if there was nothing he wanted to change but cautiously suggested that they review aspects of his life to see if there were any areas he was dissatisfied with. School was "okay." Friends were "okay." Home was "okay." Finally Sammy mentioned that he was sick of the constant supervision by the aides at school. The social worker learned that Sammy was supervised because of an incident of sexual acting-out that had occurred two years earlier. Thus the target problem was identified: Sammy does not want supervision. The social worker, Sammy, school officials, and foster parents devised a plan to reduce supervision gradually, provided that Sammy changed his behavior in specified ways. His behavior would be monitored regularly to determine further reductions in supervision. The foster parents and school personnel reported that they were "astounded" by the changes in Sammy's behavior following the intervention.

Mrs. Bradford, an elderly, disabled, African-American woman, resided in her own apartment in a residential facility for the aged. She approached the social worker for help, stating that she no longer felt safe in the building. By exploring in detail the conditions that had changed and produced the diminution of a sense of security, the social worker learned that the client had had a "falling-out" with one of the administrators with whom she had previously been visiting almost daily; she was also receiving fewer visits from a member of the janitorial staff with whom she had been friendly. Through the process of exploration, the client decided that her actual target problem was loneliness. Following the initial contact, Mrs. Bradford "made up" with the administrator and janitor on her own, and the problem was resolved to her satisfaction.

3.5.1 CHECKLIST FOR EXPLORING TARGET PROBLEMS

> — 1. Do I have information about all the areas identified in this section? (See list of questions above.)
> — 2. Does the available information suggest intervention strategies or tasks?

3.5.2 EXERCISE FOR EXPLORING TARGET PROBLEMS

The ability to explore is probably the most essential social work skill. Because of its importance, a considerable amount of time should be allotted to practicing it. Use the general instructions for role plays provided in section 3.1.2. The goal of the person enacting the role of social worker is to learn as much as possible about one target problem. The "client" should cooperate by responding to questions but should not help the "social worker" by volunteering information that has not been sought.

When the role plays, including feedback, are completed, "social workers" write, in list form, everything they know about the problem. This list is then given to the "client" who checks off all accurate items and returns it to the "social worker." The list is then compared to items listed above to identify missing information. Since different problems require somewhat different information, a useful final step is to spend about ten minutes listing additional information that could be sought. This list should be retained for the next practice session concerning problem specification.

A common mistake is usually revealed in this practice session, which is to begin to intervene before you have adequate information. All participants in the role play should be alert for this possibility and identify it as soon as it occurs. During this practice session, do nothing to change the problem! However, a useful way to critique your ability to explore is to consider whether the information you have obtained suggests some intervention alternatives or tasks. If it does not, you need more information.

3.6.0 DEVELOPING THE PROBLEM SPECIFICATION

One aspect of professional practice concerns accountability. Accountability refers to our ability to evaluate the impact of our services. Within task-centered practice, this is accomplished by using a procedure called problem specification. Problem specification has been integral to this model of practice since the inception of TC in the late 1960s. The importance of accountability has now been recognized by the Council on Social Work Education, which accredits schools of social work. The Council has mandated that all students learn the skills necessary to evaluate their own practice. Evaluating one's own practice entails determining whether the interventions are having the desired effect, that is, whether the client's problems are being resolved.

In addition to enabling us to evaluate the effectiveness of our intervention, problem specification also directs treatment. It does so by identifying the specific conditions of the problem that must be changed if the client is to experience the relief sought. Thus problem specification is a crucial element of task-centered practice.

A problem specification is developed for each target problem. The first step is to determine the manifestations of the problem, that is, how the problem displays or reveals itself. Consider, for example, a problem of depression. This problem, and others, will manifest itself differently with different clients. For one client, Mrs. Gordon, the manifestations were as follows:

1. inability to sleep;
2. frequent crying bouts at work;
3. inability to do housework or errands; and
4. lack of social engagements.

The manifestations, like the target problems, are determined by the client. If the list of manifestations is complete, then the elimination of them should produce the end state the client is seeking. To practice accountably, a second step is needed. We must determine the frequency, severity, or duration of the manifestation before intervening so that we can evaluate the effectiveness of the intervention. Before we secure this information, we need to know which of these dimensions—frequency, severity, or duration—the client is concerned about. For example, a couple's concern about their fights may be related to severity: One of them ends up in the emergency room. Or it may be related to frequency: They have ten to twelve each day. Finally, it may be related to duration: They do not speak to each other for days following a fight. Occasionally more than one dimension will be of concern.

Another decision must be made before data can be gathered. The worker must decide on the appropriate length of the baseline. Baseline data refers to the frequency, duration, or severity of the problem before intervention. Baselines can last a day, a week, a month, or any other period of time. The length of the baseline is determined by the approximate frequency of the problem. A baseline of only one day might be sufficient for a problem that occurs many times during a day. A baseline of at least one month would be necessary for problems that occur only a few times a month.

Once the manifestation(s) is identified and the appropriate baseline period determined, the necessary information can be secured. This can be done in two ways. The first is to collect concurrent baseline data. This means that the client—or someone else—is asked to keep track of the frequency, severity, or duration of each manifestation. The person who is monitoring the phenomena is usually provided with some means to record it. A simple sheet of paper with the days of the week labeled at the top is usually sufficient for measuring daily frequency.

The second way to measure the problem before intervention is to collect data ex post facto. This is sometimes called a retrospective baseline. Data gathered ex post facto are data collected "after the fact," which means that the client—or someone else—is asked to indicate the frequency, severity, or duration of the problem during the previous day, week, or month. The danger of relying on collecting data ex post facto is that the person providing the data might not accurately recall events. Thus it is important to explore the past specifically and with cues that might jog that individual's memory. The social worker might begin by asking what the person did yesterday. Once a complete description of the day's activities is obtained, the worker would ask about the occurrence of the problem: "Did you cry while getting dressed for work? While eating breakfast? While driving to work? During your conference with your supervisor?" and so on.

Data collected ex post facto are generally used in task-centered practice, as they have the advantage of allowing the practitioner to begin to intervene immediately. Sometimes, however, concurrent data need to be gathered. This occurs when those who are in a position to observe the problem manifestations are unable to provide the necessary data. If a problem is targeted but other problems have priority, gathering concurrent data will not delay intervention because work on the problems of higher priority can begin immediately.

Securing the data for each problem manifestation completes the problem specification procedure. Returning to Mrs. Gordon, the complete problem specification for her problem of depression was as follows:

1. inability to sleep: client has slept an average of four hours per night during the past week;
2. frequent crying bouts at work: client has cried an average of twice per day during the past week;
3. inability to do housework or errands: client has spent only an hour on these activities during the past week; and
4. lack of social engagements: client has not had a social engagement in two weeks.

The measures in the preceding example concern frequency and duration. When the important dimension to be measured is severity, a useful strategy is to help the client develop a self-anchored rating scale. The worker chooses an even number of points for the scale (assume 6 for this illustration) and asks the client how he or she feels when most depressed, for example. This description becomes number 6 on the scale. The client is then asked how he or she feels when least depressed. This description becomes number 1 on the scale. The client continues to describe each point on the scale alternating between the extremes. The scale is typed, and the client is asked to use it regularly to rate his or her mood. The specification of the manifestation of feeling depressed might then be the following: The client's average daily rating of feeling depressed during the past week is 2. A more detailed description of the development of self-anchored rating scales and their use can be found in most research texts.

It is probably apparent that the completed problem specification enables us to evaluate progress. For example, we can simply inquire, at each contact with the client, about the number of hours he or she slept per night. If the specifications are not improving, we know that our interventions or tasks must be altered.

The example provided by work with Mrs. Gordon concerns an affective or emotional problem. Specifications for behavioral or interpersonal problems are similar to those for affective problems. However, specifications for role and resource problems are somewhat different.

Academic underachievement provides an illustration of role problems. One student's problem of failing math had the following specification:

1. homework: client turns in two of five homework assignments per week;
2. knowledge: client knows multiplication tables through five; and
3. tests: client scores between 30 percent and 50 percent on weekly quizzes.

The manifestations for this kind of problem are identified by using deductive logic. The social work starts with the conclusion—passing academic courses—and determines the activities necessary for success. The client's performance of these activities is then measured. When a manifestation involves skill or knowledge, it is useful to have clients demonstrate their ability in your presence. Regarding one manifestation identified above, multiplication, the client was asked to solve sample problems to assess where the knowledge deficit occurs. Sometimes social workers rely on teachers' assessments or general academic tests. We have found that the latter are insufficiently specific and that the former are sometimes unreliable.

To illustrate resource problems, consider the following problem: The client's housing is inadequate. The specifications include the characteristics that describe adequate housing for this client. In this case, they were as follows:

1. size: client needs two bedrooms;
2. location: must be within two blocks of transportation to the city; and
3. cost: cannot exceed $350.00 per month, including utilities.

With a resource problem, data gathering consists of determining the necessary characteristics of the needed resource. Data describing severity, frequency, or duration are not required. By identifying the characteristics of the resource that are needed, we are able to evaluate the extent to which the resource provided met the client's needs.

The final step in developing many of the manifestations is optional but recommended. It entails graphing them over time. This procedure makes changes visible and is reinforcing for clients when the phenomena begins to change. The result, as some readers might recognize, is similar to single-subject research designs (SSDs). More information about SSDs is available in most research texts. It should be noted that graphing is appropriate for manifestations that occur regularly, which would include most behavioral and emotional ones. For example, all the manifestations for the problems of depression and underachievement previously described are appropriate for graphing, whereas those for the problem of securing adequate housing are not.

Brief, self-administered instruments (often referred to as rapid assessment instruments) that measure depression, anxiety, lack of assertiveness, and so on, may also be useful in problem specification. Such instruments, which usually take only five or ten minutes for clients to complete, help pin down the client's problem in objective terms, provide a baseline for measuring change, and often reveal facets of the problem that may not have emerged in the client interview. Moreover, if the test is normed, the severity of the client's problem can be compared to that of others. Of course, you must be able to locate an instrument that fits the client's problem, and the instrument would have to be administered regularly. A wide range of available instruments are described in Corcoran and Fischer (2000).

Finally, the concern for evaluating change on an ongoing basis must be emphasized. Many research and treatment efforts include evaluation only at the end of contact, when it is too late to alter our interventions and help clients attain their desires.

3.6.1 CHECKLIST FOR PROBLEM SPECIFICATION

— 1. Have I identified all the manifestations that are important to the client for each target problem?
— 2. Do I know the frequency, duration, or severity of each manifestation before intervention?
— 3. Have I established a baseline period for each manifestation?
— 4. Have I begun to graph the data so that the client and I can "see" changes as they occur?

3.6.2 EXERCISE FOR PROBLEM SPECIFICATION

Examine the information obtained during problem exploration, the previous role play, and try to write the problem specification. Continue the role play with the same participants and obtain any necessary additional information to complete the problem specification. Because this skill is the most difficult one to grasp, problem specifications should be submitted to the instructor for his or her review and feedback. If time permits, it is useful to attempt to specify a couple of types of problems: affective, role, or resource.

3.7.0 GOALS

Goals are the explicit, desired end points of intervention. They are determined by the client and stated in quantifiable terms whenever possible. The process of problem specification simplifies goal setting. In fact, for resource problems, the specification is the goal. For other problems, goals can be set by asking the client the desired frequency or duration for each problem manifestation. Goals for Mrs. Gordon and the problem of depression described earlier were as follows:

1. sleep: eight hours per night;
2. crying bouts at work: none;
3. housework and errands: four hours per week; and
4. social engagements: one on Friday or Saturday night, one weekday lunch date, and two telephone conversations per week.

While, in most cases, setting goals based on problem specifications is sufficient, it is often wise also to set goals based on the target problem statement. For example, a client like Mrs.Carter, who identified the problem as not having custody of her children, might accomplish all goals based on the problem specification but still not receive custody of the children. Sometimes this occurs because all relevant manifestations have not been identified. The job then is to determine the other manifestations that require attention. Sometimes this occurs because collaterals have not kept their part of the bargain. Forceful advocacy or negotiation or both is then in order.

Some goals cannot be reached within time-limited treatment. For example, a client's goal might be to graduate from college. We then ask the client to specify the smallest change the client and social worker could accomplish together that would indicate that the client would achieve the ultimate goal. In this case, the goals might be (1) passing all courses during the current quarter; and (2) obtaining a B average for the current quarter.

It is important that the client determine the goals. Client-determined target problems ensure that we "start where the client is." Client-determined goals ensure that we stay with the client.

3.7.1 CHECKLIST FOR GOALS

— 1. Has the client set a goal for each problem manifestation?
— 2. Will I be able to determine when this goal is reached?

3.7.2 EXERCISE FOR GOALS

See the exercise in section 3.8.2, below.

3.8.0 CONTRACTS

The preceding work is summarized in a contract, which is an explicit statement about the agreements reached between social worker and client. These agreements include the problem statements, problem specifications, goals, participants, number of sessions, and frequency and length of sessions.

Contracts may be either oral or written. Since the evidence about which type of contract is most effective is mixed, experimenting with both types is probably useful (Klier, Fein, and Genero 1984; Levy 1977).

Contracts not only provide a clear statement of agreements but also a means for the social worker to check the extent to which initial phase work is complete. Sometimes social workers discover that they do not know what the client's goal is with respect to one of the problems or problem manifestations or that they do not have enough information to evaluate change, for example. This information can be acquired during the next session. In general, checking after each session to determine missing data is useful.

3.8.1 CHECKLIST FOR CONTRACTS

Does my contract with the client include an agreement about the following issues:

— 1. number and scheduling of sessions;
— 2. fees, if applicable;
— 3. participants in sessions;
— 4. target problem;
— 5. problem specifications; and
— 6. goals?

3.8.2 EXERCISE FOR GOALS AND CONTRACTS

Using the general instructions for role plays, practice contracting and goal setting. These role plays can be brief if you continue with the role play for problem specification. If that role play cannot be continued, the "client" should volunteer the information regarding target problems, priorities, and problem specification. If time permits, you may want to practice both oral and written contracts.

3.9.0 ASSESSMENT: PERSON, PROBLEM, AND OTHER SYSTEMS

Clearly assessment in TC emphasizes the assessment of problems. This is a dramatic change from more traditional models of practice in which assessment focuses on the client. However, we must also know something about the context of the problem. When the primary system is an individual, important aspects of the context are the dimensions of individual functioning described in section 2.2.0 ("Theoretical Base"). The dimensions include health, and physical and intellectual functioning; information and knowledge; resources; stage of development; roles; cognitions; self-concept; environmental contingencies; skills; stress; and social support. Some of these dimensions must be considered early in treatment and with every client. Health and resources are among these. The extent to which we explore the others will depend on the target problems. For example, the concept of roles will be most useful when the target problems involve the client's inability to meet the expectations that accompany the client's position as parent, spouse, or worker. However, because we do not know with certainty at this juncture which dimensions are pertinent to which problems, it is probably wise to consider each of them at least briefly. We should do so with the intent of identifying special strengths or barriers to resolving target problems.

In task-centered generalist practice we consider the impact of other systems on the problem; the impact of the problem on other systems; and the role of other systems in solving the problem. Clients should be asked about all three of these considerations regarding each problem in relation to each system level, that is, family, community, and organization. When considerable interaction exists between a problem and another system, we should reconsider our decision about working primarily with the individual. In some cases, we might choose to supplement our work with the individual by also working with another system, at least on a limited basis. This often occurs when problems concern organizations. Social workers frequently intervene to obtain exceptions from a particular organizational policy for individual clients, for example. In other cases, it might be advisable to change from working with an individual to working with another system. The most frequent switch is probably from the individual as the primary system to the family or marital system.

When the decision to work with an individual as the primary system appears to be correct, collaterals must still be considered. As described in chapter 1, collaterals are people who are involved in the lives of our clients. They can be family members, friends, or other professionals, such as physicians or teachers or social workers in other agencies. Often they act as representatives of other systems. In TC, we do not hesitate to contact or work with collaterals on behalf of our clients provided the client agrees.

Collaterals should be considered early in our work with a client, especially when they have power over the client. For example, when working with Mrs. Carter, who had lost custody of her children, it was vital to know the standards the court would apply in decisions about returning custody. It is also critical to secure favorable recommendations from the child welfare workers involved. The case of Sammy, described earlier, illustrates that we sometimes need to reassure and be accountable to collaterals. Contacting these collaterals early in our work will prevent misdirected efforts that will ultimately discourage the client. The early involvement of collaterals also protects the client from unpleasant surprises. The child who does not realize that we are in contact with teachers might be tempted to put an unusually rosy interpretation on his or her academic achievements.

Important collaterals can be identified by asking ourselves, "Whose cooperation will be necessary to resolve the targeted problems?" Cooperation can be as minimal as simply providing information. Discussion of involving collaterals with the client should include our rationale for involvement and limits to confidentiality. All contacts with collaterals should be reported to the client.

3.9.1 Checklist for Assessment: Person, Problem, and Other Systems

— 1. Am I fully informed about the client's health?

— 2. What special strengths or barriers exist in the client or the situation? How are these likely to affect intervention?

— 3. Is the client struggling with a particular developmental issue? How does this affect intervention?

— 4. What is the impact of the family, organization(s), and community on the client and the target problems?

— 5. What is the impact of the problem on the family, organization(s), or community?

— 6. Are the family, organization(s), or community important to resolving the problem?

— 7. What other systems should be included? How?

— 8. Who are the collaterals who should be involved? Is the client satisfied with their involvement?

4

THE MIDDLE PHASE OF TREATMENT

4.0.0 COMPONENTS OF THE MIDDLE PHASE

The middle phase of treatment is the phase during which intervention occurs. Intervention is defined as deliberate and specific attempts to resolve target problems. As previously indicated, phases are not primarily defined by the number of interviews that have taken place. That a client has been seen five times does not mean that work is necessarily in the middle phase. Rather, phases are defined by the type of treatment activity. The initial phase of treatment consists of gathering necessary information and reaching various agreements with the client about the nature of the treatment endeavor. The middle phase begins as soon as attempts to resolve problems occur. It is possible for the initial phase and the middle phase to overlap. For example, the worker has to intervene immediately during a crisis even though all the desirable information has not been attained.

The major middle-phase activity in TC is the use of the Task Planning and Implementation Sequence (TPIS). This sequence consists of a package of activities, including generating tasks, eliciting task agreement, planning the details of task implementation, establishing rationale and incentives for task performance, analyzing obstacles to task performance, simulating the task, summarizing the task, reviewing task progress, reviewing problem status, and revising unsuccessful tasks. These activities are described in detail in this chapter.

Other middle-phase activities include using time limits and revising assessments. Occasionally we encounter clients who consistently do not implement the tasks, and sometimes clients identify new problems during the middle phase. All these issues are discussed in this chapter. In addition, the use of eclectic practice and work with collaterals are considered.

4.1.0 THE TASK PLANNING AND IMPLEMENTATION SEQUENCE

The Task Planning and Implementation Sequence (TPIS) was both developed and tested by using empirical methods. Beginning with the idea of tasks as the major vehicle for reducing target problems, interviews were scrutinized to learn how social workers used tasks. The activities discovered were articulated in the TPIS. The effectiveness of these activities was then examined. Social work students were asked to plan two tasks with a randomly selected client. The students used all the TPIS activities with one of the tasks and none of them with the other task. (Tasks were randomly assigned to the conditions.) It was found that tasks in the TPIS condition were completed significantly more often than the other tasks (Reid 1975). This research suggests that all relevant TPIS activities should be used with each task planned.

A task is an action performed for the purpose of reducing target problems. Originally tasks were defined as activities the client performed outside the session. The rationale for requiring that the client perform tasks is that clients should take action on their own behalf. The rationale that tasks be performed outside the session is that important changes are located in the real-life settings in which problems occur.

However, experience with this approach indicated the need for both practitioner tasks and session tasks. Practitioner tasks are developed when the client cannot perform the necessary activity. For example, acquiring a service from another agency might require a referral from the practitioner. Practitioner tasks are also used when delay or hardship will result if the client is asked to perform the activity. For example, clients without telephones have a difficult time contacting social workers who are often away from their offices or in interviews. For convenience and because client tasks are usually preferable, it will be assumed that the client performs the tasks unless tasks are specified as practitioner tasks. Occasionally, however, cases will require that the practitioner perform most or even all of the tasks.

Session tasks are most frequently used when the treatment unit consists of a family or group. Frequently family members, for example, need to learn new ways to communicate with one another. Session tasks facilitate practicing new skills. Again, for convenience and because out-of-session tasks are usually preferable, it will be assumed that tasks are performed outside the session unless they are specified as session tasks.

4.1.1 GENERATING TASK ALTERNATIVES AND SELECTING A TASK

Generating task alternatives is the first activity within the TPIS. It consists of brainstorming with the client about actions that might be taken to alleviate the target problem. Often it begins with a question like, "What do you think we could do to reduce the fighting between you and your mother?" The social worker attempts to engage the client in problem solving. It is important to elicit as many alternatives as possible from the client. During this step alternatives should not be evaluated, because evaluation tends to reduce the number of alternatives suggested. The social worker also suggests as many alternatives as possible.

Once a list of alternatives is generated, one or more of them must be selected for implementation. Often the client is asked, "Which one should we try first?" Usually the choice will be obvious or the client will have a strong preference. Occasionally it will be necessary to discuss the relative merits of some of the alternatives. Selection of an alternative has not proven to be difficult. As with target problems, the client has the final word on task selection.

Social workers sometimes have difficulty thinking of task alternatives. When this occurs, it is almost always because they have insufficient information about the problem, and thus the problem must be re-explored (see section 3.6.0). Fortunately identifying alternatives has become less challenging with the publication of *The Task Planner* (Reid 2000), which contains many innovative potential tasks for many problems. It also contains background information about the problem and references for further reading. For example, suggestions from *The Task Planner* for the problem of depression in adults include the following: "consult with psychiatrist to assess need for antidepressant medication"; "identify modifiable factors, especially stressors"; "select a stressor that you think you can change and take at least one step to change it"; "identify resources and coping mechanisms"; "keep track of things you enjoy and accomplish"; "undertake an activity that results in mastery or pleasure"; "increase your social activities"; "identify thoughts and beliefs that might add to your depression"; "identify beliefs and assumptions that underlie depression"; "learn social skills to improve interpersonal relationships, including assertion and conversational skills"; "set realistic, attainable goals"; "identify 'messages' from important figures in the past that may be contributing to depression and attempt to act in ways that would modify these messages"; "identify role disputes and role transitions that might be contributing . . ."; "identify difficulties in establishing satisfactory interpersonal relationships, attempt to understand factors contributing to these relationships, and take steps to resolve them"; and "express your feelings" (102–4).

Most task suggestions are followed by an elaboration that explains why the task might be useful and a description of the practitioner's role in implementing the task. The elaboration and practitioner role for the task of identifying role disputes and transitions are as follows:

> Elaboration: Interpersonal role disputes (e.g., conflict with marital partner or employer) and role transitions (e.g., loss of job) can lead to depreciated self-esteem and demoralization and hence can be factors in depression. Practitioner's Role: Help client carry out the identification process, develop understanding of the problem, and devise a plan of response. For example, the client may have to mourn the loss of a cherished role before he or she can replace it. (Reid 2000:104)

As useful as *The Task Planner* has proven to be, it is not a panacea. Tasks must fit the client's situation and therefore have to be individualized. Tasks drawn from *The Task Planner* are suggested by the social worker while generating alternatives. Sometimes the ideas will be unfamiliar to the client, and so we must be prepared to explain what they are and why they might work.

The number of tasks chosen in a session will depend on the demands of the target problem(s), the abilities and resources of the client, and the time available. The social worker should avoid overburdening the client. While tasks are generated and selected with the clients' resources in mind and are generally not extremely difficult, they nevertheless often require a new behavior from the client and new behaviors require some concentrated effort. Often tasks can be arranged sequentially. For example, it has been found that children with academic difficulty experience greater success if tasks are spaced. Thus the first task might be to acquire an assignment notebook. During the following week a task to record all assignments in the notebook might be planned. Finally, a task to spend a certain amount of time doing homework each night can be developed. If you are in doubt about the number of tasks selected, you might say to the client: "I wonder if we are asking you to do too many things this week" or "I know you are eager to get this problem solved, and I wonder if we should try another task as well as this one."

Once tasks have been selected, the most useful attitude to convey concerning task difficulty is this: "This might be somewhat difficult, but I think you can do it." With most clients, avoid conveying either that you expect the client to fail or that the task is very easy. Many of our clients feel helpless in the face of their problems and will be discouraged by the former belief. The latter belief might produce increased feelings of inadequacy if the task is not accomplished.

Gary, a fifteen-year-old, illustrates a situation in which the social worker was very dubious about the client's ability to complete selected tasks. He had severe behavioral disorders and was in a special school. Gary's target problem was the following: "I seek negative attention from others." The social worker was able to elicit several task alternatives by asking Gary what he thought could be done to deal with the problem. He suggested that he call "time out" for himself when he was upset. What else might work? "I can stop interrupting." Anything else? "I could not feed into the group's negative behaviors." Any other ideas? "I could stop telling white lies." The social worker also suggested some alternatives: keeping his hands to himself, using a lower tone of voice, avoiding any loud belching or throwing of food.

4.1.2 ELICITING AGREEMENT TO PERFORM THE TASK

The client's commitment to perform the task is important. In one study, it was found that only 30 percent of tasks were fully performed when client commitment was rated as low or neutral, whereas 63 percent of the tasks were fully performed when the commitment was rated as high (Reid 1978:250). Thus the social worker should be sure that the client is willing to try to perform the task. Sometimes clients will agree to a task, but we question the degree of their motivation. We have found with most clients that it is best to suppress our skepticism initially as long as clients express some degree of willingness. There are two reasons for this. First, our judgments about client motivation are often wrong. For example, 30 percent of tasks were performed even when commitment was rated as low or neutral. Second, we will have more evidence about the possibility of a commitment problem at the next interview when tasks are reviewed. If, however, you will not be seeing the client again, it is best to discuss his or her hesitancy about doing the task immediately.

Usually implicit agreement is obtained during the process of selecting a task from an array of alternatives as described in section 4.1.1. Nevertheless, making this agreement explicit is advisable: "This is the task you want to do this week?"

Returning to the case of Gary, he selected the following tasks: reduce interruptions to two times per class and call a brief time out for himself once during each class. The social worker was very pessimistic about Gary's ability to implement these tasks but kept her reservations to herself. Much to her surprise Gary frequently implemented his tasks, and his behavior was rated by Gary, his teacher, and herself as "substantially improved" at the end of treatment.

4.1.3 PLANNING DETAILS OF TASK IMPLEMENTATION

Planning the details of task implementation eliminates possible misunderstandings about what is expected. It also helps to ensure successful task completion. Finally, it conveys our seriousness about the importance of task completion to the client.

This activity consists of determining specifically what is to occur. These are some of the questions to consider:

1. *Who* is to do *what?*
2. *When* are they to do it?
3. *How often* are they to do it?
4. *How long* are they to do it?
5. *Where* will it be done?
6. *With whom* will it be done?

Not all these questions apply to every task. For example, the question about how often the task is to be done does not apply to a task that will only be done once.

Conversely, unique details will need to be planned for some tasks. A child identified his target problem as being bullied by another child. He and the social worker planned a task for responding to the bully. For the task to be successful, it was critical that the client not only knew what to say but how to say it: "Stand straight and look the bully in the eye." Necessary details for homework tasks often entail where to keep the homework so "the dog doesn't eat it." Adults planning social tasks often need to consider who they want to approach, as well as how and when they want to approach another person. With this and other interactional tasks, it is also useful to plan how clients will react to the response of others. What should they say if their invitations are refused, for example.

Unfortunately all possible details cannot be listed for consideration because tasks are so varied. The process of identifying important details consists of thinking through the task performance with the client. The social worker's questions might proceed something like this: "So you want to ask your boss for a raise. I wonder when the best time to ask him might be." "How will you arrange to get some private time with him?" "Do you know of anyone who has gotten a raise? How did that person approach him?" This process will identify many details that merit consideration.

There will, of course, be times when an important detail is overlooked. This will be apparent when either the task is not performed or performed unsuccessfully and will be reported at the next interview.

Overlooking a detail is not usually critical with tasks that are to be performed recurrently, because you have the opportunity to correct the oversight for the following week. Consideration of details is most important for tasks that ideally should be performed only once, such as asking for a raise. Of course a request for a raise can be repeated, but then it would be even less likely to be successful; the employer would feel the need to defend his or her position, and the client would be even more reluctant to be assertive. Perhaps the best advice is (1) be aware of tasks that should be performed only once; and (2) take time to consider all possible details of such tasks, even spreading the planning time over two or more weeks, if necessary.

Many details of task implementation are planned with Mrs. Carter and Ronnie Paige (the reader will recall that the work with these clients is described in detail at the end of chapter 5). The details planned with Mrs. Paige for working with collaterals are particularly interesting. Try to identify them. Details for Gary's task of not interrupting concerned recording the frequency with which he did so. He was given a chart with a space for each class period. Each time he interrupted, he made a check in the appropriate space. The teacher's aide also had a copy of the chart, and she, too, recorded his interruptions. At the end of the school day, Gary and the aide went over the charts together to resolve discrepancies.

4.1.4 ESTABLISHING RATIONALE AND INCENTIVES

As used in TC, rationales and incentives serve the same purpose, but they are not identical. A rationale is a reason to do the task. An incentive is a concrete reward for doing the task.

Both rationales and incentives provide motivation to perform the task. The most minimal use of this activity consists of reminding the client of the reason for performing the task. Usually the reason is related to solving the client's target problem: "I know it's hard for you to ask for a raise, but, as you said, your biggest problem is to have enough money to live on and to afford a few goodies in life" or "Doing homework might be a pain but, as you said, you really want to avoid summer school." If there are multiple reasons for performing a task, the client should be reminded of all of them. An alternative way to use rationales is to ask the client to provide them: "What are we hoping to accomplish with this task?" When a task is particularly onerous or when the client is a child, incentives can be powerful.

Two general rules apply to the use of incentives. First, the incentive or reward must be something the client wants. This does not mean that it has to be large or expensive. Gold stars or stickers often act like miracle drugs with young children. Second, the dispensing of rewards must be clear and systematic. In other words, you and the client must know how much of what reward will be provided for how much of what behavior. If the reward for attending classes is use of the family car, how many classes must the client attend for each hour of car use, for example. The issue of timing must also be considered when using incentives. With young children, rewards usually have to be more immediate than with older clients. Finally, careful planning is necessary when progress is heavily dependent on incentives the social worker provides because the problem might revert to its original condition when contact ends. Possible strategies include teaching the client to self-reward; locating a collateral who is willing and able to provide the reward; fading, which entails providing rewards intermittently; or replacing rewards with social reinforcers like praise. The last two strategies must begin at least several weeks before work terminates.

Rationales for task performance should always be employed. However, you may often be in doubt about the necessity for incentives. This is particularly true with adult clients. We have found that consulting with the client is advisable in these situations: "Asking for a raise is difficult. I wonder if it would help if we planned a special treat that you could look forward to after you do it?" If you think that the task will be difficult for the client and that the client is likely to reject an incentive, you might try to be somewhat more persuasive: "When I have something difficult to do, I usually plan to reward myself with something special after I've done it. I think this might help you, too."

Often the greatest difficulty in using incentives is our negative societal bias. Teachers and parents often say that children should engage in certain behaviors because "it is right" or that a child "shouldn't need rewards." Adults apply the same attitude to themselves. In fact, most of us would cease working (or reading this book) immediately if a reward in the form of a paycheck (or college credit) was not forthcoming. When we encounter negativity about rewards, we gently remind people of why they go to work in the morning. Another strange phenomena is our preference for punishment over rewards. Most of us are comfortable nagging, threatening, and scolding. In fact, these behaviors come naturally. Human interaction would be more pleasant and effective if we replaced nagging and threatening with praising and rewarding.

For Mrs. Carter, the desire to have her children returned to her was so strong that additional incentives were unnecessary. When her motivation flagged, Mr. Rooney had only to remind her of this. This is often the case with adults. With children and adolescents, in contrast, we have seen hundreds of cases in which incentives were effectively used. Ronnie Paige illustrates this, as does Gary. When Gary was asked what might encourage him to complete his task, he suggested money. Since this was not feasible, he suggested chocolate bars.

4.1.5 SIMULATING THE TASK BY USING STRUCTURED IN-SESSION ACTIVITIES

In individual treatment, structured in-session activities are used to simulate the tasks clients are to perform outside the session. Simulating the task is done to ensure that the client knows how to perform the task and has the skills to do so. The three forms of simulation are rehearsal, role play, and guided practice.

Rehearsal is the simplest form of simulation. It consists of asking the client to perform the task in the session: "Tell me what you are going to say to your boss."

In a role play, the social worker assumes the role of the other person and a conversation is practiced. Role plays are readily usable when working with children. Many adults seem hesitant to use them, however. Often with adults we are limited to rehearsal, although sometimes a rehearsal turns into a role play. This occurs when the social worker poses a response the other person might make that the client must be prepared for.

Guided practice is most frequently used when more than one client is present, as in couple or family treatment, and when the problem concerns interaction. It consists of having the clients practice the task with one another. This gives the social worker the opportunity to refine task performance. Occasionally it is used with individual clients when the task is complicated. Carla, a six-year-old girl, was constantly being sent to the principal's office for behavioral problems, in spite of her being a very bright and delightful child. Her teacher, however, was inconsistent, moody, and erratic. The task became to predict the teacher's moods so that the child would behave well when the teacher was in a bad mood. Performing the task required Carla to (1) record what she thought was the teacher's mood; and (2) indicate whether her prediction was correct. (Once she learned to assess the teacher's mood, the task became to sit in her seat and be quiet when the teacher was in a bad mood.) This was a complicated task for a young child. The social worker combined role play and guided practice to teach her the task. He alternately pretended to be a happy or a mad teacher and then guided Carla in using the recording system they had developed together. It should be noted that we recommend using the simplest task possible. In this case, the uncooperativeness of the teacher and parents forced us to use the task described. Fortunately it was extremely effective.

4.1.6 ANTICIPATING OBSTACLES TO TASK PERFORMANCE

This activity consists of reviewing, with the client, any contextual factors that might interfere with the client's ability to perform the task. Epstein (1988) has articulated several kinds of obstacles, as well as suggestions, for circumventing them. Among the obstacles are several types of deficits, including resources, reinforcement, and skills or capacity. Another type of obstacle is adverse beliefs the client has, such as the belief that the situation is hopeless or the task is too hard. Finally our own attitude, especially a negative one toward the client, can be an obstacle. Perhaps the most common obstacle concerns lack of opportunity to perform the task. This usually occurs when the task is to be done in relation to another person, and the other person is unavailable.

Obstacles based on deficiencies are often dealt with by either providing what the client lacks or revising the task so it is not dependent on the deficiency. Thus we provide resources, reinforcement in the form of rationale and incentives, and skill training. For example, a client's task was to read the "help wanted" ads daily in the newspaper. The social worker discovered that the client did not have the money to buy the newspaper and that no one in his building purchased a daily paper. She learned that the local library made the paper available. The task then became to go to the library and read the ads. The six-year-old with the behavioral problem described above did not have the skills to predict and record her teacher's behavior. The social worker rehearsed with her until the skills were established. It is absolutely essential that the client has both the resources and skills to perform the task. Otherwise failure is assured.

Adverse beliefs are dealt with openly: "You seem to believe that nothing will make a difference." If clients doubt their ability to perform the task, one of two strategies is commonly used. First, the task can be scaled down either in amount or frequency. To scale down the amount, you break the task down into subparts. To scale down the frequency, you might ask the client to perform the task only once or twice rather than daily, for example. Second, support while performing the task can sometimes be provided. Family members or friends might be able to accompany the client to the hospital. The social worker can go with the child to talk to the teacher. Another strategy is to employ an intervention specifically designed to deal with the obstacle. For example, a task consisting of positive self-statements to improve self-esteem enhanced task performance with one client (see section 4.7.0 for more details).

In the event that the obstacle is fear, it is always wise to ask clients what they think will happen if they do the task. Often the dreaded result seems less dreadful after it has been articulated and discussed. Sometimes the fear is rational. A child who talks to his or her parents about a problem might be in for a severe beating. In these cases, it is important that we learn about the potential consequences so that we can develop a different task.

Some beliefs, of course, cannot be modified. Often these are religious or cultural beliefs, such as the rejection of medical treatment by Christian Scientists. Immutable beliefs circumscribe our alternatives, and we simply have to do the best we can within the limitations. It is sometimes wise to consult an expert who shares the client's beliefs to determine if there are other interpretations of the belief or other avenues for resolving the problem of which the client is unaware. Including a trusted authority as a collateral can be useful. A woman diagnosed as schizophrenic was adamant that her fourteen-year-old son be committed to a psychiatric unit because he was masturbating—a sin, she believed, that would condemn him to hell. The reassurance of social workers and psychiatrists did not alleviate her extreme distress about the behavior. Fortunately her minister was willing to become involved, and he was persuasive.

Finally, for some clients, we are the obstacle. This occurs when we disapprove of the client's target problem, or we doubt our client's capacity to impact the problems. Honest examination of our own attitudes and consultation with others is in order. When our negative attitudes are unchangeable, it is probably best that we refer the client to someone else.

Many external obstacles were confronted in the work with Mrs. Carter. One of them is apparent in Mr. Rooney's attempt to help her obtain public housing. Other obstacles entailed working with collaterals. An external obstacle for Ronnie Paige was that his teacher did not supply the rewards—in this case, gold stars—for his work. Mrs. Carter also identified an internal obstacle that caused her to drink in the past: "See, I've been so weak all my life til I just can't stand to hurt nobody. I would let them hurt me and then go and get drunk."

4.1.7 SUMMARIZING TASKS

Summarizing occurs at the end of each interview in which one or more tasks have been developed. It simply consists of restating all the tasks to be done during the week, including the details of implementing them. Often the client is asked to provide the summary. This gives the social worker the opportunity to check both the client's recall and understanding of the tasks.

In cases where a great many tasks are involved, a "Task Review Sheet" can be used (Rooney 1981). This sheet contains three columns of information: Date, Task, and Task Review. The date refers to the date the task was planned; the task is written in the column headed Task; and the extent to which the task was accomplished is recorded under Task Review. Both the social worker and client should have a copy of the Task Review Sheet.

The Task Review Sheet is also an excellent way to document work, especially client efforts. It is a particularly valuable tool when work is mandated. Mr. Rooney was able to obtain many extensions for Mrs. Carter and demonstrate her efforts to the court based on the evidence provided by the Task Review Sheet.

4.1.8 REVIEWING TASK PROGRESS

Once the process of developing tasks has begun, every subsequent interview should begin with task review. Task review consists of determining the extent to which all tasks were implemented. As in all the TPIS activities the emphasis is on specificity. The social worker wants to learn exactly what the client did, how often he or she did it, the results of performing the task, and problems the client might have encountered. This information will enable us to decide whether the task should be continued, modified, or discontinued. In addition to obtaining a description about task performance, it is sometimes helpful to have clients rate their performance on a scale. The scale we have used includes the following four points: none, partial completion, substantial completion, and fully completed. An additional rating—no opportunity—is used for situations in which the occasion for the task did not arise. The scale cannot take the place of a description of task performance, however, because it does not elicit enough information to revise tasks that are less than fully completed.

Clients should also be asked if they did anything else during the week to alleviate the target problem(s). Often clients will not do or have the opportunity to do the planned tasks, but they will do something unplanned to modify problems. Unplanned efforts are to be commended. It seems that engaging clients in the problem-solving process starts them thinking about possibilities.

It is important to review all tasks and to do so early in the interview. This activity communicates our seriousness to the client. Ignoring the task review has the same effect as the teacher who assigns but does not collect homework: Students stop doing it.

When tasks have been successfully implemented, task review gives us the opportunity for heavy doses of praise: "That's terrific!" "You must be proud of yourself." However, clients who do not implement tasks are not punished. Instead, we look for what interfered and revise tasks accordingly (see section 4.2.0). There are a small number of clients who consistently do not perform the tasks. Procedures for work with them are discussed in section 4.2.0 ("Revising Unsuccessful Tasks") and section 4.3.0 ("Nonperformance of Tasks"). Ms. Kane's work with Ronnie Paige provides excellent examples of reviewing task progress and, the preceding activity, summarizing.

4.1.9 REVIEWING TARGET PROBLEMS

This activity is often intermingled with task review when tasks have been at least partially accomplished. The object of problem review is to determine whether doing the task has had any impact on the problem. Perhaps the client purchased an alarm clock (task 1) and set it every night (task 2) but still is late to work in the morning (target problem). If this is the case, task revision is in order (see section 4.2.0). When tasks are successful, and depending on how they are planned, an entire problem or a problem manifestation might be eliminated.

Problem review is carried out by referring to the problem specifications developed during the initial phase of work. As an illustration, we will return to the problem specification developed in section 3.6.0. The client, Mrs. Gordon, was depressed, and her manifestations entailed the number of hours she slept (four hours per night), the number of times she cried at work (two times per day), the amount of time spent doing housework or errands (one hour per week), and the number of social engagements she experienced (none in two weeks). In each interview, after tasks have begun to be implemented, the social worker reviews each manifestation to determine whether they are changing in the desired direction. For this client, it was important to learn whether she was sleeping more than four hours per night; crying fewer than two times per day at work; doing housework and errands more than one hour per week, and having social engagements. This process enables the social worker to determine whether problems are being resolved and which aspects or manifestations of them require further work. When clients are implementing their tasks and progress is not evident in a reasonable amount of time, the treatment approach should be reconsidered.

Unplanned activities that the client performed for the purpose of alleviating the target problem should be considered in the same way that planned tasks are considered. Did they impact the target problem? Did they impact the problem manifestations? What remains to be done?

If graphing progress was not begun in the initial phase, it should begin now. A simple line graph for each manifestation will make changes readily apparent. Furthermore, when progress is occurring, these graphs are very reinforcing for clients. They are also effective for demonstrating changes to collaterals, who are sometimes reluctant to recognize progress.

When tasks are planned sequentially, it is unreasonable to expect that the first few in the series will eliminate even one manifestation, let alone an entire problem. For example, if a child is having academic difficulty and the first task is to record assignments in an assignment notebook, the successful completion of this task alone is unlikely to change the status of the target problem.

4.1.10 CHECKLIST FOR THE TASK PLANNING AND IMPLEMENTATION SEQUENCE

___ 1. Did I engage the client in generating task alternatives? Did I also suggest task alternatives?

___ 2. Did the client choose the task to be implemented? Did he or she explicitly agree to the task?

___ 3. Did we plan *who* was to do *what, when, how often, where, and with whom?*

___ 4. Did we review the rationale for doing the task? Did we include incentives? If not, should they be included?

___ 5. Was simulation used? How was it used?

___ 6. What obstacles to task performance were identified? Did we plan for each of them?

___ 7. Did we conclude by summarizing all tasks? Did I use a Task Review Sheet? If not, should I have used it?

___ 8. Were all previously planned tasks reviewed? Have tasks been revised appropriately based on information from the review?

___ 9. Were each of the problems and problem manifestations reviewed? Should tasks be changed based on the information provided?

4.1.11 EXERCISE FOR THE TASK PLANNING AND IMPLEMENTATION SEQUENCE

On a small sheet of paper or index card, list the activities included in the task planning sequence: generating alternatives, eliciting agreement, planning details, establishing rationale and incentives, simulating the task, anticipating obstacles, summarizing, task review, and problem review. Using the general guidelines for role plays (see section 3.1.2), practice using the Task Planning and Implementation Sequence. The written list of activities can be used as a prompt. If this is not a continuation of a previous role play, the person playing the client will have to provide a brief description of the target problem and manifestations.

4.2.0 REVISING UNSUCCESSFUL TASKS

Tasks can be unsuccessful in two ways. First, sometimes they are not completely implemented. Second, sometimes they are implemented but do not have the desired effect on the target problems. Information gathered during task review will reveal whether implementation or impact is wanting.

Common reasons for lack of implementation include the following:

1. expectations were unclear;
2. opportunity for implementation did not occur;
3. an unanticipated obstacle emerged, including skill deficit; and
4. client motivation was insufficient.

Each of these common impediments will be discussed.

Task review will suggest the reason why the task was not implemented or was implemented incompletely. If you are in any doubt about the reason for lack of implementation, asking the client to role play what he or she did with respect to the task can be helpful. When the issue is unclear expectations, these can usually be clarified easily. The task is not changed in these cases, but the client's understanding of it is.

Sometimes tasks are not implemented because the opportunity to do so did not arise. This is particularly common when the tasks concern ways to respond to another person's behavior. Sometimes the other person is either not present during the week or does not display the behavior that the task is designed to address. Usually these situations require that the task be continued until the circumstances occur.

Unanticipated obstacles will usually fall into one of the categories identified in section 4.1.6. The task then must be revised to accommodate the obstacle.

When client motivation is the issue, the strategy is to repeat the rationale and consider incentives (see section 4.1.4). This entails reminding the client of the reason for doing the task. It also entails a reconsideration of the use of incentives. If incentives are not being used, including them is advisable. If they are being used, the incentive is probably not sufficiently rewarding for the effort involved. In this case, two options are available. The amount of effort required by the task can be scaled down, or the incentives can be increased.

Occasionally a client will express a desire to continue a task without modification even though he or she has never tried to implement it. We have found that implementation sometimes does occur when the task is continued once. Implementation is rare, however, when a task that has not been attempted is continued more than once.

The other situation that requires task revision occurs when the client has implemented the task, but the task has not had the expected impact on the target problem. Frequently, in such cases, more than one phenomena is maintaining the problem, and the task only dealt with one aspect of it. For example, Shirley was often late for school. The first tasks were to purchase and use an alarm clock, which she did. However, Shirley continued to be late for school. In the process of reexploring what occurred during the morning, the social worker learned that the client had trouble deciding what to wear or discovered that what she planned to wear was dirty or needed ironing. A new task was developed to rectify this aspect of the problem: Shirley is to put out her clothes for the next day before going to bed. In cases like this, the original task is continued while a new task is developed. Of course, all the TPIS activities should be done with respect to the new task.

Sometimes tasks do not have the desired impact because others do not respond to them as we hoped they would. Bosses reject requests for raises; parents reject requests for extended curfews; child welfare workers reject requests from parents to visit their children in foster care; and so on. In these circumstances, the nature of the appeal can be changed: Instead of simply asking for an extension of curfew, the child offers to do certain chores, for example. A change can also be made in terms of who makes the appeal. Sometimes the social worker, a parent, or a group will be more successful than the individual client. In some situations, when clients are being denied their rights, it is necessary to escalate the pressure. For example, Ronnie Paige's sister, Olivia, was not allowed to graduate from the eighth grade because of her poor attendance, even though she was a superior student in every other way. When her mother was unsuccessful in persuading the principal to change his mind, the social worker, Ms. Kane, tried. When she, too, was unsuccessful, she referred the family to legal aide. Fortunately legal aide was successful. Other examples of task revision can be found in the Paige and Carter cases.

Obviously, when the first task does not have the desired impact, the answer is not to quit but to generate new or revised tasks. The information gathered during the implementation of the first task will be helpful in planning later ones.

However, situations will arise in which no tasks are effective. Sometimes the result will be a new target problem. The client who cannot get a raise may decide that he or she must look for a new or second job in order to survive. When this occurs, we return to the beginning by specifying the problem and generating new tasks.

The process of revising tasks is similar to that of generating them. The client is fully involved and must explicitly agree to the revisions. If revisions are major, the social worker may need to employ all TPIS activities, including planning details, analyzing obstacles, establishing rationale and incentives, simulating, and summarizing.

4.2.1 CHECKLIST FOR REVISING UNSUCCESSFUL TASKS

___ 1. Did the problem occur because the task was not implemented as designed or because the task did not have the desired effect on the target problem?

___ 2. If the task was not implemented, was it because expectations were unclear, opportunities to do so did not arise, unanticipated obstacles occurred, or motivation was insufficient?

___ 3. Did the revision of the task take into account the reason it was not implemented?

___ 4. If the task was implemented as planned but did not have the desired impact on the problem, what other tasks are needed? Should other systems be involved?

4.2.2 EXERCISE FOR REVISING UNSUCCESSFUL TASKS

Continue the preceding role play for the Task Planning and Implementation Sequence. Assume either that one of the tasks was not implemented or that it did not impact the target problem. Revise the task or plan a new one.

4.3.0 CONSISTENT NONPERFORMANCE OF TASKS

Occasionally we encounter clients who perform no tasks at all no matter how carefully and cooperatively the tasks are planned or revised. Three possible reasons may account for nonperformance. First, the client may not be interested in changing the selected target problem. Second, the client may not be interested in working with us. Third, the client may not want to change anything. Once the reason for nonperformance is identified, the appropriate action is fairly obvious. If the client is not interested in the target problem, we identify the problem that does concern the client. If the client does not wish to work with us, we find someone with whom the client does want to work. If there is nothing the client wants to change, we terminate treatment.

The challenge for the social worker confronted with nonperformance is to identify the reason for it. Like all other TC activities, this is done through a frank and open conversation with the client.

We start with the assumption that we have not identified the correct target problem: "Since you haven't been doing the tasks, I wonder if this is really the problem that concerns you the most." Sometimes clients freely volunteer that, indeed, another and more pressing problem exists. With other clients it is necessary to review all the problems that were mentioned during the initial phase of treatment, as well as new ones. A review of the content in sections 3.4.0 and 3.4.1 might help to identify a more appropriate target problem. When a new target problem is identified, all the initial phase work—exploration, specification, and so on—must be done with respect to this new target problem.

If we cannot identify a new target problem and yet our client seems unhappy or troubled, we ask if he or she would be more comfortable seeing someone else or using a different agency. Sometimes clients have a preference about the worker's gender, age, race or ethnicity, or religion. Sometimes clients do not want to receive psychosocial help from a particular agency. A teenager, for example, might be embarrassed to see the school social worker. A parent might not want to share his or her frustrations with the job of parenting with a worker at a child protective agency. Offering the client the opportunity to change workers or agencies must be done carefully. Clients often fear that they will hurt our feelings if they request or accept referral to another worker. The worker might say, "I think you really want things to be different in your life but that you would be more comfortable talking to someone else. Other social workers are available in this agency, and other agencies exist that help people with concerns like yours. Tell me what kind of person you would feel most comfortable with." Occasionally the worker will have to tell the client directly that his or her feelings will not be hurt. If the client agrees to a referral, the social worker should do everything possible to locate the kind of practitioner the client desires. The client should also be reassured that the social worker will still be available in case the referral is not suitable.

If nonperformance is the result of the client not wanting to make any changes at this time, we suggest termination. The idea of terminating contact might be anathema to social workers who interpret uncooperativeness as resistance that must be "worked through." In TC we do not assume that resistance is ever present. We do believe that the most effective strategy for dealing with obstacles from any source is to ally ourselves with the expressed interests of the client. Sometimes this alliance will result in early terminations. The suggestion to terminate should be made in a nonjudgmental or nonpunitive manner. We should also leave the door open for the client's return: "If you decide at any time in the future that you want to work on these or any other problems, I would be happy to meet with you." Occasionally you will encounter clients who identify target problems and implement tasks once they realize that the alternative is termination.

In some cases, the client may not want help, but termination is not possible. This most often occurs in child welfare or correctional settings where client supervision has been mandated. In these cases, the social worker tells the client that he or she will need to continue to check in regularly but that work on problems will be abandoned until or unless the client wants help. Again, this explanation should not be made judgmentally or punitively.

4.3.1 CHECKLIST FOR CONSISTENT NONPERFORMANCE OF TASKS

___ 1. Is the client not performing tasks because the selection of target problems is inaccurate, the client does not want our help, or the client does not want help from anyone?

___ 2. Have the appropriate corrective actions been taken: retargeting problems, referral, or termination?

4.3.2 EXERCISE FOR CONSISTENT NONPERFORMANCE OF TASKS

Continue the preceding role play. This time, assume the client has not performed any tasks. Determine the reason and take the appropriate action.

4.4.0 NONTARGETED PROBLEMS: RESTRUCTURING

Occasionally a new problem will emerge during the course of work on targeted problems. This might occur in several circumstances. The client may experience an emergency, such as a health problem or a housing or employment crisis. Or a preexisting concern may become more serious. For example, a parent might be aware that a child is having difficulty in school, but a suspension or a particularly bad report card could heighten the severity of the problem. Sometimes the client becomes aware during work on targeted problems that another problem is preventing the solution of those that have been targeted. For example, the client who is unable to employ certain kinds of tasks might realize that he or she has a self-esteem problem. Finally, on rare occasions, a client might "test" us with a relatively minor problem when a more important one exists. After trust has been established, the client shares the important concern.

Regardless of the reason why a new problem appears, the procedure is the same. Clients are asked explicitly if they want our help with this new problem. If they do, they are asked to reprioritize; that is, to decide where this problem ranks in importance compared to those problems that have already been targeted. When clients want to work on the new problem immediately, we employ the initial phase activities with regard to the new problem (see sections 3.5.0, 3.6.0, 3.7.0, and 3.9.0). The contract is revised (section 3.9.0), and new tasks are developed. When clients choose to add the new problem *after* work on the current one is completed, we can often do the initial phase work on the new target problem *while* continuing middle-phase work on the current one.

This procedure is called *restructuring*. We simply change the structure of our work to accommodate the new target problem. An important advantage to TC is its flexibility in dealing with client concerns.

We have noticed two kinds of errors that are made when new problems arise. The first is to ignore the problem. Sometimes workers are so consumed with existing target problems that they simply do not hear the new ones. At other times the worker hears them but decides independently that they are unimportant. For example, Patty, an elementary school child, was unable to concentrate during a particular interview.

She frequently referred to her torn blouse. Finally, the worker responded and asked if she would like to get the tear repaired. After a trip to the office where sewing supplies were kept, a few stitches were inserted and Patty was again able to concentrate on solving the previously identified target problems. This example illustrates how small problems can interrupt work if they are not resolved. It also illustrates that restructuring is sometimes very brief.

The second error occurs when workers *assume* that clients want our help with new or newly shared problems. Marilyn, a woman in her mid-twenties, was productively working on target problems. However, she frequently mentioned her deceased father. She reported that she kept his picture on her dresser and talked to it each evening. The worker, somewhat forcefully, began to suggest tasks related to her father. Marilyn refused to attend any more treatment sessions. The correct procedure would have been to ask Marilyn if she wanted the worker's help with her feelings about her father.

Two skills distinguish the expert task-centered practitioner from the novice. One is the ability to be flexible in restructuring work to meet client needs. The other is the ability to identify target problems in difficult circumstances (see section 3.5.1). Both these skills can be developed with practice. Both require a high degree of collaboration with clients.

4.4.1 Checklist for Nontargeted Problems

___ 1. Has the client mentioned any nontargeted concerns?
___ 2. Have I asked if these concerns should be targeted and with what priority?
___ 3. Have I employed the necessary initial-phase activities: exploring, specifying, and goal-setting? Have I revised the contract?

4.4.2 Exercise for Nontargeted Problems

Continue the role play for the task planning sequence (see section 4.1.11). As tasks are being planned, the person assuming the role of client must mention a new concern. Mention it subtly, like most clients do. If the "worker" does not pick up on it, be more obvious. See how often it must be mentioned before the "worker" addresses it. Once the "worker" has heard it, he or she should begin to practice the skills identified in this section.

4.5.0 USE OF TIME LIMITS

The establishment of time limits occurs during the initial phase of work (see section 3.3.0). The two middle-phase activities regarding time limits concern (a) using them, and (b) altering them.

Using time limits during the middle phase is simple. It consists of reminding the client *during every interview* of the number of sessions that have been conducted and the number that remain. We say something like, "Let's see, this is our sixth interview so we have four more after today." With a young child, this is accomplished by marking off days on a calendar.

Altering time limits is somewhat trickier. Alteration can mean either reducing or increasing the number of sessions.

We consider reducing time limits when the target problems have been solved in less time than was anticipated. It might seem that the rational approach when problems are solved is to terminate. However, sometimes a client who has worked hard and enjoyed the experience views this as punishment. Therefore the procedure, as always in TC, is to ask clients what they want to do with the remaining sessions. Some adults will want to terminate. Some will want to use the remaining sessions (or some fraction of them) to discuss other matters of concern to them. Others will want the security of checking in for the remaining sessions to be sure the problem is resolved. Children and teenagers often want to complete all the sessions even if the remaining time is spent playing games or chatting.

Two criteria determine whether we should extend the time limits. We will extend them if (1) the client has been performing the tasks; *and* (2) either a new target problem emerges or there is reason to expect that existing target problems will be resolved with an extension. In other words, we would not extend the time if the client was not actively working. Nor would we extend the time if nothing remained to be worked on. An extension consists of setting a specific number of additional sessions, usually no more than four to six. There are, however, some notable exceptions like Mrs. Carter. Work required several contract extensions largely because of the slowness of the bureaucracy.

Either clients or practitioners can initiative extensions. Practitioners do so when the two criteria described above are met. They explain the rationale for the extension. Usually clients agree. If a client disagrees with the suggested extension, we accept their decision.

Actually social workers rarely initiate extensions, because clients generally do so first. When the client initiates an extension, we explore the reasons for it. What benefits does the client expect to gain from an extension? We also ask how many additional sessions the client wants. If the client's expectations are reasonable, and if the two criteria stated above are met, we would agree to an extension for a specific number of sessions. However, if the client initiates an extension early in the middle phase, we try to postpone the decision: "I would prefer to complete our contract and then decide how many more sessions we need. Is that okay?" The reason for postponing premature initiatives is that time limits seem to lose their motivating power if they are amended too readily. On rare occasions we may need to agree to an extension before we are sure that the criteria will be met. This occurs when the client is anxious about the time limits or when the collaborative relationship would be seriously impaired by refusing.

4.5.1 CHECKLIST FOR USING TIME LIMITS

___ 1. Am I reminding all clients, at each session, of the number of interviews remaining?

___ 2. Do I have any clients who would benefit from a concrete reminder such as a calendar?

___ 3. Have I extended treatment or indicated that I would do so when (a) the client was not performing tasks, or (b) no unresolved, targeted problem remained?

4.5.2 EXERCISE FOR USING TIME LIMITS

Practice of this skill can easily be included in any of the middle-phase role plays.

4.6.0 REVISING ASSESSMENTS

The middle-phase activities generate a great deal of information about the clients and the problems. Depending on the problem, these activities sometimes generate a great deal of information about the other systems and about collaterals. The continual accumulation of information means that assessments should be continually revised. We suggest that assessments be reconsidered after each contact.

Because of the collaborative, problem-solving nature of TC, we readily learn about the client's problem-solving skills, which are revealed as we observe the client's responses to the Task Planning and Implementation Sequence. These skills include generating alternatives, appraising consequences, and means-ends planning. Some clients have clear deficits on one or more of these skills. This information can be used in one of two ways. First, we can compensate for the deficits by using our own skills. Thus we would generate more alternative tasks, point out the consequences to various courses of action, or plan the details of task implementation. Second, we can point out the deficits to clients and ask if they would like our help with them. If they accept our offer, the skill deficit becomes a target problem. The first course of action is appropriate when the client is a child or intellectually limited. It is also appropriate when the skill deficit is limited to the targeted problems. Many people have perfectly adequate problem-solving skills but are unable to apply them to emotional issues. The second course of action is preferable when the skill deficit is clearly one of the factors maintaining the target problems.

Depending on the type of task, we might also learn about other skills like assertiveness or sociability. It is sometimes tempting to use our observations to identify new problems. This is acceptable practice only if the client agrees! Our awareness of a problem does not mean that the client wants to work on it or wants our help to work on it. Our new observations should be used when designing new tasks, however. For example, clients with assertiveness problems might be offered some support when implementing tasks that require assertiveness. Or such tasks might become practitioner tasks. Conversely, we might observe some special skills. These, too, should be taken into account when planning new tasks or revising old ones.

Of course, new information is not limited to client skills. We are likely to learn more about the extent of stress in clients' lives, their resources, and their social support. Periodically reviewing the dimensions of functioning will help us to incorporate this new information.

Additional information about the problem is also generated. In almost all cases we learn something about the resiliency of the problem. Will it be solved readily, or do we have to redouble our efforts? In many cases we will learn something unique to the particular problem. This is often new information for both the client and the worker. For example, a task was developed with a mother to change the acting-out behavior of her son. In the course of discussing rewards with him, she learned that he was angry and afraid because he thought she was going to leave her long-term partner, a man the boy adored. The new information about the problem, like that about the client, helps to shape further work.

When the tasks require contact with other systems, we discover how flexible and supportive they are in relation to our clients. We learn about the impediments they present. This information should be used to reconsider the three questions identified in chapter 1: What is the causal or maintaining impact of other systems (family, organization, and community) on each of the target problems? What is the impact of the target problems on the other systems? Can the other systems contribute to resolving the target problems? The systematic consideration of each of these questions should enable the social worker to determine whether other systems should be involved and if, in fact, the individual is the appropriate primary system.

Finally, when collaterals are involved, we learn about the extent of their helpfulness. Helpfulness is influenced by motivation, knowledge and skill, risk taking, and position. When collaterals are insufficiently helpful, we might want to engage other representatives of the same system who have more power, knowledge, or motivation.

Of course, this must be done tactfully. When collaterals are helpful, we reinforce their efforts. Verbal expressions of admiration, thank-you notes, and extolling letters to superiors are inexpensive and always appreciated.

4.6.1 CHECKLIST FOR REVISING ASSESSMENTS

___ 1. What new information do I have about the client? What does it mean in terms of intervention?

___ 2. What new information do I have about the target problems? What does it mean in terms of intervention?

___ 3. What new information do I have about the role of other systems on cause or maintenance of the target problems? What does it mean in terms of intervention?

___ 4. What new information do I have about the impact of the target problems on the other systems? What does it mean in terms of intervention?

___ 5. What more do I know about the potential contribution of other systems to solving the target problems? What does it mean in terms of intervention?

4.7.0 ECLECTIC PRACTICE

Eclectic practice refers to using the best components of various approaches to meet the needs of a particular client with a particular problem. Surveys of practitioners in the mental health fields have found that the majority of them identify their orientation as eclectic (Garfield and Bergin 1994). TC is an ideal base for eclectic practice for three reasons. First, problems are not explained according to any particular theory in TC. This permits the worker to choose from an array of theoretical explanations—if, in fact, a theoretical explanation is needed. Second, tasks can be developed based on interventions from a variety of approaches. Third, the structure of TC prevents work from losing direction, which is the potential danger in eclectic practice.

A summary of all intervention strategies that might be borrowed from all approaches to practice is beyond the scope of this book. Fortunately the publication of *The Task Planner* (Reid 2000) makes the job of deciding what to borrow relatively easy for problems that it includes. It also contains a chapter, "Common Procedures," which describes many interventions. A few of the approaches and interventions frequently used in TC are briefly described. The reader is encouraged to learn about other practice approaches and to think about how the recommended interventions can be included in TC.

TC has borrowed most frequently from operant behavioral approaches. Among the interventions used are reward plans, including token economies, time out, and contingency contracting. These interventions are particularly useful with child-behavior problems. These interventions are so well known that they are not described here. They are at least partially built in to TC through the TPIS activity of "establishing incentives and rationale."

Respondent conditioning suggests tasks based on exposure therapy. This is an intervention used with phobias. In exposure therapy, clients are helped to confront the feared object. A client with agoraphobia was helped with TC. The tasks consisted of gradually increasing the distance and time spent away from home (see also Reid 1992).

Cognitive behavioral techniques have also been employed within TC. Among the interventions are positive self-statements and thought stopping. Positive self-statements consists of generating with the client a list of the client's positive qualities. Each quality is listed on a separate card. The client's task is to read the cards a specific number of times each day. This task is particularly useful with self-esteem problems. It was used as part of a single-subject design project with Edward, a twenty-three-year-old Native American, who completed very few tasks. It was found that, when positive self-statements were included, Edward's rate of task completion increased dramatically.

Thought stopping is used to combat negative thoughts. In one variant of this approach, the client's tasks are (1) to wear a rubber band on his or her wrist; (2) to snap the band whenever the negative thought that is to be eliminated occurs and say no; and (3) to turn attention to a predesigned positive thought.

Rationale Emotive Therapy (Ellis 1962) is similar to cognitive behavioral interventions. One worker used it to help forty-five-year old Mrs. Baker lose weight (Tolson 1988). The problem was puzzling, because Mrs Baker knew how to accomplish her goal and had done so in the past. Further exploration revealed that she was afraid to lose weight because when she was thin she was also promiscuous. Tasks were designed to help her combat her assumption that the past predicts the future.

Other behavioral approaches focus on skill training. The activities necessary to developing a skill can easily be shaped into tasks. In fact, it is often necessary to teach a skill in order to complete a task successfully.

Our knowledge about the developmental stages of human beings can also be used to generate tasks. The parent whose child is not bonding can be helped to develop nurturing tasks. Tasks based on value clarification exercises can be developed for the client experiencing a midlife crisis. Elderly clients can be given tasks to maintain their competence or to encourage reminiscing.

Finally, traditional social work activities like referrals and advocacy can be encompassed in the form of practitioner tasks.

Including some of the aforementioned tasks might require a slight alteration during the task generation phase of the model (see section 4.1.1). They can be suggested to the client during this activity just as any other task is suggested. However, because the client might be unfamiliar with some of them, they may require explanation. Explanations should be brief and expressed in nontechnical language. Avoid trying to "sell" these tasks to the client beyond saying that this strategy has been used successfully with some people with a similar problem. As always, the client has the final say in task selection.

4.7.1 EXERCISE FOR ECLECTIC PRACTICE

Learn about either another practice approach or the interventions used for a particular problem (depression, child abuse, etc.). Try to integrate the interventions with TC. This has been used as a term paper assignment.

4.8.0 WORK WITH COLLATERALS

In the preceding chapter we discussed the involvement of collaterals. When collaterals are involved, work with them during the middle phase consists, minimally, of keeping in contact with them to determine that efforts are both on track and productive. Sometimes we will ask them to become more actively involved. For example, Monique, a ten-year-old African-American, complained that she could not do her work when her teacher stood over her. In a joint conference, the teacher agreed to alter her teaching style if Monique would stay on-task. In Mrs. Carter's case, a child welfare worker was asked to gather the children who were placed in several different foster homes so that their mother could visit them.

The roles of broker, mediator, and advocate can be operationalized within TC as practitioner tasks. Social workers act as brokers when they take on tasks that involve linking the client to resources. This is, of course, a frequent activity in all approaches to social work practice. Social workers act as mediators when they take on tasks designed to resolve disputes between the clients and other people or other systems. Social workers act as advocates when they argue for the client.

Another role of social workers is common but not mentioned in the literature: public relations agent. Often collaterals hold negative opinions about clients. We can sometimes modify these opinions by providing collaterals with information about clients. Teachers and physicians, for example, are not always aware of a client's living conditions. Sometimes they are unaware of the influence of a client's culture. Sympathetic collaterals are more likely to be cooperative and helpful with change efforts.

Work with collaterals usually entails practitioner tasks. These tasks are planned in cooperation with the client, and many of the TPIS activities are employed. If there are alternatives—for example, it may be possible to refer the client to one of several agencies—these are weighed and chosen with the client. Details of task implementation are also planned with the client. They might include the date when the practitioner will perform the task, what precisely will be done or said, and when the client will be informed of the results. Practitioner tasks are summarized with client tasks at the end of the session, and they are reviewed with client tasks in the following session. These procedures are designed out of respect for the client's right to control the treatment endeavor and a desire to communicate that we take our task work seriously.

Of course, as work with Mrs. Carter illustrates, clients should be informed of all contacts with collaterals whether or not practitioner tasks are involved. If these contacts are extensive, maintaining a written record that can be shared with the client is helpful. Information is not provided without considering the issue of confidentiality.

4.8.1 CHECKLIST FOR WORK WITH COLLATERALS

__ 1. Are the important collaterals in this case sufficiently involved?

__ 2. Am I reporting my contacts with them to the client?

__ 3. Am I ignoring any roles, for example, enabler, teacher, broker, mediator, advocate, or public relations agent?

__ 4. Am I developing practitioner tasks? Are they being promptly implemented? Am I reporting the results to the client?

__ 5. Have any important collaterals been overlooked?

5

TERMINATION AND CASE ILLUSTRATIONS

5.0.0 COMPONENTS OF TERMINATION

The termination or final phase of treatment in TC usually occurs in the last interview. Occasionally it will require two interviews. The purpose of the last interview is to review accomplishments, plan follow-up, and say good-bye. These purposes are fulfilled with five activities: (1) final problem review; (2) reinforcement of accomplishments; (3) future plans; (4) problem-solving skill review; and (5) reactive discussion. These skills are described in this chapter.

Before describing termination-phase skills, an explanation about the length of this phase in TC is in order. Readers familiar with long-term treatment in which clients are prepared for termination over a period of at least several months are probably surprised by the brevity of this phase in TC (or in any time-limited approach). Preparation for termination can be brief in TC because clients are informed about termination from the very first interview when time limits are explained. They are indirectly reminded of termination in each subsequent interview when time limits are reviewed. Thus, for almost all clients, termination comes as no surprise. Furthermore, the knowledge, from the outset, that contact will be limited, permits clients to determine how much they will invest in the relationship.

5.1.0 The Final Problem Review

The final problem review differs from problem reviews conducted during middle-phase interviews (section 4.1.9) in only one respect. It is more thorough. Every target problem and all specifications for every problem are reviewed. The review consists of determining the change between the problems and specifications from the initial phase to termination. If specifications are well developed and reviews have been consistently conducted, the final problem review will seem like "business as usual." Furthermore, the status of the problems will cause no surprises.

In addition to gathering the empirical information inherent in the problem review, inquiring into the client's subjective satisfaction is advisable. This can be done by asking the client to rate the amount of change for each target problem on the following scale: problem completely alleviated, substantially changed, minimally changed, or unchanged.

If collaterals are actively involved, it is wise to solicit their opinions about change before the final interview and to inform the client that you have or will do so. Actually, we recommend this procedure throughout the middle phase as well. It prevents the uncomfortable consequences that inevitably occur when clients mislead us about either the extent to which they have employed tasks or the extent of problem change. It is most useful when authority figures are involved (teachers, physicians, parole officers, and so forth).

5.1.1 Checklist for the Final Problem Review

> __ 1. Did I review all target problems and all specifications?
> __ 2. Did the client rate outcome for each problem?
> __ 3. If collaterals are involved, did I secure their opinions concerning a change in the target problem?

5.1.2 Exercise for Final Problem Review

See section 5.3.2 for an exercise that combines practicing final problem review with other termination-phase activities.

5.2.0 Reinforcement of Accomplishments

Reinforcing accomplishments is intertwined with the problem review. As used in TC during termination, reinforcement simply means praising clients for their accomplishments. "You really did a terrific job on this problem." "It's surprising that you could do as much as you did, given the difficulty of this problem." "I know that you would have liked to see more change on this problem, but I think *you* did all *you* could to improve the situation."

In addition to praise, social workers can reinforce clients by reporting how many tasks were planned and how many were implemented, as Mr. Rooney did with Mrs Carter. Ms Kane, in working with Ronnie Paige, cleverly pointed out to him how many pages of work he had done. She knew he would be impressed by such big numbers. Social workers can remind clients of the positive consequences of solving target problems: "What is wonderful is that, as you said, now that you are disciplining the children consistently, they are fun to be with. This will affect your relationship with them for years." Alternately, social workers can make inquiries that will lead clients to consider the impact of their efforts: "How have the changes in your job situation affected the quality of your life?"

Be generous with praise and avoid punishment. Your ability to implement this directive will depend somewhat on your own feelings about the client and the work accomplished. This is discussed further in the last section (5.5.0) of this chapter.

5.2.1 Checklist for Reinforcement of Accomplishments

___ 1. How many times did I praise the client?
___ 2. What did I say that was intended to be reinforcing?
___ 3. What else could I have said or done?
___ 4. Was the praise genuine?
___ 5. What was the client's reaction?
___ 6. Did I punish the client?
___ 7. What did I say or do that the client might experience as punishment?

___ 8. What prompted the use of punishment, and how can I avoid it in the future?

___ 9. Did I praise collaterals who were involved?

5.2.2 EXERCISE FOR REINFORCEMENT OF ACCOMPLISHMENTS

See section 5.3.2 for practice of this skill.

5.3.0 FUTURE PLANS

This activity can be intertwined with problem review and reinforcing accomplishments when the target problem has been completely or substantially changed and plans to maintain the changes are relatively simple. Consideration of the future is provoked by simply asking clients how they plan to maintain the changes. Often future plans consist of simply continuing the tasks: attending Alcoholics Anonymous (AA) meetings, doing homework before watching television, informing the public assistance worker of changes in address, or making at least one social engagement each week. With Mrs. Carter, future plans consisted of discussing how she would be able to secure beds for the children not yet returned to her custody and reviewing the procedures for informing the collaterals when she had secured the beds.

Obstacles to the continuation of task performance might be raised: "Do you foresee anything that might get in the way of continuing to attend AA meetings, doing homework, and so forth?" If obstacles are apparent, plans for coping with them can be questioned: "What will you do if that occurs?" This discussion should be brief, however, and its tone positive: "It might be difficult, but you have been able to do it in the past and you know what to look out for."

Sadly some problems and conditions simply have to be endured. When a target problem has not been resolved, clients usually resign themselves to living with it at least temporarily; change their goal, and hence target problem; or seek some ongoing support for coping with it. For example, problems in a work situation may not be resolvable, but the client might decide to become resigned to them until another op-portunity presents itself or until the children graduate from high school and the family can relocate. Resignation is an unfortunate outcome but, for the few problems with which it has occurred, clients seem able to accept it because they know they have tried every avenue to correct the target problems. The client who is unable to develop the kind of in-timate relationship that was desired might decide that he or she should build more networks of casual relationships and interests. Seeking sup-port often in the form of support groups occurs most commonly when clients learn that they or an intimate other must endure a medical prob-lem or disability. In these circumstances, social workers should praise the clients' efforts even though the problem is substantially unresolved, locate support services, and offer to be available should the client seek more help in the future.

Collaterals should also be involved in future plans. The visiting nurse, for example, will need to know that our contact with the client is terminated so that the nurse can be aware of the implications of this for his or her work with the client. Collaterals should know, too, that we will be available in the event they need us. In fact, termination of TC does not always mean that the social worker will no longer see the client. In cases in which we have a monitoring or supervisory respon-sibility, such as child welfare or parole, we will continue to see the client periodically even though our active, problem-solving efforts are terminated. This distinction, as well as plans for future contact, should be made clear to the client.

5.3.1 CHECKLIST FOR FUTURE PLANS

___ 1. Do I know how the client plans to maintain or extend accomplish-ments for each target problem?

___ 2. Is the client aware that he or she can return for additional help when and if necessary?

___ 3. Has the tone of the discussion regarding the future been realistical-ly positive and optimistic?

___ 4. Have future plans been discussed with collaterals?

5.3.2 EXERCISE FOR FINAL PROBLEM REVIEW, REINFORCING ACCOMPLISHMENTS, AND FUTURE PLANS

Problem specifications for two target problems are required for this exercise. They can be developed and written out by either the "client" or the "social worker." Those developed during earlier exercises can be used. The participants should assume that one of the problems was completely resolved and that the other one was either minimally changed or unchanged so that skill in handling both types of outcomes can be developed.

It is desirable to tape this role play.

The "social worker" should begin with the final problem review, and intertwine reinforcing accomplishments and making future plans. Be careful to allot approximately the same amount of time for discussing each of the problems. After the role play is completed, the "social worker" should listen to the tape using the checklists for each of the three activities to note missing content. The "social worker" should also use the tape to count the number of times he or she explicitly praised the client. (For an exercise concerning reliability, both "client" and "social worker" can count each occurrence of praise and compute reliability by dividing the number of agreements by the number of agreements plus disagreements.)

5.4.0 REVIEW OF PROBLEM-SOLVING SKILLS

Problem-solving skills were originally identified by John Dewey (1933). In recent years social problem-solving skills have received considerable attention from psychologists. Deficits in these skills have been found to be associated with a variety of dysfunctional behaviors (Spivack, Platt, and Shure 1976). The skills include the ability to (a) identify that a problem exists; (b) generate alternative solutions for the problem; (c) appraise consequences; (d) see a situation from another person's perspective; and (e) develop a detailed plan to implement the chosen solution.

In reviewing these skills, we simply identify them and point out how they were used in our work on target problems. (Young children might be developmentally unable to comprehend the fourth skill, to view a situation from another's perspective.) We might introduce the review by saying that, although all people have problems, what determines whether we get stuck in our problems is our ability to solve them. "Let's look at how you were able to solve the problem of __ so that you can use your skills to solve other problems when they arise. First you recognized that a problem existed. This is essential. Some people try to pretend that they have no problems, but then, of course, they can't fix them." We proceed through the skills, illustrating how each one was used with a target problem. When clients are able, invite them to participate in identifying either the skills or how they were applied: "After you identified the problem, what did we do first?" or "The next step is to think of alternative ways to solve the problem. Do you remember the possible solutions we considered for this problem?"

Among the clients who are most responsive to the review of problem-solving skills are people who demonstrate good problem-solving skills in other areas of their lives but are unable to apply them in emotional situations or young children who are just learning them. The former seem to readily understand that they possess skills that can be generalized. Some of the children get excited by and proud of the idea that they have a new skill. When a client seems to be benefiting from the review of problem-solving skills, practice can be extended by inviting the client to try to apply the skills to a new, hypothetical problem. Responsiveness does not, however, guarantee that the problem-solving skills have actually been enhanced or that they will be used in the future.

5.4.1 CHECKLIST FOR REVIEW OF PROBLEM-SOLVING SKILLS

__ 1. Did I illustrate each of the five skills with activities?
__ 2. Was the client involved in the discussion?

5.4.2 EXERCISE FOR REVIEW OF PROBLEM-SOLVING SKILLS

See section 5.5.2.

5.5.0 REACTIVE DISCUSSION

Reactive discussion consists of exploring the client's reaction to treatment and, especially, to the termination of treatment. It also includes sharing our feelings and reactions to the extent that this can be done in a way that is supportive of the client.

We begin this activity by directly inquiring about the clients' feelings about termination. Few clients who receive TC have strong negative reactions to termination. Some, like Mrs. Carter, feel a little sad. Some are mildly anxious about how they will manage without the social worker. Some are both somewhat anxious and a bit sad. Most feel a sense of accomplishment. Some feel relieved. We believe that the paucity of strong negative reactions is because clients know treatment will be time-limited from the beginning and thus are able to modulate their investment in the personal relationship while maximizing their investment in solving problems. Fortune, Pearlingi, and Rochelle (1992) found that the strongest reactions of clients terminating from a variety of types of psychotherapy are positive and include feelings of pride and accomplishment.

The one client behavior that might be interpreted as an indirect expression of concern about terminating consists of requests to alter time limits—especially requests for brief extensions. Such appeals occur rather frequently and might be understood as expressing a desire or need to control termination. We recommend that these requests be interpreted literally and responded to rationally, as described in chapter 4 (see section 4.5.0). If, however, a client asks for one extension after another and the requests are not justified by problem status, we would raise the possibility with the client that the problem is really one of termination.

While strong reactions to termination are rare, we know of one client, thirteen-year-old Sarah, who was extremely surprised by termination, even though time limits had been reviewed in each interview conducted with her. We are certain that time limits were reviewed, because all interviews with Sarah were taped and the social work student's supervisor listened to each tape. Sarah's expression of shock during the final interview when she learned that she would not be seeing the social worker again was dramatic and genuine. So was her unhappiness. Thus, even with careful preparation, a rare client might have difficulty accepting termination. In Sarah's case, her reactions were discussed, and several additional interviews were held.

Actually we have witnessed more problematic behaviors from beginning social workers using TC than from clients. TC appears to be a straightforward and readily comprehensible approach to practice. And it is. However, one aspect of the model causes beginning social workers more stress than other models of social work practice, and that is the emphasis on accountability or outcome. In TC we accept responsibility for helping clients solve problems. We also collect data so that we know whether our efforts are successful. This emphasis on accountability often produces anxiety for beginning workers who are afraid that they will not be able to help clients resolve their target problems. If treatment does not progress satisfactorily, other reactions like guilt and anger occasionally occur. Guilt results when the social workers think that they have been inadequate. Anger results when they think that the client has not cooperated. Sometimes anxiety reemerges even when work has been successful because social workers worry that clients will not be able to maintain the gains on their own.

All these negative emotions interfere with successful termination. The first step in dealing with them is to recognize what you are feeling toward the client and toward your joint effort. If you are feeling negatively at any point in treatment, talk to your supervisor before the next session. A social worker's feelings of anger, guilt, or anxiety should not be taken out on the client. It is appropriate to share mild feelings of sadness about termination, as Mr. Rooney did with Mrs. Carter, and of disappointment when goals were not reached. These should be realistic and nonpunitive. If you have been able to maintain the close collaborative rapport characteristic of TC, your reactions to the outcome of treatment and the client's reactions will likely be similar. Sharing them in the final sessions will be just one more piece in the collaborative process.

If you are supervising or consulting with someone who is learning TC, we urge you to be aware of the stress caused by assuming responsibility for problem change—especially problem change in a relatively short period of time. Some beginners in TC may need considerable support. We remind students who are anxious that (a) we are there to help; and (b) they cannot control problem change and are only responsible for using the best skills they have. When students are angry with clients for not cooperating fully, we remind them that the vast majority of people usually do the best they can in their particular circumstances and with their particular capacities and resources. If a student is experiencing acute guilt, we sometimes take this on ourselves, at least until the student is "unstuck." This can be done by saying, "This was my fault. I should have warned you that such and such was likely to occur."

We are emphasizing the stress that some students experience because many of us cut our teeth on models of practice that did not focus on problem change, and thus we might overlook the stress that is entailed. Many of us, in our student days, were able to comfort ourselves by concluding that the client was relating to us more openly or that the client had greater insight or even that the client was recalling more dreams. Fortunately or unfortunately, these reassurances are not sufficient for the student learning TC.

Another actor in the treatment endeavor who sometimes reacts badly to termination is the collateral. Because time-limited approaches to treatment are newer than long-term ones, many collaterals are unfamiliar with them. As a result, they are surprised that treatment is ending and anxious about the duration of accomplishments. Collaterals sometimes respond negatively because treatment has not produced a perfect person; that is, they believe we should continue to work with clients until problems are nonexistent.

We deal with the negative termination reactions of collaterals by explanation. The key elements in the explanation are (1) the research on time-limited treatment; and (2) the importance of the client-determined target problems to a successful outcome. We also reassure them that we or someone else will be available should the problems recur. The negative reactions of collaterals to termination are, in fact, often a testament to the effectiveness of our work.

5.5.1 CHECKLIST FOR REACTIVE DISCUSSION

___ 1. Did I inquire directly about the client's reaction to termination?
___ 2. Were client concerns about termination (if any) dealt with to the client's satisfaction?
___ 3. Did I recognize my own feelings about termination with this client?

___ 4. Did I recognize my own feelings about the outcome of treatment?
___ 5. Did I share my own reaction to the extent that it was supportive of the client?
___ 6. Did I deal effectively with reactions of collaterals?

5.5.2 Exercises for Review of Problem-Solving Skills and Reactive Discussion

1. Continue the role play begun in section 5.3.2 and practice reviewing problem-solving skills and reactive discussion. Follow the general guidelines for role plays as described in section 3.1.2.

2. Think about the client with whom work is proceeding the least smoothly. Write down, in a few words, your response to each of the following questions. How are you feeling about the client? How are you feeling about the work you have done with this client? How are you feeling about the outcome thus far? Are your responses thoughts or feelings? If they are thoughts, identify the accompanying feeling. Evaluate your reactions. Are they realistic? What might account for them? Does your analysis produce a sense of relief? Did it provide you with any new ideas or observations? If not, consult with your supervisor or a colleague who is likely to be more objective.

5.6.0 Case Illustrations

Ronnie Paige

Ronnie Paige was an eight-year-old African-American male placed in a third-grade classroom when his teacher, Ms. Walsh, referred him to the school social work intern, Ms. Kane (Kane, unpublished). He had been referred because he was frequently absent and had been incorrectly placed academically. He was unable to do any of the work and needed a special classroom. Before contacting Ronnie, Ms. Kane went to the home to visit with his mother and to obtain written permission from Mrs. Paige to work with Ronnie.

Mrs. Paige greeted Ms. Kane with barely suppressed anger. She was more than willing to permit Ronnie to receive social work services and recognized that he had learning problems, but she was angry with the schools because they had not provided adequate learning opportunities for Ronnie, and she was particularly angry about the truancy issue. According to Mrs. Paige, the principal at the school that her eighth-grade daughter, Olivia, attended had refused to permit Olivia to graduate because of her many absences. School records indicated that her daughter had missed 80 out of 120 days, but Mrs. Paige was not sure this information was accurate. The daughter was a straight-A student. Mrs. Paige thought the school's refusal to allow her daughter to graduate was highly unjust. She was the mother, and it was her right to determine whether her kids were able to go to school. In spite of several angry confrontations, she was unable to sway the principal. Her daughter was heartbroken that she would not be able to go on to high school with her peers, and her mother was afraid that she would lose interest in school. She did not want her daughter to drop out as she had. Mrs. Paige acknowledged that she allowed the children to remain at home if they were at all under the weather or even if they did not feel like going.

Mrs. Paige and her four children lived in a run-down but adequate apartment building in a poor, inner-city neighborhood. Her public assistance grant was occasionally supplemented by money from her husband, who had left the home about a year ago. He visited regularly and remained involved with his wife and children. In spite of her poverty and limited formal education, Mrs. Paige appeared to cope well. Her children were well groomed and well nourished. Her apartment was clean. She was articulate. She had hopes and expectations for the her children's future.

Ms. Kane offered to look into the situation with regard to Olivia but strongly suggested that the children get to school regularly in the interim. Mrs. Paige gratefully accepted the offer and agreed to send them to school. At the end of the interview, Ms. Kane told Mrs. Paige that she would get in touch with her during the following week to report on her contact with the principal. She would also keep her informed about her work with Ronnie.

Before meeting Ronnie, Ms. Kane had another collateral to contact: Ronnie's teacher, Ms. Walsh. Ms. Walsh reported that Ronnie was an engaging youngster; that he had been absent for 67 out of 127 days, or about 2 or 3 days per week; that he was unable to do any of the classroom work; and that her efforts to get him tested through the regular channels had been blocked by the long waiting list. Ms. Kane arranged to meet Ronnie later that day. She also observed Ronnie in the classroom for about thirty minutes. Indeed, he seemed unable to do any of the schoolwork. Instead, he played quietly at his desk.

Ronnie willingly left the classroom to meet with Ms. Kane. Ms. Kane explained that she was a social work student at the school and that she was there to help children with any problems they had in school. She also shared with him that Ms. Walsh had asked her to meet with Ronnie because he was having trouble with his schoolwork. Ronnie became crestfallen. He liked school. He liked Ms. Walsh. He was good, he insisted. Ms. Kane assured Ronnie that Ms. Walsh liked him, too, and knew he was good. She just wanted him to have some help with his work. Was it true that Ronnie had trouble doing the assignments? Ronnie was relieved. He freely admitted that he could not do *any* of the work. Would he like Ms. Kane to help him? Yes. To assure that Ronnie was unable to do the work, Ms. Kane had obtained some copies of the worksheets assigned that day. She began to go over them with Ronnie. It was immediately evident that the child could not read any of the words of the assignments and that he could not count much beyond twenty.

Ms. Kane asked Ronnie what he thought they should do about the problem. Ronnie said that he would like to have some work he could do. He didn't like just sitting there when everyone else was working. Ms. Kane agreed to locate some work. She said that that would be her "job" but that Ronnie's "job" would be to do the work when she gave it to him. He sincerely assured her that he would do it. Ronnie was indeed a sweet child who was eager to please.

Ms. Kane then raised the issue of attendance. Ronnie acknowledged that he did not come to school "lots of days" because he did not feel like it or his mother wanted him to stay home. He added that it didn't matter because he couldn't do anything in school, anyway.

Ms. Kane said that he would have to come to school to do the work she was getting for him. He agreed to do so. Ms. Kane had already told Ronnie that she had met with his mother, and she now told him that his mother would help him get to school more often. "Now you will have two jobs," Ms. Kane said enthusiastically. "You will have to do your work, and you will have to come to school." Ronnie was sure he could do them.

Ms. Kane concluded the interview by telling Ronnie that she would meet with him for about six more weeks. Because Ronnie could not envision what six weeks meant, Ms. Kane got a calendar and circled the six Thursdays that they would meet. Ronnie asked, "You mean we won't see each other any more after that?" We will see each other in school, Ms. Kane assured him, but we won't have to meet because the problems will be solved. In the meantime, she would get him work that he could do.

Ms. Kane had two practitioner tasks to do. She had to find appropriate work for Ronnie, and she had to talk to the principal at his sister's school. The work was easily located at a local educational resource center. The principal readily agreed to meet with Ms. Kane but adamantly refused to allow Olivia to graduate. Ms. Kane said that she would have to pursue the matter.

At the beginning of the following week, Ms. Kane showed the workbooks to Ms. Walsh. They agreed that Ms. Kane would assign a certain amount of work each week and that Ms. Walsh would check the work. She inquired about Ronnie's attendance. He had not missed a day since she had met with Mrs. Paige.

The conversation with the principal was reported to Mrs. Paige. Mrs. Paige said that she knew Ms. Kane wouldn't get anywhere with him. Ms. Kane asked for her permission to talk with the District Superintendent. Mrs. Paige agreed but indicated that she felt the situation was hopeless and that the school was just out to get them. Ms. Kane reported that she had obtained appropriate schoolwork for Ronnie and suggested that Mrs. Paige encourage him to do it. Finally, she congratulated Mrs. Paige for getting Ronnie to school every day for the last five days. Mrs. Paige volunteered that both Olivia and her twelve-year-old son had had perfect attendance since her conversation with Ms. Kane.

Ronnie was happy to get his workbooks during the next interview. He and Ms. Kane decided how many pages he should do in the reading book and how many in the math book before the next session. Ms. Kane also enthusiastically praised Ronnie for attending school every day. They also decided on the rewards he would earn if he did his assigned pages and continued to come to school.

Ms. Kane continued on her practitioner tasks. An appointment was made with the District Superintendent. She looked into the problem of getting Ronnie tested and learned that the delay was unacceptably long. She also learned that testing results from several private testing services, if she could obtain them, would be accepted by the school board for the purpose of providing an appropriate educational placement for Ronnie.

During the next several weeks, interviews with Ronnie followed the same pattern. Work from the preceding week was discussed, rewards were provided, and new work was assigned. In the course of discussion, a couple of obstacles were discovered. An excerpt that illustrates task review, as well as other TPIS activities, follows.

MS. KANE: Let's see what your jobs were. Okay? And we'll see if you did them. Ronnie, did you go to school? (She is reading from a list of tasks.)

RONNIE: Yeah!

MS. KANE: Did you go to school Friday? Did you put your star on the Ronald MacDonald calendar?

RONNIE: Yeah, but my mother didn't take me to Ronald MacDonald's.

MS. KANE: But your mom didn't take you to Ronald MacDonald's? You must have been disappointed. You were supposed to be able to go to Ronald MacDonald's, right?

RONNIE: Yep.

MS. KANE: Well, let's see what we can do about that. Can you remind her? Did you remind her that you were supposed to go to Ronald MacDonald's . . . and what did she say?

RONNIE: She forgot.

MS. KANE: She forgot? Or you forgot to remind her?

RONNIE: She forgot.

MS. KANE: But you did put your stars in and now you deserve a free coke, right?

RONNIE: Yeah.

MS. KANE: Okay. So you went to school Friday and Monday, and you put your stars in. And you brought your books, right?

RONNIE: Yeah.

MS. KANE: Because that was another thing you were supposed to do was bring your books.

RONNIE: I read the books and I learned them.

MS. KANE: That's good. So you brought your books. That's very good, Ronnie. And you were to read, "A Pig Can Jig," right?

RONNIE: Uh huh.

MS. KANE: And you finished . . . let me see. My gosh, you did . . . one chapter: man, Dan, ran, fan, can. Right? You did one, two, three, four, five—you read six pages! And then you went to this chapter. What are those words?

RONNIE: Man, pan, Dan, can.

MS. KANE: Good! You did a second chapter. You did it four times and you finished up to page twelve. You did twelve reading pages! Very good, Ronnie. And now you're on a new chapter and you've got some more words to learn, right?

RONNIE: Right.

MS. KANE: Okay, so you did twelve pages here and then in your workbook you did—let me count this—one, two, three, four—

RONNIE: . . . three, four, five, six, seven, eight, nine, ten, eleven, twelve.

MS. KANE: You did twelve reading pages. You did twelve pages out of your workbook. But you were unhappy because your teacher didn't put the stars on them.

RONNIE: Yeah.

MS. KANE: Did you give them to her this morning?

RONNIE: No. I told the teacher, I said, "Teacher are you going to mark my pages?" and she said, "Later," but she didn't.

MS. KANE: Okay, well maybe we should make a task. When would you like her to mark your papers? Like just before the beginning of lunch time? Like if you do five pages in school . . . When would you like her to put the stars on and help you, you know, go over the pages with you? What time?

RONNIE: Around 9:30.

MS. KANE: Okay. So that's a new job for you. Ronnie is to give his teacher his work. (She is writing the task down as she articulates it.) Ronnie, let's see how many math pages you did. You did one—

RONNIE: . . . two, three, four, five, six, seven, eight, nine, ten, eleven, twelve, thirteen, fourteen, fifteen, sixteen, seventeen, eighteen.

MS. KANE: Eighteen math pages! You did eighteen math pages! That's really very good. So you did eighteen math pages. Okay. So I'm going to give these to your teacher when we're done and see if she will grade them for you so that tomorrow morning when you come to school I'll ask her to give these back to you. She'll sign her name and she'll put the stars on it. And she's going to write down on her little page that I gave her—see, she's doing a chart, too—she'll write down: Ronnie did this many pages this week in school. Okay?

RONNIE: Uh huh.

MS. KANE: You know what? I think you're going to have a hundred pages done soon.

RONNIE: What do you mean?

MS. KANE: Because you got—well, you did six and eighteen is twenty-four pages of work. That's a lot of work, Ronnie. You did twenty-four pages of work.

RONNIE: That's cause I know some of these words here like Dan, can . . .

At the end of the interview, Ms. Kane begins to summarize the tasks for the following week. An excerpt from this discussion follows.

MS. KANE: So, Ronnie is to come to school. You're going to read the next chapter. So you have to read all these pages at home. The next chapter, see you're on chapter 3. So now you do chapter 4. Every day you do another chapter, right? (Client responds briefly but inaudibly.) All right, if you want to do two chapters, like you said. If you want to move fast, you can move fast and do more than one chapter. (Again, client's response is inaudible.) If you finish this book, you've read ninety pages. Ten more pages, and we'll have a hundred.

RONNIE: Wow!

MS. KANE: Wow is right! There's ninety-four pages in here and you've done something like twenty of them already.

RONNIE: How much is in here?

MS. KANE: Why don't we look and see (they flip to the back of the book)—318 pages!

RONNIE: Wow! I didn't know we had that much.

MS. KANE: Well, this is all your "much." Okay?

RONNIE: Yeah.

MS. KANE: So, you're going to bring your books to school tomorrow and show your teacher which chapter you read, right?

RONNIE: Right.

During these weeks, Ms. Kane continued to contact both Mrs. Paige and Ms. Walsh. Because Ms. Walsh continued to report perfect attendance, with the exception of two days when Ronnie had a cold, Ms. Kane continued to compliment Mrs. Paige for getting him to school. Unfortunately the District Superintendent, although courteous, was unwilling to override the principal's decision with regard to graduating Olivia. As a result, Ms. Kane referred Mrs. Paige to the local legal-aide clinic. Mrs. Paige promptly acted on the referral, and the attorneys were able to reverse the decision about graduation. Mrs. Paige was jubilant.

Ms. Kane managed to locate a private testing agency that had a sliding fee scale. Her last extended contact with Mrs. Paige occurred as she drove Mrs. Paige and Ronnie to the testing site. During the ride, Mrs. Paige revealed some remarkable information. About five years earlier, Mrs. Paige had lost an infant daughter to sudden infant death syndrome (SIDS). Mr. Paige had been at home with the child when the death occurred. Both Mr. and Mrs. Paige had been inconsolable, and the grief was still evident in Mrs. Paige's voice as she talked. Mr. Paige felt extremely guilty, as well as sad, because the daughter had been in his care when she died. Both Mr. and Mrs. Paige had attended weekly, outpatient group psychotherapy meetings, at a local medical center, for parents who had lost a child to SIDS. They continued to attend these meetings for almost four years and until Mrs. Paige became pregnant again. At the time, Mr. Paige became extremely distraught and left the home. He could not face the possibility of losing another baby. Poignantly, Mrs. Paige said that, now that the children were attending school regularly, she was not so afraid of "letting them go." In fact, she said shyly, that she and Mr. Paige were talking about "getting together again." Ms. Kane empathized with the pain they had experienced and praised Mrs. Paige for her new courage. She made a mental note to herself that this was one more example of behavioral change preceding psychological change.

The testing results revealed that Ronnie had a moderately severe learning disability. As a result, he was transferred to a special classroom in another elementary school.

Mrs. Carter

Mrs. Carter was a forty-year-old, African-American widow (Rooney, unpublished). She had been supported by public assistance for the past fifteen years. She had ten children, nine of whom (ages two to fifteen) had been placed in foster homes a year before Mr. Rooney, a white male, was assigned to the case. He was employed by a private agency that had been subcontracted by the public child welfare agency to work with some of their clients. The two oldest children in placement had been returned by the time Mr. Rooney entered the situation, one of them because she had run away from the foster home. Another of Mrs. Carter's children, a nineteen-year-old daughter, had been residing with relatives for some time and thus was not involved in foster placement.

Before the children were removed from the home, Mrs. Carter had been considering entering the hospital. The reason for the hospitalization is disputable, with Mrs. Carter claiming it was for surgery and a previous counselor asserting it was for alcoholism. In any event, it was recommended that she temporarily place the children so they would be cared for during her hospital stay. She agreed to do so, but then changed her mind about both the hospitalization and the placement. The counselor, who had made the recommendation, and the child welfare agency nevertheless went to court and were able to obtain temporary custody of the children. Mrs. Carter learned of this action when the police arrived at her home to remove the children.

The reasons for the removal included the following: truancy of the children, poor hygiene, Mrs. Carter's alcoholism, and concern that Mrs. Carter was unable to supervise the children. Because Mrs. Carter did not have a telephone, Mr. Rooney arrived at her home unannounced. Although she was inebriated and incoherent, she was clear about the fact that she wanted her children returned to her custody. The home smelled of urine. Piles of clothes covered the floor. The door was broken. The picture was one of overwhelming poverty.

Mr. Rooney wrote down his name and the time and date when he would be returning to meet with Mrs. Carter. He asked her to try to be sober for their next meeting and to clean the house, since they knew these were concerns of the court.

At the next meeting Mrs. Carter was sober, and both she and the apartment were much cleaner. Mr. Rooney again introduced himself and explained his role in the case. He committed himself to helping Mrs. Carter regain custody of her children. He also pointed out, however, that he is obligated to report to the court on Mrs. Carter's behavior with respect to the problematic conditions identified. He explained that, in order to obtain her goal, Mrs. Carter would have to correct certain conditions specified by the court. These included:

1. inadequate housing (she did not have a stove, a refrigerator, or hot water, and had only two pieces of furniture);
2. her drinking problem, which interfered with her ability to care for her children;
3. her children's erratic school attendance; and
4. a home that was not kept clean.

Mrs. Carter acknowledged all these conditions.

Mr. Rooney and Mrs. Carter agreed to a twelve-week contract. In fact, this was only the first of several twelve-week contracts, and work continued for fifty-five sessions over fourteen months. The length of the contact was largely necessitated by the slow workings of the many bureaucracies involved. Another complicating factor was that the subcontracts provided three months of service. A request for renewal had to be submitted to the funding agency for each three-month extension. Approximately 40 percent to 50 percent of renewal requests were granted for one extension. This case was an exception in that almost no other cases were renewed more than once. It is noteworthy that the reason so many extensions were granted was because the task accomplishments were carefully documented with each renewal request. That neither worker nor client knew whether work could continue beyond the current contract was a matter of concern and frequent discussion.

Mrs. Carter and Mr. Rooney began developing tasks to correct the conditions that would interfere with regaining custody. They also began to work on the related problem that Mrs. Carter had not seen her children for several months. Approximately three or four tasks were established in each session, and most of them were implemented. During the first sixteen sessions, eighty tasks were implemented. Fifty-five of them were client tasks, and thirty-five were practitioner tasks. Tasks were carefully recorded on Task Review Forms, for two reasons: First, with such a large number of tasks, recording was needed simply to remember them, and, second, Mrs. Carter's task accomplishments would provide evidence of her efforts to the court. This was particularly important, as the many public agencies with whom she was involved viewed Mrs. Carter as unresponsive and unreliable.

From the outset, tasks entailed the consideration of a large number of collaterals. These included three public assistance (PA) workers, two child welfare workers, the landlord, individuals connected with Alcoholics Anonymous, various foster parents, school personnel, the juvenile court judge, and various court officials including several public defenders and prosecutors, and representatives of the public housing authority. Sometimes the tasks entailed obtaining services from the various bureaucracies. For example, because Mrs. Carter had moved, it was necessary to have her case transferred from one PA office to another so that the children who had been returned could be added to the grant. Increased financial resources were vital to securing adequate housing. Transferring the case took twelve weeks. At other times, the collaterals' opinions needed to be considered in task planning because their judgments would determine whether the children were returned to Mrs. Carter. For example, tasks had to be carried out in a way that persuaded the child welfare workers that Mrs. Carter was cooperative and responsible.

Excerpts from the sixteenth and seventeenth interviews are used to illustrate the Task Planning and Implementation Sequence. The content of the excerpts pertains to the problems of securing visits with the children, locating adequate housing, and alcoholism. In the first excerpt, Mrs. Carter and Mr. Rooney discuss Mrs. Carter's desire to see her children. At the time of the discussion, she had not seen her two youngest children for two months.

MRS. CARTER: I wish you would . . . for me to see my daughter and son, and my baby daughter.

MR. ROONEY: I don't know what to do about that, because the first thing she [the social worker] is going to bring up now is that it is getting cold. And are they going to be safe here. She's probably going to be more willing for them to come to the office than to come here.

MRS. CARTER: Well, that would be all right as long as I can see them.

MR. ROONEY: Well, we can get her to do that.

MRS. CARTER: I wish you'd ask them.

MR. ROONEY: I would suggest this time—have you talked to her on the phone yet?

MRS. CARTER: Nope. I never talked to nobody on the phone.

MR. ROONEY: Well, sooner or later you're going to have to start dealing with her more often. Because you know she's got to get to know you better. Right now she doesn't know much about you and doesn't trust you very much, and you don't trust her. What I would suggest is—

MRS. CARTER: Well, I don't care nothing about her, period! I don't like her.

MR. ROONEY: She doesn't like you either.

MRS. CARTER: She doesn't have anything to do with my kids; she's supposed to bring them in.

MR. ROONEY: That's right, you have that right, so I would suggest that you—I can give you her number—you call her.

MRS. CARTER: I got her number.

MR. ROONEY: Ask her when it can be done . . . and I'll call her later—

MRS. CARTER: Okay.

MR. ROONEY: . . . to follow up. But she needs to hear from you first, I think.

MRS. CARTER: Well, she know I don't like her.

MR. ROONEY: Okay, let's go over the things we were going to do for this time. You were going to call Ms. Jordan last Friday; did you talk to her?

MRS. CARTER: No, I didn't get her last Thursday; I called her last Friday morning and they said she was out of the building—she wasn't due until 11:00—and I asked the lady that answered the phone whether my kids were coming to the office, and she said yes they are all supposed to be there at 10:30.

MR. ROONEY: And so you left then?

MRS. CARTER: Yeah, I left and went down there; I had Alma to take me down there and when we got down there we didn't see nobody but Robert Lee and Evalina. Then I saw Mr. Baldwin down the hall and I asked where was the rest of them? He said he was in an emergency meeting and Ms. Jordan wasn't in, had an emergency case.

MR. ROONEY: So they could only bring those two?

MRS. CARTER: Uh huh, that's why I can't understand. He told me Jr. and Robert Lee go to the same school and he said they stay on the same street.

MR. ROONEY: Same street?

MRS. CARTER: And Jr. lives three or four blocks from them, so why didn't he pick up Jr.?

MR. ROONEY: It may be that he just didn't . . . he doesn't always tell you what he's thinking and I don't know what he was thinking, maybe he didn't want you to have three kids over the weekend because he thought that was too many.

MRS. CARTER: Well, he should have told me over the phone that I was going to bring them home.

MR. ROONEY: Oh, I get it.

MRS. CARTER: I didn't know nothing about I was going to bring them home until I got there.

MR. ROONEY: Well, you remember I was the one who asked him earlier—I said she wants to see Robert Lee and Evalina and she wants them to come here. And he said, "Okay, no problem." And then, when I talked to you last Thursday, you told me he said to come up to the office. So what he did, he just mixed the two, changed his mind, and he agreed to have them come here. So it worked out, at least you did get them.

The first tasks established to secure adequate housing involved working with the landlord of Mrs. Carter's current apartment for the purpose of making it adequate. These tasks were implemented but were unsuccessful because the landlord was unwilling to make the necessary improvements. In fact, he threatened to evict Mrs. Carter whenever she pressured him for hot water and heat. He also told her and the other tenants to send their rent money to the gas company but refused to provide them with receipts for doing so, claiming he had limited writing skills. (One of the practitioner tasks had been to secure a receipt book for Mrs. Carter, so she would have proof that she paid her rent even though it was sent to the gas company.) It became necessary to find new housing, but this was complicated by Mrs. Carter's lack of funds and the fact that the apartment had to be approved by PA workers. Mr. Rooney and Mrs. Carter evolved a threefold plan, whereby Mrs. Carter would look for private housing on her own, they would jointly complete an application for public housing, and they would try to prevent the current landlord from evicting Mrs. Carter for nonpayment of rent. In the following excerpt certain obstacles to securing public housing are identified.

MR. ROONEY: Tell me what you were just now saying about . . . what do you think is going to happen when you make the application at the Public Housing Authority (PHA)?

MRS. CARTER: That they're not going to accept us. Because when I moved out of there I owed them $260 because they kicked me out of the apartment I was in. So I moved out but they also taken me to court to—

MR. ROONEY: Say what?

MRS. CARTER: They had—

MR. ROONEY: Since you moved out?

MRS. CARTER: Before I moved out.

MR. ROONEY: What for?

MRS. CARTER: For not paying the rent . . . I . . . my apartment was all tore up and didn't have no stove where I could cook so . . . it was a stove there, all I could use was the eyes but the oven would never come on. I didn't have no refrigerator where I could store food, so I kept telling them to give me one and they wouldn't give me one. So then when they sent me to court and the judge asked me why I didn't pay the rent, I told him. Then he sent an investigator to see why they didn't . . . hadn't gave me a stove and a refrigerator.

MR. ROONEY: So they still wanted you to pay your rent then?

MRS. CARTER: Yeah, but they would never come and fix the sink, and never would come and cut the water on. I mean I never could get them to do nothing in my apartment with me and my children what I asked for.

MR. ROONEY: So when you left, did they . . . did they try to get the money from you?

MRS. CARTER: Uh huh. I went down and talked to them, my counselor and myself, and I asked them, could I pay them so much every month and you know and he said no I had to pay all of it at one time so I didn't pay it.

MR. ROONEY: They haven't gotten in touch with you again?

MRS. CARTER: About the money? No. Not since I come from my niece [She had lived with her niece between leaving PHA and moving to her current apartment.]

MR. ROONEY: Well, sounds like you're right. That's going to make it tough. I wrote a letter—you know we talked to that man, Mr. Clark, and he told me—once he calmed down about how uncooperative you've been, then he started cooperating—he said to write a letter that might help you, and I brought you a copy.

Mrs. Carter left the apartment in approximately week 20 and lived with friends for several months until she located private housing with heat and hot water and without broken windows. Counseling sessions during that time were often conducted as Mrs. Carter and Mr. Rooney traveled to various agencies and looked for apartments. Some of the tasks included reading want ads, contacting public housing, and registering with an apartment-finding service.

Another problem addressed was Mrs. Carter's alcoholism. In addition to the task of being sober for counseling sessions, tasks to enter outpatient treatment programs and to join Alcoholics Anonymous were developed. In the following excerpt Mrs. Carter shares her moving reflections on this issue.

MRS. CARTER: See, I've been having trouble with my left side for a long time, so I went to the doctor to see what he could tell me about it. Instead of him telling me about my side, he told me about my blood pressure.

MR. ROONEY: Is he going to tell you what to eat?

MRS. CARTER: I have to go back to him in two weeks. That will be on the seventeenth.

MR. ROONEY: Well, you definitely have to watch your health. You've been trying to do so much, but you can't do it without your health.

MRS. CARTER: Doctor told me last year that I had to stop drinking. And I never did take him in my mind you know.

MR. ROONEY: That contributes to it, doesn't it?

MRS. CARTER: Yeah. All that whiskey and wine and stuff. It runs your blood pressure up. See I always did have trouble with my blood pressure, I started as a kid. And then when I started getting drunk, falling out and you know, on the street and things, wind up in the hospital—you didn't know that did you? (Laughs) Yeah, I did that a couple times last year. Got drunk and fell out on the sidewalk and wind up in the hospital.

MR. ROONEY: All I remember is the first time I met you, you were in pretty bad shape.

MRS. CARTER: (Laughs) Yeah, doctor said if I didn't stop it, I would wind up with sclerosis of the liver.

MR. ROONEY: What about now?

MRS. CARTER: I don't want to drink cause I might not survive next time I fall out. And I want to get my kids back. So I put myself to a test. I don't think its always going to be easy, but my friends— like those two just left out of here—they stone alcoholics. They just don't know it. Some friends of mine was drinking—well, they been drinking all this week. I haven't taken any of it because I don't drink and take medicine. That's one thing I don't do.

MR. ROONEY: How can you see them—stay with them—and keep from drinking?

MRS. CARTER: (Inaudible) The guy I got a crush on, he drinks, too. But it don't bother me. You know its strange, it don't bother me. It use to would make me want some, but now I just don't have no interest in it. I guess I'm going through another phase.

MR. ROONEY: A good phase.

MRS. CARTER: Yup. I don't want no more. Cause he even told me, the doctor said you can drink some, but I don't want to drink no more, period. Alcohol has caused me everything bad that has happened to me in my life. Caused me to be drunk, get my TV stole out of here, my radio.

MR. ROONEY: People take advantage of you?

MRS. CARTER: Of course.

MR. ROONEY: You see, that's the thing I think that PA doesn't know about you is that they have been here but once in five months and they don't know that you haven't been acting like the person they knew before.

MRS. CARTER: I know that.

MR. ROONEY: So what they've been trying to say to me and to you is why should we make any special efforts for somebody who is going to, you know, not be able to hold up.

MRS. CARTER: They say once you do something you always have to do it, but that's wrong. A person can change if he really wants to.

MR. ROONEY: You didn't like going to those meetings, though, huh?

MRS. CARTER: Well, I said I was going back this Saturday for sure, because when I went before, I will be honest with you, you know I always like to tell you the truth—

MR. ROONEY: I know you do.

MRS. CARTER: When I went there, I was so drunk I didn't even know what I was doing there. So I'm going back this time, so maybe I can understand what they're talking about.

MR. ROONEY: Well, it would help to be sober when you go.

MRS. CARTER: Yeah, well the first time I was so drunk, I got into an argument.

MR. ROONEY: And then you asked them why they served coffee?

MRS. CARTER: Yeah, he served a lot of coffee there now.

MR. ROONEY: That's just because they had people like you coming in there.

MRS. CARTER: (Laughs) I know one thing, its a lot of people going there so it must be something to it. Cause I know the doctor told me, don't fool myself. Over there at Mercy Hospital, he said, "Once you're an alcoholic, you're always an alcoholic." But alcoholism is a sickness just like anything else. And that's the problem—see, I've been so weak all my life til I just can't stand to hurt nobody. I would let them hurt me and then I go and get drunk and forget about it, but you don't forget about it. You forget about it while you're drunk 'cause you don't know nothing else, and when you're real drunk, you're out.

MR. ROONEY: And then?

MRS. CARTER: When you get sober, it's the same thing.

MR. ROONEY: It's the same situation right there.

MRS. CARTER: Right. So it don't make no sense to get drunk. Just stand up and speak up for your rights, that's all I say. But see, I ain't never did that because, if I had, I'd have left my husband twenty years ago, I mean before he died.

MR. ROONEY: If you stood up for yourself?

MRS. CARTER: Yup. Me and my kids—life would have been different and maybe my life would have been different.

MR. ROONEY: That's a hard decision to make though, to leave like that. You know I don't think you should fault yourself too much for it because, you know, that if you did that, you were going to have to find some way of living for you and the kids.

MRS. CARTER: We didn't have to worry cause we was on ADC [Aid to Dependent Children] then. It wouldn't have been that much difference. It wouldn't have been no different, really. Mostly, he was on us, we wasn't on him—like what you're talking about. When anybody worked, it was me.

MR. ROONEY: Well, the fact is that now—that may have been true about you and it may still be true about you sometimes, that you don't stand up for yourself—but I haven't seen it for some time. When you needed to stand up for yourself in the last several months, you've done it.

MRS. CARTER: Well, I'm trying to stand up for myself and stand up for my kids and stand up to my kids when I know they are wrong.

MR. ROONEY: That's another problem. That's something we're going to have to deal with now and we're going to have to deal with as soon as your kids come back.

Mrs. Carter made slow, steady progress with respect to the alcoholism, although she relapsed occasionally. Work on the problem of the children's school attendance was already under way when Mr. Rooney met Mrs. Carter. The children who had been returned to her were attending regularly and performing reasonably well. Tasks in this area were largely limited to securing documentation of the improvement to present to the court.

The cleanliness of Mrs. Carter's apartment improved greatly with the successful placement of a homemaker. Four different homemakers had been assigned to Mrs. Carter during the past several years, and she had asked each of them to leave.

Two more children were returned to Mrs. Carter's custody during the last month of contact. Mrs. Carter would be able to petition for custody of the children remaining in placement as she was able to secure beds for them. She had saved the money to purchase two more beds at case closing, and a petition hearing was scheduled for the following month. The work was terminated before all the children were returned, because Mr. Rooney was leaving the agency and the area and because it was unlikely that the subcontract would be renewed again.

Mr. Rooney and Mrs. Carter had become extremely attached to each other. At termination both had to try very hard "not to cry" even though it was clear to both of them throughout the case that the contract would end. Mrs. Carter was happy that her children were being returned, however, and she was considerably more confident in her ability to work with the various service providers. In fact, recognizing that his agency could not serve Mrs. Carter indefinitely, Mr. Rooney had tried continuously to establish better relationships between Mrs. Carter and the collaterals.

PART TWO *Families*

6

PRETREATMENT CONSIDERATIONS

6.0.0 INTRODUCTION

In the task-centered model *family practice* refers to work with two or more family members regarding target problems of concern to them. This form of practice is not confined to fifty-minute hours centered on family relationships. A task-centered practitioner *may* work with a family on a problem of one of its children in a manner similar to that of a conventional family therapist, but he or she may also do family work in the context of discharge planning, foster placement, providing emergency medical care, obtaining tangible resources, or setting up referrals to other agencies. Family practice may be limited to one or two sessions and may be one aspect of a case in which individual or group methods are featured. Further, our notion of family practice incorporates work with people who live together, regardless of marital status or sexual orientation.

Our explication of task-centered family practice will build on the previous chapters that have presented the basics of the model and have applied it to work with individuals. Our position is that the similarities between the individual and family versions of TC outweigh the differences. Our focus in the next four chapters will be on what is *different* about the family version. We shall attempt to pursue this focus without repeating content set forth in the earlier chapters. At points we refer specifically to this preceding content, but in general we assume that readers will be able to make their own applications of the preceding content to practice with families.

In this chapter we describe the adaptations for family practice that are pertinent to the following topics: effectiveness and replicability, theoretical base, mission and purpose, social work values, relationship, and the appropriate system for work.

6.1.0. EFFECTIVENESS AND REPLICABILITY

A considerable amount of research has concerned tests of the effectiveness of task-centered family methods. In the study reviewed in section 2.1.0 (Reid 1978), approximately one-third of the problems concerned difficulties in family relations. An extensive and independent test of the task-centered approach with family problems was carried out in a large-scale experiment with four hundred patients who had taken drug overdoses in apparent suicide attempts. Patients were randomly assigned to experimental (task-centered) and control (routine service) groups. Difficulties in "continuing" personal relationships, usually problems with a spouse, were reported in two-thirds of the cases. Research interviews conducted four and eighteen months following service favored the experimental patients in measures of change in personal relationships; differences were statistically significant at the second follow-up, providing evidence on the durability of gains achieved.

A variation of the family treatment approach was also tested as a part of the task-centered case management model for children at risk of school failure (see "The Appropriate System for Work," section 6.6.0; and "New Applications," section 1.5.0). In brief, case management teams consisting of a social worker, parent(s), the child at risk, and a teacher meet every other week to develop and implement task strategies addressed to the child's difficulties in school. On alternative weeks, the social worker meets with the family to further the carrying out of these strategies. In the main randomized trial of the model, families assigned to the case management program (n = 33) surpassed families assigned to a no treatment control (n = 38) and to an alternative monetary incentives condition (n = 41) in respect to the children's improvement in grades and attendance. However, additional help appeared to be needed to maintain the gains during the following year (Reid and Bailey-Dempsey 1995).

Single case studies, as well as research that has not used control groups, have provided additional evidence supporting the effectiveness of the family practice model (Chou 1992; Ewalt 1977; Tolson 1977; Reid 1977; Reid 1994; Reid and Donovan 1990; Rooney 1981).

Considerations concerning replicability of the model discussed for work with individuals apply as well to family practice. The resources utilized by the model are primarily the practitioner's time and effort. Unlike some family practice approaches, the task-centered model does not normally employ "co-therapists" or consultants behind one-way mirrors. The use of such resources is not precluded, however.

6.1.1 CHECKLIST FOR EFFECTIVENESS AND REPLICABILITY

— 1. Is the treatment approach effective?
— 2. Is the treatment approach likely to be effective with this particular family?
— 3. Do I know enough about the approach to be able to replicate it?
— 4. Are resources required to implement the approach available?

6.1.2 QUESTIONS TO CONSIDER

1. What kinds of evidence should be provided to support the effectiveness of a family treatment approach?
2. Some evidence bearing on the effectiveness of TC has been presented. What additional kinds of evidence would be desirable?

6.2.0 THEORETICAL BASE

In keeping with the model's eclectic orientation to theory as a whole (section 2.2.0), task-centered family practice draws on different ways of understanding the family. These include communication theory (Watzlawick, Beavin, and Jackson 1967; Verderber and Verderber, 2001);

family structural theory (Minuchin 1974; Aponte and Van Deusen 1981; Nichols and Schwartz, 2001); attribution theory (Doherty 1981a, 1981b); theories of family problem solving (Reid, Rotering, and Fortune 1989; Vuchinich and Angelleli 1995); cognitive-behavioral approaches (Dattilio 1998; Smith and Schwebel 1995); and theories of reciprocity and exchange (Jackson 1965; Ruben 1998). Such theories, together with the methods of assessment and intervention suggested by them, are drawn on selectively depending on the problems and type of family situation in the case. Many cases can be understood and treated in common sense terms; no formal theory is required (section 2.2.0). For example, Mr. and Mrs. G, both in their eighties and with serious health problems, need help to remain in their residence. The social worker and Mr. and Mrs. G undertake tasks to secure Meals-on-Wheels, a visiting nurse, special transportation, and other services. Also, with the social worker's prompting and encouragement, Mrs. G. reinitiates her relationship with her estranged sister, who agrees to help. Although any of the theories mentioned (as well as others) enhance the practitioner's understanding of the family situation, none may be necessary to bring the case to a successful conclusion.

But, in most cases, theories provide useful ways of understanding the dynamics of problems or obstacles or in generating task possibilities. From the theories cited earlier we have developed a framework of dimensions of family functioning. Each dimension is designed to capture an aspect of family life that may either constitute a target problem in its own right or is part of the context of other problems. They do not add up to a comprehensive theory of the family but, rather, are a set of perspectives (to which others can be added) that we have found to be clinically useful.

It should be noted that they pertain largely to the internal functioning of the family. The family's relation to its external environment has been covered in the ideas presented in the initial chapter. The dimensions are summarized in Table 6.1 and each is briefly described below.

Communication   Perhaps the basic dimension of family life is communication. Without it, other dimensions could hardly take place. Family problems are commonly presented as problems in communication. Even when they are not, they can often be recast as communication problems.

TABLE 6.1 *Dimensions of Family Functioning: Key Questions*

Dimension	Key Question
1. Communication	Who exchanges messages with whom about what and to what effect?
2. Conflict	Who's at odds with whom?
3. Problem Solving	How do family members resolve difficulties?
4. Control	Who's in charge of whom?
5. Closeness/caregiving	Who's close to (or avoids) whom?
6. Intrusiveness	Who's intruding on whose space?
7. Alliance	Who's on whose side?
8. Boundaries	Who's in and who's out?
9. Flexibility	Are there stable rules and how modifiable are they?
10. Beliefs	How do family members view themselves, one another, and the world?

Human communication involves exchanges of meanings. It takes place largely through three channels: (1) language, that is, written language or spoken words; (2) paralanguage, in which meaning is conveyed through vocal behavior, such as tone of voice, rather than words; and (3) kinesic communication, which comprises gestures and other forms of body language (Verderber and Verderber 2001). Like conflict, communication has both "content" and "relationship" aspects (Watzlawick, Beavin, and Jackson 1967:112). The content of a message describes its substantive meaning, but messages also make a statement about the relationship of those communicating. If a husband asks his wife to make him breakfast, and she responds by asking him what he wants, the content of the exchange concerns meal preparation. Its relationship or "process" aspect suggests the husband's dominance in this interaction. These distinctions are basic to understanding communication problems that may occur in any channel (or in incongruities between them).

The expression "problems in communication" is often used loosely to refer to almost any kind of relationship problem between family members. More rigorous and useful definitions pinpoint specific aspects of communication processes. At this level, "communication problems" is the most likely expression to be used to describe difficulties involving marital partners or parents and older children. What follows is an attempt to isolate a configuration of more common problems.

- *Criticizing, accusing/blaming*. The theme here is finding fault in the other or in each other. Problems of this type often grow out of interactive escalation. Common tendencies, especially in heated exchanges, are to attribute faults to global, stable characteristics ("You're an uncaring person"), to present catalogues of faults unrelated to the immediate issue ("gunny sacking"), and to blame the other for past wrongdoings.

- *Domineering/nagging*. Persistently telling another to do things, behave differently, and so on, in a bossy manner, characterizes this problem. This kind of communication often elicits hostile, defensive responses (especially with teenagers!). Escalations are common: The more A nags, the more defensive and uncooperative B acts, leading to increased nagging on A's part, and so on. A is likely to complain that nagging would not be necessary if B did what he or she was supposed to do. B is likely to counter that there is no need to do it, that it is none of A's business, or that he or she would do it if A would lay off.

- *Problems in sharing*. This problem usually revolves around one person's wanting the other to be more expressive and open, and to share thoughts and feelings more. Vicious cycles can develop when A presses B to be more responsive; in reaction, B may become more withdrawn, which causes A to press more. Given the evolution of sex roles in our culture, it is not surprising that family members wanting greater responsiveness from others are likely to be wives (in respect to their husbands) and mothers (in respect to their teenage sons). Sometimes the problem takes the opposite form: One partner reveals more than the other wishes to hear; one unburdens, while the other feels overburdened. Vicious cycles also occur. The more A reveals, the more B avoids communication, which increases A's need to talk.

- *Not listening/cutting off*. A person does not "hear" what the other is saying or interrupts the other's talk to present his or her own point of view. Included is "disqualification" (Watzlawick, Beavin, and Jackson 1967), in which a person's communications are not taken seriously by another.

Conflict   Conflict is the common denominator for most difficulties in family relationships. Many problems are expressed directly in terms of conflict: between marital partners, parents and children, and siblings. Problems expressed in other terms, such as poor communication or lack of intimacy, often *become* problems because family members disagree about how these aspects of their relationship should play themselves out. Moreover, conflict may not necessarily be overt. One partner may suffer the other's behavior in silence, in which case conflict is present but covert. But, in most cases, the resolution of such hidden conflicts requires that they be brought to the surface.

Conflict between family members involves intricacies of close interaction that have evolved over time. The interaction is entwined with cognitions, feelings, and behavior for which often no clear norms exist. For most intimates, it is necessary to resolve or accommodate the conflict that is disrupting interaction, since it tears at the very fabric of what intimate relationships are about—affection, caring, trust, and support.

Of course, not all conflict is disruptive. Conflict is as much a part of intimacy as closeness, and most family members largely take it in stride. Indeed, conflict serves positive functions. It can bring differences into the open, which can lead to efforts to work them out. We focus here on conflict that family members themselves cannot satisfactorily resolve.

In analyzing conflict, we are drawn first to its most obvious element: its substance or content. (We have in mind "manifest content," that is, what participants themselves say is the issue.) In some conflicts the content is the dominant feature. This is so when the issue is a major one, for example, geographic relocation or a decision to have a child. The substance of the conflict may appear minor to outsiders, including the practitioner, but may be of major consequence to the participants because it threatens deeply held values or well-established rules or, for whatever reason, stirs up strong feelings. In one case a disagreement over whether the wife should attend the wedding of her husband's disowned son (and her stepson) was the basic reason for seeking help and constituted the focus of service.

In other conflicts, the content is subordinate to the patterns of the participants' interaction. Thus, when a couple quarrels "about everything," the content of any particular quarrel becomes relatively less important. In most cases, however, several areas of conflict typically exist in which content does seem to matter; various underlying factors may contribute to these conflicts. An integrated analysis, in which the content and the relationship aspects of the conflict are taken into account simultaneously, seems to be required. Thus, in a marital conflict over how domestic responsibilities are to be shared, the practitioner must become immersed in the content of the conflict—the grubby details of who does what around the house. At the same time, the practitioner needs to be aware of the dynamics of the marital relationship. How is the couple communicating? Who is trying to control whom? What are the partners' conceptions of the roles of husband and wife?

Regardless of what it is about, any conflict is expressed through some form of communication between its participants, and communication provides the usual means of resolution. The communication styles of participants are of considerable importance in determining the outcome of a conflict. A volatile, name-calling interchange can turn a minor disagreement into a raging battle that may scar a relationship permanently. A tightly controlled interchange in which interests and feelings are suppressed may produce the appearance of a resolution while the conflict continues to fester. A reasonable but assertive interchange may bring the conflict to a mutually satisfactory solution. It is recognized, of course, that communication is the means by which feelings and thoughts are expressed. A person in a rage may use words like weapons. Moreover, a conflict can be so centered on differences in interests that how it is expressed may matter little. Be that as it may, what is said, and how, can be decisive for a range of conflicts in which participants are in some control of what they say and where some compromise is possible. If so, then learning more effective ways of communicating can be one key to conflict resolution. Thus communication training, to be considered subsequently, is an important tool in conflict reduction.

As we know, family conflicts frequently escalate, sometimes to the point of physical violence. After a certain point in an escalating conflict, participants are often unable to control their actions and the conflict itself becomes out of control. As a result, it is important to identify more readily controlled actions that typically occur early in the escalation. For example, in one case a wife would react with sullen silence when her husband was late without a good reason. The silence would provoke the husband into angry comments about her childish behavior, with resulting escalation. The husband agreed to make more of an effort to be on time and to let his wife know beforehand when he was going to be late. In exchange she agreed to refrain from hostile withdrawals.

Problem Solving   In order to function adequately a family needs to have the capacity to resolve the conflicts and other issues that arise in family life. The ways families actually go about solving problems have been studied largely under structured laboratory conditions. Little research has been done on family problem-solving processes in natural situations.

Families, left to their own devices, are not likely to follow orderly sequences of problem-solving steps, such as those used in the task-centered model or in training programs—for example, identifying the problem, coming up with alternative solutions, and selecting the best one. Even in structured training contexts, Thomas (1977) has observed that problem solving often occurs in a "non-stepwise manner" and "in fragments." This lack of fit appears to be a likely cause for the frequently observed difficulties in transferring skills learned in problem-solving training to the home (Foster, Prinz, and O'Leary 1983).

Problem solving in the home probably makes use of a variety of devices. Rational processing of possible solutions by family members would certainly be one. But other strategies also appear to be used (Reid, Rotering, and Fortune 1989). One such strategy is cognitive restructuring, such as changing one's views of the problem or of the motives of other family members. Another strategy may involve attempts to change patterns of family interaction. For example, a mother and daughter may recognize their mutual over-dependence and make an effort to become more independent of each other without articulating the problem or explicitly considering alternatives.

These ideas suggest that practitioners should be alert to the variety of ways that a family goes about solving problems. Such understanding can be used as a basis for developing tasks that fit the family's own problem-solving inclinations.

<u>*Control*</u>   Control in family interaction refers to such aspects as power, dominance, and hierarchy. Relationships can be defined as either *complementary* (with one person in a superior position and the other in a subordinate one) or *symmetrical* (both persons interacting as equals) (Watzlawick, Beavin, and Jackson 1967).

There are many visions of what is ideal in respect to patterns of control. Perhaps the current dominant view in American society portrays an egalitarian relationship between spouses with the parents exercising benign authority over their children, who are granted progressively greater freedom as they mature. Against the backdrop of this ideal type, we can consider several central issues frequently found in client families.

- *Power struggles.* Interaction is characterized by conflict over who is in control. What makes the conflict a power struggle is an explicit or implicit dispute over who has the *right* to make the final decision in given circumstances. Thus an examination of power issues inevitably leads to consideration of the beliefs the participants have about who should prevail (and why) when disagreements occur.
- *Overcontrol.* Problems of overcontrol arise in complementary relationships. Those in one-up positions exercise considerable control that is accepted by those in a one-down position. (If it were not accepted, a power struggle would ensue.) The one-down partner may have negative feelings about the arrangement. He or she may feel put upon, pushed around, and so on, but at the same time is unable or unwilling to become assertive or may be relieved at not having to make decisions. A common result is for the one-down partner to become depressed or to develop somatic reactions.

  In some cases, the one-down participant accepts the arrangement without voicing objections. Because whoever is one-up is not likely to complain, the relationship usually is not presented as a target problem. It may, however, be a contributing factor to other problems. In this category falls the syndrome of the overprotective parent and the compliant, dependent child. The child is typically seen for a behavioral or health problem and, in addition, may have some form of developmental disability that gives the parent(s) rationale for the overprotectiveness.

- *Hierarchical reversal.* A generally accepted norm is that parents should be in control of their children. A breakdown of parental authority is most likely to occur with older children and adolescents in the form of power struggles, in which parental attempts at exercising control are rejected by their offspring. In some cases parents, especially single parents, lose (or give up) the battle for control with a reversal of the usual hierarchical structure. The child or children become one-up in the relationship, a position often maintained through such coercive behaviors as temper tantrums and threatened or actual violence.

Closeness-Caregiving Closeness-caregiving is a dimension of family life identified by Green and Werner (1996). Its "most important elements include: warmth, nurturance, time-together, physical intimacy (affection) and consistency" (p. 125). According to these authors, closeness-caregiving has been traditionally embedded in family theory under the rubric of "enmeshment" (Minuchin 1974), which, they point out, also incorporates the notion of "intrusiveness." They have argued, correctly we think, that these two concepts need to be disentangled. Once this is done, closeness-caregiving can be seen as a way of describing any dyadic relationship in a family along a continuum. They posit direct associations between the dimension and indicators of healthy functioning in dyadic relationships. In other words, the more closeness-caregiving, the better. Family members at high levels of closeness-caregiving are not likely to act intrusively toward one another, although they may. Aspects of enmeshment relating to self-other confusion ("Mom, am I going to throw up?") may be more accurately seen as a boundary issue, particular since only one member of a dyad may be experiencing the confusion.

Intrusiveness In Green and Werner's (1996) formulation, intrusiveness refers generally to a negative overattachment, either unilateral or mutual, between two family members. Specific components include the degree to which one member becomes anxious or upset, when another wants to do things independently; possessiveness/jealously; extent of emotional reaction to problems in the other; "mind reading"; and expressions of hostility. Although conceptually distinct from closeness-caregiving, the two dimensions might be expected to show some degree of inverse relationship—the greater the closeness/caregiving between a dyad, the less the intrusiveness. It is possible, of course, for a dyad to be characterized by both high degrees of closeness-caregiving and intrusiveness. These two dimensions provide the core of a widely used standardized instrument—the California Inventory for Family Assessment. Factor analytic studies have supported their conceptual distinctiveness (Fanjoux-Cohen et al. 1998; Lewinsohn and Werner 1997).

Illustrations of intrusive relationships might include the overprotective parent and child and the obsessively jealous and possessive spouse. At first glance it might seem that such relationships might also be characterized by closeness-caregiving, but a more searching analysis usually reveals that the closeness is illusory. For example, a parent's overprotective intrusiveness may cause a child to become cold and distant as a self-protective response.

Alliance   Alliances are alignments or coalitions between family members to achieve a common purpose. Alliances reflect the cooperative actions essential to healthy family functioning, but certain kinds of dysfunctional alliances may bring about or maintain family problems.

- *Alliance supporting problem behavior.* Family members join together to justify, defend, or approve dysfunctional behavior of a member. Often the family is a nonvoluntary referral. (Parents blame the school for their child's behavioral problems in the classroom.)
- *Weak parental alliance.* Parents do not act as a team in interactions with their children. This may be owing to conflict between parents over issues concerning their children, or one parent may withdraw from child care responsibilities. Often in such cases the boundaries of the parental subsystem lack definition; that is, decision making about the children is more likely to involve a parent and child rather than the two parents.
- *Cross-generational alliance.* A special case of a weak parental alliance is the coalition of a parent and child(ren) against the other

parent. The coalition, which may be implicit, disrupts cooperative parental behavior and compromises the authority of both parents. (Dad consistently takes the side of his teenage daughter in her arguments with Mom.)

- *Scapegoating alliance.* Family members ally against another member, usually a child. Usually the scapegoated member exhibits behaviors that provoke the hostility of the scapegoater. However, the scapegoaters are responding to more than the provocations. They are heaping on the scapegoated member an extra margin of hostility or blame resulting from frustrations that have nothing to do with his or her behaviors.

Boundaries   While the concepts of "closeness-caregiving" and "alliance" refer to how family members come together, the notion of boundaries describes mechanisms for maintaining separateness. For family subsystems, as well as the family as a whole, boundaries suggest what is in and what is out. Thus, for the parent subsystem, a boundary rule might define interactions for parents only, such as making financial decisions. Similarly boundary rules for a sibling subsystem might exclude parents from a wide range of information that the siblings freely share with one another. Problems or obstacles concerning boundaries include overexclusiveness (e.g., a family's boundaries exclude needed input from others), excessive permeability (e.g., a child is allowed to sleep indefinitely in the parents' bedroom), and lack of clarity (e.g., parents give mixed messages about when a child can participate in parental decision making). As noted earlier, the concept of boundary can also apply to individual family members. When a boundary is too permeable, it may be difficult for the family member to distinguish self-other properties. When a boundary is too rigid, it may be difficult for a family member to share thoughts and feelings with other family members.

Flexibility   Flexibility concerns variability in the family's internal interactions and in its responses to external events. At one extreme are those families that are relatively rigid in their functioning. Patterns of interaction are highly repetitive, and family members have little capacity to respond differently to changes in environmental circumstances.

In other families, however, chaos reigns. How members relate to one another or how the family as a unit relates to the outside world is unpredictable. Fortunately few families fall at either extreme in all respects. More commonly one finds *areas* of rigidity and lack of predictability in family functioning.

Excesses in either direction are generally thought to be dysfunctional. Too much rigidity can stifle the development of individual family members and make it difficult for the family to change when change is needed. Excessive flexibility becomes equivalent to instability and disorganization, making it difficult for the family to be effective in child rearing, decision making, and other essential tasks.

Optimal flexibility (like optimal involvement) falls somewhere in the middle range. Families with appropriate flexibility may be thought of as "adaptable" (Olson, McCubbin, and Associates 1983). They are capable of altering their modes of response as circumstances warrant.

Certain levels of flexibility may be better suited for some situations than others. For example, child care workers seeking to place disturbed, acting-out adolescents in foster care or adoptive homes are likely to look closely at this dimension. A family may function well but may have fairly rigid rules that they expect a child to fit into. A child to be placed may do better in a more flexible family with greater tolerance for "crazy" behavior but still able to enforce outside limits (Kagan and Reid 1984).

In addition to characterizing family units or patterns as having a certain level of flexibility, one can examine how fluctuations are managed. Interaction patterns in families tend to vary within a permissible range. When that range is exceeded, steps may be taken to restore the pattern to a range considered to be acceptable, as was noted earlier in respect to coercive symmetry. These rebalancing maneuvers (homeostatic mechanisms) are most readily discerned when one knows how the basic pattern operates and what deviations have occurred. For example, in the interactions between a given husband and wife, a certain level of hostility is tolerated; they can express irritation with each other's behavior without disrupting their normal, good-humored give-and-take. However, when hostile exchanges exceed certain limits, for instance, are too frequent or touch on "sore spots," the normal pattern of interaction is disrupted. Both feel angry and stop talking. After a time they may draw on one of several rebalancing devices, which might include apologies, humor, undertaking an activity together, or "talking out" whatever problem has occurred. It is important to identify such devices since they reveal how problems of deviation within the system are resolved or could be.

Family Beliefs   We have considered beliefs of family members in various contexts, but up to this point the emphasis has been on problems resulting from discrepant beliefs between family members or the dysfunctional beliefs of individual members. In this section we examine beliefs that characterize the family as a unit, that is, beliefs that family members share.

One type is the family myth, a belief that is idiosyncratic to the family. *Family myths*, as we use the term, contain some distortion of reality and serve a stabilizing or protective function. For example, parents may view the social agencies in a community as conspiring to take away their children, or a family may maintain the belief that a severe, irreversible disability of one of its members is a minor handicap that can be cured. Certain myths, such as the belief that a particular child is inherently bad, can provide a rationale for scapegoating.

Family myths are rarely presented as problems by the family itself but may form difficult obstacles to the solution of actual target problems. They are not easily modified because family members reinforce one another's perceptions and collectively interpret evidence to support these perceptions.

A quite different kind of shared belief is derived from the family's cultural and ethnic identities. A Mexican immigrant family may, with good reason, view government agencies with suspicion. A middle-class black family may have a strong belief that their children should do especially well in school to prepare themselves for life in a discriminatory society. Such beliefs, based on values and experiences of group members, may be quite functional for many purposes. But they may not always fit the realities of the larger culture—a lack of fit that may become apparent in the family's inability to cope with its external environment. When these beliefs no longer capture current realities in an adaptive manner, they become open to challenge and change. However, other beliefs related to cultural and ethnic identities may be resources in the family's efforts to cope. For example, the belief found in some cultures that one has an overriding obligation to help members of one's kin may be a source of vital assistance to a family in need. Like any social work model, the task-centered approach needs to be applied with sensitivity to the beliefs and needs of ethnic minorities (McGoldrick, Pearce, and Giordano 1982; Falicov 1998; Lum 1996). But, as always, the social worker should relate to the client as a unique individual and avoid applying cultural stereotypes. Often the practitioner must serve as "a culture broker" in helping the client and those in the mainstream culture to understand each other's actions (Spiegel 1981).

As noted, these theoretical frames can be used to understand both target problems and problem contexts. For example, a problem may be presented as a power struggle. More often, however, these ideas come into play as a means of understanding obstacles to problem resolution or task progress. Thus the acting-out behavior of a teenager may be a reflection of a hierarchical reversal (in which the teen has become the controlling figure in the family). It may be aggravated by a cross-generational alliance in which a parent covertly supports the teen's misbehavior.

These dimensions are used selectively when occasions warrant. They are not routinely considered in all cases

6.2.1 CHECKLIST FOR THEORETICAL BASE

— 1. Do I need a theoretical understanding of this family to help the family resolve identified problems?
— 2. If so, have I considered the ten dimensions of family functioning (Table 6.1)?
— 3. Which dimensions best explain the family's plight?

6.2.2 QUESTIONS TO CONSIDER

1. Consider the problems you might encounter in each of the following families:
    a. an overprotective mother and a clinging, dependent child;

    b. a family in which the mother sees herself as a buffer between the children and a rigid, punitive father;

    c. a conflict between an eighteen-year-old daughter and parents in an immigrant Hispanic family about the daughter's freedom to date young men.

2. For each problem, which theoretical dimension(s) might apply?

3. What questions would these dimensions suggest for problem exploration?

4. What should be considered in relation to the family's ethnicity?

6.3.0 MISSION AND PURPOSE

The mission of social work as described in section 2.3.0 applies whether the primary system for work is the individual, family, group, organization, or community. The nature of our purpose when the family is the primary system is, however, somewhat more complicated than it is when working with individuals. Is our purpose to improve or alter family functioning? Is it to improve or alter the behavior or plight of one or more family members? In TC, or any problem-solving approach, the answer to this question will vary depending on the problem and the family's role in the problem.

Listed below are some of the reasons for seeing families or for inviting them to be seen:

1. The family requests help for the family unit;

2. The family seems to be a causal factor in problems experienced by another system, such as an individual or a community;

3. The family is an important resource for solving problems experienced by other systems; or

4. The existing problem, whatever its location, is having a debilitating impact on the family.

Thus the reason for working with any system is to resolve problems. Whether one's purpose is then to change the family or a member of the family depends on where the problem is located.

6.3.1 Checklist for Mission and Purpose

— 1. What is my purpose in working with this family as a primary system?
— 2. Is my purpose consistent with the agency purpose and the mission of social work?
— 3. Do I consistently consider the role of families in problems experienced by other systems?

6.3.2 Questions to Consider

1. Can you identify any purposes when working with a family that might be inconsistent with agency purposes or the mission of social work?

2. What kind of work are you doing or do you expect to do with families? How will this further the mission of social work?

3. When working with families, we are sometimes expected to help an individual adjust to a dysfunctional environment. When might this occur? What position would you take?

6.4.0 Social Work Values

The social work values respecting the worth and dignity of the individual, the uniqueness of the individual, and the individual's right to self-determination apply regardless of which system is chosen as the primary one. They apply equally to everyone regardless of whether the individual is a client or a collateral.

These values become somewhat more difficult to implement as the size of the primary system increases. It is hard to respect those who scapegoat others, hold rigidly one-up positions, abuse their children, or withhold affection. It is sometimes impossible to respect self-determination when the parent is a child abuser. These and other circumstances provide genuine ethical dilemmas for the social worker.

6.4.1 CHECKLIST FOR SOCIAL WORK VALUES

— 1. Do I respect all members of the family?
— 2. If not, why not?
— 3. What does this tell me about my own values?
— 4. What corrective actions are necessary?

6.4.2 QUESTIONS TO CONSIDER

1. The parents want to keep their child but you have reason to suspect physical abuse. What do you do? Why? What is the ethical conflict?
2. The family is from a cultural group that emphasizes the development of male children. The family is not in conflict about this value. What is your position? What do you do? Why?

6.5.0 RELATIONSHIP

Relationships with families, like those with individuals, are professional ones. The relationship with the family is also important as a mediating variable. Note, however, that the extensive body of research about relationships summarized in section 2.5.1 has been conducted with individuals. Thus we do not know whether effective relationships with families are also, or to the same extent, characterized by behaviors that convey warmth, empathy, and genuineness. The importance of the social worker's credibility and attractiveness has also not been examined in work with families.

The literature about family treatment suggests that concepts like "joining" are important when working with families (Minuchin 1974; Nichols and Schwartz 2001) *Joining* refers to the worker's ability to modify his or her behavior to fit the style of the family. That some conflict might exist between the family style and the relationship variables that are thought to be important is entirely possible. For example, the interaction of the family might not be characterized by warmth. In fact, expressions of warmth for a particular family might be interpreted as indications of weakness.

Until relationships with families are further researched, we can probably safely assume that the skills described in section 2.5.1 should be used but that their use will be moderated by the style of the family.

6.5.1 COMPONENTS OF EFFECTIVE SOCIAL WORK RELATIONSHIPS

See sections 2.5.0–2.5.1.

6.5.2. RELATIONSHIP IN TASK-CENTERED WORK WITH FAMILIES

In task-centered work with families the collaborative nature of the practitioner-client relationship is as critical as it is in work with individuals (section 2.5.0). However, in maintaining a collaborative orientation with families, the practitioner must contend with two issues.

One issue has to do with being collaborative in the face of conflict between family members. How does one form a partnership with a family if its members are going in opposite directions? Not easy! One principle is to try to identify common interests and relate to them. For instance, Beth and Jon are at loggerheads over whether their four-year-old son, Kevin, should go to a parochial school (Beth's choice) or public school (Jon's choice). But both may agree that they want quality education for Kevin, and Jon may accept Beth's goal that their son should receive religious training. Thus the practitioner can collaborate with the parents in helping them achieve these mutually accepted goals, perhaps through enabling them to reach a compromise about how these goals can be achieved.

Conflict between parents and children often raises a difficult challenge for practitioners attempting to relate to the family in a collaborative way. Sometimes common ground is apparent. An operational rule used in the present model, as well as in most forms of family treatment, is to give priority to developing a collaborative relationship with the parents. At least two reasons account for this: One is to provide support for parental authority; the other is more pragmatic—parental cooperation is essential for the continuance of treatment. At the same time, you should try to articulate collaborative themes that might embrace both parents and child—for example, you can show support to the child for aspirations the parents would find acceptable.

Moreover, once you have established a collaborative spirit in your work with the family, you can, for specific purposes, ally yourself with a particular family member. Thus you may support Mom's desire to give her teenage daughter more freedom even though Dad has reservations. Later on, you might support one of Dad's decisions over Mom's misgivings. As this illustration shows, specific alliances should be temporary and should involve, sequentially, different family members.

A second major issue concerning collaborative work with families has to do with the practitioner's "leadership" role. In the present model the practitioner exercises leadership primarily through facilitating the family's own problem-solving work. In this respect, task-centered family practice is in tune with recent trends toward client empowerment and self-direction (Cox and Parsons 2000; Reid, 2002). Unlike some models, the practitioner does not assume the role of an expert who takes responsibility for providing the correct "directives" for problem solution. Thus clients are given the initiative in formulating problems, and their ideas about tasks are elicited. Some families need more direction than others to achieve their own goals, as a study by Hampson and Beavers (1996) has suggested. In the present model, leadership is offered to the extent needed. For some families, you may need to propose possible solutions or suggest tasks. How much leadership is called for is always difficult to determine. Perhaps the best answer is "just enough to keep the family moving forward."

6.5.3 CHECKLIST FOR RELATIONSHIP

— 1. Did I search for common goals when family members have apparently opposing interests?
— 2. In what ways did I try to facilitate the family's own problem solving?
— 3. If I suggested to the family problems to consider or tasks to undertake, did I elicit and use their feedback?

6.5.4 QUESTIONS TO CONSIDER

1. Debbie, age sixteen, wants to quit school and live with her twenty-one-year-old boyfriend. Her parents want her to stay in school and give up the boyfriend. How do you approach the situation in respect to your goal of maintaining a collaborative relationship with the family?

2. The parents of an eight-year-old underachieving boy "have tried everything" to get him to do better in school "but nothing has worked." The father says, "You're the expert! You tell us what should be done!" How do you respond?

6.6.0. THE APPROPRIATE SYSTEM FOR WORK

We shall first consider situations in which the family is the *primary* system for work (section 2.6.0), that is, when treatment sessions routinely involve two or more family members or involve different family members sequentially. We shall then take up situations in which the family is the secondary system. Finally, we shall consider situations in which the best strategy is to form a special system consisting of the practitioner, clients, and collaterals, who work together as a case management team.

Ideally the family should be the primary system for work when one or more of the following conditions apply:

1. The problem is located within the family—for example, parent-child or marital conflict;
2. Change in the family is necessary to alleviate the problem—for example, parents are not providing an undernourished child with an adequate diet; and
3. The family is able to bring to bear resources to further problem solution or has a role in effecting a solution—for example, the involvement of adult children in discharge planning for an older parent.

We say "ideally" because effective work with the family may be difficult or impossible to engineer for a number of reasons. The family may be uncooperative or otherwise not available, too dysfunctional to participate in any meaningful change effort, or the client referred may object to family involvement. Still, if you have reason to involve the family, a concerted effort should be made to do so, even if the involvement is less than ideal (as shall be discussed shortly).

When the problem is located within the family system, work with family members who are part of the problem is especially important. Most such problems turn out to be some form of conflict. If only one participant is seen, say the wife in a marital problem or the parent in a parent-teen conflict, treatment often becomes stalled: The practitioner gets a one-sided view of the situation, often in the form of unproductive complaints from the client who is seen. The entire burden of effecting change (through tasks in the present model) falls on the client participating.

When a problem is located in a child, family involvement is almost always desirable. The family has a stake in the problem; usually the family has resources to help the child; and often changes in the family can help resolve the problem.

The family may be a secondary system in treatment for two reasons. In some situations the family should ideally be the primary system but may not be cooperative or available. Often, however, some family involvement is possible and sometimes critical. For example, in work with the chronic mentally ill, the patient and the patient's parents may be estranged; neither wants anything to do with the other. However, an adult sibling, aunt, uncle, or grandparent may be willing to become involved and may often be an important resource.

In other situations the family becomes a secondary system by design. An individual, neighborhood, or organization is the primary system, but some work with the family may have an important adjunctive function. For example, a child's problem may be located primarily in the school. The most efficient strategy may be to work directly with the child and the school system. However, family involvement is indicated because of the family's concern about the child and its need to learn what it can do to prevent the problem from arising again. A family session may be useful in helping to work out a discharge plan for an older person even though individual and group treatment may be the modalities primarily used.

Families are a part of complex social networks. In task-centered family treatment, practitioners should know how these networks bear on the target problems and which network members (collaterals) should become treatment participants. In family treatment, practitioners sometimes err by concentrating exclusively on the family on the mistaken assumption that family dynamics lie at the heart of whatever problem is under consideration. Careful problem assessment often reveals the role of the social network, especially in problems of family members that are located in systems external to the family. Thus, as a rule, school personnel should be contacted and often actively involved in the intervention process when target problems involve a child's adjustment at school.

A task-centered case management approach may be indicated when the family is involved with multiple service providers or if such providers should be involved in work on target problems (Bailey-Dempsey and Reid 1996; Naleppa and Reid 1998, 2000). Essentially a new primary system is created, one consisting of relevant family members and service providers, including the task-centered practitioner, who assumes the role of a case manager. This system, or case management team, meets regularly during the course of treatment. Client problems are identified and worked on by the team. Tasks for different team members are developed in the meetings and carried out subsequently.

For example, in using a task-centered case management approach with a frail elderly woman who needs support to remain at home, the team might consist of the elder, a close friend who lives nearby, a visiting nurse, and the social worker. The team would meet to identify what was needed to maintain the elder in her home and divide up tasks directed at meeting the need (see also section 8.9.0, "Applications to Special Populations"). In the task-centered case management approach for children at risk of school failure (noted earlier) teams consisted of parents, the child, the social worker (in the role of case manager), school personnel, and (depending on the case) the child's peers or representatives from community agencies.

6.6.1 CHECKLIST FOR THE APPROPRIATE SYSTEM FOR WORK

— 1. Why have I decided to work with the family as the primary system?
— 2. What other systems might be involved?

7

THE INITIAL PHASE OF TREATMENT

7.0.0 COMPONENTS OF THE INITIAL PHASE

For purposes of discussion in this chapter, we shall assume that the situation meets the criteria considered in the previous chapter for family treatment as the primary modality. As a rule, we think family members relevant to the problem should be seen together in both the initial and subsequent phases of treatment. Conjoint interviews are much better able than separate interviews to provide the practitioner with a sense of how family members interact and to foster family problem solving. Moreover, they set the stage for therapeutic interactions between family members, which, of course, are not possible in individual sessions.

Still, individual interviews have their place, especially for assessment purposes in the initial phase. Family members may be reluctant to share critical information with other family members present but may do so in individual sessions. Examples of such information are revelations of extramarital involvement, "hidden" habits, secret misgivings about family members, and criticisms of other family members.

When problems involve such issues, a common practice is to arrange for individual interviews in addition to joint sessions during the initial phase. These individual interviews may be full-length or brief (e.g., fifteen minutes). Briefer interviews can often be held just preceding or following joint sessions.

Another consideration is which family members should be included in treatment. In some forms of family therapy, all family members in the same household are routinely asked to participate. In the task-centered model, who is included depends on the problem. For example, if a problem is located in a child, the child and parents are normally seen; siblings may or may not be included depending on their relationship to the problem. When conflict between parents is an issue in a child-related problem, the parents may be seen for several sessions alone in an attempt to enhance the parental alliance before the children are brought into the sessions (Reid and Donovan 1990). When a case management approach is used, representatives from other systems (e.g., teachers, probation officers) may be seen with family members for specific purposes (Reid et al. 1994; Bailey-Dempsey and Reid 1996).

In most cases the initial phase of family treatment can be completed in one to four sessions. Sometimes extended initial sessions (up to two hours) may be used, especially when problems are complex and the family group is large. The activities that comprise the initial phase include explanations of role, purpose, and procedures; time limits; obtaining necessary information; targeting, prioritizing, exploring, and specifying problems; goals; contracts; and assessment.

7.1.0 Explanations of Role, Purpose, Treatment Procedures

Before the formal beginning of the first family interview, a brief "warm-up" may be conducted. The warm-up consists of casual conversations in which the practitioner encourages members present to participate. The idea is to get the family in a friendly and conversational mood. A warm-up is particularly important if children are present. If they can be brought into the conversation around their interests and activities, they are more likely to participate later on. Moreover, a warm-up can help avoid children "clamming up" completely when asked to present their views of the problem (Reid 1985). During the warm-up, the practitioner can introduce him- or herself, as illustrated in section 3.1.0.

Given that family treatment has some complexities that do not occur in work with individuals, more time is usually spent in orienting clients. We have found, however, that spending too much time in an initial orientation is inadvisable. Family members can "hear" only so much about what is in store for them (Doel and Marsh 1991). Keeping initial explanations brief and filling clients in as you go along, that is, explaining what a procedure is about when it is first used, is preferable.

7.1.1 CHECKLIST FOR EXPLANATION OF ROLE, PURPOSE, AND PROCEDURES

— 1. Do family members know my name and title?
— 2. Do they know the name of the agency and its purpose?
— 3. Do they know who referred them and why?
— 4. Do they understand that together we will work toward changing specific aspects of their situation that they identify?
— 5. Do they understand that we will work together for a specific number of sessions?
— 6. Do they understand confidentiality and any limits to it?
— 7. Did I use a "warm-up" to start the first family interview? How did it go?
— 8. What and when did I inform the family about my role and about treatment procedures?
— 9. How did the family react?
— 10. How might I have done it differently?

7.1.2 EXERCISE FOR EXPLAINING ROLE, PURPOSE, AND PROCEDURES

Apply the exercise in section 3.1.3 to a family group. The instructions in section 3.1.2 can be used for family treatment exercises so long as the number of participants is increased.

7.2.0 TIME LIMITS

If anything, the case for time limits in work with families is even stronger than it is in work with individuals. Reviews of research suggest that the effectiveness of planned short-term treatment with families is at least equivalent to family treatment of indefinite length and, as a consequence, the briefer treatment is more efficient (Koss and Shiang 1994). As Zuk (1978) has pointed out, family treatment is best seen as a short-term modality because families are generally not willing to continue in long-term treatment. Sustaining the treatment motivation and cooperative effort of an entire family, or even a family dyad, over a long period is difficult. Long-term cases often end (prematurely in the views of practitioners) when a key family member decides to quit (see section 9.5.0). Short-term contracts have the advantage of attracting families that may be willing to commit themselves to a limited number of sessions but are not willing to become involved in treatment of indefinite length.

7.2.1 CHECKLIST FOR TIME LIMITS

— 1. Did I set specific time limits with the family?
— 2. How did the family react?

7.2.2 EXERCISE FOR TIME LIMITS

Practice discussing and setting time limits, as well as explaining role and treatment procedures; also practice "warming up" in a family session.

7.3.0 OBTAINING NECESSARY INFORMATION

The same basic, demographic information acquired in working with individuals is useful in work with families. However, in cultures where families tend to be large or where family is defined as including many people outside the nuclear family, securing all the information may take too long, so you may need to be selective. Some of the information can be obtained during the "warm-up," which was described previously. Some of it can be obtained before the first interview. In family work, for example, the practitioner should know all the members of the family and household constellation before deciding on whom to include. The practitioner can obtain the remaining necessary information by means of brief questions as work progresses.

7.3.1 CHECKLIST FOR OBTAINING NECESSARY INFORMATION

Do I have the following information about the family?

— Address
— Phone number
— Identity of all members of the family constellation
— Identity of all members of the household
— Referral source
— Reason for referral
— Household income

Do I have the following information about each member of the family to be included in treatment?

— Age
— Gender
— Race/ethnicity
— Religion
— Marital status
— Parental status
— Occupation or grade in school
— Place of employment or name of school
— Source of income
— Highest level of education achieved
— Health
— Whereabouts

7.3.2 EXERCISE FOR OBTAINING NECESSARY INFORMATION

Apply exercise 3.3.2 to a family case.

7.4.0 TARGETING PROBLEMS AND DETERMINING PROBLEM PRIORITIES

(The initial step in targeting problems is to elicit, in turn, family members' views of what they would like to see changed) Normally the practitioner begins with the parents, allowing them to decide which one will begin. The practitioner lets family members express problems in their own way but may enter in to clarify what is being said and to elicit additional details. Each member's views are elicited. If a family member is reluctant to speak out—children often choose to be nonvocal at this point—the practitioner may make a "gentle" effort to elicit a response but does not press the issue.

What emerges from this process is usually a wealth of untidy information full of gaps and contradictions. In some cases a problem list can be extracted from the family's expression of dissatisfactions and complaints. Often, however, you need to *formulate* potential target problems—a procedure in which you pull together dissatisfactions expressed by different family members into provisional problem statements. These statements should try to capture what the clients are expressing. They should not reflect your own theories or opinions about what is wrong. The acid test is client acknowledgment—family members should expressly accept your formulations as describing their own concerns.

How problems are formulated depends on the type of problem. Most problems that family members present fall into one of three groups: relational problems (e.g., "We don't get along"); individual problems (e.g., "Kevin lies and steals"); and external problems (e.g., "We need better housing"). Relational problems should generally be formulated in interactive terms. For example, Mom and Lisa presented various complaints about each other and indicated that their differences lead to continual quarreling, which neither of them likes. The problem would be formulated as one of "quarreling between Mom and

Lisa" (an interactive focus) rather than in terms of the complaints of mother and daughter. This quarreling formulation would likely encompass their complaints when the content of their quarrels is specified. Putting such problems in interactional terms helps the family members to begin to assume joint responsibility for the difficulty.

Often difficulties initially presented as individual problems can be reframed in interactional terms. Thus "Mr. and Mrs. G's" complaint that "Frank wants to quit school" may become "Mr. and Mrs. G and Frank disagree about whether he should quit school." However, many problems initially presented as individual problems do not lend themselves to this kind of reframing. Depression, alcoholism, anorexia, delinquency, to mention some examples, may be best expressed as problems of individual family members, even though they may all be responsive to family interaction.

The final problem list should involve more than one family member when that is possible, so that one member is not seen as *the* problem. Either individual or relational problems involving other family members will suffice. In one case, for example, an individual problem involved the "lack of ambition" of a young schizophrenic man. He would spend most of the day at home watching television, behavior that was becoming increasingly upsetting to his parents, especially the father who had a hard time keeping his temper in check. A second problem then became the parents' difficulty in coping with their son's troublesome behavior. A third problem expressed by the son concerned his parents nagging him about "not doing anything."

Good problem statements should not only reflect the concerns of family members but should also be sufficiently detailed and specific to lay the groundwork for tasks to follow. Even though the problem may be identified with a shorthand phase, such as "quarreling between Mom and Lisa," particulars should be spelled out. What do they quarrel about? What happens when they quarrel? What are the consequences? Only some of this detail may be apparent (and need be shared) at the point of problem formulation. More is normally added in the next step, "problem exploration," considered below. As this suggests, a problem is seldom pinned down at one point in time. Rather, the practitioner's and client's joint understanding of a problem gradually unfolds as the case proceeds.

Although it is desirable that family members agree on target problems, consensus is not essential. Karen may see her husband Dave's excessive drinking as a problem, while Dave may deny that his drinking is a problem. He sees Karen's overattachment to her mother as something to be changed, whereas Karen thinks her relationship with her mother presents no difficulties. Each may not see eye-to-eye on the target problems, but each may be willing to respect the other's concerns and even to make changes, on a quid-pro-quo basis. Issues like these, in which one person experiences a problem that can only be resolved by changes in another person's behavior, are sometimes called "reciprocal problems." Being alert to them makes it possible to arrange behavioral exchanges that, often, achieve some degree of resolution fairly quickly because both parties have something to gain.

Each family member ranks each problem in terms of its importance to him or her. Generally the problem taken up first is the one family members rank first. If family members disagree, the practitioner may suggest taking up the problem where change is likely to occur most quickly or may propose working on two reciprocal problems concurrently (as in the example of Karen and Dave above).

7.4.1 TARGETING PROBLEMS IN SPECIAL CIRCUMSTANCES

When the family as a unit is a nonvoluntary recipient of service, the considerations presented in section 3.4.0 apply (see also section 8.8.0). Often in work with families, however, you may find that one family member wants your services while another (or others) may or may not.

Usually the reluctant one is central to the problem in the eyes of the one seeking help. A wife comes to an agency with the complaint that her husband is an alcoholic, or a son wants a social worker to work out a plan for his elderly mother who lives alone. Neither the husband nor the mother wants to see a social worker.

In such cases the preferred option is to try to involve the reluctant family member. The client applying can make requests, or the practitioner can do this directly. In either case the request can be put on the basis that a single interview with the reluctant family member would be useful in order to clarify the problem. Asking for a single interview only (either individual or joint) lets the family member know that continuing beyond the first contact will be his or her choice. You hope for further involvement but avoid making this an expectation. The interview, if it comes to pass, might be used to target problems in a way the reluctant family member would find acceptable as a basis for continued work. (Offering a short-term contract is an advantage here.) If this initial attempt at involvement is unsuccessful, you can continue with the client who has applied. The target problem is then framed in terms of that client's concerns and struggles. For example, "Mrs. A. is upset about her husband's drinking and is undecided about what to do." The effort to involve the nonparticipating family member continues.

7.4.2 Checklist for Targeting and Prioritizing Problems

— 1. Did I give each family member a chance to express his or her views of the problem?
— 2. Did I formulate relational problems in interactional terms? Were individual problems formulated in this way when possible? Did family members agree with these formulations?
— 3. Are different family members represented in my problem list?
— 4. Did family members rank problems in terms of their own priorities? How well did they agree?
— 5. Did I try to engage any member initially refusing to become involved?

7.4.3 Exercise for Targeting and Prioritizing Problems

Practice targeting and prioritizing target problems using instructions for role plays in section 3.1.2. In this exercise those playing the roles of family members should assume *one* of the following:

a. The family has a combination of individual, relational, and external problems.
b. Family members disagree on their problems.
c. A family member who does not want to be involved in treatment has come in for an interview.

7.5.0 EXPLORING TARGET PROBLEMS

Because family interviews are typically less structured than individual sessions, problem exploration may not occur as a separate step but rather as a part of problem targeting. In any case the purpose of this activity is to obtain the kind of data about target problems necessary to help the family develop a plan of action.

In task-centered practice generally, and in family applications in particular, problem exploration continues through the life of the case. The complexity of family problems defies easy understanding. However, enough information to serve as a basis for initial intervention needs to be gained. Further intervention will be shaped by subsequent data on the problem.

Exploration of the target problem is combined with investigation of contextual factors, including obstacles that may stand in the way of problem resolution and the resources that may facilitate it.

The practitioner is particularly alert to how the dimensions of family life, presented in section 6.2.0, might constitute either obstacles or resources. For example, is avoidance of communication about the problem an aggravating factor? Is the out-of-control behavior of the children reactive to a weak parental alliance? Are the cohesiveness and adaptability of the family resources that will help it fight racial discrimination in the neighborhood?

Although the task-centered model emphasizes "here-and-now" realities, attention is also given to historical and etiological factors. Of special interest are factors that clearly bear on the target problem. Darci, an eight year old with mild behavioral problems, is harshly treated by her mother, Mrs. O. Younger sister Blair can seemingly do no wrong. It helps to know that Darci was an out-of-wedlock child that Mrs. O never wanted, whereas Blair was born after Mrs. O was happily married to her current husband. Perhaps Mrs. O's attitude toward Darci is a reflection of her history. If so, a likely obstacle to progress on future tasks has been identified.

Such historical material is often brought up by clients because it is on their minds or because they see it as relevant to the problem. Often the practitioner may elicit it in determining how the problem began.

Sometimes asking clients if they can think of anything in the past that might have contributed to the current difficulty is worthwhile.

7.5.1 CHECKLIST FOR EXPLORING TARGET PROBLEMS

— 1. Have I adequately explored contextual factors bearing on the target problems?
— 2. What strategies or tasks are suggested by the information I have obtained?

7.5.2 EXERCISES FOR EXPLORING TARGET PROBLEMS

Adopt the exercise described in section 3.5.2 for a family interview. The "family" should make sure it has one or more contextual factors (drawn from section 6.2.0) that bear on the problem—intrusiveness, cross-generational alliance, and so forth.

7.6.0 DEVELOPING THE PROBLEM SPECIFICATION

Securing baseline data in family work makes use of the same procedures as used in individual treatment; that is, manifestations of the problem and indications of their frequency, duration, or severity are identified (section 3.6.0). In addition, for problems involving interaction among family members, observational measures may be used by having family members carry out structured communication or problem-solving tasks. For example, family members—say, a marital or parent-child dyad—can discuss a "hot topic" for five to ten minutes, either in the session or at home. Whenever it is done, the interaction can be tape-recorded for subsequent analysis. The interaction can be assessed using available scales or a measure devised by the practitioner.

A variety of rapid assessment instruments are available for measurement of family problems and functioning. The Hudson Clinical

Assessment Package contains a number of family assessment tools, including the Index of Family Relations, Child Attitude Toward Mother (or Father), and the Index of Marital Satisfaction (Hudson 1982). These instruments can be computer-scored and results graphed with an available software package (Hudson 1990). Other instruments that have proved useful in task-centered family practice include the Family Assessment Device (Epstein, Baldwin, and Bishop 1983; Miller et al. 1985) and the Diagnostic Adjustment Scale (Spanier 1976). A large variety of instruments for couples and families can be found in Corcoran and Fischer (2000).

In work with families, problem specification is complicated by the tendency for specific problems to be manifestations of larger contextual issues. Thus, in one case, the presenting problem concerned disagreement between Mr. and Mrs. F over curfew for their fourteen-year-old daughter, Jerri. Mr. F wanted to give Jerri far less freedom to stay out than her mother wanted to give her. Exploration of the problem and its context revealed a long-standing alliance between mother and children (Jerri and younger brother Ken) against the father. Mother appeared to take the role of the children's protector against father, whom the children viewed as overly strict and punitive.

If you were the practitioner, your dilemma might be stated as follows: If you were to focus exclusively on the presenting problem, you would run the risk of dealing with just a surface expression of a deeper issue. Even were the problem to be resolved, others would take its place. On the other hand, the presenting problem is the one the family wants to work on; it does not "see" the underlying pattern, and at this point you are not so sure about it yourself.

A solution for such a dilemma is the notion of a "representative problem" (Reid 1985). In the present case, the disagreement about Jerri's hours can be seen as a valid target problem in its own right but one that is representative of a larger issue—the cross-generational coalition. You can specify the problem in terms of the disagreement over Jerri's hours, but you can also suggest to the parents that it seems to reflect larger issues of disagreement about the children and that these issues may need to be addressed in the course of working on the problem. Mr. and Mrs. F, like most parents at odds about how to handle their children, would be likely to accept such a formulation.

7.6.1 CHECKLIST FOR PROBLEM SPECIFICATION

> — 1. Have I identified all the manifestations for each target problem that are important to the family members?
> — 2. Do I know the frequency, severity, or duration of each manifestation before intervention?
> — 3. Have I established a baseline period for each manifestation?
> — 4. Have I graphed the data, when appropriate, so that the family and I can "see" changes?
> — 5. Did I specify a representative problem in this case, if doing so was appropriate? If so, what does the target problem represent?
> — 6. Have I considered using a rapid assessment instrument?

7.6.2 EXERCISE FOR PROBLEM SPECIFICATION

Adopt the exercise in section 3.6.2 to a family.

7.7.0 GOALS

As noted in section 3.7.0, goals state the desired end points of intervention. Problem formulations describe what needs to be remedied and always imply a minimal goal, but they may not include a definition of what might be seen as an optimal solution. Thus the problem may be stated in terms of Howard's doing failing work in math with the implicit minimal goal of "not failing." But goals for Howard might range all the way from that minimum to getting an A in math.

Developing specific goals as a part of the initial problem statement or subsequently may be useful for motivational purposes as well as for clarifying what a satisfactory resolution might be. In fact, goal statements can be used in lieu of problem formulations, when there might be reason to avoid the latter, such as in using the model in conjunction with a "strength perspective" (Saleebey 1997) in which service is organized around goals rather than problems. However, certain cautions need to be kept in mind in work with families. Family members may agree that a certain problem needs to be addressed and on the minimal goal implicit in the problem, but may not agree on further specifications of goals. Thus all may agree that Howard needs to pass but may not agree on his level of achievement beyond that. Also, many family problems are messy and shifting; it may often be better to see how much can be done rather than try to set goals that may be premature, arbitrary, or unrealistic.

7.7.1 CHECKLIST FOR GOALS

— 1. Are goals necessary in this case?
— 2. If so, are they understood and agreed on by the family?
— 3. Will the family and I be able to determine when each goal is reached?

7.7.2 EXERCISE FOR GOALS

Role play a family session. Assume that a target problem has already been agreed on but that a goal may be helpful in pinning down a desirable outcome. In the role play, family members disagree on the goal and the practitioner tries to work out a compromise.

7.8.0 CONTRACTS

The complexities and uncertainties of some family cases often require that the contract be more general and tentative than in individual treatment. For example, you may not be sure at the outset which family members will be willing to participate and to what extent. Greater generality and tentativeness may also result from the need to accommodate the conflicting interests of different family members.

7.8.1 CHECKLIST FOR CONTRACTS (SEE SECTION 3.8.1)

Have I gone as far as possible with the family to reach agreement about the following issues?

— 1. number and scheduling of sessions;
— 2. fees, if applicable;
— 3. participants in sessions;
— 4. target problems; and
— 5. problem specifications and goals

7.8.2 Exercise for Contracts

Role play a portion of a family session in which target problems have already been formulated. Practice setting up a contract around these problems.

7.9.0 Assessment

As in TC with individuals, much of the assessment process focuses on explaining and specifying target problems. However, these problems must be understood within contexts of family functioning and the family's relationship to external systems.

How much and what kind of contextual data are obtained depends on the problems in the case. If problems are simple and readily resolved, a minimal amount of contextual data may be required. If problems are complex and ready solutions are not forthcoming, then much more contextual data may be needed. The theoretical perspectives on family functioning (section 6.2.0) are used to determine specific dynamics that may be contributing to the problem or impeding its resolution. In some cases, sessions with individual family members or with particular groups—for example, parents—may be indicated. Examination of the family's environment needs to take into account the multiple systems that impinge on each problem and how the family (and different family members) relate to these systems. The assessment process often needs to be extended to include contact with these systems. How do they view the family's difficulties? What resources and obstacles do they present in relation to resolving these difficulties. The case-management approach discussed earlier (section 6.6.0) provides an excellent vehicle for this type of assessment.

7.9.1 Checklist for Assessment

— 1. Do I have an adequate understanding of contextual factors bearing on the target problem?

— 2. What additional information do I need, and what is the best way of securing it?

— 3. What is the impact of other systems on causing or maintaining the problems?

— 4. What is the impact of the problems on other systems?

— 5. Are other systems important to resolving the problem?

— 6. What other systems should be included? How?

7.9.2 Exercise for Assessment

In a role play of a family session, the "practitioner" attempts to identify contextual factors and the impact of other systems on a target problem. The "family" determines beforehand what some of these might be and provides "clues" to the "practitioner" during the session.

8

THE MIDDLE PHASE OF TREATMENT

8.0.0 COMPONENTS OF THE MIDDLE PHASE

As in work with individuals, the middle phase of family treatment begins when tasks are used to bring about change in the clients' problems. It includes the activities that have been described in part 1: the Task Planning and Implementation Sequence, including revising unsuccessful tasks; addressing consistent nonperformance of tasks, as well as nontargeted problems; using time limits; and revising assessments. Eclectic practice and work with special populations are also described in this chapter.

In family practice, however, you are working not with just an individual but with a social system. Tasks may be undertaken by an entire family or a family unit. Moreover, two or more family members are often present in the interview. Thus family members can work on problems and develop and practice tasks in face-to-face interactions.

8.1.0 TASK PLANNING AND IMPLEMENTATION SEQUENCE

The Task Planning and Implementation Sequence (TPIS) in family practice incorporates the same steps as in individual treatment but is altered by the greater use of face-to-face communication between family members, the need to involve two or more clients simultaneously in carrying out the various steps, and by the different types of tasks to be done outside the session. Family sessions are more fluid than individual interviews. As a result the TPIS is often used more flexibly in family than in individual practice. Some typical variations will be noted. In general, ensuring that all the steps are covered is more important than covering them in the order given.

8.1.1 Generating Alternatives and Selecting a Task

Alternative task possibilities can be developed in three ways in family treatment applications. In the first method, the procedures used in individual sessions are merely extended to multiclient interviews. You ask family members to suggest task possibilities. These possibilities are clarified, if need be, through subsequent questions. You can offer modifications of the family's task ideas or suggest your own if the family is unable to think of any. In some situations, your professional knowledge or your own practice experience may provide just the right idea for a task, perhaps one that might never occur to the family. You should not hesitate to present it. For example, suppose a child is having difficulty in school. The circumstances of the case suggest that a "home notes" approach might be effective (Kelly 1990). In a home notes procedure the child's task is to take home a daily progress report from the teacher. The parents can reward progress or use the report to guide their own efforts to help the child. The family may not be aware of this procedure, or they may not know (as you do) of the teacher's willingness to use it. Often the task plan involves some combination of tasks suggested by the practitioner and the client. In any event, family members' input to practitioner-offered tasks should be invited and incorporated, if at all possible.

A variation of this method involves generating alternatives in case management team meetings (6.6.0). Usually you would normally first ask family members to suggest task possibilities and then involve other participants who may provide feedback on the client's ideas or suggest task possibilities themselves. Thus a teacher may outline what a child needs to do to be promoted. Or a representative of a housing project may be able to specify the steps a family must take to become eligible for project housing.

The client can then respond to such suggestions. As the examples suggest, one of the advantages of a case management approach in task development is to bring the family together with persons in the environment who are able to clarify the actions necessary for clients to achieve desired goals. In this process the other participants might also be asked to identify tasks that they themselves might take on to further resolve the client's problem.

In the second method, family members generate alternatives through communicating with one another. Such interactions, sometimes referred to as session tasks (Reid 1985, 1992), tend to be relatively brief (one to five minutes) and are usually structured by the practitioner to accomplish specific purposes relating to task planning and implementation.

In using family conversations to generate alternatives, you start off by summarizing the problem and asking family members (e.g., a marital or parent-child dyad) to spend a few minutes working together on ideas for actions that might resolve it. In this format, you let the family do the work. Your role is to keep them talking to one another (not to you) and to keep them focused. Your interventions are then primarily facilitative. How much you intervene, and when, will depend on the family's problem-solving style. For example, in some families problem solving may occur in the context of quarrelsome communication, replete with name calling and angry outbursts. But what sounds like an ongoing battle produces viable task suggestions. In other (probably most) families, problem solving stops when fighting begins. So some patience and careful listening on your part is needed to learn how a family goes about its problem-solving work.

After the family has come up with task possibilities and selected the most promising, you may bring their conversation to a close with a summary or perhaps explore one or more of the possibilities presented. You may also suggest additional alternatives at this point, especially if the family appears to be at an impasse. It is hoped that either the session task or the ensuing discussion will yield an external task or tasks.

(A third method consists of the social worker suggesting task possibilities based on his or her own knowledge or on pre-arranged task plans, which includes published task planners (Reid 2000). Such a plan may be offered to the family as "a possible approach that is often effective for the kind of problem you have." If the family's problem seems to fit a task plan that has been well worked-out, especially a plan of established effectiveness, it may make sense to suggest it at the outset, at the same time permitting the family to reject or modify it. A number of task plans have been developed for use in family practice to address a variety of problems that families frequently face. Several of these plans are summarized below. Others are described in section 8.9.0.

Relationship building (Disengaged or conflicted family relationships are often target problems in themselves or may exacerbate other problems.) One strategy to improve relationships makes use of *shared tasks* in which two or more family members carry out the same task together. A simple type of shared task used for relationship building involves family members carrying out mutually enjoyable activities. A disengaged father and his son may attend a sporting event. A quarrelsome teen and her mother decide to listen to music together that they both enjoy. A distancing couple may agree to have dinner out. Although such tasks may at times backfire—e.g., wind up in a quarrel rather than fun—they usually provide a means of helping family members relate to one another in more satisfying and constructive ways.

Shared tasks can also take the form of daily debriefing conversations (Berg-Cross 1997). In these conversations each participant discusses events of his or her day with the other. Such conversations can be a vehicle for sharing experiences and feelings and for developing intimacy.

Participants in troubled relationships may be helped to restore intimacy if they can respond more empathically to one another (Jones, Christiansen, and Jacobson 2000). Shared tasks might involve discussions between family members in which they discuss their own feelings without expressing anger or blaming the other. In this task (adapted from Jacobson and Christensen 1996) participants usually are encouraged to focus on their "soft" or "vulnerable" emotions, such as fear and sadness, as a means of eliciting compassionate responses.

Another approach is to make use of *reciprocal tasks*, in which actions are reciprocated or exchanged in a quid-pro-quo manner. Reciprocal tasks are based on the principle of reciprocity, a fundamental norm of family life (Ruben 1998). In many families seeking help, this norm has broken down—family members are no longer willing to act on behalf of one another. Reciprocal tasks can revive positive interactions generally.

In one kind of reciprocal task, clients agree to exchange pleasing or caring actions. Each partner lists things that he or she would find pleasing or see as an expression of caring. Each then selects a number of these behaviors from the other's list and agrees to do one or more of them during the week (Stuart 1980; Epstein and Baucom 1998).

One principle in this type of behavioral exchange is to select tasks that "provide maximum gratification for the receiver with little cost to the caregiver" (Lawrence et al. 1999). In this way the tasks are more likely to be carried out. In the context of work with couples, examples might include a good-morning kiss or putting the children to bed (Lawrence et al. 1999). Although such contracts have been used, for the most part, in therapy with couples, they can be applied to other family dyads, for instance, a parent and an adolescent.

Changing Specific Behaviors   In work with families there is often need to try to bring about change in specific behaviors of family members that other members find aversive. Reciprocal tasks can be used for this purpose. Behaviors that participants find objectionable in one another are identified. Both agree to change his or her own behavior if the other does the same. In the case of a parent and child, the child may agree on a behavioral change contingent on a reward or concession from the parent. For example, Harry agrees to let Rachel know when he is going to be late; in exchange, Rachel agrees not to be critical when Harry calls her. Daryl will spend an hour each night on his homework; if he does, Mom will allow him to stay out an hour later on weekend nights. As these examples suggest, reciprocal tasks can involve symmetrical exchanges, that is, exchanges between equals, or complementary exchanges, that is, exchanges between family members of unequal status—parent and child.

The tasks may occur in pairs, as in the examples, or participants may agree on multiple exchanges in what Stuart (1980) has called a "holistic contract." For example, each participant may list a number of behaviors he or she would like from the other. The contract is formed from exchanges that each is willing to make. As might be imagined, such tasks are often difficult to arrange successfully since the behavior of two possibly antagonistic participants must be coordinated in a way that each feels is equitable. The high risk of failure is offset by the possibility of high gain (Rooney 1978). If successful, they can often result in dramatic reversals of negative interaction.

Behavioral changes may also be brought about through *individual tasks*, or tasks undertaken by individual family members without the expectation of immediate reciprocation. When two or more family members agree to do such individual tasks concurrently, the result can be what Weiss, Birchler, and Vincent (1974) have referred to as *good faith*, or parallel, contracts. Thus Mr. R might agree to a task to control his temper; Mrs. R might agree to a task to be more consistent in disciplining their son. Although their problems may be interrelated and each may expect the other to make progress on their tasks, one person's effort is not as dependent on the other's as in reciprocal or shared tasks. Individual tasks can capitalize on the motivation of particular family members at a particular time to do more than their share to institute change. Lou, a physically abusive husband, decides he needs to change his behavior to save his marriage. Goals to achieve that change in behavior can be spelled out in terms of individual tasks without reciprocation from his wife.

Ineffective Communication Styles

Communication Communication problems refer to a range of difficulties experienced by family members in expressing themselves to one another, including quarreling, underdisclosing, overdisclosing, lack of clarity, overblaming, sidetracking, mind reading, and defensiveness. Often expressions of major differences among family members in values, interests, personality styles, behaviors, and other dimensions may underlie communication problems. However, viewing such differences as communication problems may still offer a useful way of framing issues as a basis for intervention. The tasks listed below can form the basis of helping family members acquire communication skills while they work on specific issues. The tasks can be first worked on in the session through conversations and then continued at home. Ideally family members should set aside a certain amount of time each day (or a certain time on specific days of the week) to practice communication skills while discussing meaningful issues. The practitioner helps the partners select a real issue they want to work out. However, the issue should not be so toxic that the couple is not able to satisfactorily complete the task.

- *Use paraphrasing to develop listening skills.* While discussing an issue, each partner paraphrases what the other has just said before responding (Jacobson and Margolin 1979; Verderber and Verderber 2001). For example, when Alice finishes her response, Mark summarizes (without editorializing) what Alice has just said before responding to her communication. Alice listens to his response and paraphrases it in return.
- *Express dissatisfactions with each other in as nonthreatening a manner as possible.* The skill here is in stating something undesirable in another person in a manner that conveys one's feelings and perceptions but that minimizes angry or defensive reactions on the part of the other. Beginning statements in the first person ("I statements"), followed by a specific indication of what one is upset about and an illustrative example, is a good way of disclosing problems (Gordon 1970). For example, clients can learn to say "I would like it if you would respond when I ask you a question" rather than "You never care about what I have to say." Also, participants are encouraged to use situational rather than dispositional attributions (Berg-Cross 1997). Situational attributions explain another's behavior in terms of momentary states or environmental pressures—e.g., "I think you forgot because you had a lot on your mind." In dispositional attributions, the other's behavior is explained in terms of personality characteristics—e.g., I think you forgot because you are thoughtless. The latter are more likely to provoke angry defensive reactions.
- *Use problem-solving communication skills.* The *practitioner* helps participants learn essential skills to state the problem by beginning with something positive, to be specific, to avoid derogatory terms and overgeneralizations, to express feelings, to admit to one's own role in the problem, to deal with one problem at a time, to offer

compromises, to be neutral rather than negative, and to focus on solutions (Jacobson and Margolin 1979).

- *Self-disclose in a mutually satisfying fashion.* Issues may concern:
  (1) a partner's inability to self-disclose to the other, with the result
  that the other feels deprived of necessary information or generally
  "shut out" of the other's life; or (2) a partner's self-disclosing in a
  way that the other sees as excessive and burdensome. The practitioner helps the participants to identify cues that can be used to let
  the underdisclosing partner know that more disclosure is desired (or
  less for a partner that overdiscloses). The participants practice the
  use of cues in an in-session exercise. Although generally used with
  adult couples, the task can be adapted to disclosure issues involving
  parents and (often noncommunicative) adolescents.
- *Communicate in a validating manner.* "Validation stresses responding to the emotional state of the [other] and can be expressed by
  apologizing, complimenting, acknowledging feelings of the [other]
  and taking responsibility for making the other person upset or worried" (Berg-Cross 1997:233); see also Gottman 1994). The task is
  similar to what family members try to achieve in learning to respond more empathically to one another (discussed above).
- *Communicate positives about one another.* Communication among
  family members often becomes dominated by negative or neutral
  "businesslike" exchanges. Neglected are communications that convey appreciation of the other's positive attributes or behaviors, such
  as "I do appreciate your sense of humor!" or "I am really happy
  about the progress you have made at school." A start can be made
  in the session and continued at home. In the session, family members are asked to say something positive about one another. They
  almost always can, although they may have to grope a bit. Sometimes the positives are things they have taken for granted. One
  teenager surprised everyone present, and perhaps herself, when she
  said about her much maligned father, "Why I guess he provides me
  with food, shelter, and money." If the client gropes too long, you
  may want to come in with a quick prompt to keep the task from
  backfiring!
- *Agree to disengage—e.g., one or both leave the room—when quarreling begins to reach the "name calling" stage.* Partners should

identify cues or signals to let each other know when a disengagement is advisable. They should also have in mind where they will go and what they will do during the disengagement period.

Conflict   Conflict is the common denominator for most difficulties in family relationships. Many problems are expressed directly in terms of conflict: between adult couples, parents and children, and siblings. Problems expressed in other terms, such as poor communication or lack of intimacy, often become problems because the couple or family members are in disagreement about how these aspects of their relationship should play themselves out. Moreover, conflict may not necessarily be overt. One partner may suffer the other's behavior in silence. Conflict is present but covert. But in most cases the resolution of such hidden conflicts requires that they be brought to the surface. Problems calling for behavioral change on the part of family members can often be most effectively approached in terms of conflict over the behaviors in question using the tasks outlined below. The tasks are designed to be carried out in the order given, although not all may apply to all conflicts. All but the final (implementation) task can be practiced in the session. Work on the tasks in the session should ideally involve face-to-face communication by clients, with the practitioner serving as a facilitator or coach. Once clients have mastered the essentials of the tasks, they can carry out the whole sequence at home. It should be noted that this series of tasks parallels the general Task Planning and Implementation Sequence presented subsequently. The TPIS can be consulted for additional techniques that might apply to this series.

- *Define conflict in a clear and specific way.* Before the task, the practitioner may help clients identify their conflict in general terms. The practitioner may also introduce certain ground rules to be followed for this and subsequent tasks. The following are the more commonly used ground rules: Participants should focus on the problem itself and solutions for it rather than on each other's personal qualities. In the case of disagreement, participants should attempt to make some concessions, that is, they should be prepared to accept something less than (or different from) their conception of the ideal solution to the problem. Participants should try to see positive elements in each other's proposals, acknowledge the positives, and try to build on them. Each participant should offer to take some constructive action to help resolve the conflict. Problem behaviors or possible problem-solving actions should be spelled out as specifically as possible.

- *Reveal to one another your points of view, motivations, rationales, expectations, and so on, concerning the issue.* This may involve extensive and free-ranging self-revelations if the issue is pervasive or deep-set. Revelations should be expressed in ways that respect other participants' feelings. Structured conversations between family members may be useful here as a means of letting one another know where each is coming from. For example, Kevin and Tracy are at odds over their relationship with Tracy's parents. Kevin wants more distance. Tracy likes things the way they are (quite close). In a structured exchange, each is instructed to calmly state his or her position and to give reasons for it. Another kind of structured interaction that may prove helpful is a reenactment of an instance of the conflict (e.g., a quarrel). Reenactments can often enhance family members' understanding of their motives, beliefs, and feelings associated with a conflict. During or following the reenactment, the practitioner can ask the clients to say what they were thinking or feeling at particular points.

- *Generate alternative ways for resolving conflict.* One approach is to use brainstorming (Osborn 1963) in which participants are asked to generate numerous alternatives without initially considering the quality of the choices. Then the most promising alternative is selected. Although brainstorming may produce creative solutions and may add humor to the process, it may not be the best choice for all circumstances. In many situations there may be only two or three viable alternatives, which are quickly recognized. It may be more productive to pursue these often complex alternatives in depth than to have clients spawn a number of possibilities that may be off the mark. When clients are unable to generate alternative solutions acceptable to one another, the practitioner may suggest one or more possibilities. Also draw on your own expert knowledge or clinical experience to offer possible solutions that may not have occurred to clients.

- *Offer concessions and exchanges to resolve conflict.* Unless they do so on their own, ask clients, in turn, to indicate concessions or exchanges they would be willing to make to reach a solution. A concession involves the client's giving up a previous demand. An exchange is an offer to do something for something in return. The something in return may be a concession or another behavior. If concessions or exchanges are offered but an impasse continues, use what has been offered to develop and propose a solution for the clients to consider. Also, you may conduct individual caucuses with each client alone to explore the client's position and the kind of concessions or exchanges the client is willing to make (Donahue 1996).

- *Plan implementation of the solution agreed on.* Most solutions (including many that may appear to be relatively straightforward) require some planning. Determining when the task is to be carried out is of particular importance.
- *Implement the solution.*

Tasks for Problems and Contexts   As noted earlier, problems presented by families are often an outgrowth of some larger difficulty, which can be seen as part of the *context* of the problem. A useful strategy in work with families is to develop tasks addressed both to the target problem itself as well as to the contextual factors that may be feeding the problem. For example, the target problem may concern quarreling between Alice and her teenage daughter, Jenny. Tasks directed at the quarreling itself may involve Alice and Jenny working on communication skills and conflict resolution using the task plans outlined above. But it is also apparent that the relationship between mother and daughter has deteriorated to the point that little positive interaction occurs between them. Alice makes a point of avoiding contact, spending most of her leisure time alone in her room or with friends. Alice regards Jenny as a "lost cause" and sees her own role with her largely in terms of trying to keep her out of trouble. The degraded relationship as a whole forms a central feature of the problem context. Since neither have much respect or affection for the other, minor issues tend to escalate into major conflicts, replete with name calling and followed by long periods of not speaking to each other, which, in turn, further degrade their relationship. Another set of tasks might then be directed to improving the general quality of interaction between them. In the session, Alice and Jenny might be asked what they once enjoyed doing together, which might provide some leads for shared tasks involving mutually enjoyable activities. In session interactions in which they try to identify positive aspects about each other or in which they both reveal their thoughts about the relationship and how it might be improved might set the stage for tasks at home, such as having periods of friendly "talk time" or each agreeing to try to change a behavior that irritates the other.

8.1.2 ELICITING AGREEMENT TO PERFORM TASKS

In work with families, obtaining explicit agreement from all task participants is important. In reciprocal tasks, it is helpful, as noted previously, if each participant agrees to complete his or her task even if the other fails to do so or at least to give the other a second chance. With such a commitment from both participants, the tasks are less likely to fail on such grounds as, "Jack didn't do his part so I didn't do mine." Although securing task agreement may occur at this point, it may be deferred until after the next step, when details of the task have been worked out.

8.1.3 PLANNING DETAILS OF IMPLEMENTATION

In some cases, especially if the task is relatively simple, any necessary planning will have been done during the process of generating alternatives. Often, however, you will need to make sure that sufficient details are clarified so that family members know what they are to do, and how. There is evidence that such preparation can make a difference in whether family members will carry out tasks developed in the session (Reid 1994).

How much detailed planning is required will depend not only on the task but also on the family's need for structure. As deShazer (1982) has pointed out, some families do better if the plan is more general; others want a blueprint. How the family does with the first task can often provide clues about how much planning should be done on the second. As with generating alternatives, planning may proceed through either a practitioner-led discussion or through face-to-face communication among family members.

Whatever method is used, make sure that the plan is adequately developed. (For discussion purposes, we will assume that you are working with a family that needs an average amount of structure.)

Planning is the most challenging when tasks involve two or more family members, as in shared and reciprocal tasks. In shared tasks, clarifying each participant's task may be helpful, especially when the task calls for unfamiliar activities that need to be coordinated. For example, if Mrs. Adair's adult children agree to explore care facilities for their mother, it may be worthwhile to clarify possible divisions of labor. Even a shared task that appears fairly simple, such as a couple's agreement to have dinner out, may merit some discussion. Where might they go? When? Such inquiries can help put in concrete form what may be a nebulous good intention or at least stimulate the participants' thinking about the task. As a result, the task may have a greater chance of being implemented.

In helping families plan reciprocal tasks, make sure the participants are clear about what is to be exchanged, how, and when. Suppose that Kevin, who does freelance work at home, agrees to make sure that the front room is clear of the children's toys when Marla, his wife, comes home from work. In exchange, Marla agrees to be pleasant and chatty when she comes home (rather than sullen and silent).

In respect to this task, the following might be clarified: (1) Does Kevin know when to expect Marla, or will Marla let him know if she is coming home early or late? (2) Do the children's "toys" mean all their possessions—clothes, food, and so forth? (3) What might be some examples of a pleasant greeting? (4) Who is to make the first move, and when?

As the example suggests, try to pinpoint contingencies that may affect the plan, the manner in which tasks are to be done (presumably in a way the other will find acceptable), and when and how the tasks are to be initiated. Even though clients may not do the tasks in the way planned, the process prepares them for what to expect, helps them to be prepared for unforeseen possibilities, and reinforces the importance of what they have agreed to do.

Role playing or guided practice are often useful as a means of preparing clients for performing tasks. In individual treatment, role plays for this purpose are confined to the practitioner and client (see section 4.1.5). In family treatment, many more possibilities are available. For example, in successive role plays the practitioner may first demonstrate a skill with one partner, and then with the other. The partners can then practice the skills in another session task, with the practitioner providing feedback. Family members themselves can serve as models in role plays designed to help other members prepare for tasks. For example, a father may model in a role play how he might respond to a teacher with whom his son is having difficulty. The teacher may be role played by the son. In the next role play, the son can demonstrate his use of his dad's responses in a role play in which he plays himself and the father plays the teacher.

8.1.4 ESTABLISHING RATIONALES AND INCENTIVES

Family members need to perceive their tasks as furthering the solution to problems that they have agreed exist. They also need to see the tasks as being equitable.

A rationale may be difficult to establish if clients are reluctant participants to begin with. In respect to families, reluctance may involve the family as a unit or individual members who are being "dragged in" to treatment by other members. The unwilling member of an otherwise willing family presents an issue special to family treatment. Often these reluctant members are children whom the parents wish to change. The children may be unwilling to take on tasks or only give the tasks minimal effort because they see them as solving someone else's problems.

In some cases, recalcitrant children can be helped to see how the problem is important to them. For example, through discussion with the practitioner they may see the consequences of continuing to miss classes. A tangible incentive to attend classes (extra privileges; money or tokens that can be cashed in for a reward) may be useful. Because such incentives may be less desirable than intrinsic motivation and because parents (and siblings) may have objections, you might first see if the child will do the task without them. Finally, children may be more willing to do something about "imposed" problems if action is being taken on problems in which they have a greater investment. For example, Derek may try harder in school if he sees Mom making an effort not to favor an older sibling.

A family member who sees his or her task as equitable *perceives* it to be reasonable in relation to the efforts of other family members. Tasks do not need to have the same exact weight on some scale of fairness. Family members have their own views of equity, involving complex considerations of who owes what to whom (Boszormenyi-Nagy and Ulrich 1981). However, concerns about equity may arise if one family member winds up with most of the tasks or if tasks fall mainly on family members who may already perceive themselves as doing more than their fair share.

8.1.5 SIMULATING THE TASK WITH STRUCTURED IN-SESSION ACTIVITIES

The basic methods of task simulation used in the model—rehearsal, role play, and guided practice—were set out in Section 4.1.5 and are used as described there in sessions with individual family members. When family members are seen together, these methods tend to be integrated into in-session task planning and work on tasks. For this reason they have discussed as a part of these activities (Sections 8.1.1 and 8.1.3).

8.1.6 ANTICIPATING AND RESOLVING OBSTACLES

In task-centered treatment of both families and individuals, obstacles to task completion are first anticipated and dealt with *before* the task has been attempted and then, if need be, worked on again *following* task performance. Although we focus on the anticipation phase in this section, most of what we say can also be applied to working through obstacles that arise after a task has been attempted.

In anticipating obstacles, queries about what might go wrong are asked of family members present. More specifically, you might ask clients how they might respond if certain likely contingencies were to happen. In one case, for example, Phil, a teenage boy who was living with his mother, wanted to spend more time with his father, whom he saw only occasionally. He and his mother brainstormed some possibilities in a session task. Phil thought that inviting his father to a forthcoming basketball game would be the best idea and agreed to ask him as a task. Among the questions the practitioner asked was, "What if your dad says he can't go?" By enabling the client to anticipate likely obstacles, as was done in the example, the practitioner can help broaden the client's range of responses to possible contingencies. In the present case, Phil was able to suggest alternative proposals in the event his dad did not want to (or could not) attend the game with him. Family members can also be invited to suggest what they think might go wrong with the task. Birchler and Spinks (1981) have found this procedure especially useful when the task may be sabotaged by a family member.

Types of obstacles of particular concern in family treatment are (1) beliefs that family members have about themselves, one another, or the world; and (2) patterns of family interaction. Family members' views of one another's capacities, characteristics, and intentions may work to block task performance. A wife who thinks her husband is incapable of setting limits for their daughter is likely to interfere prematurely if he falters in a limit-setting task. A husband who sees his wife as the cause of their financial problems may be reluctant to complete a task that assumes he shares some of the responsibility. Parents who believe that a teacher is mistreating their son may be at risk of failing a task that calls for them to cooperate with the teacher. If it seems likely that family members hold beliefs that may stand in the way of the task, you may wish to explore the nature of these beliefs and to help family members modify those that appear to be unreasonable or ill-founded. The process has been described as *cognitive restructuring*, a basic method of cognitive therapy that has been adapted to work with families (Robin, Bedway, and Gilroy 1994; Dattilio 1998).

In task-centered family practice, there are two basic approaches to cognitive restructuring. One is to use in-session conversations among family members as a means of resolving misperceptions. Frank, a depressed and unemployed man living at home with his parents, was reluctant to assume his fair share of household tasks, because he believed his parents wanted him to "make up" for his deficiencies by doing work around the house. He resented this "demand," especially since he believed that such duties had not been expected of his older siblings who had already left home. The practitioner asked Frank and his parents to discuss this issue. In the ensuing conversation, the parents reminded Frank of the household responsibilities his siblings had in fact carried out and (at the instigation of the practitioner) reassured him that they were happy with his efforts to find a job and were not trying to make him compensate for anything. Frank agreed that perhaps he had over-reacted and eventually agreed to do at least some of the chores.

Lila's anger toward her mother, Joyce, was interfering with their success at implementing "mutually enjoyable" shared tasks aimed at strengthening their relationship. Some exploration revealed that a good deal of Lila's resentment was based on her belief that her mother had deserted her father to marry her present husband (Lila's stepfather). Joyce broke in to state vehemently that this was not the case. At the practitioner's suggestion, they agreed to discuss the breakup of the marriage. Joyce related very convincingly a story of physical abuse at the hands of Lila's father, a story she had never told Lila. The result was the beginning of a softening of Lila's attitude toward her mom and greater success in doing the shared tasks.

The second approach is based on practitioner-client interchanges. The social worker targets a dysfunctional belief and helps the client develop a better alternative through questions and commentary (Boyd-Franklin and Bry 2000). The practitioner may ask the client to consider the evidence for or against the belief, the quality of the evidence, or alternative ways of viewing the phenomena reflected by the belief (Kuehlwein 1998). For example, Hal thought Betty should prepare dinner after they both get home from work since to do so is part of the "woman's role," and he did other things, such as house repairs. (Betty was quick to add that "house repairs and other things" were few and far between in their rented apartment.) Nevertheless, Hal was unwilling to accede to her wish that they work together to prepare the evening meal (a suggested task for him). The practitioner asked him to talk about his conception of the "woman's role" in the home. Hal presented a traditional view of the man as the breadwinner, house repairer, and the like, and the woman as the homemaker, nanny, and so on. The practitioner wondered if that notion applied completely in his case since Betty was also a breadwinner, who worked as many hours as Hal did and made almost as much money. After some discussion, Hal agreed to pitch in on the cooking as long as Betty was working, which he saw as temporary—perhaps making only a modest amendment to his belief but one sufficient to remove the obstacle to task involvement.

Common types of dysfunctional beliefs in family practice include dubious assumptions about "proper" roles of family members (as in the example above), misreading causes of behavior (e.g., interpreting silence as anger when other explanations are more plausible), exaggerations of negative characteristics of another ("He *never* does what he is told"), and convictions that minor incidents will have disastrous consequences or "ruination," as Robin, Bedway, and Gilroy (1994) have aptly put it ("If I can't see Jim on Saturday, he'll find someone else and that will be the end of our relationship!") Dysfunctional beliefs may be shared—and mutually reinforced—by particular family members or by an entire family.

Often tasks are directed at change in problems that are outcroppings of patterns of interaction occurring in relation to such dimensions as control, intrusiveness, alliance, and boundary, considered earlier. The interactive pattern may present a formidable obstacle to either the success of the task or problem change. A single mother and her teenage daughter are at odds over the daughter's involvement with a particular young man. This conflict constitutes the target problem, but exploration of the context has suggested a pattern of a controlling mother and a rebellious daughter. The issue of the boyfriend is a problem that is representative of this larger struggle. Tasks may need to be adjusted accordingly. Thus a task for the mother to "stay out" of her daughter's plan to take her boyfriend to an upcoming party may fail because of the mother's need to control. Tasks that enable the mother to exert some degree of influence yet enable the daughter to retain some measure of autonomy might have a greater chance of success. For example, the daughter might be asked to bring her boyfriend home so that her mother could meet him.

8.1.7 SUMMARIZING TASKS

As in individual treatment, summarization consists of repeating all tasks at the end of the session. If tasks are numerous, complex, or involve several family members, a written record like the Task Review Sheet can be helpful. (Practitioners may want to have a supply of selfcarbonating paper on hand or quick access to a copier so that copies can be made for participating members and the practitioner.)

8.1.8 REVIEWING TASK PROGRESS

In family practice, as in individual treatment, tasks are reviewed at the beginning of each session. Reviews take advantage of the presence of different family members who can corroborate or challenge one another's reports of how tasks went. This advantage becomes a disadvantage, however, when family members, acting collusively, distort reports of task progress. This situation is most likely to occur with nonvoluntary clients who may try to give a false impression of progress to meet the requirements of a court mandate. Thus if parents, in order to get their children back, are under pressure to demonstrate that they are no longer abusing drugs, it is not surprising that they may inflate the progress they are making. In such cases, additional evidence may be required to determine task progress—for example, verification from a substance abuse center—if, in fact, demonstration of progress is to be used to meet a mandated requirement. This kind of external verification should be set up at the beginning of the case as a standard procedure rather than introduced when clients are suspected of being deceptive.

But such situations are fortunately exceptions. In reviews of task progress, as in other components of the model, the practitioner proceeds on a collaborative basis in which the client's accounts are presumed to be valid. In this process, family members can often be used to verify one another's accounts of how tasks have gone.

Another aspect of task review unique to family practice concerns tasks involving more than one participant—for example, shared and reciprocal tasks. Although the efforts of all participants may be reviewed together, the task progress of each is recorded separately as a way of capturing sometimes considerable differences in the performances of each.

Finally, original tasks may be considerably modified or even replaced by family members. Such "reinventions" (Rogers and Shoemaker 1971) are perhaps more common in family practice than in individual treatment. (For an example of a reinvented task, see section 8.2.0 below, "Revising Unsuccessful Tasks.")

8.1.9 Reviewing Target Problems

As in task reviews, the practitioner's review of change in problems takes advantage of the input from the different family members present. Family members often volunteer their impressions of change; if not, their impressions can be elicited. In some cases, family members are asked to track changes in problems in logs or charts or to complete rapid assessment devices. If so, such material is gone over with discussion of the results.

8.1.10 Checklist for the Task Planning and Implementation Sequence

> ___ 1. Did I use all the TPIS activities?
> ___ 2. Which were not used?
> ___ 3. How could I have used those that I didn't?
> (The checklist in 4.1.10 also can be applied to a family case.)

8.1.11 Exercise for the Task Planning and Implementation Sequence

Apply the exercise in 4.1.11 to a family case.

8.2.0 Revising Unsuccessful Tasks

Whether a task is to be considered "unsuccessful" depends on its impact on the target problems. Some tasks are dutifully carried out as planned but have little impact. In other cases, the original task may be altered considerably by the clients. Such "reinvented" tasks are likely to occur more often in family treatment than in individual treatment because of the effects of family interaction on the task plan. For example, in one case a father's task was to give his son driving lessons if his son completed his homework assignments during the week. The son completed his task but the father, busy with different projects, delegated the driving instructions to his daughter, which worked out fine as far as the son was concerned. Although the father technically "failed" the task, the result was satisfactory to the son. In recording the task progress, an explanation rather than a simple rating is needed. More important, the practitioner's response to such successful reinventions should usually be positive and reinforcing. Creative problem solving by clients should be encouraged even if it departs from original task plans. (For basic techniques for revising unsuccessful tasks, see section 4.2.0.)

Sometimes unsuccessful tasks need to be revised in response to obstacles (see section 8.1.6). Modification may be indicated if the obstacle cannot be adequately resolved or if the resolution suggests a different course of action

8.2.1 CHECKLIST FOR REVISING UNSUCCESSFUL TASKS

___ 1. Did the problem occur because the task was not implemented or because the task did not have the desired effect on the target problem?

___ 2. If the task was not implemented, was it because expectations were unclear, opportunities did not arise, unanticipated obstacles occurred, or motivation was insufficient?

___ 3. Did the revision of the task take into account the reason for the failure to implement the task?

___ 4. If the task was implemented but did not have the desired impact on the problem, what other tasks are needed? What other systems should be involved?

___ 5. Did the family "reinvent" a task that was successful? If so, did I sufficiently reinforce this activity?

8.2.2 EXERCISE FOR REVISING UNSUCCESSFUL TASKS

Apply the exercise in 4.2.2 to a family case.

8.3.0 Consistent Nonperformance of Tasks

As with individuals, we occasionally encounter families that consistently do not perform tasks. Sometimes this behavior occurs because the family is achieving sufficient progress by means of work in the session. Thus the first issue to consider when families do not perform tasks is whether this is a matter for concern. In most cases, tasks are of some importance even when families work diligently during sessions. This is because tasks are the means by which progress in the office is transferred to the natural environment. This should be discussed frankly with the families.

When a family does not work productively either in or out of sessions, it is likely that, like individuals, the family is not interested in changing the identified larger problems, family members have no desire to work with us, or the family does not wish to change anything. After the reason for nonperformance is identified, we proceed, as described in section 4.3.0, to identify new target problems, refer to another professional or agency, or terminate.

8.3.1 Checklist for Nonperformance of Tasks

__ 1. Is nonperformance of external tasks important with this family?
__ 2. Is the family not performing tasks because the selection of target problems is inaccurate, it does not want our help, or it does not want help from anyone?
__ 3. Have the appropriate corrective actions been taken: retargeting of problems, referral, or termination?

8.3.2 Exercise for Consistent Nonperformance of Tasks

Apply the exercise in 4.3.2 to a family case.

8.4.0 Nontargeted Problems: Restructuring

In both individual and family forms of task-centered practice the initial plan to work on a specified target problem is likely to undergo modification as the case proceeds (section 4.4.0). Such modifications are more likely to occur in family practice than in individual treatment and are likely to take a different form. Because the focus in family treatment is a multiperson system, more forces are at work to upset the original plan.

Some families are frequently beset by unexpected problems that need immediate attention. With such families an emergency may push the target problems to the background, at least in respect to the family's concern and motivation. In these situations the practitioner and family can usually devote part of the session to dealing with the emergency, still using a task-centered approach. The remainder of the session can then be spent on the original target problems (Rooney 1981). If the emergency is really the first sign of a major difficulty, it may lead to the formulation of a new target problem, perhaps replacing one that the family regards as less important.

However, responding to the "emergency of the week" or adding and dropping target problems with abandon is best avoided. Too much scatter will usually result in accomplishing little of substance. The wiser approach is to suggest that the family deal with the emergency on its own, especially when the problem is not too serious and the family has the capacity to deal with it. This will conserve time in the session for target problems that may be more serious and less amenable to being solved through the family's own resources.

8.4.1 CHECKLIST FOR NONTARGETED PROBLEMS

___ 1. Has the family mentioned any nontargeted concerns?
___ 2. Have I asked if they should be targeted and with what priority?
___ 3. Have I employed the necessary initial-phase activities: exploring, specifying, and goal setting? Have I revised the contract?

8.4.2 EXERCISE FOR NONTARGETED PROBLEMS

In a role play, the "family" presents an emergency. The practitioner attempts to deal with the emergency without making it a target problem. In addition, apply the exercise in 4.4.2 to a family.

8.5.0 USE OF TIME LIMITS

As with work with individuals, the use of time limits during the middle phase includes two activities: reminding clients of the number of remaining sessions and adjusting this number.

Requests for extensions probably occur less often in family cases than in individual ones. This is because family treatment is more likely than individual treatment to be self-limiting (see section 9.5.0).

Time limits may be used specifically to motivate reluctant family members to stay in treatment. For example, such a family member may be willing to stick with treatment to the end if the end is in sight. A reminder that only so many sessions are left may then provide, paradoxically, an impetus to continue.

8.5.1 CHECKLIST ON THE USE OF TIME LIMITS

___ 1. Am I reminding all families in each session of the number of interviews remaining?

___ 2. Do I have any families who would benefit from a concrete reminder, such as a calendar?

___ 3. Have I extended treatment or indicated that I would extend treatment when (a) the family was not performing tasks; or (b) no unresolved, targeted problem remained?

8.5.2 EXERCISE FOR USE OF TIME LIMITS

Practice of this skill can be included in any of the middle-phase role plays for work with families.

8.6.0 REVISING ASSESSMENTS

In section 4.6.0 we indicated the importance of revising assessments in work with individual clients, as well as some considerations that may guide such reassessments. All this applies to work with families. We might add that, if anything, continually revising assessments is even more critical in family practice. Families are more complex than individuals; our original assessments are more tentative; and greater amounts of information are likely to emerge as the case progresses. As tasks are tried out and obstacles encountered, new insights are gained about the family context. It becomes clear that Joan's antagonistic, rebellious behavior is being sustained in part by an alliance between her mother and a younger sister, both of whom use Joan as a scapegoat.

Sometimes these insights need to be checked out through sessions with individual family members or a family subsystem. In one case, for example, a brief session with the children produced convincing evidence that the father had a serious drinking problem. The problem had been hinted at, but effectively denied, in family interviews.

With the exception of work with children, direct observation of the client system is used to a greater extent in family work than in individual work. It often takes time for observation to detect interaction patterns or to isolate microevents (Metcoff and Whitaker 1982), which are specific interactive sequences in family sessions that "sum up" larger patterns. Not until the fourth session does it become apparent that mother tends to speak for her youngest child while deferring to her oldest one.

Repeated use of rapid assessment instruments can also reveal patterns. In one case, for example, repeated administration of the Dyadic Adjustment Scale (Spanier 1976) with the parents provided evidence that the parental alliance was becoming stronger, which served as a basis for involving the children in family sessions (Reid and Donovan 1990).

When a case management approach is used, a large amount of assessment data is gathered regularly in team meetings. The progress of a child in school or of a mentally ill client in a group care home can be tracked by information given by teachers and caretakers.

8.6.1 CHECKLIST FOR REVISING ASSESSMENTS

___ 1. What new information do I have about the family or family members? What does it mean in terms of intervention?

___ 2. What new information do I have about the target problems? What does it mean in terms of intervention?

___ 3. What new information do I have about the role of other systems on cause or maintenance of the target problems? What does it mean in terms of intervention?

___ 4. What new information do I have about the impact of the target problems on the other systems? What does it mean in terms of intervention?

8.7.0 ECLECTIC PRACTICE

The task-centered family practice model provides a framework for utilizing the contributions of a wide range of approaches to work with families. It draws most heavily on schools that Levant (1984) has referred to as "structure/process models"—problem-solving, communications, structural, strategic, and behavioral approaches. With their emphasis on here-and-now interactional and behavioral phenomena, they fit well with the basic orientation of TC. In addition, TC practitioners may draw from other models, for example, solution-focused (Berg 1997) and narrative (Freedman and Combs 1996).

Some of the contributions from these schools have been "written into" the model and have become an integral part of it. In this category are a number of behavioral methods, such as behavioral exchanges (reciprocal tasks) and communication training; also included are certain structural methods, such as tasks to bring about contextual change.

But a great variety of problems and methods are not accommodated by TC. The principle is to go as far as you can with what the model offers and then look elsewhere. Many approaches that fit neatly into the TC framework can be found in the family treatment literature. Tasks are widely used in many different approaches and under a variety of names: behavioral assignments, instigations, directives, homework, contracts, enactments, and so on. In fact, an advantage of using TC is that it provides a single concept for a large variety of action-oriented procedures, as well as a structure for making use of them.

You also will encounter situations that call for something other than TC or a cognate approach. For example, TC may not be the best approach to helping clients clarify their life goals. TC generalist practitioners are expected to make use of a broad treatment literature to do what is needed. Also, in applications to given populations, the TC practitioner may frequently encounter certain situations not covered by TC. For such situations it is possible to design modules that can be used when such situations arise. Thus, in applications of TC to work with the frail elderly, Naleppa and Reid (1998) developed a module for helping clients with problems of grief and loss. The model is designed to permit exits to other approaches and returns. "Task-centered" means what it says—that treatment is *focused* on tasks but not that tasks are the exclusive means of therapeutic effort.

8.7.1 Exercise for Eclectic Practice

Read an article or book chapter that discusses methods used in one of the following family treatment approaches: behavioral, structural, or strategic. Which interventions can be conceptualized as tasks, and how would you fit them into the present model?

8.8.0 Work with Collaterals

See sections 4.9.0 and 6.6.0.

8.9.0 TC With Special Populations

TC has been used with virtually all types of families that appear in any number in social work caseloads (Reid 1985). In this section we take up applications to two common and challenging family types: the single-mother family and the multicrisis family. (Applications of the model to culturally diverse families may be found in chapter 16.)

Single-Mother Family   The trend toward single-mother families has shown a marked increase over the past three decades. From 1990 to 1999 the increase in their numbers has been 19 percent, in contrast to only 2 percent for two-parent families. As the last century ended, 7 percent of all households were headed by single mothers (Department of

Commerce 2000). Moreover, families headed by single women are major and disproportionate consumers of social services (Reid and DuFresne 1985).

Such family structures are not necessarily dysfunctional. In fact, they can contain many positive elements, such as absence of conflict between adults living together and opportunities for children to master challenging responsibilities. Moreover, a number of studies based on large-scale survey data (National Survey of Families and Households) have suggested that family processes, such as parent-child interaction and parental conflict, are more important in explaining problems or well-being in children and adolescents than whether the family is one-parent or two parent (Kleist 1999). Some of the findings have dramatically challenged prevailing myths about single-parent families. For example, Amey and Albrecht (1998) found that African-American youths from single-parent families were *less likely* to use marijuana and alcohol than youths from two-parent families. It is perhaps better to think of single-mother families as being structured differently than two-parent families, rather than as being essentially inferior. With such a view in mind, one needs to consider both potential strengths (e.g., lack of daily adult conflict) as well as potential vulnerabilities (e.g., the concentration of child-rearing and breadwinning roles in one person).

Of particular concern to social workers are "high-risk," single-mother families (Pett 1982). The mothers of these families tend to have difficulties with their children, a cause of stress and a frequent reason for their contact with social agencies. They are often faced with an accumulation of environmental deprivations and hardships—social isolation, poor housing, bad neighborhoods, and low income. Overinvolvement with children and difficult relationships with ex-spouses and boyfriends are frequently part of the scene. Not surprisingly, such women often suffer from emotional difficulties, especially depression, which interact with other problems. The following are offered as guidelines in working with high-risk, single-mother families concerning children's problems—the most common presenting problems that these families bring to social agencies.

Initial Phase   The practitioner tries to help the mother identify interactional aspects of the problem with her children but at the same time is sensitive to the feelings of guilt and inadequacy the mother may have. In some cases, these feelings may lead to a self-defeating attitude; in others, they may cause the mother to adopt a defensive posture and to blame the child. In-session interactions in which the parent and child express their problems to each other (or act them out) may provide a means of highlighting interactive elements while avoiding excessive focus on the mother.

In exploring problems and their contexts, attention should routinely be given to circumstances of the divorce or separation (if such occurred recently), the mother's and children's current relationship with the father (if he is still in the picture), and the mother's support network. Such factors usually have a bearing on the target problem.

Middle Phase   Basic to the use of specific tasks is the general strategy of strengthening the mother's parental role. One frequently used approach is to help the mother improve her skills in coping with her child. In using these tasks, the practitioner draws on the extensive literature on parent training. Different forms of parent training can be used with a task-centered framework . Parent-training programs for a range of specific problems, such as conduct disorder, school refusal behavior, attention-deficit hyperactivity disorder (ADHD), and sibling conflict may be found in Briesmeister and Schaefer 1998.

In adapting parent-training approaches the practitioner, when possible, helps the mother learn and practice skills with the child in the session. Tasks to be carried out between sessions are designed for each skill. Skills include (1) informing the child clearly and explicitly which behaviors are acceptable and which are not; (2) giving the child reasons for desired behavior; (3) rewarding proper behavior, when it occurs, through praise or tangible rewards; (4) setting and following through with consequences for undesirable behaviors.

A form of parent training that may be particularly helpful for single mothers is planned activities training (PAT), which has been found to add to the effects of parent training alone (Harrold et al. 1992). Single mothers need to cope alone with a range of frequently occurring, and often troublesome, activities, such as shopping trips, meals, and bedtime routines. PAT is designed to help the mother learn to plan activities in advance and to anticipate likely trouble spots. Tasks involve instructing the child in the rules governing the activity and rewarding the child if the rules are followed. PAT can be used in place of, or in combination with, conventional parent training.

Single mothers often need help to deal with the stress and anger that arises from the solo parenting of difficult children. Vicious cycles may develop. Children exhibiting behavioral problems begin to create stress for the mother, which, in turn, leads to disruption of parenting. This then results in further discord and additional behavioral problems in the children (Bloomquist 1996). For that reason, anything that alleviates parental stress or anger would be potentially useful in breaking this downward spiral. Often mothers attribute negative motives to the child's misbehavior—the child is trying to spite her, is acting like his father, and so on.

Key tasks call for the mother to learn about the reasons for the child's provocative behavior and to respond to them. For example, she may discover that such factors as fatigue, hunger, or frustration may be prompting the negative behavior. With such knowledge she may be able to react less angrily and to take action to meet the child's needs.

Another kind of task sequence, one that may be particularly useful with an older child, involves rule making. A common contextual feature in single-mother families is the mother's lack of control over her children; power struggles may be occurring or the children may have taken charge. In this sequence, the mother and child(ren) negotiate rules in face-to-face interaction in the session. Rules may concern such matters as chores, bedtime, curfews, and sibling relations. Although rules may involve changes in the mother's behavior (e.g., giving the child a chance to comply before nagging), the mother is cast as the person in charge and her position of authority is strongly supported.

Additional task plans, which include parenting children with specific problems (e.g., post-traumatic stress, oppositional defiant disorders) and coping with sibling conflict have been developed (see Reid 2000). Although these task plans were designed for all parents, single mothers, who are raising children alone, may be in special need of such aids.

The breakdown of usual parent-child boundaries, as well as tendencies for single mothers to relate intrusively to their children, are frequently encountered obstacles. Mothers often become dependent on their children for companionship or use them as confidants. Intrusiveness may be accentuated by the sheer demand of having total responsibility for child care and by lack of social contacts or interests outside the home. Such obstacles can be addressed through task sequences that help mother and child develop independent interests. Exploration of the family's social network may reveal the possibility of outside friendships or activities that can be cultivated for both mothers and children. One study found that successful single mothers developed strong networking skills that fostered the development of new relationships for both parents and children (Morrison 1995). Finally, shared tasks involving siblings may serve to strengthen the sibling subsystem as a way of reducing involvement with the mother.

Another common issue concerns the mother's own distress or emotional needs. Mothers who feel guilty, deprived, under stress, or depressed may not be able to engage in tasks relating to problems with their children. In some cases, the mother's personal difficulties will become target problems; in others, they will intrude as obstacles to child problems. If target problems involve only the mother-child interaction, it is important to be clear about focus and to resist the temptation to slip into scattered and unproductive "therapy" for the mother's difficulties. Selected concerns may be dealt with as obstacles, but the relation of them to the target problem should be explicit. In one case, for example, a single mother's efforts to resolve problems with her daughter were complicated by the mother's relationship with her boyfriend, who would interfere with her disciplinary efforts. Although the relationship was fraught with difficulties that the practitioner might have explored, she chose to concentrate on the conflict over discipline, which resulted in a single and productive joint session involving the mother and the boyfriend. If the mother wishes to deal with her own difficulties in depth, they should become target problems in a considered decision with the mother.

The mother's and children's relationship with the children's father often extrudes either as sources of obstacles or as target problems. In such situations it is useful to view the mother, children, and father/ex-spouse as constituting a "post-divorce (or separation) family," one that may, in fact, be brought together in treatment to work on such issues as custody, support, and visitation (Everett, Nichols-Volgy, and Nichols 2000). Often, however, the father may be inaccessible or the mother does not want him involved. Thus, in the typical case, direct intervention efforts may be limited to the mother and children. Tasks for the mother might include communicating with the father directly rather than through the children, attempting to help the children maintain the best possible image of their father, and helping to maintain their relationship with the father and paternal relatives, negotiating issues with the father or using court mediation to resolve them (Donahue 1996; Emery, Kitzmann, and Waldron 1999), and cooperating with government agencies to secure child support. Children may need to be helped to avoid self-blame for the divorce or separation, to disengage from parental conflict, and to accept the loss of their father's not being in the home. Tasks might include efforts to initiate contact with "abandoning" fathers. Both mother and children might benefit from psychoeducational, support, and therapy groups. Parent groups can be located through the Parents Without Partners website, which also has links to chat rooms, literature, and other resources for single mothers. Many school systems have groups for children of divorced and separated families. A review of selected programs and their effectiveness can be found in Emery, Kitzmann, and Waldron 1999).

Termination   In termination with high-risk single mothers, a frequent issue has to do with ending at the agreed-on time or recontracting, often to focus on the client's personal concerns. Recontracting is an acceptable option in the model if specific problems can be identified as a basis for work and the client expresses a need to work on them. Recontracting becomes questionable if it is offered on the practitioner's perception of the client's need without problems having been identified and if the case is continued not to work toward explicit goals but rather to gratify dependency needs (either the client's or the practitioner's).

Vulnerable Multicrisis Family   In social work literature and practice various terms have been applied to families possessing a loose configuration of characteristics: poverty; multiple problems exhibited by the family as a whole or by individual members, which might relate to material inadequacies, substance abuse, children's behavioral difficulties, or child maltreatment; and repeated involvements with service systems but an unwillingness to change (at least in the eyes of service providers). Historically the term most frequently used to refer to such families has been *multiproblem* (Geismar and LaSorte 1964), and, indeed, these families were so labeled in the first edition of the present volume. Other terms for families possessing such characteristics have included *problem poverty families* (Janzen and Harris 1997), *families in perpetual crisis* (Kagan and Schlosberg 1989), *families in "extreme distress"* (Sharlin and Shamai 2000), *families who function in a "crisis mode"* (Boyd-Franklin and Bry 2000), and the *vulnerable multicrisis family* (Walsh 1998).

Although *multiproblem* is still used as a descriptor (Knei-Paz and Ribner 2000; McNeil and Herschell 1998), the shift in recent years has been toward terms such as *crisis* and *distress* that emphasize the family's experience of turmoil and pain. Although the change in language might strike some as yet another instance of addressing a social problem by renaming it, the new vocabulary has the merit, perhaps, of helping to sensitize practitioners to the formidable stressors these families must struggle with. The new vocabulary is also consistent with trends toward a less pathological view of such families and greater emphasis on family strengths and empowerment (Reid, in press; Walsh 1998; Weil 2000). For that reason, we will, following Walsh (1998), refer to the families as "multicrisis."

Whatever it is called and however defined, the multicrisis family has always presented a serious challenge for social work and, one might add, for the task-centered model. Indeed, a frequent question raised about TC is its applicability to this type of family. The emphasis in TC on time-limited service, client-acknowledged problems, practitioner-client collaboration, and client action as a medium of change strike some practitioners as ill suited to work with multicrisis families. However, a good deal of clinical literature (see, for example, Cunningham and Henggeler 1999; Sharlin and Shamai 2000; Walsh 1998; Wood and Geismar 1989) and evaluations of some TC projects (Rooney 1981; Katz 1981) not only fail to support the notion of a poor fit but even suggest that the model in some ways may be particularly useful with this population. As Walsh (1998:258) has observed, "Action-oriented, concrete problem-solving approaches work best with overloaded families."

Since the majority of multicrisis families are female-headed (Janzen and Harris 1997), practitioners may also make use of methods outlined above for work with single-mother families. Some specific applications of these methods will be noted.

Initial Phase   As Wood and Geismar (1989) point out, multicrisis families often come to the attention of social agencies because some community standard has been violated: child neglect, abuse, or delinquent behavior of the youngsters or adults. Thus the family may see the social worker's presence as an unwanted intrusion.

Practitioners who use TC need to recognize that they may have two functions in such cases: One is an investigative/monitoring function sanctioned by a community agency or court; the other is a service function that they hope will help the family make constructive changes (Katz 1981). Investigation and monitoring are used to introduce and activate the service function.

In the investigative/monitoring role, the practitioner presents reasons for appearing on the family's doorstep (practice with multicrisis families is typically carried out through home visits). In this process, the practitioner may need to refer in one way or another to the family's presumed difficulty in meeting community standards—not the most propitious way to begin a treatment relationship! But the basic question should still be: "How can I be of help?"

A next step is to explore the family's own views of its situation, its experiences with (often complaints about) social agencies, and to elicit and respond emphatically to the difficulties the family perceives, even if it sees your presence as its only problem. Most writers agree that hearing the family out, presenting it with choices, including the choice of rejecting your help, and avoiding power struggles is important (Cunningham and Henggeler 1999; Sharlin and Shamai 2000; Wood and Geismar 1989; Kagan and Schlosberg 1989; Rooney 1988, 1992; Janzen and Harris 1997). If the family is suspicious and skeptical (often based realistically on past experiences with agencies), try to recognize the basis for their concern. As Kagan and Schlosberg (1989) suggest, perhaps the most reassuring remark you can make to a suspicious family is "Don't trust us!"

In engaging multicrisis families it is essential to adopt a noncritical, nonconfronting attitude, even though you may think that the family's problems are its own doing (Cunningham and Henggeler 1999). To avoid blaming family members for offensive behavior, it helps to focus on the *meaning* of the behavior, for example, to view an act of child abuse as an expression of the parent's frustration rather than simply as harm to the child (Sharlin and Shamai 2000) Although it is important to identify the family's strengths and involve family members as partners (Weil 2000), this should be done while presenting yourself as an expert helper. Behavior that clients might see as inconsistent with that role, such as disclosing problems of your own that may be similar to the clients, may undermine your credibility (Cunningham and Henggeler 1999).

As noted, often multicrisis families do not seek help voluntarily. Because the task-centered model is premised on the existence of a collaborative relationship with the client, the practitioner seeks ways to enlist the cooperation of the family. Writing from a task-centered perspective, Rooney (1988, 1992) outlines different means of achieving this goal.

In an "agreeable mandate strategy," you try to fit the family's conception of the problem to the court's or your agency's requirements (the mandate). Abusing parents may blame the child but can agree that the child's behavior provokes them. They may be agreeable to accept the child's annoying behavior as a target problem, hardly an ideal formulation, but one that might serve as a basis for using some of the parent-training techniques discussed earlier. In some cases, the family's and practitioner's goals are the same—for example, the return of a child from foster care. The family may agree to make mandated changes in order to have the child returned.

Another strategy involves a quid pro quo. Here the practitioner agrees to help the family with its concerns, which often involves securing a concrete resource or advocating with the school, social agencies, and the like, on the client's behalf. In exchange, the family agrees to accept help for the mandated problem. Often the exchange is not explicit. By demonstrating helpfulness to the family, the practitioner is more likely to be seen as an ally rather than an enemy, and the family may be more willing to accept his or her help in other areas.

When all else fails, Rooney suggests that the target problem can be expressed as "getting rid of the mandate." The target problem becomes getting the court or even the practitioner off the family's back. In one task-centered case that used this strategy (Katz 1981) the family made tangible progress in correcting a problem of malnourishment in one of their children. At termination, the practitioner, instead of receiving the thanks he had expected for helping the family, was rather curtly ordered to leave by the father. As the case illustrates, families can make constructive changes even though their reasons for so doing may be, at least in part, to end their involvement with a social agency.

In pursuing these strategies, you may need to point out to the family the self-defeating consequences of refusing to agree to a contract. Because the practitioner may need to take action that may be adverse to the family's interests—for example, recommending removal of a child—a refusal to cooperate, in effect, denies the family the opportunity to influence the action the practitioner may take. Still, you need to emphasize the choices the family has. Even if the choice is between involvement with you and a possible jail term for a family member, it is still a choice, and this should be made clear. If the family refuses to agree to work on any target problems, you may need to remain active on the case in an investigative/monitoring capacity; what this entails should be made clear to the family.

Most families, if skillfully approached, will accept some form of service consonant with the mandate. If so, the process of targeting problems proceeds in the way previously described (section 8.4.0).

In some cases, the family may want help with too many problems all at once. As a rule, you would do well to prioritize a manageable number of problems of greatest concern to the family (usually no more than three) but to leave the door open for recontracting (see below). Practitioner flexibility (here and elsewhere) is always important, however. Several fairly specific concrete problems (e.g., getting phone service restored) may be handled simultaneously. In such cases, a second practitioner or case aide may be an asset. If problems are complex—e.g., behavioral difficulties, it may be best to work on one at a time, starting with relatively modest, attainable goals (McNeil and Herschell 1998; Walsh 1998).

In assessing problems and context try to identify resources, usually not an easy chore in the face of the many deficits such families have. Often reframing can be used to locate resources that may be embedded in what appears to be deficits. Thus the parents' anger at the school system for treating their child unfairly can be reframed as parental concern for the child. Although the anger may be excessive and an obstacle to be dealt with, the family, as well as the practitioner, may benefit by seeing its positive side.

Family functioning may be hampered by such structural deficits as a weak parental alliance (in the case of two-parent families), diffuse subsystem boundaries with children sometimes assuming parental roles, and lack of consistent rules. However, in work with multicrisis families, such structural features become of major concern only when they constitute clear obstacles to target problems. Resolving immediate issues in these families is demanding enough. Moreover, some apparent structural deficits, such as the "parentified" child, may turn out to be functional in important respects—for example, in providing needed assistance to an overstressed mother.

Assessment also usually requires attention to the families inadequacies in areas of tangible resources. A useful assessment device is one developed by Vosler (1990)—the Family Access to Basic Resources (FABR). It provides a comprehensive review of the family's concrete resources—income, housing, food, clothing, and so forth. Although its full administration is time-consuming, it can be used as a checklist for a rapid survey.

Typically assessment will include the family's multiple involvements with social agencies. Diagrammatic devices, such as Hartman and Laird's (1978) "eco-map," can provide useful displays of family-agency relationships. Information from other agencies may need to be obtained, especially from referral or mandating agencies.

Middle Phase   The middle phase generally consists of some combination of conjoint sessions with the family, usually conducted in the home, and work with organizations and others in the family's environment. Home visits are used because of the unwillingness or difficulty the family may have in making office visits. Because the family's investment in treatment is likely to be tenuous, you want to make it as easy as possible for the family to continue.

The home visit also facilitates informal interaction—for example, having something to eat with the family. An informal climate helps make the practitioner less forbidding and thus more acceptable to the family. Home visiting has its downside, however. Families can still miss appointments by not being at home when you arrive. Sessions may need to be conducted against a background of a blaring television set, crying babies, and squabbling children.

It is helpful to keep several considerations in mind in work with multicrisis families on problems and tasks. To begin with, you should make use of the clients own strengths and resources to the extent pos- sible. Although this principle should be used in any form of task- centered practice, it is especially important with multicrisis family members, given their characteristically low sense of self-efficacy and their need to make use of "everything they have" in order to survive. Empowerment can take simple forms, such as noting a mother's orga- nizational ability in getting her three children off to school in the morn- ing (Sharlin and Shimai 2000).

Focus should be maintained on agreed-on target problems, if at all possible. Because families tend to function in a "crisis mode" (Boyd- Franklin and Bry 2000), other issues are likely to intrude. Such emer- gencies of the moment should be given only so much attention as is strictly necessary to enable the family to cope with them, and attention should be redirected to the target problems (Rooney 1981). As McNeil and Herschell (1998:262) point out, "If we were to try to deal with each new problem, little else would be accomplished." In some situa- tions, retargeting problems may be unavoidable. An emergency may be of such magnitude that work on the original problems cannot effec- tively proceed unless it is adequately dealt with (see also section 8.4.0, "Nontargeted Problems: Restructuring").

Information about potential external resources that may help the family is critical. The practitioner should bring to bear knowledge of agency and community resources and be able to help families brain- storm additional possibilities (Boyd-Franklin and Bry 2000). Such re- sources may include the extended family, neighbors, friends, and churches. For example, in one family a six-year-old boy was persist- ently absent because the mother was afraid of sending him on a long trek to school through a dangerous inner-city neighborhood. Some brainstorming about resources revealed that a nearby neighbor had older children who went to school at the same time. The neighbor was agreeable to have her children accompany the child on their way to school. This arrangement, with which the mother felt comfortable, led to a resolution of the attendance problem. Often the practitioner must undertake tasks to help the client secure resources, tasks that might include advocacy with community agencies and organizations.

Task plans often involve helping parents improve their functioning with children, especially in cases involving suspected or actual abuse or neglect. Use can be made of parent-training and rule-making approaches outlined earlier for work with single-mother families.

Multicrisis families are often involved simultaneously with several service providers, especially in cases involving risk of child placement or permanency planning. In such cases, the cast of providers might include a caseworker from the local department of social services, a school social worker, substance abuse and domestic violence counselors, a home-based prevention worker, a representative of a foster care placement agency, and a mental health practitioner (Bundy-Fazioli 2001). An understanding of issues and methods relating to interagency and interprofessional collaboration is extremely helpful (Payne 2000). Desirable as it might be generally, close collaborative relationships might not be possible or even essential in all situations. In one case, for example, a student intern was able to use task-centered methods to help a nine year old, Annette, cope with a chaotic family situation and improve her academic skills. These goals were achieved while a total of five other service providers were involved with the family regarding a variety of problems, including the mother's drug addiction, domestic violence, financial assistance needs, and an older sibling's delinquent behavior. For the intern's purposes, it was sufficient to know what was happening in the family. A high degree of collaboration with other providers (while certainly desirable) was not critical and, in any case, did not seem possible to achieve. However, when an overall plan is required, such as a permanency plan for children, then a high degree of collaboration between service providers is essential.

Termination   In work with multicrisis families, brief service approaches with preplanned end points can facilitate the engagement of the family. Reluctant to accept any service, the family may be more willing to contract for a limited number of sessions than to become involved in an open-ended relationship. But is a brief period of service adequate for such families? A way of answering this question is provided by Wood and Geismar (1989:121):

> It is not reasonable to expect most severely troubled multi-problem families, beset by environmental inadequacies as well as whatever internal problems may exist, to totally resolve or even to appreciably ameliorate all their compounded problems in a very short time span. But the urgency of their problems and the threat of community action weigh as heavily on the practitioner as on the family, creating a pressure for rapid resolution.

As Wood and Geismar suggest, the practitioner needs to distinguish between full-scale rehabilitation of the multicrisis family and what is needed and doable in the short run. Achieving far-reaching changes with such families is unrealistic as a rule, although exceptional cases can always be found. A more realistic goal is helping the family to ameliorate immediate problems, including whatever occasioned the referral. Short-term treatment may be the most efficient and, for the family, the least threatening means of achieving such goals. The social worker should expect that, in many cases, additional episodes of service will be needed for future problems. Practitioners assume that the family's motivation for change is typically "crisis bound" and that treatment reaches a point of diminishing returns quite rapidly.

Educating community referral sources accordingly is advisable. Given the enormity of the family's problems, the referring agency may expect that a treatment should be for the long term.

In some cases, of course, longer periods of service are needed. Brief treatment may not be sufficient to modify even the immediate problems, or the duration of a case may be controlled by a goal that may take some time to reach, such as the return of a child from foster care. Recontracting for additional periods of service is often used with multicrisis families, even though extending service may be successful in only a minority of these cases. Now and then extended work is quite rewarding. A case reported by Rooney (1981) and summarized in section 5.6.0 is one such example.

8.9.1 Exercise for TC with Special Populations

Read an article or book chapter about another special type of family, for example, a minority family or a blended family. What modifications in TC would you make with this type of family?

9

TERMINATION AND CASE ILLUSTRATIONS

9.0.0 COMPONENTS OF TERMINATION

In section 5.0.0 we described the five basic components of termination in work with individuals: (1) final problem review; (2) reinforcement of accomplishments; (3) future plans; (4) problem-solving skill review; and (5) reactive discussion. In this section we elaborate on special features of those components that occur in termination with families.

9.1.0 THE FINAL PROBLEM REVIEW

As would be expected, the final problem review involves eliciting opinions about problem change from all family members present. To save time, questions can be asked of the family as a group rather than of each family member individually. Discrepancies in views of change can be pursued in more detail with those family members holding divergent perceptions. Each family member notes each problem on the scale described in section 5.1.0, and may also complete one or more rapid assessment instruments. When parents have been seen apart from the children during treatment, the problem review can be conducted in two stages: a brief interview with the parents alone concerning the issues discussed only with them, followed by a review either with the children alone or with the family as a whole concerning other problems. In some situations, separate reviews with different family combinations—for example, parents, then children; one spouse, then the other—might be indicated if it is thought that clients might find it difficult to be frank if the entire family is seen together. For instance, in one case involving physical abuse of the children by the father, it was decided to have a separate review with the children since it was thought that they could be more open about the issue if seen alone. When family members are seen separately for certain purposes, it is important to bring the family together to consider aspects of termination that might affect the family as a whole. Generally, all family members who have been seen in treatment should be present at the close of the termination interview.

When a case management approach has been used (section 6.6.0) a problem review can be conducted during the final case management meeting. The review is limited to the problems dealt with by the case management team, for example, the children's difficulties in school. Such reviews have the advantage of bringing to bear information on problem change from a variety of sources. Such a review also provides the opportunity for interchange among participants who can help sort out the nature of the changes that have occurred and the remaining work to be done. Issues internal to the family can be reviewed in the final family session.

9.1.1 CHECKLIST FOR THE FINAL PROBLEM REVIEW

___ 1. Did all family members present contribute to the problem review?
___ 2. Did all family members rate outcome for each problem?
___ 3. Did I secure data on problem change from relevant collaterals?

9.1.2 EXERCISE FOR FINAL PROBLEM REVIEW

See section 9.3.2 for an exercise combining practice on final problem reviews with other termination activities.

9.2.0 REINFORCEMENT OF ACCOMPLISHMENTS

In terminal family sessions not only is it important that you reinforce the family members' accomplishments, as described in section 5.2.0, but family members should reinforce the accomplishments of one another—especially parents in giving children deserved praise. If this does not occur naturally, you can prompt family members (Mr. D, what do you think of Larry's progress in school?) or structure a session task in which family members comment on one another's attainments. The same principle applies to final case management team meetings. Team members especially should acknowledge the contribution of family members.

9.2.1 CHECKLIST FOR REINFORCEMENT OF ACCOMPLISHMENTS

__ 1. Did I praise family members for their contributions?
__ 2. Did I help family members praise one another?
__ 3. Did I acknowledge the help of collaterals and (if present with the family at the final meeting) did they credit the family for whatever successes it achieved?

9.2.2 EXERCISE FOR REINFORCEMENT OF ACCOMPLISHMENTS

See section 9.3.2 for practice of this skill.

9.3.0 FUTURE PLANS

As in individual treatment, families are engaged in planning how changes in problems will be maintained or even extended after termination. In addition, with families, plans for maintaining contextual changes should also be discussed. For example, Don's stealing, as well as his conflict with his sister, may have abated in large part because of a strengthening of the parental alliance and better communication and coordination between the parents in handling their children's problems. Such changes may be difficult to achieve and maintain, since they may involve shifts in entrenched patterns of interaction. Yet such changes may be vital to durable resolution of a range of specific problems.

When a case management approach is used, planning for the future involves all members of the case management team, including clients. For example, what can the parents, teachers, and school social worker do to help Mike continue to do passing work? The team meeting structure enables face-to-face joint planning between clients and collaterals.

9.3.1 CHECKLIST FOR FUTURE PLANS

> __ 1. Do I know how the family plans to maintain or extend accomplishments for each target problem?
> __ 2. Did I specifically discuss how contextual changes could be maintained?
> __ 3. Is the family aware that it can return for help?
> __ 4. Were collaterals appropriately involved in planning for the future?

9.3.2 EXERCISE FOR FINAL PROBLEM REVIEW, REINFORCING ACCOMPLISHMENTS, AND FUTURE PLANS

Apply the exercise in section 5.3.2 for a terminal interview with a family.

9.4.0 REVIEW OF PROBLEM-SOLVING SKILLS

The practitioner attempts to highlight critical skills used by family members during treatment and, as in work with individuals, to go over examples of how they contributed to problem resolution. Here, the practitioner should keep in mind the variety of possible problem-solving strategies that families may employ (6.2.0), including those the family may have unconsciously used. In one case, for example, a couple tended to use humor to reduce tension. Although the practitioner had encouraged them to use humor for this purpose, it had never been identified as a problem-solving mechanism. In the final session it was so identified, leading to a discussion of how the couple might use it more effectively.

When skills involve family communication, session tasks can often serve to identify particular skills and give family members the chance to demonstrate progress they have made. Family members are asked to discuss a specific issue with instructions to use particular skills. (Because it is the last session, the issue should not be a toxic one.) You can then identify the skills used in the task, giving family members appropriate praise for their use.

Attention should be given to helping clients learn to generalize skills learned during the course of treatment. Generalization is often associated with the ending phase of treatment and, for that reason, is being considered in this section, but, in fact, attention to generalization needs to be built into family treatment from the onset. If that has been the case, generalization of skills should be reinforced and extended in the termination interview.

As Fortune (2002) suggests, generalization can be facilitated through three processes. The first is to learn general principles about applying the skill, for example, the rationale for using "I" statements. A second concerns the transfer of skills from the treatment session to natural environments. In task-centered family work, communication, conflict resolution, and other skills may be first learned and practiced in the session. The transfer to the natural environment then occurs through tasks. However, in some cases, families may make apparent progress through in-session learning and practice. Consequently insufficient emphasis may be given to follow-through at home. Obviously the corrective for this is to stress tasks outside the session throughout treatment. When tasks have involved use of behavioral methods such as reinforcement and relaxation to treat problems of individual family members, the practitioner should begin to shift to self-management forms of these methods before the terminal interview (Luiselli 1998). A third method of generalization involves extending skills learned to new situations. For example, if a mother has used Parent Activity Training to cope with getting her child to bed, she might apply skills learned to shopping trips or other difficult situations. As new situations are mastered, the skill in general becomes more thoroughly learned.

The foregoing suggests that generalization must start at the beginning of treatment and not be left to its end. If generalization of critical skills seems questionable as treatment approaches its agreed on end point, the practitioner and family may wish to consider devoting what might normally be the final session to work on generalization and reschedule the termination interview to allow family members to work on skill generalization.

9.4.1 CHECKLIST FOR REVIEW OF PROBLEM-SOLVING SKILLS

__ 1. Did I identify and reinforce problem-solving skills used by the family?
__ 2. Did all family members participate in the discussion?

9.4.2 EXERCISE FOR REVIEW OF PROBLEM-SOLVING SKILLS

See the exercise in section 9.5.2.

9.5.0 REACTIVE DISCUSSION

In work with families, termination is, in some respects, simpler than in work with individuals; in other respects, it is more complex. It is simpler in the sense that the practitioner-client relationship usually is less intense than in individual treatment and hence easier to end. The problem of the client becoming dependent on the practitioner is less likely to occur in family treatment, since family members are able to continue their patterns of dependency with one another. Also, in family treatment relatively less attention is given to the clients' emotionally charged personal problems, making it less likely for the client to develop a transference reaction—for example, to view the practitioner as a parent figure. All this, of course, is relative. The here-and-now focus and time-limited structure of the model provide control for such problems in both individual and family treatment.

But termination is more complicated in the sense that ending must be arranged for a group of clients who may vary in their readiness to stop or in their need for further help. This type of issue is less likely to arise in time-limited than in open-ended treatment because of the continually reinforced expectation that service will end at an agreed-on point. But the issue does arise.

In one variation, family members disagree about the need for additional family sessions. One way to handle such a disagreement is to have family members discuss their differences in the session and try to resolve them. If this does not settle the matter, you can offer a specified number of additional sessions to work on specific issues. Alternatively you can suggest that the family attempt on its own to work on remaining problems for a set period (e.g., a month). At the end of this period another family session will be held to evaluate progress and to determine if further work is necessary.

In another scenario, one family member expresses the need to continue in individual treatment to deal with personal concerns. In some cases, these may be unrelated to the family problems that have been embarked on. In other cases, these concerns may be related to family problems but family treatment cannot be continued. For example, a marital problem has not been resolved during an eight-session contract, but the husband does not want an extension. The wife wishes to continue in order to reach a decision about whether to stay in the marriage. In either type of case, a new contract can be drawn for a specified number of sessions with the family member who wishes to continue.

When a case management approach is used, two terminal interviews may be needed. One involves the case management team and family, and brings to closure work on problems that the team has addressed. The other is with the family alone and focuses on whatever internal family concerns were dealt with in treatment; if none were discussed, this interview may be brief or omitted altogether.

9.5.1 CHECKLIST FOR REACTIVE DISCUSSION

__ 1. Did family members agree on termination? If members disagreed, how was it handled?

__ 2. Did I enable collaterals, either as part of a case management meeting or separately, to discuss their reactions to termination?

__ 3. Did I deal with my own reaction to termination?

9.5.2 EXERCISES FOR REVIEW OF PROBLEM-SOLVING
SKILLS AND REACTIVE DISCUSSION

Apply the exercises described in section 5.5.2 to a family case but build
in disagreement among family members about termination. Try to deal
with the disagreement.

9.6.0 CASE ILLUSTRATIONS

The following two cases illustrate the task-centered approach to work
with families. Both have been drawn from the Task-Centered Family
Treatment Project at the School of Social Welfare, University at Albany,
State University of New York.

The Garcias

The Garcias were referred by a local school to a community agency
serving Hispanic people. The Garcias had emigrated from Puerto
Rico two years earlier. Mr. Garcia worked as a cab driver; Mrs. Garcia, who spoke little English, stayed at home to care for their two
children, Anna, age twelve, and Robert, age eight.

The referral resulted when Anna had sought help on her own
from a guidance counselor for problems she was having at home.
She had complained to the counselor that her parents were too strict
and wouldn't let her do things that other girls did, such as sleeping
over at a girlfriend's house.

Mrs. Garcia was eager to contact the agency because of her concern about Anna's "rebellious" behavior and "her wanting to do
things that she was too young to do." Mr. Garcia accepted the referral reluctantly, responding to pressure from his wife and daughter. The family was assigned to Blanca Ramos, a social worker experienced in work with Hispanic families. She invited the whole
family to the initial interview. All interviews were conducted in
Spanish. (See chapter 16 for discussion of adaptations of the model
for Hispanic families.)

The first interview began on a volatile note. The parents were angry at Anna for having gone to the guidance counselor. By complaining to a stranger, she had violated the family's privacy. Anna saw her parents' reaction as another example of their being out of step with "what everybody does." As the interview progressed, it became clear that the parents were at odds over Anna. They both agreed she was "disrespectful" toward them, and both were fearful that she might become involved with drugs, boys, or other sources of temptation. They differed, however, over how much control they should exercise. Mr. Garcia favored strict rules, whereas his wife believed that they needed to be more flexible. Although Mrs. Garcia seemed to defer to her husband, the tension between them was obvious.

The practitioner helped the family to identify two target problems: (1) the conflict between the parents and Anna; and (2) the parents' disagreements about how to handle Anna. They agreed on a short-term contract within an eight- to ten-session range. Sessions involving Anna alone and her parents alone were to be alternated with sessions involving Anna and her parents together.

In her analysis of the problems and their contexts, the practitioner characterized the family as one in which a high degree of mutual involvement existed, which was expressed in the Garcias' concern and caring for one another. But it was currently in the throes of power struggles—between the parents and Anna and between the parents themselves. Further, a cross-generational coalition was evident, with Mrs. Garcia tending to side with Anna against her husband. Finally, the parents' beliefs and those of the mainstream American culture clashed in a number of respects, particularly regarding parental control over a preteen daughter.

In interviews involving the parents together, as well as those involving the parents and Anna, tasks to be done at home were developed through session tasks by having participants engage in face-to-face, structured problem solving, with the practitioner in a facilitative role. Using the results of their own problem-solving efforts, the practitioner helped the family members to develop home tasks.

For example, in one session the practitioner structured a discussion between Anna and her parents about Anna's wish to go to a shopping mall with her girlfriends. Anna presented her request; the parents, especially the father, questioned the wisdom of such an un-chaperoned outing. In the resulting give-and-take, a compromise (suggested by the mother) was reached, which led to a home task. The father would drive both Anna and her mother to the mall where Anna could go off with her friends. The mother would remain at the mall where she would do her own shopping and "be available" in case Anna "needed her." The practitioner helped the family to focus on the issue, encouraged the father to express his concerns, and asked for possible solutions.

Using this approach, the practitioner helped the family to develop several other tasks. The parents agreed to attend English language lessons and to consult with another Puerto Rican family who had been in this country a longer period of time. They also agreed to have regular discussions between themselves over how to handle Anna so they could present her with a united front. Anna took on tasks of talking to her parents without insulting them and, in response to her parents' wishes, of speaking Spanish more at home.

In helping the family develop these tasks, the practitioner took the role of "culture broker" referred to earlier. Thus she tried to help the parents achieve greater tolerance of the beliefs and practices of the larger culture without rejecting their own values. Her self-disclosures of her own experience as a Hispanic immigrant were particularly helpful in this effort.

Substantial progress was made on most of the tasks agreed on. Perhaps the most successful was "going to the mall," which was implemented without a hitch on two occasions. This task was particularly important, since it epitomized a spirit of cooperation and compromise between Anna and her parents.

As is typical in a task-centered case, not all the tasks were accomplished. For example, the Garcias kept putting off the task of consulting with the Puerto Rican family that had arrived earlier. Moreover, the tasks did not address all the issues of concern to Mr. and Mrs. Garcia and Anna. For example, Mr. Garcia's refusal to allow Anna to sleep over at a friend's house blocked the development of tasks related to this issue.

In the terminal interview (ninth session), the two main problems were reviewed with family members. In her recording of this review,

Blanca Ramos noted (regarding the first problem): "Disagreements still exist [between Anna and her parents], but they are not perceived as "crises" and are not handled in an antagonistic, confrontational manner." In respect to the second problem, she noted that parents were working more closely together, with less tendency to "give conflictual responses to Anna." More important, both parents and Anna thought that significant improvement had occurred.

The Sabatinis

Mr. Sabatini, a widower, age seventy-six, was hospitalized in a psychiatric ward following a panic attack and an episode of severe depression. He lived alone in a two-family house that he owned but did not wish to return to. He did not like living alone (he had not had a tenant in some time) and, in fact, blamed his anxiety and moodiness on his living situation. He preferred to remain at the hospital. He had two daughters, one married (Ruth) and one single (Mary). Although both were supportive and visited him frequently, neither wanted to take him in.

The case was referred to the hospital's Social Service Department for discharge planning. After an initial meeting with Mr. Sabatini, the social worker, Nick Natale, arranged for a family meeting at the ward. Mr. Sabatini and his two daughters agreed that the main problem was his need for a suitable living arrangement, although his emotional distress was also a concern.

Service consisted of a series of family sessions supplemented by individual contacts with Mr. Sabatini and his daughters. The initial family meetings were used to help the family, through session tasks, to begin to discuss possible living arrangements for the father, as well as disposition of his house. Home tasks called for the three family members to continue these discussions on their own during the week and to identify and visit possible facilities. The solution reached was for Mr. Sabatini to move in temporarily with Ruth and then to a group care home. Mary would move into the vacant apartment in her dad's house and rent the other one. Although the family had worked cooperatively, it had become stuck on the issue of the house. Mr. Sabatini and Mary wanted to sell it; Ruth wanted to keep it in the family. The issue was dealt with in a session task in which the three of them, at the practitioner's suggestion, discussed a range of options without forcing themselves to agree on a yes or no decision about selling the house at this time. In considering a greater variety of alternatives, the family members were able to break away from their fixed positions and thus reach a resolution. Mary, the unmarried daughter, would occupy one of the apartments of the house and rent out the other. In addition to structuring and facilitating the session tasks, the practitioner took on a number of tasks himself, including obtaining information about group homes, supervised apartments, and so forth; coordinating visits to these facilities; and helping Mr. Sabatini move into the one selected. Also, in these sessions the practitioner, using a psychoeducational approach, helped Mr. Sabatini and his daughters understand the nature and possible course of his emotional symptoms.

The review of progress in the terminal (tenth) interview revealed that Mr. Sabatini was pleased with the group home; his anxiety and depression had abated. The daughters were also satisfied with the resolution. Future issues, such as the possibility of Mr. Sabatini's moving from the group home to another domicile, including one of his daughter's homes, were discussed.

PART THREE *Groups*

10

PRETREATMENT CONSIDERATIONS

10.0.0 INTRODUCTION

As in each of the preceding parts, this one begins with a chapter that describes some of the issues and principles that must be understood by task-centered practitioners who work with groups. The topics included here are the effectiveness of task-centered groups, the kinds of clients for whom these groups are appropriate, the theoretical assumptions that underlie this kind of group work, the values that are incorporated into this practice, and the basic skills that are required of the practitioner who utilizes this approach. This chapter also discusses the decision as to whether to utilize task-centered group work with particular clients.

The chapter also incorporates the idea that task-centered approaches may also be employed with other kinds of groups, usually referred to as *task groups.* This term is a common one among group workers and refers to those groups whose goal is to accomplish a purpose external to the group, such as making a decision for an agency, raising funds, or engaging in social action.

A task-centered practitioner working with groups should be educated in the principles of group work, as well as have an understanding of group processes. Task-centered group work builds on this understanding by offering techniques and procedures whose effectiveness has either been demonstrated or is amenable to such evaluation. These techniques and procedures supplement basic group work methods, and, consequently, the latter must be understood to a greater degree than can be included in these chapters. Many practitioners with groups are also likely to organize their work around defining and accomplishing tasks and helping members do the same, but these workers describe this in terms other than those used by practitioners explicitly trained in task-centered methods.

Thus the reader who plans on doing task-centered group work is urged to become familiar with such texts on group work as Garvin (1997), Toseland and Rivas (2001), Glassman and Kates (1990), Northen (1988), and Brown (1991). These books provide information required for *all* work with groups, such as how to compose groups, help members to develop relationships with one another, create norms that are supportive of group work, utilize activities, and engage the group in problem solving. While this chapter touches on how task-centered practice embellishes these procedures, it does not present them in depth.

The reader should also study presentations on the social-psychology of groups, such as those by Garvin (1987), Johnson and Johnson (1996), Wheelan (1994), Parks and Sanna (1999), and Forsyth (1990). These discussions help all practitioners with groups to understand phenomena that occur in groups and that must be responded to appropriately for the group service optimally to succeed. These phenomena include how attractive the group is to the members (cohesiveness), the pattern of relationships among members (group structure), cyclical and noncyclical sequences of events (group processes), shared beliefs among members as to what behavior is desirable and undesirable (group norms), traditions that the group develops (group culture), how the members divide tasks among one another that are necessary to maintain the group (division of labor), and the phases through which the group proceeds (group development).

10.1.0 EFFECTIVENESS AND REPLICABILITY

More than twenty-five years have passed since the first paper on task-centered group work appeared (Garvin 1974), and, since then, several research studies have evaluated this approach. These investigations demonstrate that task-centered group work is feasible for a variety of problems and client populations.

The earliest evaluation of task-centered group work was reported by Garvin, Reid, and Epstein (1976) and was based on two projects. One was on patients in an adult, outpatient psychiatric setting; the other was on students in an inner-city school. Of the nine school groups, members in three achieved their tasks at a rating of substantial or better; members in another three partially attained their tasks; and in the remaining three, members only attained their tasks to a minimal degree. The practice in the psychiatric setting was with a group of women with reactive depression. While some women attained their tasks, others did not, and the investigators attributed this to poor task specification.

Newcome (1985) reports on an application of task-centered group work in an adult day-treatment program. Outcomes were measured utilizing Goal Attainment Scaling and were better for the group that received task-centered group services. Toseland and Coppola (1985) present their experience with elderly people. Although these authors did not use quantitative measures to evaluate outcomes, they do present qualitative findings indicative of success.

Pomeroy, Rubin, and Walker (1995) report that a quasi-experimental evaluation found that an eight-week psychoeducational and task-centered group was effective in alleviating stress, perceived stigma, depression, and anxiety among family members of people with acquired immune deficiency syndrome (AIDS).

Scharlach (1985) used task-centered group work with institutionalized elders. His report exemplifies that different authors have different ideas of what task-centered group work is. Scharlach cites the original article by Garvin (1974) but then defines the approach as being employed when "participants design and implement a group project to achieve explicit social goals" (1985:34). Garvin's work clearly defines task-centered group work as a means of helping individuals with individual tasks. This does not rule out group projects, but these are used to help individuals with their tasks.

Kilgore (1995), in a doctoral dissertation based on a developmental research paradigm, employed task-centered group work with adult male

sex offenders at a community mental health center who were court ordered to participate. Each client carried out five to six tasks outside the
group that were assigned by the group members or workers and were
intended to address an issue essential to the client's treatment progress.
There was a moderate positive correlation between task progress and
goal achievement, and all clients made gains in goal achievement. The
way that this project was carried out was problematic in that the tasks
seemed to have been imposed on members, whereas the "pure" model
calls for tasks devised by members, albeit with the help of the worker
and other members.

Raushi (1994) similarly prepared a doctoral dissertation along developmental research lines and developed a task-centered model for
work with single-mother students in a community college setting. The
model was tested with two groups in an urban setting. The focus of the
groups was on life-coping problems that impact college success. These
groups were described as "ultra brief," as one group continued for six
weeks and the other for four. This project was seen as developmental
research, since the focus was on testing the feasibility of the model and
suggesting modifications in the model rather than on evaluating client
outcomes. For example, the investigator developed a series of educational tools for task-centered group work, such as mini-lectures on the
task-centered process, handouts, flip-chart outlines, and work sheets
used by members in their task-centered work.

Although the above literature demonstrates the widespread applicability of task-centered group work techniques, it does not yet provide
as strong a scientific substantiation of effectiveness as would be desirable. This does not mean that this approach has been found to be ineffective but, rather, that the studies do not uniformly employ all the
scientific procedures that are required to place the findings on a firm
foundation.

Part of the problem is the complexity of evaluating the effectiveness of group interventions (Bednar and Kaul 1994; Brower 1989).
Many events occur in groups that can confound the findings. For example, in any experiment that involves several groups, identical
groups cannot be created and maintained over time. Each group develops different group conditions as the members interact with one

another, drop out, and fail to attend every session. The effect of these circumstances can be accounted for in the research design, but this is seldom done.

The interactions among the following—the approach to group work that is employed, the group conditions that emerge as a result of this approach, and the outcomes that ensue for the individual members—need to be studied. Group work research activities, consequently, are time-consuming and expensive. This usually requires outside funding, and, as of this writing, we know of few occasions when such funding was available for task-centered group work research. This is probably because task-centered approaches are largely indigenous to social work, and social workers have not been well represented among the decision makers of granting agencies, although this is currently changing.

As stated above, not the least of the problems encountered in investigating task-centered group work (and perhaps any approach) is a definition as to specifically what constitutes this type of group work and exactly how the practitioner and the members conducted their group. Investigators of group and other interventions try to provide these details in a variety of ways so that the approach can be replicated. One method that has been used historically is a well-constructed process record of the events that occurred in the treatment situation. Another is a manual, used before and during an intervention, that describes the sequence of events that should occur and that gives details about the information to be presented to the members, the activities to be engaged in during group meetings, the problems to be solved, and the extragroup actions to be taken by the practitioner and the members. (In well-executed research projects on task-centered or any other intervention, the intervention also needs to be monitored to determine the degree to which the manual is actually followed.)

Only a few reports of task-centered group work provide this kind of detail about the task-centered group work process (Garvin 1986; Kilgore 1995; Raushi 1994). Garvin, in his paper, presents examples of the way the task-centered group work process was specified in a project to serve seriously mentally ill clients. (Some of these procedures are described in chapter 11.) The Kilgore and Raushi publications were doctoral dissertations. Like Garvin's work, these were presented as examples of developmental research in which the outcome was more to confirm the feasibility of the models and to modify them for future research purposes than to have an intervention that has been carefully evaluated through a true experimental design.

The practitioner who utilizes task-centered group work, in addition to thinking about effectiveness, must also consider feasibility, and this involves the availability of several resources. One is whether a sufficient pool of clients is available so that enough members can be recruited for a group. (A description of the process of recruitment and group composition is provided in the next chapter.) In addition, however, groups require more meeting space than is necessary for work with only one client at a time or even for some families.

10.1.1 CHECKLIST FOR EFFECTIVENESS AND REPLICABILITY

___ 1. Have any group approaches been effective with this type of problem?

___ 2. If studies of task-centered group work with this type of problem have been reported, have they shown it to be effective?

___ 3. Do I know about and can I employ a specific set of interventions for doing task-centered work in a group setting?

___ 4. Are resources available for doing task-centered group work?

10.1.2 QUESTIONS TO CONSIDER

1. You are aware that clients with problems similar to those of your client have been helped by individual task-centered practice. Does this mean that your client can be helped by task-centered group work? Why or why not?

2. You are also aware that clients with problems similar to those of your client have been helped in groups that were served through the use of other group approaches. Does this mean that task-centered group work will also work with clients with these types of problems? Why or why not?

3. You are planning to work with a committee (such as an agency staff committee). How useful would it be to think of the ways of helping the committee through explicitly focusing on individual and group tasks?

10.2.0 THEORETICAL BASE

Task-centered group work, along with other task-centered approaches, is not connected to a particular theory of behavior. As stated in chapter 2, this model "tells you how to make changes" by "providing directives for practice" rather than providing explanations of behavior. Thus task-centered group workers use a number of theories—many that parallel those used in practice with individuals and families—to understand what is going on in their groups and what interventions might be useful. These include ego psychology, learning, role, social systems, and cognitive theories.

Nevertheless, because this is a *group* intervention, all practitioners will make use of an understanding of small group theory when using task-centered approaches in groups. This theory enables these practitioners to understand group conditions that exist at various phases of the task-centered group work process, so they can support those conditions that enhance the process and abate those that do not.

Group conditions are classified under the following headings: (1) group development; (2) group structure; (3) group process; (4) group resources; (5) extra-group transactions; (6) group boundaries; and (7) group climate (Garvin 1997:102). We shall briefly discuss each of these conditions and how they affect task-centered group work interventions. Practitioners, however, are encouraged to read one of the excellent texts dealing with groups (Johnson and Johnson 1996; Wheelan 1994; Parks and Sanna 1999; Forsyth 1990), as this will enable them to utilize group phenomena to enhance their task-centered practice.

Group Development   Groups undergo changes over time that are often predictable, and these are referred to as stages of group development. Because space does not permit an extensive discussion of these stages, we shall merely list them and highlight a few stages that have implications for task-centered group work.

Hartford (1971:67), in her list of stages, incorporates the ideas of a number of authorities as follows:

    I. Pregroup Phases
       A. Private Pregroup Phase
       B. Public Pregroup Phase
       C. Convening Phase
    II. Group Formation Phase
    III. Integration, Disintegration, and Conflict
    IV. Group Functioning and Maintenance Phase
    V. Termination Phases
       A. Pre-termination Phase
       B. Termination
       C. Post-termination Phase

[handwritten margin note: First meeting]

An important stage is "formation," which takes place at the first meeting or even the first few meetings. At this time members experience ambivalence about being in the group, interact with one another in stereotypical ways, and seek to clarify the purposes of the group, as well as their reasons for being there. The practitioner, therefore, will make sure that these issues are discussed and will utilize interventions that enhance the value the members place on the group experience.

In the beginning of the next phase, members are likely to enter into a conflict period in which they challenge some of the rules, as well as the patterns of leadership that emerged in the formation period (Garvin 1997). Practitioners will have to be particularly supportive to the members during this period in order to maintain their commitment to the group. This leads to the next phase in which members are likely to engage fully in activities that help them to accomplish the group's purposes. The final or termination phases, in contrast, place demands on members to solidify the gains they have made in the group so that they can leave the group and this group experience can come to an end.

Group Structure This group condition refers to the pattern of relationships that emerges among group members, such as who speaks to, influences, and feels attracted to whom. Since task-centered group work involves a problem-solving process in which members are asked to help one another, the practitioner has to be attentive to patterns of ` interaction that enhance or impede this process. A wide array of techniques are available to practitioners to deal with this issue (Garvin 1997:103–4).

An example of a structural condition that arose in a task-centered group occurred in a group of adolescents in a residential treatment center. Some of the members identified with the social worker and consistently supported her ideas. Another segment of the members identified with a youth who competed with the social worker and opposed her suggestions. After a while, the question of which idea was the better one was less important than whether the idea was supported by one's subgroup. In this case, the social worker pointed out to the group what was happening, and the members found other ways to give recognition to the leadership potential of the oppositional member than through their automatic rejection of the worker's ideas.

Group Process A number of phenomena in groups occur as sequences of events that are predictable or can be ordered in some way, and the term *group process* is used to describe this condition. Thus many writers have described how problem-solving processes should occur in groups so that good outcomes can be created (Garvin 1997:123–25.). Such problem solving proceeds in an orderly way from specification of the problem to a generation and analysis of alternatives to a choice among alternatives and implementation of the choice. Task-centered group work is very much a problem-solving process; thus ideas about group problem solving are highly compatible with task-centered processes.

Other group processes described in the group literature include role differentiation, conflict resolution, and value creation (Garvin 1997:107–10). All these processes are highly pertinent to the success of task-centered groups.

Group Resources   Groups require numerous resources in order to exist. These include the physical setting, equipment for group activities, and staff assistance. Task-centered groups, in addition to these resources, may also need materials related to the specific task-centered activities chosen by the group in question. For example, in a task-centered group of teenagers, the members required long sheets of newsprint on which to record their tasks, as well as their progress in achieving them, taped to the walls.

Extragroup Transactions   Groups do not exist in isolation but interact with other individuals and groups in the agency, as well as in the community. These interactions may be problematic, as when members hear of groups that are not run on a task-centered basis and wonder about this. Also, because members of task-centered groups typically are helped to perform tasks outside the group, this will have an impact on people who are not in the group and who may be called on to cooperate with the members' efforts.

Group Boundaries,   This refers to the restrictions that all systems, including groups, must set to determine who is and is not a member of the group and who is entitled to be present during group sessions. This issue can have a special impact on task-centered groups in the following ways:

1. Should a member who fails to attend several sessions and is obviously not engaged in carrying out tasks be continued in membership?
2. Can an individual join the group after it has started and then be helped to "catch up" to where the other group members are in relationship to defining and carrying out tasks?

Group Climate   This refers to the emotions that members express and that are prevalent among all or most of them, often through the process of contagion. Because task-oriented approaches are pretty much "down to business," members may become restless or bored even if they are making progress on their tasks. The task-centered group worker will watch for these kinds of emotions and will use tools, described in sections 12.1.4 and 12.1.6, to meet the needs that are stirring these emotions.

10.2.1 CHECKLIST FOR THEORETICAL BASE

___ 1. Am I utilizing a theoretical explanation in my work with the group as a whole (e.g., some aspect of group theory related to a specific group condition, such as how the group members' behaviors relate to a stage of group development)?

___ 2. If so, what is it?

___ 3. Is this explanation necessary?

___ 4. What alternative explanations might apply?

___ 5. Do the group members have an explanation?

___ 6. If so, what is it? Is it held by one, a few, or many of the members?

— 7. Is there conflict among members regarding their explanations or between the members and myself?

10.2.2 QUESTIONS TO CONSIDER

1. Which of the following explanations apply to individuals? Which to groups? Which to both?

a. Individuals are more likely to repeat behaviors that have been rewarded than behaviors that have not been rewarded.

b. When individuals wish to remain in a group, they are more likely to act in conformity with group norms.

c. Increasing the attractiveness of a group increases the *likelihood* that members will conform to group rules.

d. When individuals are exposed to contradictory expectations as to how they will behave with reference to a role, they will feel stressed.

2. What kinds of explanations would you suggest account for the following situations?

a. Many members fail to attend group meetings.

b. Many members fail to work on the tasks they have developed with the help of other group members.

c. Members appear bored during group meetings.

d. A member frequently criticizes the way another member is working on his or her tasks.

10.3.0 MISSION AND PURPOSE

In section 2.3.0 we discussed the relationship of task-centered practice to the mission and purposes of social work. We wrote of the prevention or eradication of such problems as poverty, racism, sexism, abuse, addiction, mental illness, illiteracy, and so forth. We also spoke of the special commitment of social workers to serving the disadvantaged and disenfranchised. The mission, purposes, and goals of task-centered group work are similar to those of all the other modalities through which task-centered practice is conducted.

Group work, however, has two sets of purposes—those that relate to the individuals and those that relate to the group—although the two are clearly related. Thus the purpose of one group was to help members increase their achievement in school. The purpose for one of the members was to help that member complete assignments; for another, it was to help the member secure tutoring to compensate for a lack of specified skills.

Because of the nature of group interaction, group members often fulfill purposes in addition to those fulfilled in individual treatment. These relate to certain benefits of participation in groups, such as learning to give help to peers and to receive their help, learning how to behave in group situations, receiving feedback regarding ways of relating, and developing new relationships.

The value of giving help to others should not be underestimated. People who receive social work services often have low self-esteem. This can be improved when they are not only perceived as receiving help but as capable of offering it.

10.3.1 CHECKLIST FOR MISSION AND PURPOSE

___ 1. Have I identified the group's purpose?
___ 2. Have I identified the purposes for individual members related to their group service?

10.3.2 QUESTIONS TO CONSIDER

1. What contributions do task-centered group work services make to accomplishing the mission of social work?
2. How does the fact that members are asked to help one another relate to the mission of social work?
3. If the way the group is operating helps some members but not others to fulfill their purposes, how does the worker proceed?

10.4.0 SOCIAL WORK VALUES

Task-centered group work is conducted with full respect for all the values discussed in section 2.4.0, such as respect for persons, individualization, and self-determination.

Self-determination requires that we uphold voluntary participation in groups and insist on a "contract" between the social worker and members, and that the group as a whole specifies goals as well as member and worker tasks. The worker should negotiate these tasks with members and renegotiate them whenever changes take place. A related principle is that workers may intervene in the group in ways that do not benefit all members but must not intervene in ways that can harm any member even if others would benefit.

A special issue that arises for group workers and members is the question of whose needs take precedence at any particular time: one member as opposed to another or a member versus the group as a whole. For example, one member may want help with a problem in accomplishing a task at the same time that another member wants help. Or a member may want help when the worker notes that everyone in the group appears restless and that they may need a "break" or even a short physical exercise in order to continue working on their tasks. Acting in a manner consistent with the principle of self-determination, the group worker will usually give the members an opportunity to be involved in making these decisions.

Another value issue arises when an agency requires members to participate in a task-centered group. This often occurs in prisons and psychiatric hospitals. We recommend that the social worker urge the agency to make such participation voluntary. Even when the agency agrees, however, a degree of duress may be present, such as when the members are aware that discharge from the hospital or a recommendation for parole may be influenced by such group participation.

The social worker should acknowledge these realities with members, help them to make decisions that they think are in their own best interests, and ultimately choose goals and tasks on a strictly voluntary basis. Nevertheless this is an ideal, and in the practice situation many complexities regarding self-determination arise and the worker will have to frequently examine a series of value issues in deciding how to proceed. Rooney (1992) has written an important book that expands on this topic with many references as to how task-centered principles and involuntary conditions affect each other.

10.4.1 Checklist for Social Work Values

Non-Voluntary Groups

___ 1. Have the members joined the group voluntarily? If not, what actions have I taken with regard to the principle of self-determination?
___ 2. When decisions are made in the group, how have the members been involved?
___ 3. How have I dealt with my own values when these are related to the purpose of the group or to issues that have come up in the group?

10.4.2 Questions to Consider

1. In groups, some members can intentionally or unintentionally exercise a considerable degree of influence over others, even to the point of dominating them. This often occurs through sexism (men dominating women) or racism (members from one ethnic group dominating members of another). How should you handle these phenomena when they occur in task-centered groups?

2. A member tries to pressure another to choose a particular goal or task. How should you handle this?

3. The group's purpose is to prevent child abuse. A member of the group communicates that he has given a harsh spanking to his young child and maintains that this is appropriate ("spare the rod and spoil the child"). What should you do about this?

10.5.0 RELATIONSHIP

The same considerations that we discussed earlier (see section 2.5.0) regarding relationships with the social worker apply in task-centered group work. Social workers will form relationships with individual members of the group through their contacts with them before the group starts, as well as occasional interactions outside the group even after it has begun. In addition, however, on many occasions workers will direct their remarks to individual members during the group meetings.

Even when social workers talk to all the members at once or to an individual, other members will develop feelings toward the worker that are similar to those they might have toward a worker whom they see on a one-to-one basis. All these occasions for relationships with social workers in groups should be governed by the same professional and ethical considerations that are in place in those one-to-one interactions.

10.5.1 COMPONENTS OF EFFECTIVE SOCIAL WORK RELATIONSHIPS IN GROUPS

The "core conditions" of warmth, empathy, and genuineness discussed earlier (section 2.5.1) are also important for the social worker in group situations to display, and this has been demonstrated through research (Truax, Wittmer, and Wargo 1971; Levinson 1997; Bohart and Greenberg 1997; Geertjens and Waaldijk 1998; Shamasundar 1999; Patterson 1985). In addition, however, the group worker helps the members to develop relationships with one another, and this includes each member demonstrating warmth, empathy, and genuineness to other members.

The strength of members' relationships to one another is a component of "group cohesiveness," which, in many ways, is the parallel on a group level to "relationships" on a one-to-one level. Cohesiveness is defined as "the resultant of all the forces acting on the members to remain in the group" (Festinger 1950). According to research findings, it is one of the most important variables accounting for the outcomes of group experience. As Yalom (1975:49) states: "If an individual experienced little sense of belongingness or attraction to the group, even when measured early in the course of sessions, there was little hope that he [*sic*] would benefit from the group and, in fact, a high likelihood that he would have a negative outcome."

With regard to empathy, the social worker explains the value of expressing empathy and trains members to make empathic responses to one another. This occurs through calling attention to the social worker's own empathic responses, asking members to role play empathic ways of responding, and reinforcing them when they actually do so.

The expression of genuineness has similar ramifications in group situations. In a manner analogous to expressions of empathy, the social worker helps the members to be genuine with one another. For example, if a member is likely to have a feeling toward another member, such as affection or anger, but does not express it, the worker may inquire about this or support other members doing so. In addition, if a member appears to have some thoughts about another member, the social worker will usually encourage their expression.

An issue in groups related to expressions of genuineness is "self-disclosure" (Wiener 1978). This bears on how much workers tell members about their thoughts and feelings and how much members tell these to one another. This topic can, of course, arise in one-to-one situations but is more complex in groups, as some members hesitate to reveal personal matters to peers. Social workers also differ among themselves in how appropriate they think it is for professionals to reveal anything about themselves to clients.

10.5.2 RELATIONSHIP IN TASK-CENTERED GROUP WORK

In task-centered group work, social workers have often used self-disclosure constructively by assigning themselves tasks when members are assigned theirs and then encouraging members to scrutinize worker achievements in the same way as they examine one another's. The worker then acts as a model of how tasks are assigned, carried out, and assessed. For example, in a task group in a medical setting the social worker openly assumed the task of securing a better meeting room for the group.

The same principle holds for work with groups seeking to attain changes in the environment, the so-called task-groups. The social worker is often in the role of "staffing" the group, which means assisting the members and officers of the group to carry out their functions. The worker will assume such tasks as preparing minutes, obtaining resources, and educating the members regarding their roles. We recommend that social workers in these situations make their tasks and their progress in completing them a matter of public information.

Another aspect of genuineness is the social worker's provision of feedback to members regarding their individual progress or the group's progress in utilizing the task-centered process. As we have stated elsewhere:

> The worker who withholds personal reactions to individuals in the group, as well as to the group itself, will not be evaluated by the members as having been honest with them. The worker must use judgment as to the way such reactions are shared and whether they are reflective of his or her biases in ways that are destructive to the members.
>
> Warmth is the third facilitative condition and is a rather complex one. For this reason Schulman (1978:225) divides it into two dimensions—positive regard and respect. Positive regard is the interest the worker shows in group members and their accomplishments. This means that members are given high regard despite whether they succeed in attaining their tasks, although the worker certainly hopes that they will do so. This kind of attitude is also reinforced among group members (Garvin 1997:83).

Respect relates to the members' efforts in the group. Even when they do not succeed at their task-centered activities or even if they behave in inappropriate ways, the social worker acknowledges that these problems may emerge because members are often struggling with difficult situations in their lives.

Social workers help members in task-centered groups to form relationships with one another, thus contributing to the cohesiveness of the group, in a number of other ways. These include:

1. *Helping members to discover similarities among themselves.* Most task-centered groups are composed of members who have similar problems, such as school difficulties, parenting problems, coping with aging, and so forth. When members discover that others in the group are in a similar position, a basis for attraction is established.

An example of an obvious way of doing this is to help members discover similarities in the problems they bring to the group. In one group of adolescents, however, members discovered that they lived in the same neighborhood and went to the same school. In a casual conversation during a break in the meeting, they discovered that they liked the same kinds of music.

2. *Helping members to talk to one another.* This may seem like a fairly obvious principle, and yet frequently members tend to address their comments to the worker. The task of the social worker in task-centered group work is to assist members to *help one another* to define and accomplish tasks. As the members develop an understanding of this principle, they are likely to develop very positive feelings toward one another.

An example of this occurred in a group in which the members addressed all their questions to the practitioner. When one member asked if the group could take a break, the practitioner suggested he ask the other members if that was what they wanted. Later in the meeting, a member asked if they could have coffee during the meeting. The practitioner again suggested that she ask the members what they thought. After some discussion, they agreed that this was a good idea. The practitioner then suggested that they discuss whether they would take turns bringing it to the meetings or contribute money to a coffee fund or whether they had other suggestions.

3. *Helping members to become good listeners.* The group worker will watch for situations when members appear not to have heard

what others have said or not to have heard it accurately. Sometimes it is sufficient merely to point this out. At other times workers will use a group exercise, such as asking members for a limited period of time to repeat the previous comment before making their own contribution to the discussion. Members will develop better feelings about one another when they perceive themselves as heard and understood by other members.

For example, in one group in which the above ideas did not work, the group worker asked the members to discuss why they seemed to have difficulty listening to one another. One member thought that they were competing with one another too much for the attention of the group. Other members agreed that this was a problem in the group. Another member said that they should take turns observing for this problem so that the group could discuss it further should it occur again.

We also indicated above (section 2.5.1) that task-centered social workers "must be able to keep work progressing," and this requires the skill of directiveness. This was defined as "the extent to which the practitioner structures intervention by controlling the topic of discussion." This is especially important in working with groups, as the worker is faced with a number of individuals who, at times, may each want to pull the discussion in different directions.

The social worker must decide which comments contribute to the group's movement toward the goals of task-centered group work and which do not. He or she will tactfully respond to a member who digresses so that the digression will not occur, while ensuring that the member does not feel rejected. The worker may even use these occasions to help members to understand how to focus discussions. The group as a whole may also be involved in making decisions as to which direction to proceed in when conflicts over this arise.

As we stated earlier (section 2.5.2), the distinguishing characteristic of the TC relationship is its highly collaborative nature in which social workers and clients see each other as partners. This is clearly true of task-centered group work, with the additional idea that *all* the members and the group worker should become partners engaged in problem solving as equals.

10.5.3 Checklist for Relationship
(Use Role Play or Tape of Group Session)

___ 1. How did I express empathy? What attempts were made to foster expressions of empathy among group members?

___ 2. How did I express genuineness? What attempts were made to foster expressions of genuineness among group members?

___ 3. How did I express warmth? What attempts were made to foster expressions of warmth among group members?

___ 4. What efforts did I make to keep discussion focused? How successful were they?

___ 5. Which skills need improvement? What other skills would I like to add to my repertoire?

___ 6. How am I going to improve or add skills?

___ 7. If the group was one created to accomplish changes outside the group, was I able to convey a sense of support to members to the degree appropriate to my role (such as staffing the group)?

10.5.4 Questions to Consider

1. A group member seeks to monopolize the entire session by talking about his problems with task completion? What interventions might help with this?

2. A member tells the group members that he had once abused his child. Members react to this story with horror, and the individual concerned says "Maybe I don't belong in this group." How might you respond to this?

3. One member talks much less than other members. How might you increase this person's participation in the group?

10.6.0 The Appropriate System for Work and Identification of Collaterals

As we have implied throughout this chapter, we believe that any type of client problem, under some circumstances, might be helped through task-centered group work. We think, consequently, that other factors enter into the decision as to whether to offer this service. One of these is whether the client wishes to be part of a TC group as opposed to participating in one-to-one TC work. This decision should be made, however, in an informed manner in which the client has a chance to learn adequately about both individual and group approaches.

An exception to this (see part 2 of this volume) is when family approaches are appropriate because the problem is embedded in family transactions and might best be solved by tasks accomplished by individuals in the context of their families or by tasks in which several or all family members are engaged.

Individuals may wish to work on tasks with the help of peers in groups, but enough members for a group might not be available or those who are available may not share enough similarities to form a cohesive group. Research should be done, however, to determine how dissimilar task-centered group members can be and yet work together to help one another do TC work.

People may or may not be appropriate for task-centered group work for other reasons. A valid circumstance for offering a group would be when the tasks heavily involve relationships with others. The group offers a good setting to practice accomplishing such tasks, as well as securing feedback on tasks that deal with relationships. On the other hand, groups should be avoided when an individual cannot tolerate sharing the worker's attention with others or disclosing his or her problems with others.

The same issues discussed above (section 2.6.0) regarding collaterals applies to task-centered group work. People who have identified the client's problems also can be collaterals, and the worker can engage them as allies in either supporting clients or modifying systems external to the group. Social workers have even formed groups of such collaterals (such as schoolteachers or parents) to support their efforts on behalf of group members.

Even when the group's purpose is related to changes in systems outside the group, the social worker may need to work with systems other than the group. A social worker who was defined as providing assistance to a board committee was asked by that committee to meet with representative groups of the staff to obtain their views of agency policies that required modification.

10.6.1 QUESTIONS TO CONSIDER

1. Why have I decided to invite a particular individual to join a task-centered group?
2. What other systems might be involved?
3. Who are the important collaterals in the other systems?
4. What modality (individual or group) might I use to work with these collaterals? Why would I choose that modality?

11

THE INITIAL PHASE OF TREATMENT

11.0.0 COMPONENTS OF THE INITIAL PHASE

The initial phase of task-centered group work for the purpose of helping individuals deal with problems might take longer than task-centered work with families because of the amount of time needed to establish what each member's problems and goals are. This phase can even take longer than usual if the problems brought by members are complex, if the groups are large (for example, some groups have as many as ten members), or if, for reasons discussed below, more time is required to define each person's problem and goal than is typically the case. The initial phase of task-centered group work includes some procedures that are similar to task-centered work with individuals and families: explanation of the roles of group worker and members; purpose and treatment procedures; obtaining necessary facts; targeting problems and determining problem priorities; exploring the target problem; developing a problem specification and a goal statement; setting time limits; contracting; and making assessments. For these procedures, we assume that the reader is familiar with one-to-one procedures described earlier (see chapter 3) and will primarily indicate how the group setting produces some differences from the one-to-one setting.

Certain additional procedures must be accomplished in task-centered group work that have no parallels in the individual or family practice situation. Some must be accomplished before the first meeting, and these include determining group composition, preparing members for the group, and preparing the physical setting. Others are accomplished after the group has been convened, such as developing group norms, determining the group's structure, processing issues associated with group formation, and determining initial group goals and tasks. In this section we shall comment on procedures of the initial phase of task-centered group work that do not parallel individual work, and then continue with a discussion of how other procedures found in individual and family work in this phase are conducted under group conditions.

Group Composition   The way that social workers select members for a group based on specific characteristics is referred to as *group composition*. Examples of compositional decisions include creating a group that consists of all women or one that is made up of an equal number of black individuals and white individuals or one comprised entirely of adolescents who are failing in school. Because the group's composition has a major impact on its outcomes, that composition should be related to the purposes the social worker and agency have for forming the group.

One obvious compositional principle is to select members whose problems relate to the purpose of the group. By "purpose of the group," we mean the kinds of problems the agency and worker expect will be dealt with in the group. Obviously a group to help students with school difficulties should recruit students with such difficulties. Beyond this principle, however, a number of member attributes should also be considered. One of the most important of these is the sex of group members. Social workers should avoid forming a group in which men or women constitute a small minority, such as one or two members. Such an individual may have little in common with other members and may come to be seen as a "representative" of a larger set of people rather than as an individual.

On the other hand, social workers may appropriately compose a group of all men or all women because the problem may relate to sexual identity issues. For example, a task-centered group was formed of women who were unemployed. Their tasks required that they challenge stereotypes about women in the workplace, and they were not likely to feel comfortable working on this issue in a mixed-gender group.

Social workers should also be aware of gender dynamics that are likely to occur in groups so that the worker can deal with these if they hinder the group's progress. One such dynamic is the likelihood that men in mixed groups will compete with one another for the women's attention. Another example is the tendency of many women to defer to the opinions of men and to permit them to take a dominant role in groups. Davis and Proctor (1989:221–50) discuss many of these gender-related conditions, as well as group work approaches for dealing with them.

Social workers should also be sensitive to cultural issues that arise in groups, particularly as these relate to people of color. Such members may suffer when workers and other members do not understand the values inherent in their culture, as well as the experiences members have had with oppression in the larger society (Davis and Proctor 1989). Davis (1984:97–109) discusses such issues as the uncomfortable feelings of whites when they do not comprise a large majority in a group, as well as the corresponding feelings of comfort blacks have when they are not severely outnumbered.

Other issues confront Asian-Americans in groups. Chu and Sue (1984) and Ho (1984) comment on the kinds of self-disclosure these individuals are likely to engage in when participating in groups, as well as how they commonly react to various types of worker interventions. Several writers have also commented on the value of composing groups entirely of members of one ethnic group because of the similar issues they face and because of the ways such groups could strengthen identity (Acosta and Yamamoto 1984).

In addition to race and gender, group workers take behavioral characteristics of members into account in composing groups. Such characteristics include how much a person talks, how aggressive the member is, how well (or poorly) the person does in school, or how motivated the person is to join the group. Group members must be attracted to the group (group cohesiveness) in order to continue to attend group sessions, and one basis of attraction is the presence of members who are seen as similar to oneself.

A proposition we have found useful in composing groups is to invite a member to join a group who differs from others on behavioral (such as how much one talks or the severity of the problem) and demographic (such as age, sex, ethnicity) characteristics as long as the individual has some of these characteristics in common with others in the group (Garvin 1997:59–60). The group worker can manage these kinds of compositional issues by inviting additional members to join the group who share characteristics with a member in question. In many circumstances, however, the pool of potential members is not large enough and the worker will often settle for a less than optimal group composition as an alternative to no group service at all.

As we have noted, task-centered methods can also be adapted to work with other kinds of groups than those created to help members with their problems. The compositional issues that arise in a committee, for example, consist of whether the members are sufficiently representative of the constituencies concerned with the work of the committee and whether the members possess the skills and resources the committee requires to accomplish its purposes.

When group workers see that the composition is problematic, they can take measures to overcome this, such as selecting a particular coworker, making use of a programmatic tool such as a film, or helping the member to have other opportunities for beneficial interactions with others who share that member's characteristics.

Preparation of Group Setting   The worker must also prepare the physical setting for the group as the room requirements for a group are different from those for an individual. The room must be large enough for all the members to be seated comfortably. If role playing or other programmatic tools are to be used, sufficient room has to be available for these to occur. Group workers typically arrange chairs in a circle as this conveys the idea to members that they are expected to communicate with and try to help one another.

11.1.0 EXPLANATION OF ROLE, PURPOSE, AND TREATMENT PROCEDURES

The procedures for explaining who you are, what the agency is, how you should be addressed, and so on, are no different whether the client is being offered individual or group treatment, and the group worker also deals with the client's feelings about these matters. A reason for the similarity is that clients who are referred to a task-centered group are first interviewed on a one-to-one basis.

This pregroup interview is conducted for the following reasons:

1. Clients need to be screened so that those who are not appropriate for a group experience can be offered other forms of service.

2. Clients need to be prepared for the group experience.

3. By telling clients about task-centered group work procedures before the group meets, the group work process can be accelerated. Clients enter the group already somewhat prepared to work together on defining problems, goals, and tasks.

4. In groups created to bring about changes outside the group, potential members will also be informed of the group's purposes and asked whether they wish to be in a group to accomplish those purposes. Their specific roles, if known, should also be identified.

How we determine whether the client is appropriate for group service was discussed in chapter 10, but here we shall touch on other aspects of the pregroup interview. We prepare clients for the group experience by talking with them about their previous group experiences and asking how they felt about them. When these experiences have been negative, we might indicate how task-centered group work will differ from the previous experiences. Examples of how members help one another to define goals and work on tasks may also be provided.

Clients may have concerns such as whether they will like or be liked by other group members and whether they will be pressured to reveal matters they prefer to keep private. The social worker will reassure them that these questions are typical of individuals who are considering joining a group and that group members are not pressured to say or do anything.

The worker also explains the purpose of the group as proposed by the agency. As we indicated earlier, the purpose relates to the kinds of problems the group is expected to address. It is, of course, conceivable that one or more members will not agree with the purposes the agency suggests. They then have the right to propose changes in group purpose and to remain in the group or leave it based on the outcomes of an effort to negotiate purpose. In any case, the members are likely to clarify the purpose of the group and to make it more specific to their individual purposes and needs.

An example of a discussion of purpose occurred in a group of persons with problems in child rearing. In this group, the worker indicated that the agency's purpose for the group was to help members learn child-rearing skills that would help them be more effective parents. One member asked if that purpose could include receiving support from other members in carrying out activities suggested in the group. The worker and other members thought this made sense, and this idea was added to the statement of group purpose that was written on the invitation to join the group. Another member said that her main purpose was to find ways of working out her disagreements with her husband about child rearing. The worker and other members did not see this as a purpose for this group. The member consequently decided she really wanted to be in a couples group whose purpose was to improve communication.

The social worker presents a brief summary of the task-centered group work process. First, the worker states the number of group sessions that will be held. As in individual work, the idea of target problems is explained and the client is helped to identify, at least in general terms, what his or her target problems are likely to be. Here, however, unlike in individual treatment, the client, after actually meeting other group members and learning about their problems, may decide to pursue different ones than those proposed in this pregroup interview. This may occur because the level of trust in the initial phase of the group is greater or less than the client anticipated. Such a change, however, does not obviate the value of considering target problems in the pregroup interview as it helps members to understand the nature of problem definition and to begin the selection of the problem(s) to be worked on.

In the pregroup interview, social workers also explain to clients that after the group members help one another to select their target problems, they will work together to define tasks. In some cases, as with target problems, the client may anticipate some tasks. In other situations, just having some idea that this is what the group members will work toward is sufficient. The same principle holds true for tasks as with problems, that is, members may change their minds once they experience the reality of the group, who the other members are, and what they are like.

Above all, the social worker should try to convey to clients that the main idea behind the group is that it exists to provide "mutual aid"—that members will help one another. Members, it is hoped, will come to understand that this affords more opportunities for help than those provided by a worker acting alone; moreover, members can help others, as well as being helped, and thus gain a sense of empowerment by participating in this type of group experience.

11.1.1 CHECKLIST FOR EXPLANATION OF ROLE, PURPOSE, AND PROCEDURES

___ 1. Do clients know the purpose of the group?

___ 2. Do clients know why they are being referred to a group?

___ 3. Do clients know that they will be working together with other group members toward changing specific aspects of their situation?

___ 4. Do clients understand that they will be asked to accept help from other group members, as well as offer help to them?

___ 5. How do clients feel about being in a group? Have positive feelings been reinforced and negative ones ameliorated or at least acknowledged?

___ 6. Do clients understand that the group will meet for a specified number of sessions?

11.1.2 EXERCISES—GENERAL INSTRUCTIONS

The same instructions presented earlier (section 3.1.2) apply. A difference, however, is that because "clients" are being prepared for a group, the students will need to determine the kind of group being created and the kinds of clients being recruited for the group. For example, in one class the students decided that they would create a group of teenagers who were having school difficulties. The potential pool of group members consisted, then, of such individuals. This part of the exercise is also useful in helping the students better understand how to conceive of group purposes.

11.1.3 EXERCISE FOR EXPLAINING ROLE, PURPOSE, AND PROCEDURES

The students should practice explaining role, purpose, and procedures, as well as dealing with the client's feelings about being in a group. At times, class members might benefit by talking with one another before or after the exercise about their previous group experiences and how these have colored their own feelings about selecting members for and facilitating groups.

11.1.4 ESTABLISHING GROUP NORMS

During the first few group meetings, the members and the group worker establish norms that, for better or worse, often continue for the life of the group. We have referred to some of these earlier, namely, confidentiality and attendance. In addition to these, workers seek to instill the following:

1. The sanctity and rights of all members should be valued. Thus members are not pressured to say or do anything that they do not wish to say or do.

2. Every member's contribution to the work of the group should be appreciated.

3. Members should seek ways to have caring feelings toward one another.

4. Members should find ways of cooperating rather than competing with one another.

5. The group should seek ways to help rather than exclude members who some find "difficult." As Glassman and Kates (n.d.:14) state: "It is a group that may choose to struggle with such a member and to develop fuller ways of coping with that individual [that strengthens] itself as a collective."

Group workers, like all social workers, place a high value on self-determination. This extends from the members' voluntary group participation to the members' choice of problems, goals, and tasks. The group as a whole also has a degree of self-determination, but this must be balanced against the interests of the individual members, as well as those of the agency and other groups within it. In practice, this can lead to many situations in which these entities must negotiate with one another in ways that are respectful of the rights of all concerned.

An especially noteworthy issue is that members sometimes tell one another information outside group meetings and may even collude with one another in avoiding bringing this information to the worker's attention or to the attention of other group members. Group workers tend to handle this by asking members to create a rule that conversations between members outside the group meetings be reported to the group. This is a more realistic request than forbidding contact outside the meetings—a rule that tends to invite deception.

Group workers help group members establish group norms in various ways. Listing these is difficult because the worker's decisions in this respect are made with each group's unique circumstances in mind. The worker might suggest norms to the group in its first meeting by providing members with a written list for discussion or by verbally mentioning and discussing each one. In other circumstances, the worker will wait until a group member or group event makes discussion of the norm appropriate.

Whatever the circumstance, the group worker should be aware that a norm stated by the worker does not become a *group norm* until the members agree to it. The worker's statement only has the status of a "worker rule" that members may accept or oppose. The emergence of a group norm, which is a rule of behavior that has the support of all or most of the members, typically requires that the members discuss the proposed norm and determine that it is to their benefit to follow it.

Example: In a group of substance-abusing women, the worker proposed a series of norms to the members. These norms were listed on a sheet of paper and each member was provided with a copy. The specific norms were as follows:

- Members will not use any substances on the day meetings are held; they will therefore not come to the group under the influence of a substance.
- Members will work to discourage other members from using substances.

- Members will tell the group about their struggles to abstain from substances.
- Members will tell the group when they have failed in their efforts to abstain.
- Members will not say anything outside the group about what other members say or do in the group, including mentioning the names of other members to people who are not in the group.
- Members will not act in an aggressive manner to other members, either verbally or physically.

The members spent most of the meeting discussing these norms. They questioned what the word *substances* meant and specifically asked if this meant cigarettes or coffee (it did not). They also were very concerned about what would happen if they came drunk to a meeting. A lot of confusion was present around the words "aggressive manner," and the group decided they would have to discuss this again at the next meeting.

11.1.5 THE INITIAL GROUP STRUCTURE

The term *group structure* refers to the pattern of relationships among the members. Aspects of structure are who talks to whom (communications structure); who likes or dislikes whom (sociometric structure); who influences whom (power structure); who performs which tasks for the group (role structure); who contributes the most to defining and accomplishing group tasks (task leadership); and who contributes the most to reducing tensions and promoting group cohesiveness (social-emotional leadership).

These aspects of structure have a particular character when a group begins. The group worker should be aware of this character and how it impacts the initial phase of task-centered group work. For example, the initial communications structure tends to consist of members talking primarily to the worker, who must counter this by urging the members to talk more to one another. The worker might remind the members that they are also expected to help one another and that the group worker is not the only one who may have ideas and suggestions.

The initial sociometric structure is likely to consist of members being drawn to others who are like themselves in obvious ways, such as age, sex, or ethnicity. The group worker will encourage members to get to know others who are less like themselves. The worker may do this, for example, by subdividing the group for problem-solving discussions and, with the agreement of the members, arranging for a different composition of the subgroup each time this is done.

When the group begins, the most influential members may be those who talk the most at that time. The worker anticipates that this will change and, consequently, urges the group to rotate group positions and group task assignments so that power and leadership do not become defined too early.

11.2.0 TIME LIMITS

The generalization stated earlier (section 3.2.0) that "short-term treatment is at least as effective as treatment of indefinite length and probably more effective" is as true of group as of individual approaches (Garvin 1990). We also find that task-centered group work takes about the same number of sessions as the individual approach, and we have conducted task-centered groups that lasted between eight and twelve sessions.

In contrast to individual or family work, we have not known of any task-centered groups that lasted for fewer than eight sessions, as it takes several meetings for every member to have an opportunity to select and specify problems and to determine goals. Some variation exists, moreover, depending on how many members are in the group. Obviously four can take turns in less time than it takes for eight members to do the same.

Task-centered group workers have also devised procedures to accelerate the process. One of these is to subdivide the group into pairs or triads. The members in the subgroup help one another determine goals, select tasks, and so forth. While this is happening, the worker circulates as a consultant to such groupings and calls the whole group together to discuss common issues and concerns.

As with individual and family work, a task-centered process can be introduced into other types of groups for a specified number of sessions. Generally this is advisable when groups have reached a plateau and members do not seem to be working on important individual issues. Groups that have done this include support groups for severely mentally ill and developmentally disabled people, parent education groups, and groups for people with physical disabilities.

It is also as true for group as individual or family treatment that adding sessions for a specified reason is easier than subtracting sessions from the number that has been promised. This should not be indicated in advance, however, as this would convey the idea that the social worker is unsure of what she or he is doing and that the members may be less capable than they are of accomplishing this work. It is also possible, in some groups, for members who have completed their tasks to terminate from the group while others continue a while longer.

Another issue that arises in task-centered groups in regard to time is that some members might be ready to move to another phase of the process while others are not. The group worker in these circumstances may have to give some members additional time between sessions. When this is undesirable, some members might volunteer to help other members "catch up."

Time-limited, task-centered groups may, in fact, be an important type of service in the current funding environment in which insurance companies, as well as many agencies, set firm limits on the number of reimbursable sessions. Such carriers may fund group treatment for a sufficient number of sessions because rates are lower for group treatment than for individual services, and this model of treatment is oriented to the determination of clear outcomes as well.

11.2.1 CHECKLIST FOR TIME LIMITS

___ 1. Have I set a specific number of sessions for the group?

___ 2. Will the group require some procedure so that all members will have an opportunity to receive the feedback they need at every session? What might this be and has it been explained to the members?

___ 3. Are all members likely to proceed together through the various task-centered phases? If not, what interventions might I use to help members to be involved in similar phases of the task-centered process?

11.2.2 EXERCISE FOR TIME LIMITS

This and other skills described in this chapter can be practiced by creating, in a simulated way in the instructional setting, any type of task-centered group. The learners should practice explaining time limits to the "members" of this group.

11.3.0 OBTAINING NECESSARY INFORMATION

Some of the information described above (section 3.3.0), such as age, ethnicity, religion, marital status, reason for referral, and family constellation, is secured from the client in the pregroup screening interview. These pieces of information help the social worker to develop the kind of anticipatory empathy that we described earlier. In addition, however, this information helps the worker to *compose* the group.

In addition, the group worker must decide and help the client to decide how much of this information the client is likely to tell other group members. At the beginning of the first group session, it is customary for members to introduce themselves to others. Sometimes workers specify what may be revealed; at other times, workers invite members to introduce themselves and reveal whatever information each is comfortable with at that point in the life of the group. One technique that groups employ is to have members interview each other in pairs and then introduce each other. Remember that some members may not be comfortable sharing certain information about themselves until they feel more secure in the group, and this should be acknowledged and respected.

In children's and even some adult groups the introduction process can be made into a game, such as having members repeat the names of those who have already spoken before giving their own. Such devices may be useful to help members get to know one another when the group is large.

11.3.1 Checklist for Obtaining Necessary Information

__ 1. Do I have the information identified in section 3.3.1 about each group member?

__ 2. What information am I going to expect members to present to one another at the first meeting? At later meetings?

__ 3. What techniques will I use to help members give information about themselves to other group members? What techniques will I use to help members recall the information they have received from other members?

11.3.2 Exercise for Obtaining Identifying Information

A student can role play a client being interviewed for basic information. The class members can discuss how much of this information is likely to be expressed in a group during the first meeting. A major issue for the class to discuss is how much information will the client need to present in the group at particular times: at the beginning, when selecting a target problem, and when determining a task.

11.4.0 Targeting Problems and Determining Problem Priorities

As is the case with individual and family task-centered work, a major value of task-centered group work is that the client determines the target problems. As stated above, this process begins in the pregroup interview but is only concluded in the group when clients experience the full impact of the group situation and the nature of the other group members. Many groups are composed of people with similar problems, and clients' initial statements of their problems might be used to select an appropriate group.

At the first group session, members are asked to make lists of potential target problems, and these may be written on a blackboard or poster board so that members can visualize one another's problems. During this process each member's remarks will influence what others say. Some members may not wish to indicate problems that are quite different from the problems of other members. On the other hand, a statement of a problem by one member may encourage others to state a similar problem. A member may even state a problem that is nonexistent in order to appear similar to others in the group.

The social worker must understand certain underlying group processes that create some of the situations noted in the above paragraph. These include pressures to conform that emerge in group situations, as well as facilitative processes that occur, such as when the presence of others helps group members to express something about themselves that otherwise might have been difficult to say. Workers may call the group's attention to these processes when they hinder treatment in order to help them find ways to overcome them. Several group work texts provide more details than we have space for here as to how this may be done (Garvin 1997; Toseland and Rivas 2001; Glassman and Kates 1990). Briefly stated, however, the social worker may confront the group with the process that is causing the problem and ask the members to try to find a way of changing it before proceeding with the business at hand.

Prioritizing problems raises an issue that is not present in individual task-centered work. For example, a member may allocate a high priority to a problem because it is similar to those of other group members. This may be a good idea, as members with similar problems often strongly empathize with one another, choose like tasks, and quickly identify barriers to task accomplishment. Nevertheless, unlike family work, group work does not necessarily require a common focus as each member can work on a different problem and receive some group time for this work.

On the other hand, allowing the problem priorities of one member to affect those of another is not always advisable. This is the case when the problems of one member are urgent or when one member's problems stand in the way of another member solving the one chosen first.

Some clients are better able to target problems in group than in individual treatment because of the example set by other group members. The members who are quicker to understand the concept of "problem" as separate from "goal" provide models for those who are slower to grasp this concept. Moreover, because members often come from similar life situations, they may be able to intuitively spot one another's problems. This is a result of common cultures, language, occupation, and experiences with the same institutions.

11.4.1 TARGETING PROBLEMS IN SPECIAL CIRCUMSTANCES

Alternative issues in targeting problems may arise when working with so-called natural groups, that is, groups that social workers offer to help that were in existence before any social work intervention, such as teenage clubs or groups living together in a residential facility. In many ways this kind of work is similar to work with families inasmuch as the members have bonded together for a mutual purpose before the worker appears and may continue after the worker leaves.

As is true, also, in work with families, the social worker has to find ways to be accepted into the group inasmuch as relationships already exist among the members before the worker's entry. Social workers sometimes handle this issue by performing a concrete task for the group or forming relationships with high-status group members.

We will provide two examples of problems that arise in natural groups. One kind of problem relates to individual members who perform specified tasks for the group but do not do so adequately. An example of this is an individual who is selected to write the minutes of the group and does not understand what this entails. This individual might accept the task of learning how to perform this function better.

The second type of problem that natural groups pose to social workers relates to the needs of the group as a whole rather than to those of individuals. Examples of this are problems in attracting members, securing resources, and dealing with conflict among members. Under these circumstances, the worker might introduce the idea of tasks that members can undertake collectively on behalf of the group. This introduces another level of complexity into task-centered group work, but this is inevitable given that the worker must simultaneously consider the needs of the individual members as well as of the group as a whole.

11.4.2 CHECKLIST FOR TARGETING AND PRIORITIZING PROBLEMS

___ 1. What problems were noted by the client before the first group session? Is the client likely to choose the same problem when he or she meets the other group members?

___ 2. How did the identification of problems by some group members affect the selection of problems by other members? Was this helpful in view of the problems that each member stated before the first session?

___ 3. What role will I take with respect to how the members are affecting each other regarding problem selection?

___ 4. Should I support members in selecting problems that are similar to those expressed by others or should I even confront this selection?

___ 5. If the group has been created to change some condition outside the group, did I help the members to prioritize these problem conditions and to select an appropriate one by this means?

11.4.3 EXERCISE FOR TARGETING AND PRIORITIZING PROBLEMS

Select several students to role play clients who have some problems similar to those of the other clients but some that are dissimilar. Types of clients who might create this kind of situation are the following:

1. parents who are having difficulties with their children;
2. adolescents with school difficulties (some involve problems with peers and some do not);
3. physically disabled clients;
4. recently unemployed clients.

In this role play, students acting as group workers will help the clients identify their problems. The "clients" will then role play group members discussing their problems in a group in order to select a problem to work on first.

11.5.0 EXPLORING TARGET PROBLEMS

In section 3.5.0 we described the kinds of information needed about the target problem in order to plan an intervention strategy. The same kind of information will also be sought in task-centered group work. Instead of group workers asking for this information on a one-to-one basis, however, they help members to ask this of each other.

To accomplish this, the group worker instructs the members about problem exploration. One way of doing this is to model the process. The worker selects a member and asks the group to observe how he or she asks that member about the problem or about contextual factors relating to it. Because a member may find it overwhelming to have too many people asking questions at the same time, the member may select just one other member to be the "primary" person to do the questioning. Other members may add their questions when invited to do so by the member whose problem is being explored.

Alternatively, the group worker may list questions that are required to explore the problem on newsprint. Members can use this as a guide to presenting information about their problems to the group.

Remember that a problem may have different meanings to different members. The worker should point this out so that members will be less likely to make inaccurate assumptions about one another's problems. Some tension around this issue is unavoidable in groups. This is because while it is desirable for members to have similar problems, for the reasons noted earlier, the similarity does not mean that people's problems will ever be identical.

At times the client's problem is shown through the member's behavior in the group, and other members can help specify it from their own observations. Members may also know one another outside the group and will provide information from that perspective. An example of the use of observations made during a group meeting involved a client who was unsuccessful in his efforts to form relationships. Other group members commented that he seemed uninterested in them; left meetings hurriedly, affording no chance for informal interactions; and never made eye contact with them.

11.5.1 Checklist for Exploring Target Problems in the Group

> ___ 1. Do group members have sufficient information about the problem exploration process to help one another explore problems?
>
> ___ 2. Have members been helped to explore whether their own views about other members' problems are accurate or are a result of their own assumptions?

11.5.2 Exercise for Exploring Target Problems

A simulated group should be set up involving a set of persons who are learning about task-centered group work. One role player, who is assigned to be the "worker," should help the others to explore the problem of one of the "members" of the group. The "worker" should use one of the approaches described in this section. The "members" should then make a list indicating everything they know about the problem. This list should then be given to the focal member who checks off all accurate items. The trainees should discuss what may be the reasons for any omissions or distortions.

After the role play, the group should discuss any occasions when the members began to move inappropriately from a problem exploration process to a *change* process. The group should then discuss ways that this would be handled in an actual treatment situation.

11.6.0 Developing the Problem Specification

In section 3.6.0 we explained the content of a problem specification. The same information is sought in task-centered group work, and the group is utilized to help each member to specify his or her problem. Thus the group worker explains and illustrates the concepts of frequency, severity, and duration. The group worker will then utilize one of the following group procedures:

1. The worker asks each member to take a turn allowing the group to help the member specify a problem.

2. The worker divides the group into pairs, and each member of the pair takes a turn helping the other to specify a problem. The worker either personally monitors the process or the outcome or reconvenes the whole group so that each member can "report." The worker helps the group to clarify or expand on any member's report that requires this additional work. (In some groups, three-person or four-person subgroups can be used instead of pairs.) The worker makes a decision on the size of the grouping based on how similar the members are to one another and how capable they are of conducting themselves appropriately in subgroups.

The group also helps members to collect baseline data. The group worker explains this concept to the group members and either rotates around the group to help members plan a way of collecting baseline data or utilizes the same subgroups that were used for problem exploration. If each person takes group time for these processes, this will considerably extend the short-term nature of task-centered work. Thus workers invariably utilize the subgroup arrangements we have discussed so that much of this work can occur simultaneously among the members.

Under those circumstances when the problem is manifested during sessions, members may collect baseline data on one another. Members may also possibly simulate situations to collect baseline information by creating role plays. In one group formed to help members to initiate relationships, the members role played meeting a person whom they wanted to know better. Members rated the role players on a simple observation form provided by the worker. As members learn to use these kinds of instruments, having each member keep a folder in the group room in which his or her charts are kept would be useful.

In some circumstances, using subgroups is difficult. This may be true when the membership consists of young children or people who are mentally disabled. Under these circumstances, the group worker may secure one or more assistants to help the subgroups.

Group members may also have more patience in dealing with these processes if the worker provides "time-outs" from the work. One worker accomplished this by introducing such program tools as games, music, or preparation of refreshments at intervals during sessions.

11.6.1 CHECKLIST FOR PROBLEM SPECIFICATION

___ 1. Have I identified all the manifestations of members' target problems that are important to each member?

___ 2. Do I know the frequency, severity, or duration of each group member's problem before intervention?

___ 3. Has a baseline period been established for each group member?

___ 4. Has a graph of the data been created for every group member?

___ 5. What approach did I create to enable each group member to have an opportunity to specify his or her problem?

11.6.2 EXERCISE FOR PROBLEM SPECIFICATION

Continue the role play created above for problem exploration in a group and help the "members" to obtain any additional information that is required for problem specification. Pay special attention to the group's ability to tolerate the process without becoming bored or exhausted. Note any signs of these difficulties. At these times you may find it desirable to interrupt the role play and consider programmatic tools to overcome the difficulty. The role play should then be resumed but with the solution to the "group problem" in place.

11.7.0 GOALS

The task-centered group worker helps the members to help one another determine goals in a manner analogous to the way members help one another to specify problems. This may be done in some circumstances, as we have indicated, by giving each member a turn in the group or by creating subgroups for this purpose. Keeping the same subgroups that were created for the previous purpose may be advantageous because of the familiarity subgroup members have with one another's situations. On the other hand, some groups prefer changing subgroups from time to time to secure new ideas or to become acquainted with the issues facing a larger circle of members. In groups formed to accomplish changes in the environment, the worker will also help the members to define the goals the group seeks to attain in the environment.

We have also found that less time is needed than one might think to do a "round" of the entire group for these kinds of activities. This is because members learn a great deal from hearing how others specify their problems or choose their goals. They also see similarities between their problems and those of others so that they can "piggy back" on the ideas of others and tailor the ideas of others to fit their own circumstances. The danger is that some members may do this inappropriately because, for example, they are fearful of being different or are anxious that their information will not be as well stated as that of others. The group worker should consider these issues and help members to overcome these pressures for conformity that arise in all group situations.

11.7.1 CHECKLIST FOR GOALS

___ 1. Has every group member set a goal for each problem manifestation?
___ 2. Are the goals stated in such a way that achieving the goal can be ascertained.
___ 3. Did pressures for conformity affect the creation of goal statements? How were these overcome?

11.7.2 EXERCISE FOR GOALS

The group created for problem specification can be continued into the goal phase with either a short intermission for a discussion of that process or a longer period such as might occur between class sessions. This is desirable because the work already done on problem specification would have to be repeated in order to create the database for goal setting.

The participants should be helped to be sensitive to the group's ability to proceed immediately in view of the time and energy spent giving attention to each member, either in the group as a whole or in subgroups. One of the logistical problems group workers always face is to gauge how long members can patiently listen to one another without

becoming bored and how long a member can tolerate sustained attention to him- or herself.

In addition to the use of program tools (e.g., the introduction of a
game or role play or refreshments) at appropriate intervals, the group
worker should reinforce the members' accomplishments. This can be
done by offering rewards at stated intervals, such as when all problems
are specified or all goals are created. Such rewards have been in the form
of special refreshments or the introduction of a pleasurable activity.

At times, group workers have found it useful to make the reward contingent on everyone finishing his or her work as required by the phase.
Workers should be aware, however, that this can create too much pressure on some individuals to "finish" in dysfunctional ways. The worker
should walk the narrow line between permitting that to happen versus
stimulating the group to give special help to members who need it.

11.7.3 GROUP GOALS AND TASKS

Group work has two levels of goals—individual goals and group goals.
Similarly tasks are on two levels—individual tasks and group tasks. Individual goals were defined earlier as the desired end point of intervention with respect to individual members. This desired end point is
chosen with reference to the member's problem. Groups also encounter
problems that must be solved in order for the group to function well,
and group goals are the end point the group seeks in order to solve the
group's problem. In groups created to achieve some change in the environment, the end point of group activity is also termed a group goal.
These goal-defining activities are complicated because members may or
may not agree with one another as to what the group's problems and
goals are.

An example of a group problem is when a group's meeting room is
too small for the group's activities. The group's goal is to secure an adequate room. The group's task is to assign members to make inquiries
as to the availability of other rooms. Another example of a group problem is when only a few group members do most of the talking. The
goal is to spread the communication more broadly among members.
The group's task is to select and carry out a means to do this. In this

latter example, it is conceivable that members may disagree on the problems, the goals, the tasks—or all three! The group worker's task in this case is to help the group members find some way to resolve their disagreement and then deal with the tensions in the group that were a consequence of the disagreement. The worker may do this by discussing the problem with influential members of the group, by identifying and removing the barriers to agreement, or by waiting to pose the issue until the group is ready to focus on it.

This process occurred in a group in a correctional setting. The members in this group disagreed about the existence of a problem identified by the worker who stated that members were reluctant to challenge members who were resistant to serious work on tasks. These members, week after week, reported no progress on their tasks. Members acted as if this was solely the fault of difficult environments rather than in the members' motivation to perform tasks and resolve problems. The worker thought this was another example of norms often found in correctional settings in which members referred to "doing your own time" in which inmates believed they should not get into the "personal space" of other inmates. The worker told the group of his explanation of this reluctance to challenge one another. The members collectively agreed that the worker was "right on" and that this issue must be discussed. This led to fewer disagreements among group members about the obligation to challenge one another when their commitments to accomplish tasks were not honored.

11.8.0 CONTRACTS

Workers with task-centered groups develop contracts with the members similar to those created in individual work. As stated earlier, these contracts include problem statements, problem specifications, goals, number of sessions, and frequency and length of sessions. Group workers, however, on occasion, have developed additional types of contracts that grow out of the group situation.

One of these is a contract that the members create with one another. In these contracts, which may be written or oral, members typically pledge to one another to keep confidential all personal information presented during group sessions. They may also formally commit themselves to help one another define and complete tasks. Members should also develop an agreement as to who will be notified when a member will arrive late or miss a meeting.

Two members may also develop a contract with each other. This occurs, for example, when pairs of members agree to become "buddies" in order to help each other specify problems, create tasks, and so forth. Buddies may even have a contract in which they agree to help each other between sessions with problems they may have in carrying out tasks (such as by providing verbal reinforcement).

11.8.1 CHECKLIST FOR CONTRACTS

___ 1. Is each member aware of and in agreement with the following elements of the contract: (a) number and scheduling of meetings; (b) fees, if applicable; (c) target problems; and (d) problem specifications and goals?

___ 2. Are members aware of one another's contracts?

___ 3. Has an appropriate contract been developed among the group members?

___ 4. Will additional contracts within pairs or other subgroups be required?

11.8.2 EXERCISE FOR CONTRACTS

The contract is a logical outgrowth of agreements that members reach regarding problems and goals, as well as the conditions for work such as frequency and length of meetings, fees for services, and so forth. This exercise, consequently, may be a continuance of the one described in section 11.7.2. The students may, however, experiment with alternative forms, such as (1) having an oral contract in the form of a summary of each member's agreements; and (2) maintaining a written summary of these agreements in a group "file" or even on newsprint that can be displayed from time to time as necessary. The members can also role play situations where the members see what they can remember about one another's contracts.

11.9.0 ASSESSMENT

The generalist practitioner should identify a wide range of assessment issues that pertain to the problem situation with which he or she is concerned. These may include, depending on the circumstances, assessment of individuals (see section 3.9.0), families (see section 7.9.0), organizations (see section 14.3.9.0), and communities (see section 15.3.9.0). Group workers and members have the opportunity to use the group setting as a source of assessment information in all these circumstances. That many social situations in which problems are embedded can be simulated in the group makes the group setting opportune for gathering assessment information. For example, one member's problem was his difficulty in dealing with his teachers. The problem specification indicated that he objected to most of the teacher's assignments although other students thought these were fair. Role plays were set up in the group so that the member could show others how he reacted to the teacher.

Larger system problems can also be simulated in the group. One social worker, for example, working with a staff group, asked the members to simulate a staff meeting and each member was assigned a staff role. In a community organization group, another social worker was preparing the group to handle a confrontation with the city government. A meeting with government officials was simulated, and some group members were assigned to role play such officials.

Another kind of assessment information is available when a member's behavior in the group exemplifies the problem. For example, one member's problem was that she failed to receive the help she needed from her fellow students. The other group members noted the ways that she avoided asking for help from any of the other group members.

As implied in the preceding paragraphs, task-centered group workers are likely to work with other individuals in the environment on behalf of group members. As was stated in section 3.9.0, this type of work is referred to as work with collaterals, and these can be family members, friends, and other professionals. It is as important in task-centered group work as in individual and family work to contact collaterals early, with the group member's permission, so as to prevent unexpected and often negative reactions from them, to enlist their support, and to add their views to our assessment picture. As a general rule, workers will seek to secure permission from the members to share collateral information so other members can consider the information when they offer help. Under certain circumstances, however, a member might wish the social worker to keep collateral information confidential, such as when the information might have a negative impact on another member.

11.9.1 CHECKLIST FOR ASSESSMENT

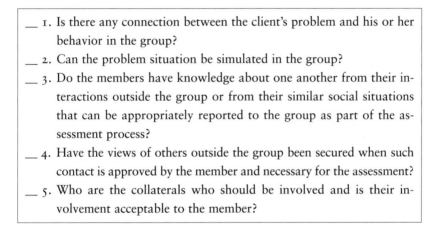

__ 1. Is there any connection between the client's problem and his or her behavior in the group?

__ 2. Can the problem situation be simulated in the group?

__ 3. Do the members have knowledge about one another from their interactions outside the group or from their similar social situations that can be appropriately reported to the group as part of the assessment process?

__ 4. Have the views of others outside the group been secured when such contact is approved by the member and necessary for the assessment?

__ 5. Who are the collaterals who should be involved and is their involvement acceptable to the member?

12

THE MIDDLE PHASE OF TREATMENT

12.0.0 COMPONENTS OF THE MIDDLE PHASE

The middle phase in task-centered group work is similar to that phase in one-to-one and family work in that the members work to resolve their target problems. As with individual work, the middle phase might begin at different time periods in different groups depending on the length of time members need to define their problems and goals and to complete the other initial tasks needed to create their group, as described in the preceding chapter. The middle phase in group work is analogous to that in individual treatment in that the group seeks to accomplish changes outside the group, and many of the group worker's facilitation activities are similar to those in individual treatment.

Although the time for the middle phase to begin may vary among groups, this particular phase will occur in group work, as was stated in the last chapter, after a longer period than in individual work. Another feature of task-centered group work is that all members may not be ready to work on resolving their problems at the same time. The group worker will find it difficult to help some members begin to implement tasks while others are still struggling with their goals, and we will now provide information on how to deal with this.

A number of solutions to this problem are possible. One is to encourage members who have defined their goals and who are willing to help other members to do so, perhaps through a buddy system. Another is to work with some members, either individually or in small subgroups, out-side the group. This is not our first choice, because it may interfere with the entire group becoming a cohesive system. Still another alternative is to give some members "homework" that they can do outside the group to complete their choice of goals (or of any other assignment). If this is a frequent problem, it may be advisable to create a workbook that guides members through some of the steps required by this model.

The group members in task-centered group work also follow the Task Planning and Implementation Sequence. They generate, select, agree on, and plan how they are going to implement and secure incen-tives to perform tasks. They also analyze obstacles to task perform-ance, review task progress, examine the status of the problem after the task has been performed, and, on occasion, may need to revise tasks when accomplishing the task does not reduce or eliminate the problem.

In task-centered group work, unlike task-centered practice with in-dividuals and families, members help one another in all aspects of the TPIS. Also in work with TC groups, considerable use is made of tasks during group sessions (session tasks) to enable members to learn how to accomplish tasks outside the session. These tasks usually involve changing the ways that a member interacts with other members; they may also involve role-playing responses in relevant situations or en-gaging in some aspects of problem-solving processes. In these respects the group treatment model differs from treatment of individuals but re-sembles family practice, in which session tasks are also widely used.

Task-centered group work provides an opportunity for workers to draw on a variety of approaches to group work to help members achieve their goals, that is, they function in an eclectic manner. Social workers also must draw on knowledge of how to work with special populations and how to work with collaterals when engaged in this form of practice, issues this chapter also examines.

12.1.0 THE TASK PLANNING AND IMPLEMENTATION SEQUENCE

Task-centered group work includes both client and practitioner tasks. As with individual and family task-centered practice, the practitioner will perform tasks for clients and for the group as a whole that they cannot do themselves or cannot do in a timely manner. The practitioner with groups also performs tasks for the group, as well as for members, that the group as an entity cannot accomplish. These include arranging for the group to meet in an appropriate space, securing other resources the group requires, and creating conditions in the group so that the group is optimally helpful to its individual members.

As just stated, session tasks are even more likely to occur in task-centered group work than in individual work and perhaps even more than in family treatment. This is because the group's character as a social situation enables it to be an effective laboratory for practicing tasks. For example, a member whose task was to initiate conversations with others could engage in this behavior within the group. This need not even be thought of as "practice" because other members are "people" in the same sense as persons outside the group are. Nevertheless, as was stated in chapter 4, tasks are most likely to be created for accomplishment outside the group.

12.1.1 Generating Task Alternatives and Selecting a Task

Members of a task-centered group are likely to use brainstorming in order to generate tasks in the same way as clients in one-to-one situations. Brainstorming is a technique in which all members are encouraged to suggest a task, and no discussion or criticism of these suggestions is allowed until all have had an opportunity to make their contributions. The group is an excellent place to brainstorm because members will suggest alternative tasks to one another. This process may benefit other members in similar situations, especially when their tasks are similar.

The group worker must help members guard against evaluating alternatives prematurely, as this is likely to happen in group situations in which brainstorming is used. The worker may also ask members to write down their alternatives and read them to one another while the worker writes them on newsprint or a blackboard. This will enable members to react quickly to the ideas of others rather than focusing on having their own alternatives read.

The group worker will then involve the members in evaluating the alternatives. This process is usually done after every member has a list from which to choose rather than at the time each member creates a list. This is a useful method because ideas that might benefit one member and not another are not thrown out too early. When the final choice is made, it must be the one the member in question wishes to pursue inasmuch as it is that member who must actually take the action and assume whatever risks are involved.

As stated in section 4.1.1 the number of tasks, their sequence, and their spacing depends on the nature of the problem and the characteristics of the member. In individual work, the practitioner and the client have the judgment of the two of them to draw on to guide this decision. In task-centered group work, members often understand better than the social worker how difficult it will be to accomplish tasks because they are "in the same boat." The worker and the member being focused on should therefore elicit other members' opinions when making determinations about tasks.

In task-centered group work, as in other modalities of task-centered work, members and workers can use *The Task Planner* (Reid 2000). Virtually all the task planners in that volume have relevance to group work (for example, alcoholism, anger management, anxiety, lack of assertiveness, to name a few).

The other members, on the other hand, may have their own reasons for thinking that a task is too easy or too difficult. The worker must guard against this. Members can be asked whether they have the other member or themselves in mind in making a judgment and, if the latter, how it influences their judgment. All or most of the members rarely have the same distortions in their judgments about such matters as the difficulty of the task. If, in the social worker's estimation, the members are colluding in some way to promote or discourage a particular task inappropriately, this should be addressed. The cause of this problem in terms of group conditions should be analyzed as it may cause difficulties in the selection of tasks for other members as well.

An example of planning tasks occurred in a group of people struggling with problems of depression when the members had reached the point at which they were choosing their tasks. The members had decided that they would work with one member to help her or him choose a task before moving on to the next member. Alice's problem was that she was depressed most of the day and responded to this by seldom leaving her house. She had been retired for about six months and was also having difficulty accepting this change in her life. Before her retirement, her primary outside interest was her work as a bank cashier. The group worker suggested that the members, as well as Alice, brainstorm some activities with which she could involve herself outside the home. As a start, the worker asked her what were some things she liked to do or always hoped she might do when she had the time. Alice said that when she was young, she once took a course in embroidering but never continued with this interest. She always had wished she knew how to play bridge. The worker asked if the other members had any other ideas of activities; her tasks would then be to learn about ways of pursuing these activities and then following up on one of these ways. One member suggested a support group for retired persons, and another suggested a choral group since Alice had a melodic voice.

The worker listed these ideas on the blackboard in the room. Alice was asked to rate each as 1 = Very interested; 2 = Somewhat interested; or 3 = Uninterested. She rated bridge as 1, embroidery as 2, a support group as 2, and a choral group as 3. Based on this, the worker wondered if the bridge group was her first choice, and Alice said that it was. The worker asked if she had any idea of tasks that she might carry out in this respect. She said that she could call her local high-school adult education program to see if it had a bridge class. Another member suggested that she also call the local YWCA. Alice thought this made sense and said that she would make these calls. The worker asked her to report on this at the next meeting, and the other members said that they looked forward to hearing from her on this. (Work with Alice will be used in some of the remaining portions of this chapter.)

12.1.2 ELICITING AGREEMENT TO PERFORM THE TASK

In individual work, the agreement is one between the social worker and the client. In task-centered group work the agreement should be between the member and the other members. This reduces the "authority" of the group worker in this area and the likelihood that members will resist performing a task because of an interpersonal problem with the worker. The group worker helps the members to be aware of the nature of this contract by pointing out that members are not committing themselves to the worker but to one another. When an intermember issue arises, the worker can act from a "neutral" position to mediate the issue.

An agreement between one member and the other members that the member in question will perform a task increases the value placed on task performance over a worker-member agreement. Such an agreement also gives all members an investment in whether the task is carried out and, consequently, promotes their interest in helping the member to overcome barriers to task implementation. In the example provided in the preceding section, not only the worker but also the other members asked Alice to report back at the next meeting regarding the carrying out of the task.

12.1.3 PLANNING DETAILS OF TASK IMPLEMENTATION

The details of task implementation in groups will be planned to the same degree as they are in individual work, as described in section 4.1.3. Some additional resources exist, however, in groups and families to help the members plan such details.

One of these is the opportunity to role play task implementation in the group. At a later point in the process, such role plays might be used for a different purpose, such as to help the member acquire skills needed to implement the task. At this point, however, the role play is used for planning details. For example, in one group a member was determining details as to how she would carry out a task to protest her denial of admission to an educational program. During the planning of the role play, the members helped her to determine the points she wanted to make. After the role play, in which a member played the admissions officer, the members identified still other points that became apparent after the actions of the "admissions officer" were noted.

The members can also suggest details from their own experiences with performing analogous tasks. In a task-centered group in which severely mentally ill members were focusing on problems in the use of leisure time, one member wished to learn to play a musical instrument. A subtask was to secure the instrument. Members indicated the ways they had gone about accomplishing similar activities, such as looking at want ads, visiting flea markets, and placing a notice on the bulletin board of the agency itself.

12.1.4 ESTABLISHING RATIONALE AND INCENTIVES

The rationale for the task, as with other dimensions of task-centered group work, is often generated by other group members. In fact, the social worker would be unwise to assume responsibility for creating the rationale in group situations, as this unduly elevates the worker's status and, consequently, increases the likelihood that a task will come to be seen as one the worker imposed on the member rather than a solution to a problem that the member arrived at with the *help of other group members*. The worker helps the members to help one another establish a rationale by the way he or she engages the members in discussion with one another.

The members are likely to create the rationale when similarities among their tasks exist. As members see approximate but not exact similarities, we have found that the underlying reasons become more apparent. This occurred in a task-centered group of people recovering from severe mental illness. A number of tasks in that group had to do with the use of leisure time. One member's task was to enroll in an art class, another's was to join a self-help group, and a third person's was to start going to a drop-in social center. One member said that she now saw how the members tasks "actually got them involved in doing something they would enjoy doing when the group ended."

Incentives are important in all efforts at task accomplishment. In fact, we argue that the issue is not whether incentives will exist but rather whether the incentives will come from "outside" the client or from "inside," in the form of the client's satisfaction from having accomplished something. Nevertheless, groups offer many opportunities for external incentives.

One source is the social worker who can offer praise or even tangible rewards. Another, and one of the most potent reasons for using a group, is the multiplicity of incentives that can come from other members. The sense of accomplishment can be visible as one watches a member's pleased expression as other members join in to express their happiness about the member's having completed a task or even having started one.

In addition, the entire group can receive incentives. One of these can be a pleasurable event toward the end of a group session to reward the members for their work during the session. This often is in the form of refreshments or a pleasurable activity, such as a game, an opportunity to listen to music, or a video-tape whose content is related to the group's purpose. Another incentive is offered when all the members have reached a predefined stage of task accomplishment. Social workers should be aware, however, that in group situations a group reward stimulates the members to bring pressure on the slower members to move ahead so the entire group can have the reward. Depending on the circumstances, this may or may not be a valid pressure to expose the members to. For example, a high school student group was rewarded with a trip to a basketball game when all the members had defined their tasks. One member had difficulty thinking of a task he could accomplish in a class with a particularly uncooperative teacher. The other members tried to discourage him from coming to the group for fear his difficulty would delay their obtaining this reward.

12.1.5 Session Tasks (Simulation)

All the methods referred to in section 4.1.5 for simulating or practicing the task (rehearsal, role play, and guided practice) are used in group situations but with some nuances derived from the group context. Rehearsal in group situations also requires the client to tell other group members how he or she will perform the task. The client can tell this to all group members at the same time or the group can be subdivided into sets of "buddies" in which two members take turns rehearsing with each other. Alternatively, the group can be subdivided into members who have similar tasks, as each may then be particularly interested in how others in the subgroup plan on carrying out the task.

In role-play situations, the group worker is most likely to ask members to portray the other person(s). The group offers the advantage of allowing role plays of multiperson situations so that the replication of these situations can be very realistic. The worker is consequently able to move from a role play to guided practice by either offering feedback on the role play or stepping in to model a behavior that the client is having trouble enacting. Groups provide another possibility for guided practice because many tasks involve social interactions and these may actually occur naturally in the course of the group's social exchanges. The worker may anticipate this and say such things as: "Next time you want help from another member in the group, will you directly ask for it from that person because that is similar to your task with your teacher—to ask for help when you need it."

In the example cited above in which members were struggling with depression, the member, Alice, who wanted to learn to play bridge did enroll in a bridge class. She came to the next group meeting, however, in a rather despondent state. She had attended the class and discovered that most of the others already knew one another and quickly formed foursomes. She happened to be the only one not involved in a foursome. The instructor therefore suggested that she watch one group, but she thought this was not the same as actually playing and was certainly not as interesting. The group members discussed this, and several thought that she should have asked the instructor to work out an equitable way of dealing with this issue, such as rotating the members of teams several times during the evening. Alice said she could not imagine herself doing that. The group worker thought that this would be a good time for a session task, namely, for Alice to role play this situation. The worker suggested, however, that another member might "play" Alice and demonstrate how this might be done, and Alice agreed. Bob thought he could do that, and the other therapy group members agreed to represent the bridge class. Bob was effective in approaching the teacher (played by the group worker) to ask for a change in procedures. The "teacher" did so and the other "class members" assented to the change. Alice then took over her own role and was effective in doing the same thing. The worker led a short discussion in which Alice was first praised and then the group considered alternatives should the actual class not be so willing to change procedures.

12.1.6 ANTICIPATING OBSTACLES TO TASK PERFORMANCE

That other members of the group have similar tasks or problems is an advantage in anticipating obstacles. These members can be asked what might stand in their way if they were to undertake the task. While it would be discouraging to focus on the "negative" by listing every problem that could occur in trying to perform the task, at least a brief discussion in the group of such problems is desirable. Members can also help one another by indicating how they would overcome these obstacles. Again, their insights that derive from having been in similar situations can be valuable.

Some of the other approaches to overcoming obstacles mentioned in section 4.1.6 can take on added potency in groups. The issue of adverse beliefs was described in that chapter and in sections 6.2.0 and 8.1.6. It was suggested there that these be handled by either scaling down the task or by providing support.

While such actions can be taken in groups, another tactic is to challenge the adverse belief directly. For example, a member of one group had accepted the task of starting conversations with others at work as a means of initiating friendships. He believed he would be rejected every time and that this would prove that no one could like him. The group members challenged these beliefs by pointing out that he had made friends in the group and that to believe he was unlikable because of a rejection was irrational. This approach has been extensively discussed by Ellis and Dryden (1987). A group is an especially potent place to challenge adverse beliefs because the members see one another as struggling with similar problems and situations, and believe, therefore, that each one knows "what it's really like."

Another common obstacle is when members feel anxious when they contemplate engaging in the task. For this reason, social workers should be prepared to help members learn ways of relaxing if this will help them accomplish their tasks. Sometimes the reminder to take a few deep breaths before embarking on the task activity is sufficient. At other times members should be taught relaxation exercises. These require that the social worker secures training in relaxation procedures, which involve instructing members on how to alternate the tensing and releasing of various muscles (Smith 2001; Poppen 1998). Another approach that can help members relax when a course of relaxation training is not feasible is to instruct them on how to regulate their breathing, such as by counting breaths (Fahrion and Norris 1990).

Members can also provide direct support to one another in accomplishing tasks. This support might involve the use of buddies in the group whom one calls when encountering an obstacle or discussing the obstacle at the next meeting and securing the help needed to overcome it.

12.1.7 SUMMARIZING TASKS

Use of a task summarization procedure in task-centered group work is essential because when a number of members are each performing one or more tasks, these are difficult for the members and group worker to recall. Usually each member's task is listed on a large sheet of paper and posted before each meeting. A standard form can also be used, but all members cannot easily view this simultaneously.

12.1.8 REVIEWING TASK PROGRESS

As is true for individual task-centered work, each group session, after tasks have been determined, should begin with a review of progress. The task-summarization sheets should be used for this purpose.

Members will tell one another in specific ways what they did and how often they did it. The group worker will prompt the members to help one another to be specific by posing certain questions to the group, such as, "Did you understand exactly what Alice did?" Some groups may use subgroups or pairs for this reporting after the worker is certain that the standard of specificity will be upheld. The worker should also help group members to praise one another regarding task progress.

While the group worker understands that punishment for nonperformance is undesirable, this may be less obvious to members. This should be the occasion for the worker to explain this principle to the members and to offer alternatives, such as those discussed in section 12.2.0 (Resolving Unsuccessful Tasks) and section 12.3.0 (Consistent Nonperformance of Tasks).

12.1.9 REVIEWING TARGET PROBLEMS

Because of the time needed for each member to report on task progress, the time remaining may be insufficient to engage in problem review, that is, to see if even partial performance of the task is alleviating the problem for which the task was devised. Nevertheless, task accomplishment can be reinforced if the worker periodically devotes part of a meeting to problem review. The worker should time this review to occur when he or she has reason to believe that a sufficient number of members have changed their problem situation in a positive direction.

Premature problem review in groups can create a "contagion effect" in which members who are discouraged "spread" this feeling to others. The ultimate effect is to reduce group cohesiveness; even the continuation of the group could be threatened. The opposite effect, however, will occur when "the time is right." Members who have not experienced improvement in the problem situation might be stimulated to renew their efforts because of the success of other members.

The social worker must, however, guard against some member feeling so outdistanced that the member gives up. If there is danger of that happening, the worker might provide support to that member, even including an individual session with the worker or with another member outside the group session or in a meeting of "buddies" during a session.

12.1.10 CHECKLIST FOR THE TASK PLANNING SEQUENCE

___ 1. Did the group encourage each member to generate alternatives as well as suggest some alternatives? Did I encourage the group to do this?

___ 2. Did the clients each choose a task to be implemented, and did each make a commitment to the group to carry out the task?

___ 3. Did the tasks describe *who* was to do *what, when, how often, where,* and *with whom?*

___ 4. Did the group members review with one another their rationales for doing their tasks? Did the members provide incentives to one another? Do I think it desirable to add incentives to the ones that I will supply?

__ 5. Did we use simulations in the group? What types?

__ 6. Did the members help one another to define obstacles? Was this done in such a way that it was encouraging rather than discouraging to the members concerned?

__ 7. Did I help the group create a means for summarizing each member's task? What form did that take?

__ 8. At the beginning of each session, did the group review progress made on each member's task since the previous session?

__ 9. Did the group also review problems that members encountered in accomplishing their tasks? Did the review indicate the need for changes in the definition of the tasks?

12.1.11 EXERCISE FOR THE TASK PLANNING AND IMPLEMENTATION SEQUENCE

One of the skills involved in task-centered group work is to manage the planning of tasks with several people. Role playing this process is useful in order to learn how to keep the state of each person's task planning in mind, how to gauge the patience of group members for working on one another's plans, and how to help each member make use of material generated by another member. Task planning in groups may take several sessions so that a role play should also allow for several "sessions." In classes that last several hours, the instructor might have one "session" and then work with the students to plan the next "session" in the light of the experience with the first. If time allows, the next "session" can then be enacted.

12.2.0 REVISING UNSUCCESSFUL TASKS

The same reasons that tasks might be unsuccessful in individual work also occur in group work. The group worker will try to reverse this by using all the ideas expressed in section 4.2.0 in the context of the group. The group can impact this process in several ways.

First, a group member will likely be faced with others whose tasks are being successfully carried out and whose problems are being resolved.

This can have both positive and negative effects on the member. The positive effect is that the others may serve as role models who demonstrate the value of carrying out appropriately defined tasks. Their encouragement may be all the member needs to "catch up." The negative effect occurs if the member becomes discouraged when hearing about the success of others and then decides "this is not for me." This effect can be prevented in some cases if the group worker warns the group early in the task planning process that each member has unique circumstances, that some will make progress more rapidly than others, and that this can be discouraging.

Second, as stated earlier, an advantage of the group is that members are likely to have similar situations, and this helps them empathize with difficulties other members have in accomplishing their tasks. They can often see solutions to overcoming barriers or can generate alternative tasks even more easily than the social worker. They also have developed an investment in one another's success because they have worked closely together in defining problems, generating tasks, and so forth. This can create a high degree of patience and support as members help one another overcome barriers to success.

A problem arises when some members need help carrying out tasks while others need to create alternative tasks. Our preferred solution is to create subgroups devoted to each process that meet simultaneously during a group session. We have also, on occasion, met with members individually to help them rework their tasks so that their phase of work is in line with that of the other members.

12.2.1 CHECKLIST FOR REVISING UNSUCCESSFUL TASKS

___ 1. Was the task not implemented or did it not have the desired effect on the target problem?

___ 2. If it was not implemented, was it because expectations were unclear, opportunities did not arise, unanticipated obstacles occurred, or motivation was insufficient?

___ 3. Did the other group members empathize with the individual whose task was unsuccessful?

__ 4. Did the other group members invest themselves in helping the person in question either to find a way to overcome a barrier or to pick a more appropriate task?

__ 5. If the lack of success of one member placed that member too out of phase with the other members, what means did I use to help the member's work again be coordinated with that of the others?

12.2.2 EXERCISE FOR REVISING UNSUCCESSFUL TASKS

Continue the preceding role play for the Task Planning and Implementation Sequence. Assume that either one of the tasks was not implemented or that it did not impact the target problem. Work with the group to help the member revise the task or plan a new one. Be especially attentive to the effect of this process on the other members and on the group as a whole. If members have a negative reaction to the revision experience, plan a way of dealing with this.

12.3.0 CONSISTENT NONPERFORMANCE OF TASKS

In section 4.3.0 we discussed the reasons for nonperformance of tasks in individual task-centered work. These included the client's lack of interest in changing the problem selected, the client's disinterest in working with us, or the client's wish to have nothing changed. In addition to these possibilities, a fourth exists in task-centered group work. Some factor related to the group might make it difficult for the client to perform his or her task.

One such factor would be that the client does not trust the group to be helpful or supportive. This may be true because of some group condition, such as one or more of the members rejecting the client. In this case, the group worker will try to work with the other members to discover and remedy the source of this rejection. The client may also perceive rejection even when it does not exist—often because of some previous experience that causes the client to distort the current situation.

The worker should try to help the client realize that this kind of distortion is occurring.

It is also conceivable that the situation cannot be remedied. One common source of this is a compositional one in that the client may perceive the other members as so dissimilar to her- or himself that they cannot understand what the member is seeking to accomplish and cannot make helpful suggestions. In these situations the client should be offered another group, if one is available. If not, the client should be given the option to continue treatment on a one-to-one basis.

Another condition associated with nonperformance of tasks is that the member is being rewarded for nonperformance by the amount of attention the member is receiving. Thus members may spend a lot of group time exploring the client's reasons with him or her, and this is gratifying to the client. One way of handling this is to point out what is taking place. Another is to work out an agreement between the client and the other members that the client will be rewarded by group attention when some progress is made in carrying out the task but not until then. The "behavioral" principle utilized here is that performance rather than nonperformance should be reinforced.

An example of dealing with task nonperformance occurred in the group of people struggling with depression described above. Alice had agreed, as we reported, to enroll in a bridge class. She also had been helped to deal with not being included in the foursomes that were created. This worked, and she was included in bridge games. In one group session, she reported that she was dropping out of the bridge class and was also considering leaving the task-centered group. The worker suggested that the members discuss this with Alice. They asked Alice about what was happening in the bridge class, and she said that the other people seemed to know much more than she did about bridge. One member asked her how long they had been taking the class, and she said that everyone else had taken it at least once before. The other members thought that she would feel differently after she had taken the class at least once. She thought about this, and said "I guess I should try a little longer." She also stopped talking about leaving the task-centered group.

12.3.1 CHECKLIST FOR CONSISTENT NONPERFORMANCE OF TASKS

> ___ 1. Is the member not performing tasks because the selection of target problems is inaccurate, the member does not want help from this group, or the member does not want help from anyone?
>
> ___ 2. Have the appropriate corrective actions been taken?
>
> ___ 3. If a member is not performing his or her tasks, what group conditions might be contributing to this?
>
> ___ 4. Have appropriate steps been taken to modify these group conditions?

12.3.2 EXERCISE FOR CONSISTENT NONPERFORMANCE OF TASKS

Continue the preceding role play but instruct one member to convey to the group that she or he has consistently not performed any tasks. Ascertain the reason and take the appropriate action. Be sure to include an analysis of group factors that contribute to this in your analysis.

12.4.0 NONTARGETED PROBLEMS: RESTRUCTURING

New problems can arise for clients in task-centered group work, as well as in individual work, and thus the client may have to interrupt work on the selected problem in order to work on the newly identified one. The new one may arise as a result of a crisis in the client's life or of an unforeseen event. The complexity in the group situation is that the other group members may inappropriately ignore problems that should be worked on or inappropriately give attention to problems that should be ignored, at least for the present.

The social worker may point these inappropriate responses out to the group. In the simplest of circumstances the group members recognize the error and continue in an appropriate way. At other times the worker's comments on this issue will lead to conflict among the worker, the client in question, and/or the other members. This is not an unusual event in group work but requires experience and skill on the social worker's part to unravel the sources of conflict and determine an appropriate response. In some group situations the group members are perceptive enough to cooperate with the worker in determining the source of the conflict, as well as the solution to it.

When the social worker and group concur that the newly identified problem should be worked on, the group will help the member through the phases described in 11.5.0, 11.6.0, 11.7.0, and 11.9.0. If time does not permit this, in view of the group's responsibilities to all the members, some of the other approaches described in this chapter should be used. These include the use of a buddy, subgroup meetings during group sessions, and individual sessions with the member outside the group. Members who have learned how to specify problems and create tasks may even do this as a homework assignment. For highly literate members, a workbook can be devised to "walk the member" through these phases.

12.4.1 CHECKLIST FOR NONTARGETED PROBLEMS

___ 1. Has a group member mentioned any nontargeted concerns?

___ 2. Have I helped the group to ask if these concerns should be targeted and with what priority?

___ 3. Do the group, the member, and I agree on how the nontargeted concerns should be approached?

___ 4. If we do not agree, how have I sought to attain agreement?

___ 5. Have we employed the necessary initial-phase activities: exploring, specifying, and goal setting? How has the group responded to a return to these activities, and how have I handled its response?

12.4.2 EXERCISE FOR NONTARGETED PROBLEMS

Continue the role play for the Task Planning and Implementation Sequence (see section 12.1.11). As tasks are being planned, one of the role players should be designated to mention a new concern and should be instructed to mention it subtly. If the role player does not perceive the worker or group as responding appropriately, he or she can escalate the way the problem is introduced. Once it is heard by the worker, she or he should practice the skills identified in this section.

12.5.0 USE OF TIME LIMITS

As in individual work, the social worker reminds the group members during each meeting of the number of sessions that have been conducted and the number that remain. It is less likely in group than in individual work that each member will complete his or her task in fewer than the number of initially contracted sessions. This is because, however simple the tasks may be, each member only receives a proportion of group time.

As in the case of individual work, however, in the rare situation in which work is completed early, members are given the option of determining whether they wish to continue for the allotted time. Because the members have usually developed relationships with one another, it is likely that they will want to continue and they will undoubtedly generate issues to discuss.

The more typical situation is that of a member who completes his or her task before the other members do. We recommend that the social worker anticipate this and, in the beginning, ask each member to contract to remain for all the sessions. This communicates to the members that they are not only there to complete their tasks but *to help one another*. This kind of commitment is necessary in order to create a group in which members trust one another.

Because of the time needed to give attention to each member, an extension of time is more likely to be requested. As with individual work, we recommend that the decision on this be postponed if requested too early because of the impact this has on the motivating force of time limits. On the other hand, group members who become too anxious about time will not give an adequate amount of attention to one another and the effectiveness of the task-centered process in the group can be jeopardized. Any extension, however, should be for specified periods of time in order to maintain the potency of time limits.

12.5.1 CHECKLIST FOR USING TIME LIMITS

> __ 1. Have I reminded the group members at every group meeting of the number of group sessions remaining?
>
> __ 2. How am I working with individuals so that they can be at the same phase of the task-centered process as the other members of the group?

12.5.2 EXERCISE FOR USING TIME LIMITS

Instruct a member during one of the middle-phase role plays to raise the issue of time limits. Practice handling this situation in ways that appear appropriate to you under the given circumstances.

12.6.0 REVISING ASSESSMENTS

New information will be generated about the clients, their ways of coping, and their problems during group sessions. The group situation, in fact, itself generates information as the social worker observes the way the member interacts with other members. The worker will also acquire information from the member, as well as from other sources about other systems in which the member is involved. This may lead to the social worker revising his or her overall assessment of the member and the member's situation and to a modification in the nature of the member's task. It may also enable the member and worker to identify unforeseen problems in external systems and to create goals and tasks to deal with these.

All this information will be useful to the social worker in devising ways to be helpful to the client during this phase. A source of complexity is the question as to how and whether the other group members are involved in examining such additional information. Our approach to this is to draw the attention of group members to such information only if it is relevant to their efforts to help a member overcome barriers to task accomplishment or to revise a problem or task.

In the group for depressed clients, used as an example in this chapter, Alice continued to have difficulty with her bridge class. She continued to report that she felt inferior to the other bridge class members. The worker concluded that she had a strong tendency to make depreciating comments about herself and to act on the basis of these comments (sometimes referred to as low self-esteem). The worker discussed this with Alice during a group session, and Alice agreed that this constituted another problem. She agreed on the task of saying to herself, when in a situation in which she made negative self-attributions: "I am capable of learning new skills."

12.6.1 CHECKLIST FOR REVISING ASSESSMENTS

___ 1. What new information do I have based on the client's ways of participating in the group?

___ 2. What new information do I have based on what clients have said to one another outside the group and which was subsequently reported to the group?

___ 3. Should I call the group's attention to this information?

___ 4. Should I modify my interventions in the group in light of this new information?

___ 5. Should I modify my interventions in the environment external to the group on the basis of this information or should I help the client to do so?

(The checklist in 4.6.1 may also be applied.)

12.7.0 ECLECTIC PRACTICE

As the reader must be aware of by now, the task-centered model enables practitioners to incorporate techniques from many different approaches into their practice. This is true of task-centered group work. While, again, we cannot discuss every possibility, we can mention some that are used most frequently.

One of these is social skills training, which is a type of practice that employs many behavioral techniques. The basic social skills model utilizes the following steps (Liberman 1988; Rose 1977):

1. An interpersonal problem is described.
2. Problem-specific behavioral goals are created.
3. A way of responding to the problem situation is described as a result of group discussion; this way of responding may operationalize a set of values, such as the value placed on assertiveness.
4. Group members (sometimes group workers as well) role play the described way of responding to the problem situation (i.e., a model is presented).
5. The role play is analyzed in terms of the degree to which it demonstrates the way of responding created in (3).
6. The member undertakes to practice the desired behaviors in another role play.
7. Feedback is given as to how the member enacted the principles.
8. If necessary, the member engages in another role play so as to come closer to an enactment of the principles.
9. Additional feedback may be given.
10. The member is given the assignment to handle the situation outside the group by employing the skill that has been role played.
11. At the next meeting, the member reports on the use of the skill outside the group.
12. If necessary, the member repeats the cycle beginning at (3).

Social skills training differs from task-centered group work in one major way, namely, the behavior is prescribed to the member rather than representing a task largely created by the member with consultation from others. In some cases, however, the creation of a task might be similar to the process involved in the acquisition of a skill. On the other hand, some tasks may not involve learning social skills, such as completing homework, setting aside time to spend with one's children, or applying for a job. On the other hand, all three of these examples could involve the acquisition of a social skill—namely, responding to a teacher, communicating with a child, or interacting with a job interviewer.

Another approach often incorporated into task-centered group work is training in problem solving (Garvin 1997:166–67). Since task-centered work involves a great deal of problem solving, it is often advisable to teach group members how to engage in group problem solving. We have done this by listing the following principles on a blackboard or other media, explaining them to members, and having members practice them on some simulated problems:

1. Goals to be attained through problem solving are specified.
2. Information is sought to help the group members generate possible solutions, as well as to evaluate such solutions.
3. Alternative solutions are evaluated.
4. One alternative is chosen.
5. The details for carrying out the alternative are planned.

A third approach comes from traditional social work models of group work, namely, the use of program media (Middleman 1981). Social workers with groups have used such content as games, dance, dramatics, food preparation, art, drama, and trips to achieve group work goals. These media can have two major uses in task-centered group work. One is to make the group sessions more enjoyable and the group more attractive to its members. For example, in a task-centered group for seriously mentally ill members, every session incorporated at least one game as well as refreshment preparation and consumption.

Another use is that the skills required to carry out tasks and identify and overcome barriers to task accomplishment can sometimes be best taught through one of these media. For example, a way for parents to communicate with young children was taught by playing games with the parent group; an assessment of possible barriers to accomplishing tasks in a school setting was accomplished by having the students produce a picture of their school's activities; and a group was helped to remember the steps in specifying tasks by making up a song about this.

12.7.1 EXERCISE FOR ECLECTIC PRACTICE

Learn about another practice approach for work with groups (e.g., gestalt groups, behavioral groups, self-help groups such as Alcoholics

Anonymous). Try to incorporate the interventions employed into some aspect of the task-centered group work process.

12.8.0 WORK WITH COLLATERALS

In group work, as with other forms of task-centered practice, the social worker is likely to interact with other systems, such as group members' families, friends, fellow employees, or teachers. Sometimes this work is done on a one-to-one basis, such as when a worker checks with teachers to learn about how well student members of a group are accomplishing their tasks. The students will have given their permission for these encounters. At other times, the social worker will interact with others on a group basis, such as convening the parents of students in order to obtain their support for the program. Still another option is to move from group work to task-centered family work when that modality is required in order to achieve the service goals.

When the social worker interacts with these other systems, he or she may still operate in a task-centered framework in which these "others" wish to assume tasks and may even want the worker's help in accomplishing tasks. Under other circumstances, another modality might be required, such as when the social worker is serving as an advocate, mediator, or broker for the group member; in section 4.9.0 we conceptualized the performance of these roles as practitioner tasks. A detailed discussion of these roles is beyond the scope of this volume but can be found in Garvin(1987:169–71).

12.8.1 CHECKLIST FOR WORK WITH COLLATERALS

___ 1. Might certain people be appropriate collaterals for several or all members of the group (e.g., teachers or employers)?

___ 2. Have I considered how work with collaterals will affect group processes?

___ 3. Have I conveyed to the group members my practitioner tasks in work with collaterals?

___ 4. Have any important collaterals been overlooked?

13

TERMINATION

13.0.0 COMPONENTS OF TERMINATION

Termination in task-centered group work is similar to that in individual and family work in that it typically occurs in the last session but may take place over several sessions. The purpose of termination in the group situation is similar to that in individual work. As we stated in section 5.0.0, the purpose of individual termination is "to review accomplishments, plan follow-up, and say good-bye." The difference in a group, however, is that the members help one another in the termination process. They bid farewell to one another as well as to the group worker, and members of a task-centered treatment group may even create a self-help, support group that continues after the end of the task-centered group.

As in individual work, the practitioner reminds the members about termination from the first group session, as well as in the pregroup screening session. The time limit in the group also encourages group members to consider how much they invest in the relationship both with the worker and with the other members.

Another issue for group work is that some members may terminate before their work is done, before the time the group is scheduled to end. In view of this, we have a requirement that members attend one session after they decide to terminate to discuss this with the group. This is explained to the members in their pregroup interview, as well as in the first group session. When this is not done, members invest energy in worrying about why the member left, whether they had done something wrong, and so forth. In addition, a problem in the group that led to the member's desire to terminate may be identified and resolved.

13.1.0 THE FINAL PROBLEM REVIEW

All the activities described in section 5.1.0 are carried on in the group situation. The members are asked to help one another thoroughly to determine changes that have taken place in the problem situation since the initial phase. Because they have been engaging in a more limited problem review during earlier sessions, this process should be familiar to them. As with individual work, the members can use the following type of rating: problem completely alleviated, substantially changed, minimally changed, or unchanged.

We have also used a "goal attainment scale" approach to evaluation of task-centered group work (Kiresuk and Garwick 1979). If this approach is to be used, it must be introduced when members set goals. At that time members, with the assistance of the worker, help one another to create an individualized 5-point scale for each goal. Each scale point is defined by specific examples of change in the goal state. The five points are (1) most unfavorable outcome thought likely; (2) less than expected success; (3) expected level of success; (4) more than expected success; and (5) most favorable outcome thought likely. Numerical ranks can be assigned to each scale point and used for a variety of purposes, such as comparing groups by calculating an average score for all the members of the group (Garvin 1997:194).

Group members will contribute a great deal to this review, especially when they can observe one another in situations outside the group. Such members might include students in school who share classes together or clients in a community mental health center who participate in other group activities at the center.

The practitioner should be aware, moreover, of some problems that can occur in groups around this process. Members, at times, seem to make an implicit agreement with one another to "go easy," and this may lead to overestimating the amount of progress each has made. Practitioners, when they sense that this is occurring, should point out to members that the problem review is for their benefit in planning to secure future help that they may need and that this requires that members respond realistically to the problem review.

Members of a task-centered group created to attain changes in the environment will have some analogous activities. They will ascertain whether the problem in the environment has been ameliorated and the environmental change goals achieved. They will also assess how effectively the group has functioned as an entity in order to achieve these goals. These types of groups are typically created in organizations (such as agency committees) or in communities (such as a committee in a community organization agency).

An example is from a group of clients recovering from severe mental illnesses. The group had reached the point of termination and was engaged in a final problem review. They had agreed, at the suggestion of their worker, to use the scale mentioned above: problem completely alleviated, substantially changed, minimally changed, or unchanged. Four members were still in the group at this time. The group began with eight members but two were rehospitalized, one lost interest in the group, and one moved from the area. The following is information on their respective ratings:

Randy. Randy's problem was that he was living in a shelter and he wished to live in his own apartment. By the end of the group, he was living in a group home. He still wished to have his own apartment but lacked the resources to pay rent. He also needed some help in structuring his daily activities. The group agreed with Randy that his problem had "substantially changed."

Sue. Sue's problem was that she was living with her sister who had little room in her small apartment, and, consequently, Sue was sleeping on the living room sofa. At the end of the group, Sue was seeking roommates so that she could share the cost of her own apartment. She concurred with the group that her problem was "minimally changed."

Bob. Bob's problem was that he did not have enough skills to obtain employment. He had explored various vocational programs and planned to enroll in one that trained people for simple clerical work, such as filing and simple data entries. The group and he agreed that the rating would be "minimally changed," but if he actually enrolled in and attended the program, then the rating would be "substantially changed."

Ruth. Ruth's problem was that her medications made her very drowsy and lethargic. This prevented her from engaging in recreational or educational activities as she would fall asleep during the activity. She had discussed this issue with her doctor, who had altered he dosage of the medication. This seemed not to lead to any recurrence of her symptoms and also enabled her to feel wide awake most of the time. The group and she agreed that her problem was completely alleviated.

13.1.1 CHECKLIST FOR THE FINAL PROBLEM REVIEW

> __ 1. Did I help the members collectively to focus on each individual's problem status as it changed from the initial phase to termination?
> __ 2. Did we review all target problems and all specifications?
> __ 3. Did I secure the opinions of collaterals, if involved?
> __ 4. Did I help the members to understand the purpose of the problem review and therefore the importance of being as realistic as possible regarding one another's problem status?

13.1.2 EXERCISE FOR FINAL PROBLEM REVIEW

See section 13.3.2 for an exercise that combines practicing final problem review with other termination-phase activities.

13.2.0 REINFORCEMENT OF ACCOMPLISHMENTS

In addition to the praise offered by the social worker, members should be helped to reinforce one another. This can take several forms. One is for members to be asked to indicate to one another what they particularly appreciated about the way others accomplished their tasks. Focusing on one member at a time and encouraging other members to provide feedback to that member can accomplish this. Alternatively, one can ask each member to comment on other members while he or she "has the floor."

Another dimension to this process in task-centered group work is to reinforce the members for the way they have helped one another and for their having taken responsibility for the group. This reinforcement often takes the form of praise from the social worker, who may say something like "I think you did a great job of helping Jill when she seemed so worried about being able to carry out her task." While this kind of mutual aid is not the reason they had been referred to a task-centered group, it may be an important skill they have acquired that they can take from the group and bring to future group experiences.

13.2.1 CHECKLIST FOR REINFORCEMENT OF ACCOMPLISHMENTS

__ 1. How did I help the members to praise one another?
__ 2. What were their reactions to giving and receiving praise?
__ 3. If members made comments that were punishing, did I limit this? Did I find some way to ameliorate the effects of punishment?
__ 4. Did I reinforce the way the members helped one another, as well as how they contributed to the group during the previous sessions?
__ 5. Were collaterals, if involved, reinforced for their contributions?

13.2.2 EXERCISE FOR REINFORCEMENT OF ACCOMPLISHMENTS

See section 13.3.2 for practice of this skill.

13.3.0 FUTURE PLANS

Working on future plans in groups includes several dimensions in addition to the aspects of planning discussed in section 5.3.0. An obvious one is that group members help one another to devise these plans. This ability to aid one another is again a consequence of members working on similar problems and tasks. In fact, several members are likely to have identical future plans and to decide to pursue these together. Examples of this are accompanying one another to an Alcoholics Anonymous meeting, doing homework together, or planning social engagements with one another.

Members can also draw on this similarity in their situations in identifying obstacles that other members will have to overcome to continue performance of old tasks or to create new ones. For example, in a group in which members had problems completing school assignments, it turned out that several of the members had an uncooperative teacher who failed to give adequate reinforcement for completion of assignments. The members reminded one another about this and agreed to reward one another for completing assignments no matter what the teacher did. These rewards were to take the form of treating one another to soft drinks on the way home from school.

In task-centered group work, all or some of the members may decide to continue the group as a self-help or support group after the task-centered group terminates. Such a support group might meet less frequently than the worker-led group but might continue to help members perform tasks. A support group might also help members live with problems that cannot be changed, such as someone's death, a permanent disability, or even the reality that we all grow older.

If members decide to continue on this basis, the social worker can help establish such a group in a number of ways. These include the following:

1. Help the group decide on the time and place of meetings.
2. Help the group decide on a leadership structure. This includes whether a permanent or rotating chair will be appointed and whether other officers will be required.
3. Train the officers regarding how to create an agenda for meetings, how to act as a "gatekeeper" during discussions, and how to deal with conflict. Bertcher (1994) presents a good discussion of group leadership techniques that can be used as a training manual for this purpose.

Social workers can also make themselves available for consultation with self-help groups when problems arise. At times, the worker may resume a more active role that even extends to facilitating another Task Planning and Implementation Sequence.

In groups seeking to achieve environmental change, the group may need to continue in order to resolve new problems. Alternatively, the group may recognize the need for new groups to be formed in order to deal with these problems. The social worker will facilitate either or both these processes.

13.3.1 CHECKLIST FOR FUTURE PLANS

___ 1. Have I helped the members to help one another create future plans?
___ 2. Have I helped the members to identify ways they can help one another with future plans after the task-centered group terminates?
___ 3. Is the creation of a self-help or support group composed of some or all the task-centered group membership appropriate?
___ 4. If the answer to (3) is yes, have I helped the members to establish that group?
___ 5. Were collaterals appropriately involved in future plans?

13.3.2 EXERCISE FOR FINAL PROBLEM REVIEW, REINFORCING ACCOMPLISHMENTS, AND FUTURE PLANS

Problem specifications for each "member" are required for this exercise. Those developed earlier can be used. Information should be supplied as to which problems were completely resolved, which partially resolved, and which not resolved at all. A range of degrees of solution should be included in the exercise.

The role player functioning as the social worker begins with the final problem review, and he or she should help the members combine reinforcing achievements and making future plans. Afterward, the students should analyze the session using the checklists provided.

13.4.0 REVIEW OF PROBLEM-SOLVING SKILLS

In section 5.4.0, we indicated that reviewing problem-solving skills with individual clients is useful. So, too, will a review of *group* problem-solving skills benefit some clients in a group situation. This is because people have many opportunities to engage in group problem solving.

This review is intended to help members overcome some common errors in group problem solving, such as proposing the adoption of solutions before either adequate information has been collected or an appropriate evaluation of alternatives has been accomplished. The group worker facilitates the review by bringing in the materials on group problem solving that were used earlier. These materials are illustrated by drawing on the problem-solving experiences that have occurred in the group.

13.4.1 CHECKLIST FOR REVIEW OF PROBLEM-SOLVING SKILLS

> __ 1. Did I illustrate each of the five skills (see section 5.4.0) with events that occurred in the group?
> __ 2. Did I facilitate the participation of all group members in the discussion?

13.4.2 EXERCISE FOR REVIEW OF PROBLEM-SOLVING SKILLS

See section 13.5.2.

13.5.0 REACTIVE DISCUSSION

Group members engage in the same kind of reactive discussion described in section 5.5.0. In addition to the feelings we identified there, clients also have feelings about leaving one another as well as leaving the group as an entity. These feelings are often mixed. The clients are typically pleased about having undertaken their tasks; they may also feel relieved that they will now have the time available for other pursuits that had been taken up by group sessions.

On the other hand, even though the feelings people have on the termination of a short-term group are not as intense as those experienced when ending a long-term one, group members tend quickly to identify with and have caring feelings for one another. It is helpful for members to acknowledge this for many reasons, such as enhancing the members' capacities to relate to one another and to deal with other terminations. The group worker might also point out that one's memories of the other members of the group may remain for a long time.

In view of these feelings that group members have for one another, group workers use several procedures to assist in this aspect of the termination process. One method is to have a short intermission in the last session in which members freely move about the group saying good-bye to one another. Another is to have a "round" in which each member is invited to express some feelings about terminating with the group and with one another.

As in the case of individual and family task-centered work, clients in groups sometimes ask for an extension in the number of sessions. This is a more complex issue than in individual work because of the number of people involved. Such an extension is requested in two typical types of situations. One is when the amount of time that was needed to work with each individual's tasks has exceeded the original estimate. In this event, it will be obvious to the members and the worker that a specified number of additional sessions is desirable. The other type of situation occurs when the request for extension comes from one or more members but not from everyone. In these circumstances, the group worker will have to decide if an extension for some but not all members is necessary. If so, the worker might continue meeting (again for a specified period of time) with a few members or even just one member. When this is done, the worker should consider and deal appropriately with the feelings of those members who terminate first.

One approach we typically use at the end of the group is to introduce a "ceremony." This may be as simple as a final "round" in the group in which each member has a chance to say a few last words. It may, on the other hand, be more elaborate, such as a modest graduation or a party.

Social workers have feelings about terminating with groups that adds another dimension to their feelings about the same process with individuals. This is because workers can have feelings about the group as an entity. Some groups have been especially gratifying because the members were very cooperative and their enthusiasm for the group was evident. In contrast, some groups have been frustrating because of a lack of enthusiasm or a great deal of conflict or a lack of completion of tasks. The workers should examine their reactions to these kinds of conditions and determine how their feelings are likely to affect the termination process. Even in unsuccessful groups, a sound termination process may make it more likely that members will accept future group services that may be more functional for them.

13.5.1 CHECKLIST FOR REACTIVE DISCUSSION

__ 1. Did the clients have an opportunity to terminate with one another through an expression of thoughts and feelings about their experience together?

__ 2. Did I recognize my own feelings about terminating with the group in addition to feelings I had about terminating with individuals?

__ 3. Did I consider utilizing a closing ceremony with the group?

__ 4. Did I terminate with involved collaterals?

13.5.2 EXERCISES FOR REVIEW OF PROBLEM-SOLVING SKILLS AND REACTIVE DISCUSSION

1. Continue the role play begun in section 13.3.2 and practice reviewing problem-solving skills and reactive discussion.

2. Think about a group you have facilitated (or, if necessary, a group of which you have been a member). How did you feel about the group? How did you feel about the work you did on the group's behalf? How did you feel about the outcome of the group's efforts? Evaluate your reactions. Are they realistic? What might account for them? Did your analysis provide you with any new ideas or observations?

13.6.0 CASE ILLUSTRATION

We shall now provide an extended example of the various stages that occur in a task-centered group. The group chosen for this illustration was created to help clients of a community mental health center. These clients all had been discharged from short stays in mental hospitals where they had been admitted because of severe mental illnesses such as schizophrenia or bipolar affective disorder. They were deemed to be appropriate for a task-centered group because they were sufficiently recovered from the acute stage of their mental illness to be able to give and take help from others. Furthermore, they each had a problem area they wished to work on, such as finding housing, securing part-time work, or arranging for child care as a single parent. It should also be noted that the potential members had expressed a desire to meet other people, as each felt socially isolated.

Case Study

The practitioner, Shirley Anderson, began the process of planning the group by meeting with several case managers who worked with patients who had been discharged from mental hospitals. She learned that the majority of the clients who would be eligible for the group were between the ages of twenty-five and forty-five, and she decided to limit the group to people in that age range. She then interviewed the social workers to determine which potential members were currently committed to working on a specific problem, and this led to identifying about twenty-five clients. Ms. Anderson further determined that she would like to have equal numbers of men and women and of black and white members in the group so that no individual would feel isolated by virtue of his or her culture or gender. The practitioner also wanted to include a few members who could express their ideas, as she wanted to ensure that the group would have some leadership potential. Based on these considerations, Ms. Anderson identified fourteen individuals she wanted to invite to the group. She was not too concerned about the number, as she had learned from experience that several clients would not be willing to join the group, would not be free at the time the group was scheduled, would have transportation problems, and so forth.

Ms. Anderson then phoned all the individuals who were selected. She explained briefly on the phone about the task-centered group and asked if the person would be willing to discuss this further in her office. All but one agreed to do this.

In the individual interviews, Ms. Anderson talked to the clients about the kinds of problems they might be willing to work on in the group. She also explained the task-centered group work process, such as the selection of problem, goal, and then task. She gave a few examples of these items so that members would have specific ideas to relate to. She also gave some brief information about who the other prospective group members were, such as their sex, ethnicity, and the types of problems they were likely to want to work on in the group.

In the pregroup interview, Ms. Anderson also described the reasons for doing task-centered work in a group. She explained that the members had similar problems, so they would be able to identify with one another. And because of their similarities, they would undoubtedly have useful suggestions to give one another. They would be likely to encourage one another, and, when matters did not go as well as they had hoped, they might have suggestions for overcoming that too.

Some of the members, as they were seen in these pregroup interviews, expressed hesitation about being in a group. One woman said that she had found members of a previous group to be cold; a man said that a woman in one of his previous groups had tried to get him to date her when he did not want to do this. Ms. Anderson discussed with the first client the idea that group members can be cold but that she hoped to help the members overcome some of their initial shyness and discomfort that led to this kind of reaction. With the second client, she indicated that if something like this should happen, perhaps she could help him to find a comfortable way to deal with the situation. After these discussions, both these clients decided to join the group. Most of the other clients she interviewed said that they liked to be in groups and were looking forward to this experience.

At the first meeting, Ms. Anderson helped the members to become acquainted with one another by dividing them into pairs. Each member of the pair was asked to find out the name of the other and something about that member that he or she wanted the others to know about. In this way it was learned that one member liked to play the piano, another liked to watch baseball, a third was happy because her mother had just returned home from a hospital stay, and a fourth said that she was just happy to be invited to join a group.

After these introductions, Ms. Anderson again explained what a task-centered group was. She reviewed the ideas of selecting problems, goals, and then tasks. The members had many questions to ask. One member asked what would happen if she changed her mind on the problem she selected. The worker said that this was possible. She hoped, however, that people would change their problems for good reasons, such as a major change in their circumstances, rather than because they encountered some difficulties. Another asked if she could pick the same problem as someone else picked or if everyone had to choose a different problem. The worker answered that several people could pick the same general problem but that the members would find that no two people are identical and so there are likely to be differences in how they experienced their problems. Another asked what would happen if he missed a meeting. The worker answered that she hoped the member would call before, if possible, so the other members wouldn't worry. In any case, the members would probably ask that person, when he or she returned, what had happened. As can be seen, the practitioner gave answers to each question; she also pointed out that at times the group would be asked to provide answers since the group also belonged to the members and so she was not the only one to be called on to solve problems that arose in the group.

Ms. Anderson then introduced the idea of group norms. The main ones she talked about were confidentiality and commitment. Under the latter topic, she said that she was asking members to commit themselves to attending the group for the twelve sessions for which it was scheduled and to come on time and stay until the group was over—each session would last for one and a half hours. If a member needed to miss the meeting, the member should call the social worker to let her know. Ms. Anderson then handed out a card to each member with her phone number on it. She asked if the group members wished to propose any other rules. One member said that she didn't think anyone should be forced to say or do anything if the member didn't want to. This was discussed, and all the members strongly agreed on this principle.

Ms. Anderson praised the group members. She said they had been working hard to understand the group's purpose; they had also asked very good questions. She suggested that they take a short break and share some coffee and cookies that she had brought for refreshments. These were served, and the members appeared to enjoy relaxing and not saying much although a few comments were made, such as how nice the room was, how good the cookies were, and how they wished they could meet more frequently than once a week.

The above events took about one hour and Ms. Anderson suggested, after the refreshments, that the members begin the process of selecting the problems that they were going to work on in the group. They would not be asked to do this at this meeting but rather they could begin a group list that would indicate some of the kinds of problems from which they could chose. She taped a sheet of newsprint to the front wall on which she had already written two problems. One was not having enough things to do with one's time. The other was finding a better place to live. She asked the members to suggest additional ones. The following were added to the list: having a medication prescribed for one's mental illness that one didn't like; not having finished one's schooling; not getting along with a roommate; and having a case manager one didn't like.

Ms. Anderson noted that Sam, one of the members, seemed to be having trouble staying awake during the meeting. She commented that he seemed very tired, and he replied that he was receiving a new medication that did this to him. (He was also the member who listed problems with medication as his problem.) Another member frequently left the room saying that he had to use the bathroom. The worker suspected that he found it difficult to sit still for long periods, but she wasn't sure how to handle this and determined to ask her supervisor for suggestions after the meeting.

At the end of the session, Ms. Anderson briefly summarized the kinds of things that had happened at the meeting: the members had gotten acquainted, had learned more about task-centered group work, and had begun the process of selecting the problem on which they would each focus. She concluded by noting that, at the next meeting, they would make decisions on the problems they would work on, as well as what their goals might be with relationship to the problem.

At the second meeting, all the members were present except Donna. Ms. Anderson had learned that Donna had become extremely distressed during the week and had to be admitted to the hospital, and she made this known to the group.

Ms. Anderson then explained that the first order of business this week was to choose their target problems, as well as to engage in "problem exploration." She explained that problem exploration consisted of providing the kind of information that will enable the member, with the help of the group, to choose goals that can be attained and to anticipate difficulties that may be encountered in trying to deal with the problem.

Ms. Anderson then asked which member would be willing to be the first to work on selecting a problem. Frank volunteered to go first, saying that he had thought a lot about this. He said that his problem was that he was living with his sister; her house was crowded, and he had to move out as soon as he could. The social worker said that this seemed to be an appropriate problem to work on. She asked Frank if he had other problems. He said, "I sure do," and mentioned finishing school and getting a job. He said, however, that these would have to wait until he had solved his housing problem. The worker and the other members commented that this made sense.

Ms. Anderson indicated that she would use Frank's problem to illustrate the problem exploration process. She asked Frank such questions as where he had lived before he was hospitalized (he had been a college student and had lived with roommates); how he would pay for the rent (he receives a disability grant from the government and could also get some help from his parents); what kind of living situation he would like (he would like to live with roommates again); and what he has already done to solve his housing problem (basically nothing). She also asked some questions related to the topic of problem specification. These included whether he has experienced a housing problem like this one before (no) and how long he has been living with his sister (three months).

Ms. Anderson engaged in a similar process with the other members, but space does not permit us to include these. In fact, we shall continue to focus on how Frank proceeded in the group in order to illustrate the various phases of the task-centered group work process.

The process of selecting, exploring, and specifying each member's problem took up the remainder of the session. Ms. Anderson summarized each member's problem at the end of the session and indicated that, at the third session, the members will consider their goals with relationship to their problems and begin the process of choosing the tasks they will carry out to attain their goals.

Ms. Anderson began the third session by indicating that the group's first accomplishment would be to help the members determine their goals with relationship to their problems. To help the members think about goals, she brought a goal game to the meeting. This game, which Ms. Anderson herself had created, consisted of a game board much like that used in Monopoly. On spaces interspersed among blank ones various types of problems were written. When a member moved his "piece" around the board (a spinning wheel determining the number of spaces) and landed on one of these spaces, the member had to state a goal. At least two other members had to agree that the goal was appropriate and, if this occurred, the member moving the piece was awarded a poker chip. The winner of the game was the person with the most chips. The members enjoyed the game, and Ms. Anderson had to be a little forceful in calling the game to an end after everyone had taken several turns.

Again, we shall illustrate this process of selecting goals by describing what happened with Frank. Several members asked Frank questions: how soon did he want to move, what kind of housing was he looking for, and how much rent could he pay. Through these questions, Frank determined that his goal was to move into new housing within two months; the housing would be an apartment with at least two others; the rent would be no more than $250 a month from each person, and each would pay his share of utilities. A similar process was carried out with each member. Because of the time spent on the game, two sessions were needed for all the members to determine their goals. It should be noted, too, that the members' choices of problems and goals, as well as a commitment to work on tasks to attain these goals for the remainder of the sessions, constitute the treatment contracts for all members. Ms. Anderson listed these commitments on large sheets of newsprint that were attached to the wall before each meeting, but this was as "formal" an arrangement as she thought necessary for this particular group.

Ms. Anderson then explained that during the next session the members will be helped to plan tasks that will assist them in reaching their goals. She complimented the members on having gotten this far and suggested that they celebrate this attainment with some refreshments that the agency had made available.

While all members worked for the next two sessions on specifying their tasks, we shall continue our illustration of how Frank did this. In a discussion with other members, Frank concluded that he should create a list of the various ways to look for an apartment and another list of the criteria for an acceptable place. He then will have to rehearse the skills required for handling an interview with a potential landlord and roommates, and then enact this interview in "real life." Final tasks will include negotiating terms once housing has been located and, finally, moving in.

Each of these tasks was then planned in detail, as well as the comparable tasks for the other group members, and this took several sessions. In our limited space we shall provide a few examples of how a few of Frank's tasks were planned. With reference to his list of places to look in his search for an apartment, the other group members provided many of the suggestions. These included looking at the housing bulletin board maintained by the community mental health program, reading the want ads in the paper, consulting the housing specialist in the mental health agency, and looking at the bulletin board in the local supermarket. Frank accepted these ideas and listed them on his newsprint sheet (all members had one and these were posted on the wall each week).

With reference to role playing an interview with prospective roommates, several members of the group volunteered to participate. In the role play that ensued, Frank was asked whether he would do his share of cleaning, whether he could pay his share of the bills on time, and whether he had any habits that might be annoying to the others. Time-outs were taken during the role plays as

Frank indicated that he did not know how to handle some of these questions and needed advice from the other members and the social worker. It should be noted, incidentally, that after all the members had defined their tasks but before they implemented them, Ms. Anderson helped them to plan a party for themselves to celebrate attaining this stage of the task-centered group work process.

During the process of defining tasks, Ms. Anderson also asked members to anticipate obstacles they might meet in performing their tasks and ways of overcoming these obstacles. In Frank's case, for example, he anticipated that potential roommates might object to his playing his stereo. Several of the members suggested that he secure a pair of earphones to use for listening if others did not like his choice of music.

During the next several sessions, Frank and the other members reported on their progress in accomplishing their tasks. At times members failed to follow through on tasks; the group members sought to identify the reasons for this and to overcome problems in accomplishing tasks. At one point, for example, Frank became discouraged and indicated that for now he might give up the idea of moving into his own place. The members learned that he had become fearful of being on his own and that he was making many statements to himself of the dangers of this kind of housing. The members helped him to see that his fears were irrational and suggested alternative ways of viewing his situation.

Not all the members fully accomplished their tasks, and two such members dropped out of the group before they had solved the problems they were working on. Frank, however, was successful in completing his tasks and attaining his goal of moving into an apartment.

At the group's final session, each member reviewed his or her goal and the task accomplishments related to the goal. Attention was also paid to helping members consider the kinds of help that they might desire from the agency in the future. Frank said, during that discussion, that he was bored much of the time and wished he was involved in more activities. Ms. Anderson indicated that a "Use of leisure time group" was being planned by the agency and that a task-centered approach was being considered for the group. Frank said that, based on his success with this group, the worker should "put my name down" for the leisure time group.

After each member's accomplishments were evaluated, Ms. Anderson introduced a "round" in which the members expressed how they felt about the group terminating. Most said that they would miss it. They did not think that they would miss one another, as almost all the members planned to attend other activities in the agency and so they thought they would have many opportunities to see one another again. They also knew that they would have other contacts with Ms. Anderson, because she conducts many other agency activities.

PART FOUR   *Larger Systems*

14

TASK-CENTERED WORK WITH HUMAN SERVICE ORGANIZATIONS

Bageshwari Parihar

14.2.0.0 INTRODUCTION*

This chapter is primarily addressed to the social worker who is responsible for the management of a human service organization. The opportunities for social workers to assume administrative roles have proliferated with the dramatic increase in the number of human service organizations in modern society. These organizations have distinctive attributes and problems that set them apart from other types of formal organizations (Vinter 1963; Hasenfeld 1983; Weiner 1990; Patti 2000).

[*The numbers used to identify topics in chapters 14 and 15 are the same as those used in part 1 except that they are preceded by either the number 14 or 15. Thus section 14.3.0.0 deals with the same topic as section 3.0.0. To locate related content in parts 2 and 3, change the second number (3 in the above example) to correspond to the appropriate chapter number, as follows:

Individual	Families	Groups
2	6	10
3	7	11
4	8	12
5	9	13

Thus the topic of section 14.3.0.0 is also addressed in sections 3.0.0, 7.0.0, and 11.0.0. Because of the comparative brevity of these chapters, some topics are not addressed; however, the topics that are included are numbered to parallel the earlier sections.]

Their purpose is to maintain or enhance people's well-being. The technologies they employ are designed to provide services and resources for altering behavior and attitudes. They are also distinguished from other formal organizations by their characteristic tasks and clientele.

The unique characteristics of human service organizations indicate a need for the development of a system of management that is particularly relevant to them. The task-centered management model (TCM) presented in this chapter is expected to meet this need. This model of practice was developed during the 1980s. It was motivated by the desire to identify an approach to administrative practice that was similar to a clinical problem-solving approach. It was anticipated that such an approach would ease the difficult transition from clinician to administrator, a transition that many social workers make.

The social worker who moves into a management position can be employed at any of the three levels of administration: (1) administrator/executive, who has overall responsibility for the functioning of the organization; (2) middle manager, who has responsibility of a department or unit; and (3) supervisor, who by virtue of seniority and professional expertise has the responsibility to supervise or guide a given number of staff and to assure staff training and quality service delivery.

The role definitions of these positions indicate that, while an administrator is usually answerable to a board of directors or a higher administrative authority, he or she attempts to accomplish organizational goals with and through people at different levels of organizational hierarchy. Examples of executiveship include the executive director of a comprehensive mental health center and director of a state-level department (e.g., public aid, public health). The middle managers, on the one hand, report to the administrator and, on the other hand, manage supervisors, direct service providers, and maintain functional contacts with the service delivery community. The higher administration has little or no contact with the service delivery context (Havassy 1990). This indicates that, structurally, middle managers are at the hub of many activities and systems, both internal and external, playing a pivotal role in translating organizational goals into service delivery. They frequently find themselves faced with conflicting expectations and demands of superiors and subordinates (Havassy 1990; Perlmutter 1983). Examples of middle managers include the director of a treatment center for substance abuse, program manager in a mental health center, and director of the social service department in a hospital.

In this chapter the term *administrator* will be used for the chief executive of an organization, and the term *manager* for the head of a unit or department. It may be noted, however, that these terms are not used uniformly across all types of human service organizations.

The social worker who is in an administrative position is responsible for organizational problem solving and therefore is in the best position to implement the task-centered management model. An understanding of organizations and skill in working with them is important for all social workers, however, because much of their professional time is involved in negotiating with organizations, internally or externally, on behalf of their clients. This is particularly important to generalist social workers who are most likely to reach beyond their own organizations in order to help their clients.

External social workers usually impact organizations indirectly, probably most often by identifying problems. Sometimes external social workers who perform liaison functions will be invited or allowed to operate in a key role in another organization for a limited time and over a limited arena. This is most likely to occur when the social worker is acting as a case manager, and an organization involved with the client requests help (see section 2.6.0). For example, the manager of a day care center brings the problems of coping with a chronically mentally ill client to the attention of the mental health worker who is the case manager. The social worker is then able to set up a meeting with all involved parties to define and specify the problem, identify tasks, and plan their implementation.

Often social workers will be involved in resolving intraorganizational or interorganizational problems. The former occurs when a problem involves more than one department in an organization; the latter, when the problem involves more than one organization. In other situations, an understanding of how organizations operate might help social workers gain cooperation even though they are distant from any management role.

This chapter contains a description of the TCM model, including its development, the theoretical base, nature of relationship, time limits, and the task planning and implementation sequence. Institutionalization replaces termination in the management model for reasons that will be explained. The chapter concludes with a case illustration.

14.2.1.0 EFFECTIVENESS AND REPLICABILITY

The management model described here is the result of using a developmental research paradigm to generate a practice technology based on scientific knowledge (Thomas 1978, 1984; Reid 1979; Rothman 1980). Consistent with developmental research, an established model (TC) was chosen as a basis for the new endeavor. Among the reasons for choosing TC are that it has distinct methods of problem solving, it has been demonstrated to be effective, and it is articulated in researchable constructs. TC also has the advantage of many practitioners now being familiar with it. This is particularly significant because social workers often move from the practitioner role to the administrative role, and this movement is frequently characterized by role discontinuity (Patti 1983; Hart 1984; Perlmutter 1990). It is expected that a management model with strong ties to an already familiar clinical model will minimize this discontinuity.

Field testing required a conceptual framework of human service organizations; a preliminary version of the model; an administrator's guide; and data collection instruments, including recording guides and follow-up questionnaires. This material was provided to administrators at seven field sites, and each was asked to apply the model to six different management problems. The data collection instruments and follow-up interviews provided information that has been incorporated into the model and is included in this presentation of it. In general, the administrators who implemented the model and the staff members who were involved in the process found the model to be functional and effective (Parihar 1984).

One of the recent innovations in the development of TC is a model for field instruction and staff development (Caspi and Reid 1998, in press). This model is relevant for work in organizations because it can provide direction for those in a supervisory capacity with students or staff. The results of a pilot study indicate that the consumer evaluations were highly favorable.

Developmental research is not, however, confirmatory. Neither the TCM model nor the field instruction/staff development model have been subjected to controlled studies of effectiveness.

14.2.2.0 THEORETICAL BASE

The TCM model is not dependent on any particular theory of organization. However, a number of concepts have been identified that can be useful to understanding and working with human service organizations. The concepts are drawn from several different theoretical perspectives, including organizational analysis, social systems theory, and management theory (Parsons 1957, 1960; Schein 1970; Bennis 1966; Hersey and Blanchard 1982; Perrow 1970; Lorsch 1976; Gibson, Ivancevich, and Donnelly 1982; and Hasenfeld 1983). Within the management arena, two schools of thought are included: scientific and human relations. The concepts important to understanding organizations, as they relate to TCM, include system and subsystem, leadership, authority and power, technology, organizational structure, external environment, goals, and communication. They are described, respectively, below.

System and Subsystem   In the social systems perspective, human service organizations are viewed as adaptive, equilibrium-seeking systems that exist in an environment and maintain continuous exchanges with it. In this perspective, for example, clients are the "input" received from the environment and on which the organization applies its technology or conversion process. They are also the "output" that is connected back to the environment. While the technology is highly professional and internal to the organization, the client is the major link between the organization and environment in that the client comes as a community member and goes out as a "product" of the organization (Hodge, Anthony, and Gales 1996; Holland 1995).

In view of this perspective, we have conceptualized human service organizations as comprising three major interlinking and interacting subsystems: (1) the environmental subsystem; (2) the technical-professional subsystem; and (3) the client subsystem. We maintain that problems in day-to-day functioning can arise in any of the subsystems or service components and that it is the responsibility of the administrator to institute problem-solving tasks. One must be aware, however, that each problem or action can affect other parts of the organization; decision making and problem solving never occur in isolation.

Leadership　Executive leadership usually functions at the highest level of the organization and is involved in policy decisions that basically determine the fundamental characteristics and attributes of the organization (Parsons 1960). Whether such decisions are made individually or with a policy-making board will be subject to the type and size of the organization, as well as other internal and external conditions (Brilliant 1986; Austin 1989). Also, the nature of executive leadership and function will depend on the stage of development of the organization (Perrow 1961). For example, an executive's role in the founding stage of the organization will have to do with mission, purpose, and the need to justify its existence, and not necessarily with the details of its operational procedures.

Most of the management writers seem to agree that leadership, at any level, involves influencing people toward goal achievement (Hersey and Blanchard 1982; Koontz and O'Donnell 1968; Tannenbaum 1987; Wolk, Way, and Bleeke 1982). This process of influencing is not only limited to hierarchical relationships such as superior/subordinate but can also include network relationships in the larger interest of the organization.

Two leadership styles have been identified: (1) authoritarian leader behavior (directive, concerned about output); and (2) democratic leader behavior (relationship oriented, nondirective, concerned about people). However, since TCM is an integrated model emphasizing both structured specificity and participatory involvement, we subscribe to Blake and Mouton's (1985) work on the managerial grid, which shows that concern for people and outcomes are mutually complementary, and to House's (1971) work on path-goal theory, which shows that different kinds of leader behavior (directive, supportive, participative, and achievement-oriented) can be practiced by the same person in different situations. This refers to situationally relevant leadership that can work with and through people collaboratively subject to the nature of the problem. For example, an administrator using

TCM and confronting the problem of staff burnout might involve staff in all aspects of the problem-solving process. However, when confronting a problem in the administrator's domain like budgeting, he or she might solve it independently.

Authority and Power   Authority is essentially role related. It is based on the position one occupies in the organizational hierarchy. *Authority* refers to the rights, prerogatives, and discretion sanctioned to each role position, and *power* implies capacity for action expressed through authority. In other words, to say that an executive has final decision-making authority is to say that he or she has veto power, a power that comes from the authority vested in the position.

In human service organizations, for the most part, the highest authority is with the board of directors. The executive's authority is directed to the internal and external elements of the organization that impinge on service delivery, which is usually the goal of the organization. The exercise of power is accomplished vertically, between superiors and subordinates (Austin 1989). However, the proximity to service provision that is centered around needs and crises can give staff a sort of "clinical power base" that generates in them a sense of power over clients and their lives. As Crozier (1964) indicated, anyone who handles uncertainty (problem/crisis) usually gains a sense of power regardless of one's position in the organizational hierarchy.

TCM subscribes to the notion of role positions based on the division of labor, structure of tasks, and authority relationships. At the same time, it emphasizes staff involvement, agreement, and communication in decision making and problem solving.

Technology   A technology may be conceptualized as a set of procedures used to bring about change in the raw material (client) in a predetermined manner. The technology is capable of being transmitted and thus makes it possible to train service providers to carry on the tasks of the organization. The extent and pervasiveness with which the technology is applied is based on (1) the extent to which the outcomes are tangible and well defined; (2) the degree of stability and predictability of the raw material; and (3) the degree of knowledge about cause-and-effect relations in the raw material (Perrow 1967). Because the raw material in human service organizations is human beings, these conditions are unlikely to be present in any uniform or consistent manner. Therefore the technical system in such organizations tends to be nonroutine and variable.

Human service organizations in general and treatment organizations in particular usually seek qualitative changes that cannot be precisely determined nor can a perfect consensus exist on the desired outcomes. For example, abstractly stated perceptual, attitudinal, and orientational changes present difficulties in assessing the outcomes, as well as in defining the process of change. The problem is mainly because of the variability and unpredictability of the client systems.

Three major categories of human service organizations with accompanying technologies have been identified: people-processing, people-changing, and people-sustaining (Hasenfeld 1983). People-processing organizations simply evaluate persons/situations and connect them to agencies for indicated services. The core technology used here is "the system of classification and disposition" (Hasenfeld 1983:135). Examples of such organizations are college admissions offices and psychiatric diagnostic clinics. The first one deals with "normal" clients and the last one with "malfunctioning" clients.

People-changing organizations, on the other hand, attempt to bring about behavioral changes through the use of change-oriented technologies. These technologies primarily consist of "structured staff-client relations" (Vinter 1963:6). Examples include schools and psychiatric treatment centers. Again, as in people-processing organizations, they can be concerned with either "normal" or "malfunctioning" clients.

People-sustaining organizations essentially attempt to maintain people by protecting them from financial or health-related problems or catastrophes. Examples include income maintenance programs like Aid to Families with Dependent Children and custodial care in nursing homes.

Organizational Structure   *Structure* refers to a set of rules and regulations, a hierarchy to facilitate policy-making, resource and staff allocation, and specialization of functions. In other words, structure provides organizations with a format, a system, and a process to function and accomplish their goals without duplication and chaos. It ensures their continuation and effectiveness. According to Perrow, "every organization of any significant size . . . exhibits more or less stable patterns of behavior based upon a structure of roles and specialized tasks. Bureaucracy, in this sense, is another word for structure" (1970:50).

The structure of organizations depends largely on the type of materials they work with and the kinds of tasks they perform. Thus human service organizations have attempted to develop a structure that is consistent with their clientele and technology. This process involves decisions regarding (1) the division of work (differentiation of service units or departments); (2) the delineation of work procedures (job definitions, communication processes); (3) coordination (integration and delegation of efforts); (4) evaluation (measurement); and (5) the creation of a favorable environment (rewards and incentives) (Gibson, Ivancevich, and Donnelly 1982; Johns 1996; and Lorsch 1976).

External Environment   The environment is the larger, societal context in which organizations exist. The organization and the environment are in continuous interaction. The generic environment can be conceptualized as a set of all the elements external to the organization that affect its structure and operations and that are, in turn, affected by the activities of the organization (Hall and Fagen 1956; Hall 1977). As such, each existing organization may constitute a part of the environment of other organizations. The task environment is composed of the external elements that are related to a particular project or, in TCM, a particular target problem.

The environment requires adaptation by the organization. It can present constraints as well as opportunities; it can restrict as well as facilitate. For example, a community might support the location of a school in its midst but reject the placement of a drug treatment center. The presence of competing organizations can have a powerful effect on organizational behavior. As a result, management must attend to environmental adaptation as well as to internal functioning in order to ensure survival and effectiveness (Austin 1989; Hasenfeld 1983; Weiner 1990).

Goals   All organizations have goals because they are established to achieve some purpose. Despite the importance of goals in the life of an organization, they have remained conceptually imprecise. Goals are usually the official statements about an organization's intentions. Sometimes such statements reflect the views of administrative elites rather than the organization as an entity. As a result, two sets of goals may be present: organizational ones and personal ones (Gross 1968). Goals can also be categorized as official or operative (Perrow 1961). Official goals are the general and publicly stated purposes of the organization, and operative goals are the ends sought through the actual operating policies of the organization. Inconsistencies may exist between them.

In human service organizations, lofty statements of intended goals that express humanistic values are common. Such goals are often difficult to operationalize. Furthermore, the variability among recipients of service and the unpredictability about human need requires fluid rather than static goals. Specific goals can be thought of as situationally relevant and time-bound. TCM uses specific goals in relation to target conditions so that goals can be measured and maintain the focus of effort.

Communication   Communication is crucial to human transaction, and its importance in clinical areas has been discussed (see section 2.5.0). It is equally important for management because none of the administrative roles and functions can be carried out without communicating.

Communication refers to the flow of information and decisions through the organizational structure. Communication moves vertically and horizontally. The structure of an organization should facilitate communication in both directions.

Communication has two functions in problem solving: securing information and sharing decisions. Because TCM emphasizes collaboration, involvement, and agreement as fundamental characteristics of participatory management, a free flow of communication is essential.

In addition to formal communication, informal communication occurs. Social workers should be aware of informal communication and acknowledge it. Informal communication can be a problem if information is distorted. Too much reliance on it can indicate that the amount of formal communication is inadequate.

14.2.3.0 MISSION AND PURPOSE

The mission for social workers employed as managers or administrators of human service organizations is no different than that for social workers employed elsewhere. However, those who are employed to manage organizations do have an additional purpose: the maintenance of the organization. The danger in this added purpose is that organizational maintenance will take precedence over serving the clients. Some of the ways managers can guard against this phenomenon are included in various aspects of quality assurance. The purpose of quality assurance is to identify and correct problems in service delivery on an ongoing basis (Coulton 1991). The activities within quality assurance are utilization review, client care monitoring, staff growth and development, patient record and documentation, and program/facility evaluation.

14.2.4.0 SOCIAL WORK VALUES

Baum and Parihar (1984) suggested an evaluative model for work in organizations that consists of four variables: efficiency, effectiveness, enactment, and *ethics*. Ethics include fairness (equal treatment to all), justice (impartial judgment based on fact and reason), respect (consideration of the client as an individual with dignity), and participatory democracy (the equal involvement of everyone).

As previously described, managers hold power and authority. Their decisions and behavior can influence the quality of life of both the employees and the recipients of service. Furthermore, clients cannot negotiate for themselves and they—particularly indigent ones—may have no choice over where they receive service. For these reasons, it is imperative that those in positions of authority are fully committed to an ethical code of behavior.

14.2.5.0 RELATIONSHIP

As in clinical areas, the concept of relationship is important in management. The management process is a human one, and one of the most important skills the manager possesses is the ability to work with others (Gibson, Ivancevich, and Donnelly 1982; Hersey and Blanchard 1982). Although informal relationships can and do occur among and between different functionaries, in an organizational context, relationships are essentially role specific, especially between administrators and staff members and between staff members and clients. This means that organizational relationships, like clinical ones, are professional; that is, they are formed to facilitate the attainment of goals.

The attributes of relationship have been discussed at length in the preceding chapters. They are applicable here as well but with due regard to the organizational context. It may be noted that relationship permeates the entire management process and that the quality of relationship seems to influence organizational climate, communication, staff support, and outcomes. Relationships with external entities (including networking) are also important because they affect the environment's acceptance of, and confidence in, the organization. Thus an effective administrator must know the value of good relationships both to promote internal operations and to counteract external uncertainties.

In addition to the relationship skills identified in preceding sections, eight techniques of task-centered intervention have been described (Reid 1978). The five that are often employed in TCM are exploration, structuring, encouragement, direction, and explanation. Exploration is used to obtain information and involves eliciting information from the organizational actors. It can include direct questioning, surveys or questionnaires, or brainstorming. In addition to eliciting information, exploration often stimulates thinking about the problem and the ways to solve it. Structuring refers to the administrator's effort to focus conversation on the problem and to bring staff functions to bear on its resolution. It may include guided interaction during staff meetings and setting the agenda. Encouragement most often takes the form of supportive statements and is done to reinforce cooperative behaviors and attitudes. Direction includes all behavior in which the administrators use their authority, including supervision, policy statements, directives, assignments, and suggestions. Essentially it is used when the administrator acts in a supervisory capacity. In contrast, explanation is used when the administrator acts as a teacher. It consists of conveying professional knowledge and information. It should be noted that, in an organization, these techniques pertain to all verbal or written communication directed from the individual responsible for administration to the different organizational actors (Parihar 1984).

14.2.6.0 THE APPROPRIATE SYSTEM FOR WORK

TCM focuses on the organization or agency itself with the expectation that enhancing the functioning of these entities will indirectly impact the quality of service to clients. Decisions must be made about which subsystem (or which combination of subsystems) are necessary to alter a particular problem. As described previously, the subsystems include the client subsystem, the technical-professional subsystem, and the environmental subsystem. Initial decisions about the primary system are based on the description of the problem provided by the "perceiver" or "informer." For instance, if a problem is identified within the context of the environmental subsystem, which may include the community, government or regulatory agency, third-party payers, or other complementary or competing services, this will be the most appropriate subsystem with which to work. If the problem entails the provision of services, the technical-professional subsystem will become the primary one. Problems identified by the client subsystem usually involve one or both of the other subsystems. For example, resolving issues related to the availability of clinical services might require the participation of professionals to design the services and an external agency to fund them.

In TCM, collaterals are the members of the subsystems who are involved in resolving the identified problem. They can include members of the staff who represent the technical-professional subsystem, representatives of external agencies or groups (which might include clients), or representatives of other departments within the organization. Developing contacts or networking is a crucial part of the managerial role.

In identifying collaterals, both internal and external support need to be assessed. A useful technique is to develop a list of those who are likely to be supportive, those who are likely to be neutral, and those who are likely to be hostile to a particular project. The lists will include names of individuals, departments, and organizations. In the event that the amount of support seems insufficient, ways to increase it or to neutralize opposition must be considered. Perhaps some of the neutral actors can be persuaded to take a supportive position. Perhaps a common concern can be identified. The important collaterals can then be identified based on the amount of their power and persuasiveness. For example, an administrator of a hospital-based alcoholism treatment center was charged with the responsibility for the construction of a new physical plant for the facility. This project met with a strong public opposition mainly because of the stigma about the addictions field. The project was delayed while an effort to mobilize public opinion was mounted. This effort included (1) engaging local organizations and holding community meetings; (2) distributing brochures and hospital bulletins describing the center's mission and goals; (3) utilizing local newspapers and press conferences; and (4) organizing a public hearing through the help of local leaders and politicians. A sufficient number of actors who were previously neutral became supportive, and the construction project was completed.

14.2.7.0 CHECKLIST FOR THE PREINTERVENTION PHASE

___ 1. Do I understand the organization, including levels of administration, organizational structure, mission and goals, and patterns of leadership, power, and communication?

___ 2. Are my goals consistent with those of the organization as well as the goals and mission of my profession?

___ 3. Are staff and clients treated with respect and included in decision making?

___ 4. Do internal and external relationships foster the work of the organization?

___ 5. Have collaterals been identified and engaged?

14.3.0.0 COMPONENTS OF THE INITIAL PHASE

The components of the initial phase that have been developed in the TCM model include time limits, obtaining necessary information, targeting problems, developing the problem specification, goals, contracts, and assessment. Each are briefly described and illustrated below.

14.3.2.0 TIME LIMITS

The use of time limits in TCM differs in several ways from their use with individuals, families, and groups. First, they are defined by the problem rather than the amount of contact. Second, they tend to be longer. Third, they are determined somewhat later in the process. Fourth, there may be more of them.

Obviously time limits are not used to define the amount of contact in the TCM model because contact is ongoing. Rather, they are used to determine time lines for the accomplishment of various activities in relation to a particular target problem. Related to this is the number of time limits and the time at which they are set. Since resolving organizational problems might require several sequential activities, the administrator and staff might set one time limit for developing a plan to solve an identified problem, another for implementing the plan, and a third for reviewing the implemented solution. For example, a problem of lack of follow-up care for clients was identified. A time limit was established for developing a program of follow-up care. Another time limit was established to indicate when the program would be in operation. Finally, a date at which the program would be evaluated was determined. Not only are a number of time limits utilized, but the last one may not be determined until the problem is well on the way to being solved.

Time limits will vary greatly across problems. This is because organizational problems vary in complexity. Furthermore, the resources that can be devoted to solving a problem vary across organizations and across problems. Nevertheless, time limits serve the same purpose as in work with other systems: They keep problem-solving efforts moving.

14.3.3.0 OBTAINING NECESSARY INFORMATION

Since our own organizations are familiar to us, obtaining necessary information is not really a distinct activity when problems and their resolution reside entirely within the organization. It is, however, pertinent when we must involve other organizations. Some of the basic information about an organization includes its auspices, mission, rules or regulations regarding service provision, powerful actors, sympathetic actors, resources and source of support, size, and clientele. For example, when we seek services from another organization for a client, the minimal necessary information includes the services the other organization provides and the procedures for acquiring them. If we are trying to build a network of services that will be used on an ongoing basis, additional information is necessary, including the quality of services provided and the names of cooperative actors.

Although this activity is most important when working with external organizations, the consideration of pertinent organizational data should not be ignored entirely when working within our own institution. It can serve as a check on our enthusiasms as when a hospital social worker identified a need for abortion services and temporarily forgot that the auspices of the hospital were Roman Catholic.

14.3.4.0 TARGETING PROBLEMS

A target problem in an organization is anything that impairs organizational functioning, that can be described in observable terms, and that can be acted on by the administrator/manager either independently or in collaboration with others. Organizational problems may be identified by any number of people, including the administrator, staff, clients, or other service providers. Thus they may be identified internally or externally. The problem(s) may be brought up individually or collectively. Finally, they might be identified in or outside staff meetings.

Some examples of potential target problems are as follows: (1) the increased caseload is responsible for staff burnout; (2) the money allocated for staff development is inadequate; and (3) aftercare services are inadequate and inconsistent.

The administrator must then attempt to evaluate the validity of the problem. Are the perceptions of the problem identifier accurate? Are others likely to agree? What are the consequences of ignoring the problem? Administrators can respond in one of three ways. They can accept the problem as valid and employ the activities described in this chapter (or use some other problem-solving strategy). They can gather additional information before committing themselves to solving the problem. In this case, they are temporarily redefining the problem as one of needing to assess a particular situation and they can use TCM to do so. Finally, they can decide that the problem is not valid and choose to ignore it. When administrators incorrectly determine that a problem is not valid, they are likely to encounter it directly or indirectly on other occasions. Obviously a problem does not become a target problem until it is accepted—at least by the administrator. Once its importance is established, its acceptance as a target problem is likely.

Some problems cannot be solved by the administrator alone. In these situations it is desirable to have an agreement among the various actors that the problem exists and merits attention. A variety of strategies can be employed to reach agreement. These include improving understanding by sharing information and mutual exploration; negotiation and compromise; appealing to overall goals of the agency; identifying a common cause; and confrontation. An example of disagreement about the target problem occurred in a community mental health center. Staff identified a problem of burnout caused by heavy caseloads. The administrator did not believe the center was understaffed. Further exploration revealed that, indeed, the center was not understaffed, but there were brief periods of increased intakes when staff were overworked. To everyone's satisfaction, the problem was redefined and procedures for coping with increased intake were implemented.

If agreement cannot be reached, it is the administrator's function to define target problems and target conditions, utilizing input from the actors, and notify all concerned of the decision. This is referred to as "agreement by administrative directive" (Parihar 1984:28). Because the administrator is ultimately responsible for decision making, he or she holds the same power to accept or reject target problems as does the client in work with individuals. This does not mean that decision making is necessarily centralized or autocratic. In fact, the use of agreement-reaching strategies is strongly recommended in order to make use of staff input and avoid problems of staff alienation.

During the developmental phase of the model, described in section 14.2.1.0, efforts were made to develop a list of organizational problems.

These efforts included reviewing the minutes of staff meetings and asking staff members to identify problems. The resulting problem list follows:

1. community's opposition to expansion;
2. staff conflict;
3. role conflict;
4. role performance;
5. staff-client relationships;
6. dissatisfaction and other problems with rules, policies, and procedures;
7. client dissatisfaction;
8. inadequate resources;
9. differences about therapeutic orientations;
10. supervision issues;
11. accountability and quality assurance; and
12. problems with other organizations.

(Parihar 1984)

This list is expected to develop into a more refined classification as experience with the model increases. For now it can be used as an aide to problem identification.

Another method for classifying problems is based on the level of complexity involved, that is, the number of causative variables and their contribution to the problems. Problems with a few known causative variables are labeled "simple problems," whereas those for which the causative factors are not precisely known are labeled "complicated." Both these problem types can be further identified as either recurring or nonrecurring. For example, a problem of staff burnout because of heavy caseloads is a simple, recurring problem. It is considered simple because the problem has a known cause, and recurring because it occurred whenever intakes increased. A directive to absorb another program presented a complicated, nonrecurring problem. It is considered complicated because the motives for the directive were unknown, and a hidden agenda was suspected. It is nonrecurring because it occurred only once. These classifications can be helpful in problem specification and task planning.

14.3.6.0 DEVELOPING THE PROBLEM SPECIFICATION

As with work with other systems, the conditions or manifestations that need to be changed must be specified in order to resolve the target problem. To do so, the nature and circumstances of the problem need to be explored. Because organizations are ongoing systems replete with structural elements, analyzing contextual information is particularly important. At a minimum such information will include (1) the origins, history, and development of the problem; (2) prior attempts at managing this or similar problems; and (3) the results of such efforts. This information may be sufficient for simple, recurring problems. For complicated, nonrecurring problems, a more complete contextual exploration and analysis is necessary.

For example, the conditions that produced the simple, recurring problem of burnout in the community mental health center were found to be the following:

1. longer peak periods of intakes and an influx of case openings;
2. lengthy intake process continued to be followed even during peak periods; and
3. lack of time for consultation and work with continuing clients.

A newly appointed administrator in a child welfare agency encountered a nonrecurring problem: a sizable deficit in the agency's budget. His fact-finding efforts involved review of financial documents, interviews with concerned staff, and an audit by the accountant at the corporate level. It resulted in identifying the following specifications:

1. failure to secure appropriate resources; and
2. lack of a system of financial control or accountability.

14.3.7.0 GOALS

The process of goal development relative to each target problem is essential in establishing a direction for problem-solving activities and in evaluating outcome. In work with organizations, developing specific action objectives related to each of the problem specifications is also useful. These action objectives should be focused, specified in realistic terms, and meaningful. Agreement about goals and action objectives among those involved is desirable. It can be reached by use of the strategies identified in section 14.3.4.0. Once goals and action objectives have been established, a tentative time frame for their achievement may be developed with a target date (or dates) for task review.

The specification of precipitating factors of a problem leads to target conditions (those aspects that must be changed), and action objectives are developed relative to each target condition. It is important to see that all specified parts of a problem are addressed. In regard to the example of staff burnout described earlier, the following action objectives were identified:

1. develop a strategy for handling increased caseload during influx of intakes;
2. develop a simplified intake process;
3. increase the amount and quality of supervision and encourage staff to reflect on their work positively; and
4. attempt early intervention for high-risk cases.

The action objectives were developed by the supervisor on the Intake Unit who volunteered to do so. A time limit of two months was set to prepare a contingency plan that would be discussed during the staff meeting.

The action objectives for the budget deficit were as follows:

1. balance the budget;
2. establish a system to control expenditures; and
3. generate additional resources.

This problem did not involve other staff members. The administrator and the accounting department were responsible for the goals as well as the specifications. It became clear, however, that the deficit was the target problem, but the free spending environment and the lack of financial restraints were the contextual factors. It may be noted that changes in the status of a problem can be achieved either by working on the target problem, by changing contextual factors, or by altering elements of both (Reid 1985). This is an important consideration for task planning.

14.3.8.0 CONTRACTS

A contract involves two people or parties who agree to do agreed-on tasks toward an agreed-on goal in an agreed-on manner. It provides direction and a means of assessing whether agreements have been fulfilled. A contract has the potential to deter ambivalence and procrastination and to promote goal-directed behavior.

In a democratic style of decision making, agreement is an essential prerequisite. We develop agreements for the following reasons:

1. to avoid centralized and autocratic decision making;
2. to avoid voting on issues when voting might result in splitting the staff; and
3. to promote communication and discussion.

Frequently contracts or agreements in organizations take the form of day-to-day memorandums or minutes. More formal contracts can be used between the administrator and an employee whose work is inadequate, with external experts whose services are being purchased, and with other agencies when services are being shared or coordinated.

Whether agreements take the form of memorandums or formal contracts, they should be specific as to who will do what, when, and so on. They should also be monitored.

14.3.9.0 ASSESSMENT

As in TC with other systems, in TCM the assessment of the problem is accomplished by means of the problem specification. Assessment must also consider contextual factors, however. The important contextual factors for organizations are identified in section 14.2.2.0 ("Theoretical Base"). They include systems and subsystems, leadership, authority and power, technology, organizational structure, the external environment, goals, and communication. One should consider the problem, its manifestations, and plans for remediation in light of these characteristics. For example, solving the problem of a low census of clients on an alcoholic inpatient unit required careful evaluation of the programs of external agencies that provided the same service. A problem that entailed the interpretation of admission criteria to the same unit was found to be the result of a lack of knowledge in one of the professional subsystems—the emergency room staff.

The involvement of other systems, as well as the collaterals who represent those systems, also need to be continually assessed. Attempts to resolve a problem of lack of space were derailed, because another department had competing demands for the desired space and these demands were overlooked. In another situation, a representative of an agency, who was included in planning a service delivery network, was found to have insufficient influence within his own agency.

Assessment, in organizations, also refers to accountability. Depending on the complexity of the organization, much reporting might be required. In addition to the minutes of staff meetings, reports might include annual ones, quality assurance, strategic planning, and program evaluations. Although much of this reporting is not specific to the resolution of particular target problems, the various reports often provide information that either identifies problems or provides important information about them. Furthermore, careful documentation of the problem-solving efforts, including tasks implemented, can provide evidence of the effectiveness of a department or agency and thus can be included in some of the reports.

14.3.10.0 CHECKLIST FOR THE INITIAL PHASE

___ 1. Do I have sufficient information about the organization and its environment in order to proceed?

___ 2. Are all relevant actors in agreement about the definition of the target problem?

___ 3. Are the manifestations of the problem identified, and do I have the data necessary to measure changes in them?

___ 4. Is the goal shared by all those involved? Is it clear and measurable?

___ 5. Have staff members been involved appropriately?

___ 6. Did I set time limits appropriate to the nature of the problem, including multiple ones if sequential activities will occur?

___ 7. Are agreements being recorded in the minutes? Are any formal contracts necessary?

14.4.0.0 COMPONENTS OF THE MIDDLE PHASE

The components of the middle phase that have been developed in TCM include the TPIS, revising unsuccessful tasks, and the use of time limits. Each are briefly described below.

14.4.1.0 TASK PLANNING AND IMPLEMENTATION SEQUENCE

Two types of tasks have been developed in TCM. These are administrator and staff tasks. The mix of these two types across problems varies considerably and is dependent on the nature of the problem. Administrators will decide to resolve some problems independently and thus will perform all tasks. Generally, when a problem is an administrative one, like the budgeting problem previously described, administrators take an active role in task planning and implementation. For other problems, all tasks will be assumed by the staff. Still other problems will require a combination of staff and administrator tasks. In addition to being responsible for the administrative tasks designed to resolve target problems, the administrator guides the problem-solving endeavor.

Sometimes, in work within organizations, problems can be resolved by changing some element of the context. A target problem might be that clients are not receiving a necessary service, for example, parent-skills training. The relevant contextual factor might be that the staff is unfamiliar with this method of intervention. The problem might then be solved by retraining staff or by hiring new staff or additional staff members who are skilled in parent training. In this example, changing the context is likely to take more time than solving the problem directly by either referring families to another agency or hiring a part-time consultant. However, this approach has the advantage of assuring that the desired skills will always be on staff and thus available to the agency's families. Of course the approaches can sometimes be combined. In this example, a consultant might be hired to retrain staff *and* see families while training is in progress.

In the problem of the budget deficit, work was done on both the problem and the context. Staff members were acquainted with the problem. They agreed to limit expenses by not submitting any requisitions and to promote use of agency services in the community to generate more revenue. The fee schedule and collection system were revised. A system outlining financial procedures and accountability was established to mitigate the free-spending climate in the agency. No one could buy or order anything without the prior approval of the administrator.

As the examples illustrate, an overall strategy must be decided on before tasks are delineated and assigned. Such a strategy is analogous to the use of "task strategies" in work with individuals and families (Reid 1992). When staff members are to be involved in carrying out the strategy in the form of tasks, it is wise to include them in planning and selecting the strategy. Their input and collaboration is valuable, and they are more likely to become invested in implementing the strategy. When this occurs, the process proceeds as a collaborative team effort.

14.4.1.1 GENERATING TASK ALTERNATIVES AND SELECTING A TASK

The process of generating either alternative tasks or strategies, as noted previously, can be accomplished by the administrator working alone, by the administrator and the entire staff, or by the administrator and some smaller group of staff members. Participants can volunteer or be chosen by the administrator; the choice is determined by the nature of the problem and the size of the staff.

An important difference between organizational and clinical work is that in organizational work authority clearly rests with the administrator. This has several implications for the process of generating and implementing tasks. First, it means that the administrator has veto power over a particular task or strategy. Second, tasks are sometimes accepted by staff members who are not particularly enthusiastic about them. Although this is sometimes necessary, it should occur as infrequently as possible. Third, some staff members might shape their contributions in order to please the boss. They might withhold ideas for tasks or strategies for fear they will meet with disfavor. Or the converse might occur: One or more staff members might try to make themselves indispensable by volunteering to do more than is appropriate.

The effective administrator, while accepting his or her legitimate authority, will try to minimize the negative effect of power imbalances by encouraging the contributions of everyone involved.

14.4.1.3 PLANNING THE DETAILS OF TASK IMPLEMENTATION

The activities pertaining to planning task details and analyzing obstacles are similar to the work with other systems but some differences do exist. First, the administrator might perform these activities alone. Second, they apply to the overall task strategy as well as to the implementation tasks. Third, planning details is often less crucial in TCM because of the general competence of all involved and because the individuals selected to implement the tasks are often chosen on the basis of their special expertise or knowledge in the area. The detail that is most likely to require consideration is timing. This issue arises, as was evident in the example of staff burnout, when several people are undertaking different tasks that must be performed sequentially.

14.4.1.4 ESTABLISHING RATIONALE AND INCENTIVES

The use of incentives can be a powerful administrative tool. Dysfunctional organizations are often characterized by irrational incentive systems. For example, the administrator at one agency was concerned about increasing the amount of client contact. However, even a cursory examination of behavior revealed that several staff members who had the least client contact (1) received the largest raises; (2) were appointed to important departmental committees; and (3) spent more time interacting with the administrator than staff members who had much more client contact. Obviously, despite all the exhortations, staff members did not increase their client contact as this behavior was not rewarded.

Sometimes administrators even punish the behavior that is desired. Some of us were asked to train all the social workers in a particular agency in TC. Surprisingly workers resisted using TC in spite of their supportive verbal comments. Why? Because the administrators who wanted the workers to learn TC based staffing on the number of open cases. If the staff used TC or any time-limited intervention, they would close cases and lose staff. Obviously staff members were not going to put themselves out of work.

Frequently rationales and incentives for task implementation are apparent to the staff. In the problem of burnout previously described, the rationale for the tasks was that they would lessen the amount of work; that is, something that was undesirable—too much work—would be taken away, and hence performing the tasks would be reinforced. However, sometimes performing the task is, in fact, burdensome. One of the tasks necessary to resolve the budget deficit, generating revenue, was onerous because it meant an additional job demand on staff members. In order to deal with this, the administrator used two types of incentives. First, he took the staff into his confidence by sharing some of the details of the problem. Second, he set up a reward or bonus for the person who generated the most revenue for the agency. Other incentives that might have been used include training, funding conference attendance or outside consultation, reduced caseload, and increased salary or overtime pay. Getting on the boss's good side is also a silent incentive for some staff members. Incentives are particularly important when performing the task entails some form of punishment, such as increased work.

14.4.1.6 ANTICIPATING OBSTACLES TO TASK PERFORMANCE

Obstacles to task performance in organizations can take many forms. Among them are differing perceptions among the various actors about the problem and the task, resistance to change, and concern for self-interest. An obstacle identified in the budgeting problem that was previously described concerned the perceptions of the funding source. To deal with the deficit, the administrator had to return to the funding source for additional revenue. The obstacle was that, because of the mismanagement of the budget in the past, the organization was likely to have little credibility. The administrator dealt with the obstacle by presenting the funding source with detailed data and by distancing himself from the previous administrator and the problem of mismanagement. The result was that additional revenues were granted *after* monitoring mechanisms were installed. As this example illustrates, potential obstacles to solving organizational problems are often identified by carefully considering the likely reactions of the various actors.

14.4.1.7 SUMMARIZING TASKS

Task summaries in organizations are often found in the organization's minutes, since problems and tasks are often discussed in staff meetings. Decisions about problems or issues that are made elsewhere can be announced in staff meetings and thus also appear in the minutes. At times, the nature of the issue might warrant strict confidentiality. It is up to administrators to determine what they can share with staff. When information must be restricted to a few people, separate memorandums are useful. We believe it is good administrative practice to require minutes for all meetings and to review them carefully. They are valid pieces of documentation.

14.4.1.8 TASK AND PROBLEM REVIEWS

A review of task accomplishment is essential to evaluate progress. Dates for reviewing task progress should be set at the time of task planning. Tentative times for problem review can sometimes be indicated during goal development. These times can then be reaffirmed during task planning. However, decisions regarding the time frame are subject to the nature of the target problem and the type of intervention. Tasks designed for simple, recurring problems can often be reviewed during scheduled staff meetings. Tasks designed for complicated, nonrecurring problems (including those that require long-term or continuous effort) are also reviewed at predetermined intervals, but the review is likely to occur during special meetings devoted to the target problem. Crisis-oriented problems also usually require special meetings. During meetings, each actor is asked to report on what he or she has accomplished either verbally or in writing. When written reports are required, the reports describe task accomplishments.

In work with individuals, families, and groups, the function of task review is to determine (1) if tasks are being accomplished; and (2) if tasks are having the anticipated impact on the target problems. In organizational work, it is sometimes not possible to determine, on an ongoing basis, whether tasks are affecting target problems until all of them are accomplished. Earlier, an example pertaining to providing families with parent-skills training was described. With this kind of problem, impact is not evident until all the myriad tasks required to establish and implement a training program are achieved. Nevertheless, inquiring about the state of the target problems during task review is useful because an unpredicted change in the problem may arise or a related problem might develop. Either condition would require replanning.

Of course once all tasks are implemented, a thorough problem review similar to that used when working with other systems must be conducted. The same scale for evaluating problem change can be employed: no change, minimal change, substantial change, and complete alleviation. Sometimes evaluating each target condition or manifestation is also useful.

14.4.2.0 REVISING UNSUCCESSFUL TASKS

When tasks are unsuccessful, careful evaluation is required. Because people other than the administrator often assume tasks, the first consideration should be the extent of implementation. Others may be less skillful, motivated, or have fewer resources than was anticipated. They may have encountered obstacles. The administrator has one option that workers with clinical systems often do not have, which is to reassign the task to another person or group. When tasks are not implemented because of a lack of resources or obstacles, the tasks can be redesigned to account for these factors. One of a leader's functions is to instill hope, and this is particularly important when tasks are not fully implemented because the actors are discouraged.

When tasks are fully implemented but do not result in sufficient problem change, the reason for disappointing results needs to be identified. In cases when the goals or time frame were overly ambitious, expectations can be scaled down or time limits extended. When efforts to secure a desired problem change fail because of a change in the problem or new information about the problem and its context, tasks should be revised. Occasionally we find, after careful evaluation, that a problem is unsolvable or cannot be solved by the organization. In that case, the procedure is either to drop the problem or to bring it to the attention of those who have the power and resources to resolve it.

14.4.5.0 USE OF TIME LIMITS

A reminder about deadlines to those who have assumed the responsibility for task implementation is advisable. This is particularly important if the interval between planning the task and the time limit for implementing it exceeds one or two weeks. Reminders can take the form of follow-up correspondence or informal inquiries about how the task work is progressing.

14.4.6.0 CHECKLIST FOR THE MIDDLE PHASE

___ 1. Are there an appropriate mix of administrator and staff tasks?

___ 2. Are staff members adequately knowledgeable about TPIS and included in implementing the activities?

___ 3. Are necessary incentives in place for staff who are carrying extra responsibilities?

___ 4. Am I adequately monitoring task completion and the recording of decisions in the minutes?

> ___ 5. Am I providing sufficient supervision when obstacles are encountered or when tasks are not implemented?
> ___ 6. Are participants being reminded of time limits?

14.5.0.0 INSTITUTIONALIZATION REPLACES TERMINATION

Termination does not occur for the social worker employed as an administrator of an organization until he or she leaves the organization. Work on most problems is not completely terminated because problem areas are periodically reviewed. Instead, the strategies used in resolving target problems become an ongoing part of the organization. This is referred to as "institutionalization." For example, the administrator of the alcohol treatment center who encountered community resistance to plans for the construction of a new facility learned the importance of being visible in the community and remaining connected to its needs. As a result, he instituted a community advisory board and an industrial advisory committee, which became ongoing components of the organization. Sometimes the successful strategies become standing policies of the organization and can be used when similar problems arise in the future. As such, proven intervention strategies become a frame of reference for future use or can be reemployed under similar circumstances.

14.5.6.0 CASE ILLUSTRATION

This illustration occurred in a hospital-based treatment center for substance abuse. The administrator was a social worker with overall executive responsibility for the center.

INITIAL PHASE

Problem Identifier   Administrator and staff.

Target Problem   Failure of outpatient, ongoing therapy groups intended to provide continuity of care.

Specifications

1. Number of patients attending outpatient group therapy continually declined to the extent that the groups had to be disbanded.
2. Groups were begun without a clear purpose other than to meet the demands of the funding source.
3. Groups were unlimited with respect to time.
4. Discontinuity occurred when the therapist running the group was not available.
5. Groups had to be scheduled to avoid conflicts with other activities over available space.

Goals/action objectives

1. Set up a committee (action objective) to define the purpose of the outpatient therapy groups (target specification).
2. Employ time-limited groups (action objective) to reduce dropout (target specification).
3. Establish co-therapy teams (action objective) to eliminate discontinuity (target specification).
4. Arrange for consistently available space (action objective) to avoid scheduling conflict (target condition).

Time Limits   The outpatient clinic manager was asked to develop problem specifications, a goal, and action objectives "as soon as possible." The task was completed in one month.

Middle Phase

Task Planning and Implementation   The committee and the administrator decided that the purpose of the outpatient therapy groups was to provide support. A number of tasks had to be accomplished in order to develop support groups.

Generation of Tasks   Tasks were developed by the administrator and outpatient clinic manager following discussions with staff during staff meetings.

Staff tasks

1. Stress the importance of support for continuity of care to inpatients at the time of discharge (to be done by inpatient counselors).
2. Staff and begin outpatient groups (to be done by the outpatient clinic).
3. Assign two counselors to each group for continuity (to be done by the outpatient clinic).
4. Conduct groups that will meet once a week for twelve weeks and inform patients that anyone who misses more than three meetings will be dropped from the group (to be done by the group leaders).
5. Evaluate and make disposition plans for further care for each patient by the twelfth week (to be done by group leaders).

Administrator tasks

1. Coordinate activities of various treatment units.
2. Provide consultation as needed.
3. Provide resources (space).
4. Monitor activities to see that tasks are being accomplished.

Obstacles

1. *Space.* The administrator found a day and time when a room was consistently available.
2. *Apprehension based on previous experiences.* Linkage of patients from inpatient to outpatient was expected to provide a steady flow of clients and diminished some of the apprehension.

Time limits

1. Three months to begin first group.
2. Subsequent review dates to be decided.

Problem Review   The group began in two months even though it was anticipated that three months of lead time was necessary. Patients were attending the group sessions.

INSTITUTIONALIZATION

The outpatient support groups became an ongoing part of the treatment program. In addition to the development of the groups, it became clear that programming cannot be done in isolation and that the involvement of other parts of the organization is required. Thus not only a program but also a procedure was institutionalized.

15

TASK-CENTERED WORK WITH COMMUNITIES

Gregory L. Pettys and Kollengode R. Ramakrishnan

15.2.0.0 INTRODUCTION*

The previous chapters have explored the use of a task-centered approach with individuals, families, groups, and organizations. Attention is now given to the community as a unit for social work intervention. Communities caught up in the society in which we live are becoming increasingly more complex. We live in an era when human rights, access to medical care, equal employment opportunities, even the physical environment require active protection and sponsorship.

Families no longer committed to one job are moving in and out of our communities. Likewise, the labor market requires a mobile work force willing to relocate for advancement and promotion. National and international mobility are changing the composition of our communities as they become more culturally diverse. Understanding the environment in which our clients live and work has never been more important. This chapter outlines an approach that uses TC to address the problems and needs of a neighborhood or community.

Given the crucial roles social work plays in working with individuals in their environments, community organization takes on an essential but often neglected role. A review of the literature demonstrates that numerous approaches have been used to enact macrolevel change

[*See the footnote to chapter 14 regarding the numbering of the sections in this chapter.]

through community organization. In an effort to develop conceptual clarity, Rothman and Tropman (1987) have classified these various community organization approaches into three discrete styles of intervention: *locality development, social action,* and *social planning.* These approaches have subsequently been referred to as the three models of community organization.

Locality Development   This model emphasizes citizen participation and focuses on the process of developing indigenous leadership, rather than on specific tasks for accomplishment. Based on structural functional theory, the model defines the cause of social problems as a result of social disorganization brought about by rapid industrial and technological development. The locality development model is one of the original approaches to social reform, and appealed to both community organizers and political leaders. This model assumes the community to be in decline and alienated, lacking in relationships and democratic problem solving. It was essentially produced for developing nations and for people in the American ghettos who remained poor and downtrodden. It was theorized that change could only endure if local people were involved in the planning of their own community. The goal in this approach is to integrate and empower the community through a collaborative effort of a broad cross-section of community members. Some of the principles of community development include democratic procedures, voluntary cooperation, self-help, development of indigenous leadership, and education (Dunham 1963).

In spite of political directives for individual self-help and self-involvement in program development, local community programs often received insufficient funding to be effective. The agencies that were created to train indigenous leaders and encourage citizen participation became bureaucracies that failed to deliver what they promised to the people at the grass-roots level. Likewise, the model was criticized as being conservative and fostering the maintenance of an ineffective status quo. For example, neighborhood clubs for poor youth received insufficient funds to succeed and failed to address the real problem of racism. The result was a general disenchantment with the locality development model.

Social Action   The social action model evolved as a radical alternative to the locality development model. Based on conflict theory, this model assumes that the plight of society's outcasts is the result of an imbalance of power—a struggle between those who have the power and those who do not. Change, in this model, comes about only by organizing the powerless into a unified body that will be able to exert influence on those in power. Many of the successful tactics of the civil rights movement in the 1960s were based on the social action model.

Advocates of this model challenged the traditional community organization method for its conservatism and hesitancy to jeopardize societal equilibrium. Some grass-roots leaders, such as Martin Luther King Jr., Gandhi, and Saul Alinsky, advocated a nonviolent, civil disobedience approach. Others openly incited members to use conflict. Despite its acceptance among grass-roots organizers, social action did not receive positive public opinion because of the use of conflict to bring about change. Furthermore, bureaucracies and agencies stifled social action organization, deepening the division between community organization and government social planning.

In spite of its general unpopularity, social action as a community organization approach continues today as a tool when collaboration and negotiation fail to bring about change (Staples 1984; Zander 1990). Despite the model's usefulness as a systematic, goal-oriented activity, the concept of careful, comprehensive planning was seen as essential. Such planning became crucial for long-term goal achievement, which social action failed to consider. Therefore social planners developed the social planning model, which uses more expertise than the locality development model, and less confrontation and more thoughtful planning than the social action model.

Social Planning   The social planning model involves rational problem solving. Expert professionals, often bureaucrats, working in elite-sponsored social agencies, guide the planning process where influential community members have central policy roles and consumers are relegated to client and recipient roles. Social planners gather and analyze data and projections, and function as program planners and evaluators. Planners use the rapidly expanding database related to social concerns and produce studies, reports, and recommendations. Modern social planning can be highly technical.

The professional agency-based social planning model not only separated the practitioners from the consumers but also created a division in community organization practice. The early leaders in social work community organization insisted on keeping the discipline as a vocation and not moving toward making it a profession, in reaction to what the Charity Organization Society (COS) leaders had done within direct practice around the turn of the century. This reluctance to professionalize community organization practice resulted in relegating leadership during the "Great Society" era of the 1960s to professionals outside social work.

Social planning alone falls short of achieving its goal. In this model practitioners, often working for an elite-controlled bureaucracy, are viewed as the experts. The planner is trained in the technical tasks of collecting, analyzing, and interpreting data; managing large bureaucracies; and writing technical reports. Planners often focus on substantive issues on a short-term basis, rather than long-range comprehensive planning. Often such planners lack skills in the interaction process and avoid developing indigenous leaders. Instead they impose personal values on the targeted community.

Because each of these three models derived from a specific theory of change, structural functionalism, conflict, or problem solving, they were thought of as distinct and separate. Recently they been integrated and elaborated into a paradigm of community intervention (Cnaan and Rothman 1986; Rothman 1996). It has been recognized that it is possible to use one, two, or all three models in a specific community project.

Task-Centered Community Organization   Similar to the current elaboration of Rothman (1996), task-centered community organization views the three traditional models as tools or techniques to use in order to bring about desired change. Individually, none of the models is sufficient to organize a community successfully to bring about effective changes. The task-centered approach incorporates the social planning model's use of experts and technical tasks to create a comprehensive intervention, and the locality development and social action models' use of organizing local citizens to become involved in planning those programs that will affect them.

Mobilizing a community and developing strategies and convictions among people require two major interrelated concerns: the technical tasks and the interaction processes (see section 15.2.5.0). Much of the disillusionment and ineffectiveness of community organization today is a result of organizers' and planners' inability to mesh properly the technical tasks and the interaction process. Currently the notion that locality development, social planning, and social action are companion models is gaining more acceptance. Task-centered community organization effectively organizes these three models into a workable and efficient social work approach to intervention.

Community and Community Organization   Clarification of the terms *community* and *community organization* is in order. In general, *community* can refer to two different units: (1) community as locality or place specific; and (2) community as function or purpose specific. Community as locality specific refers to "that combination of social units and systems that perform major social functions having locality relevance" (Warren 1983a:28). This community can comprise the inner-city neighborhood, as well as the nation as a whole.

Edward Moe describes the locality specific community as a "system of systems" (1959:29). A community, even a small one, includes many different institutions and organizations with formal and informal subgroups that develop within them. For example, inner-city neighborhoods can have a complex system of protection (i.e., gangs) or health care (i.e., folk healers). These organizations and groups are social systems, and they are part of the social system of the community.

The community as a social system is implicit, whereas formal organizations are explicit. The boundaries of a "community" are not as clearly defined. This is true both of the community system as a totality, as well as its various elements, such as the goals of the people who live in the community, the prescribed means of achieving goals, and their underlying values (Parsons 1960). Organizations are subsystems within a community and are necessarily related to one another rationally or deliberately.

Community as function or purpose specific includes functional systems or groups brought together because of a common cause (i.e., individuals with AIDS, the elderly, individuals concerned about nuclear waste, or citizens concerned about pornography). A community of citizens has, as its purpose and function, a common "glue" that holds it together. Where the participants live is immaterial. Panzetta (1983) refers to this as a "when" community. Such communities come together for a period of time for a common pursuit, such as Mothers Against Drunk Drivers, Special Games Unlimited, or Bikers Against Child Abuse.

Numerous definitions of *community organization* are in the literature. The definition used in this chapter is that of Kramer and Specht (1983:14):

> Community organization refers to various methods of intervention whereby a professional change agent helps a community action system composed of individuals, groups, or organizations engage in planned collective action in order to deal with social problems within a democratic system of values. It is concerned with programs aimed at social change with primary reference to environmental conditions and social institutions. It involves two major interrelated concerns (a) the *interactional processes* of working with an action system, which include identifying, recruiting, and working with the members, and developing organizational and interpersonal relationships among them which facilitate their efforts; (b) the *technical tasks* involved in identifying problem areas, mobilizing the resources necessary to effect action, and assessing the outcomes of programs.

This definition unifies both the technical tasks of the planning model and the interaction processes of the locality development model. While aspects of traditional community organization incorporate task-centered principles, an overall framework of task-centered community organization needs to be developed incorporating (1) a comprehensive assessment; (2) specific, measurable goals and strategies; (3) prioritizing of target problems; (4) establishing time frames for tasks; (5) active use of interaction skills to promote indigenous community participation; and (6) the professional use of social workers in technical tasks and interaction skills.

Community organization can be divided into the four phases of task-centered work. The first section will address preintervention issues concerning theory, goals, values, and the appropriate use of community organization. Following this section we will address the initial phase, the middle phase, and the termination phase. This chapter is by no means an exhaustive survey of community organization theory and practice, yet it will provide readers with a framework to understand this level of intervention.

15.2.1.0 EFFECTIVENESS AND REPLICABILITY

One of the pitfalls of early social work practice was the nondiscriminating acceptance of numerous intervention theories, practices, and techniques that were either contradictory to the values of social work or not empirically proven to be effective (Fischer 1973). Therefore increased attention is now appropriately being given to issues of practice effectiveness. As mentioned in previous chapters, the task-centered approach has been found to be very effective in working in other modalities, and it is sensitive to using a variety of established techniques and methodologies.

Although minimal research has been done on the effectiveness of a task-centered approach to community organization, related research provides encouragement for organizing community intervention under this approach. Various task-centered principles have been applied successfully to community organization in a variety of settings. A brief review of some of the community organization literature reported nationally and internationally may prove helpful in understanding the possible effectiveness of incorporating a task-centered approach to community work.

Internationally the United Nations has played an important role in this by emphasizing citizen participation and the use of indigenous leaders within its urban and rural planning and development projects. As a result of the UN policies, a number of developing nations have implemented a social planning model at the national level and a locality development approach within the local context.

Two major weaknesses have been noted in these organizing efforts. First, social development is often assumed to be a painful process, and therefore planning tends to be long term, "in the belief that far-reaching social change produces tensions and maladjustments—which are to be avoided at all cost" (Khinduka 1987:357). Second, some of the inadequacies of the community organizing efforts internationally have been because of a failure to operationalize terms and develop concrete tasks (Midgley et al. 1986). Those areas where tasks have been specified have noted success.

International models that separate social planning and locality development tend to produce long-term projects nationally because of a lack of input from the citizens, and unspecific tasks and goals locally because of a lack of direction and training from the government.

One notable exception is the Vikas Mandals (neighborhood councils and community halls) programs that were established in India. These programs incorporated two essential elements of a task-centered approach: self-determination (in the form of citizen participation) and specific tasks.

The Vikas Mandals were essentially people's institutions established by the government to encourage citizen participation in specific community improvement projects. These programs facilitated the emergence of indigenous leaders, many of whom had never undertaken such responsibility previously. Some of the tasks these programs undertook included mediation, conflict management, solving minor problems, educational classes, immunization programs, children's clubs, reading rooms, outings, and so forth (Chatterjee 1962; Kaul 1976; Kaul 1988).

Another example of a successful community organizing project that emphasized both professional planning and self-determination is the Local Community Service Centers (LCSC) project, which occurred in Canada. Positive results were reported after a two-year research project (Cawley 1996; Gulati and Guest, 1990). The approach is based on the premise that natural helping networks are important and that efforts should be made to create and support them. Social workers' tasks include motivating individuals, groups, and communities to take an active role in the community and in the process of change. Users are viewed as citizens and partners in the provision of services, not clients or passive beneficiaries of services. A great deal of work is done on preventive work and education, as well as remedial projects. Gulati and Guest (1990) indicate that LCSCs have a high public and user approval rating (85 percent in some locales).

The LCSC project is task-centered in that it takes a holistic, multidisciplinary approach (rather than emphasizing only one of the three traditional models), and it also emphasizes citizen participation.

Richardson et al. (1983) have also implemented a community development model, which is similar to a task-centered approach, with positive results. Richardson et al. worked in a small community to promote "family life education" as a preventative and treatment approach to child abuse and neglect. Their use of short-term tasks was effective in achieving their goals while at the same time promoting citizen involvement.

Steiner and Mark (1985) implemented tasks with a community group for a mass-withdrawal campaign against a bank in protest of a planned mortgage interest increase. This project emphasizes the success of a community project that is short term and task specific. Steiner and Mark's study also illustrates some of the divergent community problems that can be effectively solved through thoughtful organizing.

A recent example of a successful task-centered community organization project resulted in the development of Special Games Unlimited (SGU), an organization for children who suffer from physical disabilities without cognitive limitations (Crump et al. 2000). These children are ineligible for Special Olympics. Using a task-centered approach with social planning and locality development features, the authors, under the direction of K. R. Ramakrishnan, successfully established an organization that would meet their needs for physical activity. SGU will be used to illustrate TC community organizing in later sections of this chapter.

Another important issue to consider is whether the results of a project can be replicated. In order for social work to develop knowledge and generalizations about community intervention, the strategies must be clearly defined so others can implement them and analyze them. David Thomas (1980), who has had extensive experience in community organizing in London, England, states that researching and replicating research in community work has inherent difficulties. His main finding in analyzing research in community organization is the existence of tension between the researcher and community worker. He refers to this as the "politics of research." On the one hand, researchers tend to be interested in rigorous procedures, explicit goals, and objectivity; on the other hand, the community workers are committed to flexibility and intuition in the field, nonspecificity and openness of goals, and subjectivity and self-interest in documenting the success of their work.

Likewise, politics are involved if the community project is funded by an outside sponsor. Often pressure is applied on the researchers or community organizers to embellish their findings in order to satisfy the needs of the scrutinizing sponsor. Therefore results may be misleading and prevent other practitioners from replicating the community project. Another difficulty in replication is the variability of resources, including financial, available to community organizers from one project to the next. Yet practice principles can still be generated that will be helpful to other social workers.

15.2.2.0 THEORETICAL BASE

In its strictest sense, theory is defined by its ability to explain and predict. Theory is important to practitioners as it provides a map with which to organize the variables involved in their work. As is mentioned in section 2.2.0, the task-centered approach is not tied to specific theory but, instead, is a heuristic, problem-solving approach that utilizes techniques and strategies that have been shown to be effective. Emphasis is on utility and usefulness, rather than what is "true" or "real."

Currently three major perspectives are being developed as a theory base for community organization. The first is based on the social systems perspectives (Holland and Petchers 1987; Parsons 1960; Warren 1983b). The social systems perspective deals with the functional interactions of organizations, bureaucracies, and communities. Particular emphasis is given to the various functions of systems: adaptation and growth, goal attainment, system maintenance, and integration. The social systems perspective focuses both on the interaction at the local level, or horizontal level, and at the extracommunity level (state, federal, international), or vertical level.

The second approach is based on an ecological perspective (Germain 1985). The ecological perspective focuses on the interactions between different units of the system and the system as a whole. The ecological perspective provides a holistic view of the community, including the functional and dysfunctional relationships between and among its members in their situations and environments. This perspective addresses issues of natural habitat, ecosystems, diversity, continuity, balance, holism, adaptation, well-being, interaction, and transaction.

The third approach addresses the issue of power. Meenaghan, Washington, and Ryan (1982) define power as "the ability to move somebody or some group or organization to do something they may not want to do" (117). Biklen (1983) also looks at community organizing from the perspective of power. By examining power and power structures within a community, organizers are able to address the forces that are able to impede or facilitate their efforts.

Among the various approaches and models developed for community practice, the task-centered approach attempts to unify the best features of locality development, social action, and social planning. Rather than starting with a given theory of the community or target group, a task-centered worker begins with the facts and data that are available and then moves to any formal theory that may help explain the facts.

15.2.3.0 MISSION AND PURPOSE

As mentioned in earlier chapters, *mission* refers to the collective humanitarian cause of social work. From an ecological perspective, this mission is the improvement of transactions between persons and their environments, transactions that promote equity, freedom, and social justice for all. Social workers are the best prepared to carry out this mission through their use of both microlevel and macrolevel interventions.

Kramer and Specht's (1983) definition of community organization, cited earlier, indicates that the purpose of community organization is to help organize the "community action system" (i.e., the individuals, groups, or organizations involved in the change process) in order to bring about change within the environment. Change can occur at local, state, national, or even international levels. Change can occur through innovations in policies or procedures within various organizations and agencies; through the diffusion of knowledge and information to all sectors of the population; and through an alteration in resources, services, and programs (Monkman and Allen-Meares 1985).

Mission and purpose, used with overall goals and specific tasks, provide a road map that guides social work interventions. Without a clear understanding of the mission and purpose of the community task, the organization will not arrive at its destination. Likewise, social workers need a clear understanding of their values and the values incorporated within the community.

15.2.4.0 SOCIAL WORK VALUES

Values are what guide the social work profession to accomplish its mission and purpose. Social workers believe in being clear about their values and using those values as markers along their destination. We believe social work needs to use its value system as a guide in choosing theories, interventions, and policies. Much has been written about social work's inappropriate acceptance of faddish theories and techniques without questioning both their effectiveness and their underlying value base (Bloom 1969).

The previous chapters have expounded on social work's values for the dignity and worth of individuals, for the uniqueness of the individual, and for the right to individual self-determination. These values represent a positive and optimistic view of humankind. Although some individuals' *behaviors* may not be consistent with their own worth and dignity, nevertheless we believe that individuals still possess these qualities and therefore require our respect.

Microlevel theories and interventions draw on these values to develop treatment goals and plans. Interventions are contracted with individuals, families, and groups with careful attention not to violate the profession's core values. Interventions at the macrolevel are designed to change the environment and improve interactions between people and the social system. Macrolevel values also need to be enumerated and used as a guide in developing interventions at a community level (*community* meaning local, national, and international arenas).

Consistent with the ecological perspective, macrolevel values should include a respect for environments and social systems without assuming hostile intentions to aspects of the larger system. At the same time, social workers must address issues of oppression, poverty, and discrimination. Macrolevel values need to adhere to putting an end to global oppression. With such a value base in place, community organization will become a powerful tool for peace and for confronting the challenges of AIDS, homelessness, the exploitation of children interna-

tionally in labor camps, immigrant women in sweat shops, family violence, and the list goes on.

Just as individuals need to be approached with an attitude of respect
and dignity, communities and organizations also need to be viewed positively. Social workers need to choose macrolevel theories that hold a positive and optimistic view of environments. Although some environments
may have policies and practices that are inconsistent with their own
worth and dignity, nevertheless, as with individuals, we believe that environments still possess these qualities and therefore deserve our respect.

Task-centered community organizers need to establish priorities that
acknowledge the social environment in a positive manner. Gandhi is a
good example of a macrolevel worker whose values and techniques
showed respect and optimism for society, culture, organizations, and
the whole of what makes up a community (Ramakrishnan, Balgopal,
and Patchner 1990). Gandhi denied the necessity of tension between or
within systems: "If all is one, then in their natural state relationships
must be harmonic" (Walz, Sharma, and Birnbaum 1990:21).

Social work ethics extends recognition of diversity and promotion of
cultural pluralism, which allows for the equal coexistence of various cultural groups within a host society. At present, the world community is un-
dergoing tremendous demographic changes and, as a result, is becoming
more heterogeneous. Therefore community organizers will increasingly
work with culturally diverse communities. Incorporating a value of cultural pluralism will lead to a respect for client uniqueness, and sensitivity
to culture, ethnicity, and diverse lifestyles. Therefore workers will focus
on the strengths of the various populations rather than manipulating
them to adapt involuntarily to the dominant value system. This respect is
operationalized through active participation of community members to
develop their own tasks and outcomes. These community members can
represent the indigenous population, businesses, government, and other
groups with a vested interest in the community and its development.

15.2.5.0 RELATIONSHIP

Community organization occurs within a web of relationships including those among the leadership group, with community groups, and

with other agencies or organizations that serve similar purposes. In order to be effective community organizers, social workers require good interpersonal skills and knowledge. Interpersonal skills at a macrolevel are unique and differ from the traditional clinical skills (genuineness, respect, empathy, controlled emotional involvement, and so on). Some major differences exist between microlevel and macrolevel relationships, and these need to be explored.

Torczyner (1983) identifies relationships based on three strategies, namely, conflict, collaboration, and negotiation. Torczyner defines conflict relationships as those in which "the parties involved reject compromise and the pursuit of common interests and instead heighten their differences in pursuit of their ends and become polarized" (1983:169). Conflict represents one end of a relationship continuum. At the other end is collaboration.

Collaboration entails minimizing one's differences and, instead, focusing on common interests and goals that may be actualized through cooperation. Collaboration includes seeking to establish the positive intentions of each party involved, affirming the mutual goals, and then working together in the interests of the goal.

Negotiation falls in the middle of the continuum. Negotiation is used to minimize certain differences between groups and to develop certain agreements and mutual goals. "Negotiation begins when conflict or collaboration is no longer desirable, and they may be used to end a conflict or to set the stage for collaboration" (Torczyner 1983:170).

While many social workers are uncomfortable with conflict, those engaged in community organizing must be able to use it. Conflict is often part of raising the issues in a community that become target problems (Kirst-Ashman and Hull 2001). Johnson (1997) suggests that it can help to explore problems and to improve the quality of problem resolution and decision making.

According to Bisno (1987), macrolevel practice requires an understanding that not all relationships are based on a shared goal (as is the case in microlevel practice). Often groups have opposing goals that will not respond to a clinical skill, such as empathy. Another characteristic of macrolevel relationships is that social workers will have obligations to more than one group, such as professional organizations, bureaucracies, the social movement, and themselves.

Another difference Bisno points out between micro- and macrolevel relationships is the motivation for interaction. At the macrolevel, "transactions may be entered into in order to secure an advantage (e.g., material gain, policy, professional gain, power, status); to expedite a task; or even because of legal necessity" (Bisno 1987:148).

Bisno further indicates that the community organizer plays a multiplicity of roles: advocate, mediator, colleague, coordinator, planner, negotiator, motivator, adversary, and researcher. All these depict the versatility needed to interact with a complex community. Therefore a variety of roles and skills are utilized at the macrolevel depending on the project and the need.

Community workers will often interact with a variety of individuals and target groups. To be effective, the worker needs to match the language and metaphors of the person being approached. One organizer lamented: "When we picketed at the state capitol everyone showed up in their cut-offs and purple hair, the legislators had a hard time thinking we were serious!" Likewise, walking into a housing project, with a business suit and briefcase in hand, to organize a group for improved housing standards may communicate that this is a middle-class project of which they may want no part.

Once a relationship is developed it needs to be maintained, whether by personal contact, a telephone call, or a letter. Let the target individuals know you are still around. It may mean brunch in the morning with a community or business leader, then working at the soup line at the homeless shelter in the afternoon, and then attending a public hearing regarding a nuclear dump site at night. But maintaining an active profile is key, particularly when working with individuals who have many other projects demanding their time and attention.

15.2.6.0 THE APPROPRIATE SYSTEM FOR WORK AND IDENTIFYING COLLATERALS

When social workers become involved at a community level, they have already identified the problem as being more than an individual issue and more than a family or group concern. Rather, the social worker sees the need to work at a community level by empowering the community of concerned individuals and facilitating a better response to their needs from the environment (businesses, government, other consumers, and so on).

An example of this can be seen in the activities of one social worker who works in a private outpatient clinic. While working in individual therapy with a woman dealing with depression, it came to the worker's attention that the woman, who was receiving Supplemental Security Income (SSI), was actually losing benefits each year. The woman described how each year the Social Security office would give her a cost-of-living increase. However, the state offices were aware of this and subsequently deducted her food stamps and her medical benefits. Her landlord likewise increased the rent of her apartment. She figured that her cost-of-living increase cost her about a hundred dollars a month, and she wanted to know if she could refuse her increase.

The social worker recognized that resolving the problem provided an opportunity to empower the client through the introduction of community organization strategies. The woman was put in contact with a local state representative sympathetic to these kinds of issues. She was advised to contact the local chapter of the National Association of Social Workers and become involved in lobbying for changes in state policies. This example illustrates how social workers can empower clients by intervening at various levels. It also demonstrates that all workers need to be knowledgeable about existing community organizations and community organization strategies.

Within the task-centered approach, the group of concerned citizens becomes the client group or the nucleus that forms the leadership and core of the organization. This nucleus becomes the means for involving others. "A nucleus is defined as a small group of serious-minded citizens who should have the following traits: (1) a knowledge of and trust in one another; (2) a concern about local problems and a desire to improve conditions for all members of the community; and (3) an ethical sense of right and wrong" (Zastrow 1982:539). The community organizer will want this "nucleus" to be representative of the entire community of concerned consumers (professionals, minorities, women, school officials, church leaders, and so forth).

In identifying collaterals, a list needs to be developed delineating those individuals and groups that will support the endeavors of the organization and those who will be resistant to the objectives (see Table 15.1). In other words, a list of the key actors and players is needed. Who is affected most by the situation? Who benefits from the situation? Which special interest groups would become involved? Who are the leaders involved (formal and informal)? What resources are available? Who would benefit from the proposed changes? The answers to

TABLE 15.1 *Checklist of Key Actors*

Those who will support the project	*Those who will oppose the project*
_____	_____
_____	_____
_____	_____
_____	_____
_____	_____
_____	_____
_____	_____
_____	_____
Those who will be positively affected	*Those who will be negatively affected*
_____	_____
_____	_____
_____	_____
_____	_____
_____	_____
_____	_____
_____	_____
_____	_____

Actors to consider: schools, churches, local businesses, farmers, minority groups, local formal leaders, politicians, unions, professional organizations, national interest groups, media, experts, government agencies, and so on.

these kinds of questions will help identify the collateral groups who will become involved. For example, the SGU group thought that potentially competing organizations like Special Olympics might react negatively to their efforts. The committee concluded: "The better road for us to travel . . . was to use other special programs . . . as a strength as opposed to competition. By working together, our two programs would be reaching every child with a physical and/or mental disability" (Crump et al. 2000:6).

Nearby nuclei, groups that may be sympathetic to the cause of the community organization, may provide assistance, support, or perhaps legitimacy to the organization. The formation of coalitions with nearby nuclei helps diffuse some of the power of the groups that are resistant or likely to oppose the efforts of this new community organization.

15.2.6.2 CHECKLIST FOR PRETREATMENT ACTIVITIES

___ 1. What is the purpose of this project?

___ 2. Is it compatible with social work mission and values?

___ 3. How will effectiveness be measured?

___ 4. Is a theoretical understanding of the problem necessary? If so, which theory(ies) is most relevant?

___ 5. Does the nuclear group adequately represent important segments of the community?

___ 6. Are relationships within the nuclear group and between the group and others in the community likely to facilitate cooperation?

___ 7. Have those likely to support or oppose the project been identified?

___ 8. Have strategies to cope with those likely to resist been identified?

15.3.0.0 COMPONENTS OF THE INITIAL PHASE

This section outlines some of the unique qualities of the task-centered approach to community organization in the initial phase. The main aspects of this phase include (1) compiling a detailed description of the problem by gathering necessary information; (2) establishing goals;

(3) prioritizing goals and tasks to develop a strategy of operation; (4) making specific, although flexible, time frames to stay on task and evaluate progress; (5) finalizing a comprehensive assessment of the problem along with a systematic intervention plan; and (6) developing a budget for the project.

The community organization group will pass through the initial, middle, and final phases, and the social worker needs to be aware of these phases, their transition, and the role he or she is required to play during these phases (Burghardt 1979). The three phases are not fixed, as organizations may revert back to former stages before advancing to the next phase. Because of the focus on "community-determination" (self-determination of the community) with the task-centered approach, the social worker will need to follow the organization's lead. This can mean that a program that has been carefully planned may need to be altered or eliminated if it does not meet the needs of the organization.

A case illustration will facilitate the description of task-centered activities as they pertain to community organization during the initial phase.

Mary, a social worker with the state's child protective services agency, handled many abuse and neglect cases when they were initially reported. In her work she became aware that her community had no resources for adult sexual offenders. As part of her job, she often went to court to recommend that an offender be removed from the home as a precondition for the child's return to the home. However, Mary was frustrated by the court's lack of awareness of the need for treatment for the offenders.

Because of the need for further education in treatment services for offenders, as well as the development of efficient treatment programs, Mary decided to organize a group from within the legal and therapeutic communities to address this need. Mary discussed this with Omar, the assistant state attorney, with whom she had a good working relationship. Together they began making informal contacts to others in both the legal community (lawyers, judges, probation officers) and the therapeutic community (therapists, psychiatrists, director of the local community mental health clinic). This informal networking formed the initial organization (the nucleus) to begin addressing the need for services for adult sexual offenders.

The subsections below will follow this case to demonstrate how Mary worked with others in the community to begin to define the problem and the goals of the organization, and to gather information.

15.3.1.0 ROLES, PURPOSE, AND INTERVENTION PROCEDURES

The beginning community organizer often becomes frustrated because, in spite of his or her best efforts, the group does not seem to get focused and on task. The problem tends to be a lack of awareness on the social worker's part of the organization's different developmental stages. The initial phase consists of an orientation to the group and an exploration of the problem. Brager and Specht (1973) refer to this stage as the *socialization stage* to emphasize the need of members to develop a relationship with one another. This stage also encompasses identifying and analyzing the change opportunity, and setting goals and objectives (Kettner, Daley, and Nichols 1985).

Outline for an Initial Meeting
1. Allow time for socialization.
2. Ask for introductions of each member. Consider using name tags and lists of names.
3. Explain the purpose of the meeting and the agenda.
4. Explain the general purpose of the task group and begin discussing measures of effectiveness.
5. Discuss mission and values.
6. Discuss format of meetings and the task-centered process, including time limits and the budget.
7. Establish basic rules, which may include that members be required to do the following:
   a. attend meetings;
   b. ask questions;

      c. actively participate;

      d. remain open-minded;

      e. share responsibility;

      f. critique ideas, not people; and

      g. keep meetings within the time limit.

  8. Discuss the roles of the community organizer and the members.

  9. Discuss the next meeting and make assignments as needed.

10. Provide refreshments.

The community worker will bring together the nucleus, identified in section 15.2.6.0, which will form the leadership and core of the organization. The initial meeting of the nucleus sets the stage for the organizing process. It is important that the initial meeting is organized and kept to the established time limit. A sample agenda is outlined above. During this initial socialization phase, the first task of the leader is to form relationships of trust and to build a working coalition. Therefore time needs to be allocated for socializing. The overall purpose of the task group needs to be explained, as well as the task-centered process. Members of the task group may not have organizing experience, and therefore basic rules will also need to be established and agreed on.

One of the group's initial concerns, which the social worker will need to address, is whether the concern is worth their time and energy. Is intervention possible? Will intervention make a difference? Without a sense that the group can indeed play a part, the objectives will seem too overwhelming. Therefore the worker will need to facilitate the group's exploration to identify and analyze the target problem.

A community organizer will be most effective during this phase by focusing on interpersonal relationships within the organization. Bales (1950) refers to this as the *socio-emotional leader*. The socio-emotional leader focuses on interpersonal relationships among the group and is less concerned about specific tasks. Although the social worker will need to use technical skills to stay focused on completing the specific tasks, these skills are merely secondary in the initial phase. This is a time to build rapport and trust. The later stages of task-centered community organizing will require a more task-oriented style of leadership.

The community organizer has two significant tasks during this initial phase: gathering information (see section 15.3.3.0) and beginning to develop an organizational structure through coalition building. Depending on the nature and complexity of the problem, the structure may vary from only a few officers to a formal structure with a constitution, bylaws, and a number of subcommittees. Careful selection of subcommittee members is important. Members of the executive committee, drawn from the nucleus, should chair these subcommittees to provide feedback and to promote commitment and enthusiasm to the task at hand, as well as to the organization's overall goal.

At this stage, the leadership may need to be trained in conducting meetings, keeping records, allowing members to air differences, making other members feel important, and keeping their interest in the project alive. The chair of the subcommittee also plays an important role in the dissemination and diffusion of information to the organization. The community organizer and chairs of the various subcommittees also need to think in terms of training and developing indigenous leaders. The main objective is the facilitation of community empowerment. The community must believe that this is their organization. It must experience a sense of esprit de corps.

The core of the executive committee is then encouraged to examine the problem and narrow it down to a specific manageable task that can be accomplished within a given time frame. Such a process will require much discipline on the part of the organizer and the members of the organization.

In the case example, Mary and Omar began making as many contacts as they could within the legal and therapeutic communities in order to generate as much interest as possible. One way they found to generate interest among local therapists was to explain that the results of their findings would produce a referral list to be used by attorneys, judges, and probation officers. Monthly meetings were held with the executive committee, as well as the larger organization, to discuss the role and purpose of the task force.

Mary became frustrated during the meetings because at times it seemed nothing was being accomplished, no one was able to stay on task, each person appeared to have his or her own personal agendas to pursue. Mary began to realize that her first task as committee head was to facilitate the development of a working relationship among members of the organization. She found herself spending a lot of time between meetings "putting out fires" and addressing individual concerns. In time, however, she found that the work paid off and she began to feel a working coalition develop.

The SGU group members found that many roles were required in this phase of work. They acted as initiators, facilitators, coordinators, educators, and advocates.

15.3.2.0 TIME LIMITS AND BUDGETS

To maintain the interest of the organization, specific tasks need to be assigned to individuals or subcommittees. Burghardt (1982) suggests that the following tasks are appropriate for the initial phase: (1) sub-committee and steering committee meetings; (2) phone calls and individual follow-up; (3) forum/general meeting preparation; (4) flyer preparation; (5) mailings; (6) distributing leaflets; and (7) fund-raising work. These tasks can be made specific, and realistic time frames can be established. Tasks need to be more than mere "busy work," however; a clear rationale about how the tasks relate to the overall objectives should be made explicit.

The initial phase of organizing, which is the most important and time consuming, can be awkward. This phase requires understanding and patience. Both members and community organizers want to see results. However, the group as a whole is not ready for the action tasks that usually occur in the middle and final phases. Community organizers have a good tool with which to maintain group interest and also to gather information for the organization's project(s). This tool is the careful use of time limits. Establishing time frames for tasks helps the group remain on task, as well as providing feedback and important evaluation information.

Time frames are to be used as guideposts and not as a stick. The community organizer will need to allow for flexibility in establishing time frames. As guideposts, time limits can be used to provide feedback concerning the progress being made toward reaching the objectives. If some tasks are continually not being completed, then the group needs to reassess the task or the time frame to ensure that expectations are appropriate.

Establishing appropriate time frames also reduces the temporal gap between planning and implementing a task. When this temporal gap is brief, control of the project is maintained. Community members will have the plans and tasks fresh in their minds, which will conserve energy and maintain the momentum generated during planning meetings. Unanticipated environmental factors also have less opportunity to intervene or respond to the change efforts (Kettner, Daley, and Nichols 1985:213).

Time limits need to be flexible during the initial phase because members are still new to working with one another, and the problem is not yet well defined. For example, Mary did not realize how difficult it would be for her to locate an accurate mailing list of all local social workers, psychologists, psychiatrists, and counselors. Her time frame for completing this task changed twice before being completed. By setting time limits, though, Mary knew she would need to report her efforts to the committee at the required time. This kept her focused and motivated to try to have at least some new information for the group each time a report was due.

A concern that dovetails with time limits is the issue of a budget. Often financing a project will guide or be guided by time limits. Costs will have to be estimated and financial resources identified. Fundraising efforts may have to precede other activities. The SGU group imposed a time-limit by setting a date for "The Games." As with many first-time efforts, they found it difficult to project a detailed budget but were able to secure financial assistance from a local agency and individuals. By using a corp of volunteers they were able to reduce costs.

15.3.3.0 OBTAINING NECESSARY INFORMATION

One of the technical tasks of the community organizer during the initial phase is to gather information about the target problem. Important questions to ask include the following: Who are the leaders (formal and informal) of the various systems within the community (at the local, state, national, and international levels)? What is the power structure of the various systems? What resources (financial and human) are available? What sectors of the community need to be represented in the organization? Will the planning take place in an open-forum atmosphere? Is membership open, closed, or limited? What are the sources of resistance? How are they to be minimized?

Information can be gathered from experts, public hearings, community and political leaders, and so on. Some information may include service statistics (utilization data, caseload data, grievance data, and so on), as well as social indicators (unemployment, crime, schooling, income, and so forth). Surveys may also be used to gather information and assess the problem (Kimmel 1983). Martí-Costa and Serrano-García (1987) have indicated that using a combination of qualitative and quantitative methods is desirable "since a more precise view of reality is obtained" (366).

Checklist of Systems for Assessment

1. Total System: How does the total system contribute to the problem? How does it contribute to the solution?
   a. Demoralization and disintegration of total community?
   b. Decision problems of the total community?
   c. Inadequate resources for the total community?
   d. Problems with formal organizations?
   e. Difficulties in social adaptation?
   f. Friction based on demographic characteristics among subgroups (allogenic conflict)?
2. Subsystems: How do subsystems contribute to the problem? How do they contribute to the solution?
   a. Demoralization and disintegration of subsystems?
   b. Decision problems among subsystems?
   c. Inadequate resources for subsystems?
   d. Problems with formal organizations?
   e. Difficulties in social adaptation among subgroups?
   f. Allogenic conflict as a factor among subgroups?

The above checklist can be used to gather necessary information. Answering these questions will help focus the group on targeting the problem.

In the case example, Mary and the group began to gather important information about the problem that they had not expected. They began to realize some sharp philosophical differences within the therapeutic community. Those professionals who worked from a family advocacy model differed sharply from those operating from a family systems perspective. One model focused solely on protecting the victim, whereas the other focused on preserving the family. These differences, if not understood, could have undermined the efforts of the organization. With this information, Mary was able to emphasize the contributions of both approaches and could establish a working relationship between these two groups.

The SGU group discovered many disparate organizations serving very specialized populations, for example, providing one sporting activity for children with one particular disability. They were unable to locate any organization that served their population: children and adults with a variety of physical challenges but with IQs above 70. Thus they were able to demonstrate a need for their project.

15.3.4.0 TARGETING PROBLEMS AND DETERMINING PROBLEM PRIORITIES

Similar to interventions at the microlevel, a community organizer tries to involve significant constituencies and community members in identifying the target problems. In the community-organizing context, such involvement has been referred to as *citizen participation*. Involving diverse groups often generates differences and conflicts. Rather than shying away from such conflicts, the organizer will need to mediate and negotiate between the parties in order to generate a healthy dialogue. This process will then facilitate identifying the problems, prioritizing them, and agreeing on the most efficient and effective means to resolving them.

Reid (1978) developed a classification system to be used in targeting problems on an individual, family, and group level. The classification system at the microlevel enumerates eight types of target problems: (1) interpersonal conflict; (2) dissatisfaction in social relations; (3) reactive emotional distress; (4) decision problems; (5) problems with formal organizations; (6) difficulty in role performance; (7) inadequate resources; and (8) psychological or behavioral problems not classified elsewhere. Using the spirit of Reid's classification system, we will outline a similar schema for macrolevel assessment, which will facilitate the development of a generalist model for viewing the total system.

Our classification takes into consideration the various dimensions of communities. According to Roland Warren (1983a), communities differ from one another along four dimensions: (1) autonomy from extra community units; (2) the extent to which the service areas of the community coincide or fail to coincide; (3) psychological identification with a common locality; and (4) the extent to which the communities' horizontal pattern is strong or weak. These four dimensions can be classified into six categories, described below, which are similar to Reid's (1978) classification for micro-level, task-centered practice.

1. *Allogenic conflict.* Allogenic conflict refers to friction or discomfort experienced by individuals, groups, and communities because of significant and notable differences among themselves or with the larger society (Balgopal and Vassil 1983). Unlike intrapersonal and interpersonal conflicts, allogenic conflict states that members' allegiances to groups based on gender, age, religion, ethnicity, race, and the like, are in themselves part of the stresses and strains of contemporary life.

Differences can be implicit (personal beliefs, values, and so forth) as well as explicit (skin color, gender, style of dress, and so on), and often create tension and conflict between the members. Respecting these differences not only reduces the degree of conflict but also allows diversity without it becoming labeled as deviancy.

2. *Difficulties in social adaptation.* This community problem refers to difficulties in role performance, which includes expectations involving roles and tasks. Groups often do not know what is expected of them, and when they do know, they do not have the skills and capacity to perform in order to meet the larger society's expectations. For example, Native Americans have traditionally had a difficult time adapting to European Americans' expectations because it required that they sacrifice their self-respect and their culture.

Another example are those individuals who were moved into housing projects. The expectation of white, middle-class America was that these poor individuals should be grateful for this benevolent gesture.

What America discovered instead was that these individuals felt no identity with the projects. The poor were never involved in the planning process and therefore were unable to voice their preferences and opinions.

When the positive roles of individuals and society complement each other, this usually leads to greater mutual satisfaction and growth. However, when the roles are negative and noncomplementary, such as society's role expectations for women, minorities, or the underclass, then the transactions between individuals and their environment become dysfunctional. It is not social work's purpose simply to help people adapt to societal roles or to perform all expected tasks. Rather, social workers empower communities of oppressed individuals to organize (Monkman and Allen-Meares 1985).

3. *Problems with formal organizations.* This refers to difficulties the client group is experiencing with an organization, private or public. Such difficulties could range from the city not picking up garbage from poor neighborhoods to banks refusing to give loans to people living in poor areas (also known as "redlining"); from discriminatory practices of businesses and government agencies in hiring and retaining minorities to neglect of health care services to the poor. Problems in this area often lead the community organizations to develop tasks to change policies or procedures at whatever level is required: internationally, nationally, or locally.

4. *Inadequate resources.* Resources can be defined as people, organizations, or institutions to which one may turn for support or help. Currently resources are diminishing while competition for resources is increasing. Resources may be available supplies or the ability of a group to deal with a situation effectively (Monkman and Allen-Meares 1985). Resources could range from financial resources and political clout to the availability of recycling centers, educational programs on the environment, newsletters, and so on.

5. *Decision problems.* This problem category includes difficulties in making specific decisions often related to major changes in the life of the target population or client group. Whether to have a nuclear plant or expand an existing nuclear facility is a major decision in the life of a community. In the short run, it could mean thousands of jobs and millions of dollars to a declining economy. Yet, in the long run, it also

means environmental pollution, serious health hazards, and a "decapitated" land for future generations. The communities of England's Central Lake District have decided to keep the railroads and other types of commercial enterprises out of the area so that the place can be free of environmental pollution and its natural beauty preserved.

In some cases, the target population may have to decide whether to "put up or shut up" or fight a few elites. Such elites, because of their control over the local business and politics, impose their values on the community. Minor opponents are no match for these elites. Any major collective opposition is threatened by the action of the elites to eliminate jobs and take away monies from local banks. For people who refuse to be trampled, this is decision time.

6. *Demoralization and disintegration of community.* This area is concerned with general feelings, such as depression or anomie of the target population, rather than events precipitating the feelings. The closing of an air base, a plant shutdown, suicide by a number of people, murder and other types of violent crimes, all can have a tremendous negative effect on the emotional well-being of communities. Demographic changes can also be the cause of anxiety and depression in rural communities or communities composed predominately of elderly citizens.

After potential target problems are identified, the next step is to prioritize them. The number of problems to be worked on by the organization depends on the size and motivation of the group and the complexity of the problems identified. Most community organizations can only handle one problem at a time. If there is great interest in dealing with more than one problem, then the use of subcommittees can help organize those who want to work with specific problems.

In the example of the Sexual Offenders Task Force, the targeted problem was one of inadequate resources. The organization realized that no one in the community had any real expertise about treating offenders, and therefore they made educating the community their first priority. Following this educational goal, they would address themselves to working toward developing a treatment program. Another goal that emerged was to develop a collaborative working relationship both within and between the legal and therapeutic communities. The population served by the SGU group was allogenic conflict. Allogenic conflict naturally arises between those with physical disabilities and the larger society. For example, physical education classes in secondary schools did not provide activities suited to their situations.

15.3.5.0 EXPLORING TARGET PROBLEMS

Identifying a problem is not sufficient in itself to begin planning a strategy of intervention or a goal. More detailed information needs to be gathered in order to develop an informed plan. Questions to be asked include the following: How is the system contributing to the problem? Who are the victims? How many victims are there? What is the financial, physical, and emotional costs of the problem? What is the severity of the problem? Who are the stakeholders involved? In other words, who are the key players? How is the problem impacting on the disadvantaged and special populations? Who are the promoters of the problem? Who benefits from the problem? Who are those who fund the problem? Who will be affected by the problem's resolution? Who else has worked on the problem? What were the barriers faced by those who worked on the problem earlier?

Answering these kinds of questions will help the organization to understand the problem, its development, and the factors that maintain the problem. An essential question to consider is what effect the resolution of the problem will have. Will it mean the elimination of jobs? Increased federal spending and taxes? Anticipating these effects will help in developing goals and alternatives. Also, the organization will be better prepared to deal with opposition to the project.

The Task Force gathered information from other communities regarding their treatments and legal approaches to adult sexual offenders and was able to use this information as a means of supporting more empirically sound treatment approaches. Costs of developing various treatment programs were examined. Funding sources were also explored that would fund an educational conference, as well as a treatment program. Further, information was gathered on the number of men convicted of sexual assault crimes who were unable to find adequate treatment programs.

15.3.6.0 DEVELOPING THE PROBLEM SPECIFICATIONS

As outlined in section 3.6.0, problems need to be made specific and measurable to enable the worker to evaluate the impact of specific interventions. The questions asked in the previous section will make the problem both specific and measurable.

Community interventions can be evaluated by the extent to which problem specifications are changed or modified. As will be mentioned in later sections, evaluation is valuable in determining the need for further organizing and suggesting how the intervention can be generalized to other communities.

In the Sex Offender Task Force example, the organization realized that the community lacked viable treatment approaches for sexual offenders; therefore attorneys and probation officers were ill equipped to deal with this population. This could be easily measured by reviewing a sampling of court orders for sexual offenders.

15.3.7.0 GOALS

The goals of a task-centered community organization effort should be specific, understandable to all involved, attainable within the agreed-on time schedule, and measurable. The community members' active participation in all aspects of goal setting is desirable.

The process of goal development is the same as that of targeting and determining problem priorities and problem specifications, discussed in the earlier section. It is important that agreement on goals be reached by consensus through discussion and information sharing by the total organization.

Generally one goal is developed for each problem identified. Each goal needs to be directly related to the problem specified. The chances of concerted effort toward goal attainment will depend on how realistic the goals are. For example, community action programs of the 1960s designed to wipe out poverty in the United States were unrealistically ambitious and did not produce their ultimate objective. The poor results had a demoralizing effect on both the organizers and the consumers.

Whether the goals developed are task goals or process goals, they all should be (1) specific and mutually acceptable to all concerned; (2) small enough to be accomplished, yet large enough to give members a sense of accomplishment; (3) consistent with agreed-on objectives and values; (4) sufficiently attractive to gain target systems' commitment, cooperation, and investment of time; (5) time-limited; and (6) amenable to evaluation and measurement.

The social worker should allow the committee to develop the goal. During the initial phase, the goal may change several times before the group feels committed to the specified goal. Once the goal is delineated, the next task is to establish a working time frame. Establishing a time limit will help focus on specific tasks and thereby advance the committee to the middle phase of development.

In the Sex Offender project, the primary goal of the Task Force became the development of a conference targeted to the legal and therapeutic communities. The conference date was set and a couple of possible locations selected. The director of the community mental health clinic prepared a grant to the county mental health department to help fund this conference. Speakers from other communities were solicited, and they included a well-respected psychiatrist who specializes in this field and attorneys who discussed the legal aspects of dealing with sex offenders. In the SGU project, the goal was to sponsor a one-day event that would include indoor and outdoor activities.

15.3.8.0 CONTRACTS

The use of contracts has become a key dimension in social work intervention. As used in social work, contracts are fluid and dynamic, rather than static and set in stone. Contracts evolve just as the relationship between the social worker and the organization evolves. Contracting is used as one method of operationalizing citizen participation and involvement in the community project. Not only do contracts encourage participation, but they also outline responsibilities of all members involved and provide a measure of accountability.

Contracting is ongoing throughout the organizing process. Generating contracts is a process that includes the establishment of ground rules and the delineation of tasks (Croxton 1974). Establishing ground rules is the first step in negotiating a contract. This step determines the organization's need for service, the roles of both the social worker and members of the executive committee, the degree of involvement required of both, the degree of power held by both, and the possibility for renegotiation or termination of the contract by joint agreement. This is the process part of the contract.

The second part of the contracting phase, delineation of tasks, spells out strategies to be used, who is to perform what tasks, and who is responsible for the performance of those tasks. During the initial phase, task contracts may include such assignments as generating a list of legislators and how they voted for a particular bill or agreeing to attend all meetings.

Contracts can be either informal (verbal) or formal (written). Generally contracts made at the macrolevel should be formal, written, and explicit. The contractual agreement is made between the social worker and organization with which he or she is working. Developed in concert with the other members of the executive committee, the contract should be specific enough to leave no room for misunderstanding or misinterpretation. Terms used in the contract may need to be explained, particularly if jargon is used.

Two kinds of contracts may be used by the community organizer: primary contracts and secondary contracts (Balgopal and Vassil 1983). The primary contract is made between the social worker and the members of the organization. It includes the ground rules and a delineation of tasks. The ground rules explicate the need for service, the amount of time involved in the project, a delineation of the power structure, and the possibility for renegotiation or termination of the contract by joint agreement of the participants.

The delineation of tasks includes mention of the selected goal(s), target problems, and the tasks and strategies to be implemented. This part of the contract also needs to address who will perform what tasks and the responsibilities involved in the performance of those tasks.

Secondary contracts are agreements formed with various subgroups or individuals within the community organizational structure, as well as any agreements made with various coalitions or outside parties (Churchill 1966).

As the Sexual Offenders Task Force became more focused on the target problem and interventions, contracts became a vital part of the organizing process. Formal contracts were written for the conference presenters. Informal contracts were made within meetings among members regarding assignments. Contracts were carefully prepared so as to outline the expectations and agreements of relevant parties. When members of the executive committee would begin to give an excuse as to why an assignment was not completed, an ongoing joke was to remind them of the "contract." SGU needed written contracts with the supporting agency and a university that donated the use of its facilities. They also needed signed waivers of liability for each participant.

15.3.9.0 ASSESSMENT

Once the necessary information has been gathered, the problem specified, and the goal articulated, the community organizer is prepared to complete an assessment. Many federal agencies require that a formal written assessment be completed as part of the planning process or as a precondition for grant support (Kimmel 1983). As mentioned above, the assessment evaluates the interactions between individual community members and their environment.

Assessments outline the information gathered to determine the nature of the target problem within the given community. The assessment is used throughout the planning process to ensure that tasks are developed to respond to the needs of the community.

Assessments should specify the consequences of actions taken, such as (a) who will be affected by the goal, and how; (b) who will be opposed to the goal, and why; (c) who will be supportive of the goal, and why; and (d) what will be the ecological impact, both short- and long-term?

In the case illustration of the Task Force, the information gathered in the previous steps was compiled and used as a basis for a grant proposal to the county mental health department. The information contained in the grant proposal was thorough and well represented the time and energy put into the project. As a result, funding was granted to help pay the expenses of the educational conference.

The conference became a springboard for the development of various treatment approaches to deal with sexual offenders. Mary's organizing efforts also paid off in terms of developing a better working relationship within the legal and therapeutic communities.

15.3.10.0 CHECKLIST FOR THE INITIAL PHASE

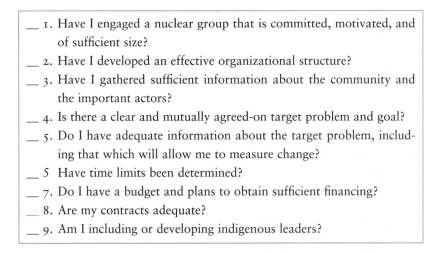

> ___ 1. Have I engaged a nuclear group that is committed, motivated, and of sufficient size?
>
> ___ 2. Have I developed an effective organizational structure?
>
> ___ 3. Have I gathered sufficient information about the community and the important actors?
>
> ___ 4. Is there a clear and mutually agreed-on target problem and goal?
>
> ___ 5. Do I have adequate information about the target problem, including that which will allow me to measure change?
>
> ___ 5 Have time limits been determined?
>
> ___ 7. Do I have a budget and plans to obtain sufficient financing?
>
> ___ 8. Are my contracts adequate?
>
> ___ 9. Am I including or developing indigenous leaders?

15.4.0.0 COMPONENTS OF THE MIDDLE PHASE

The middle phase of community organization is the stage of task development and implementation. Now the social worker begins to use more task-oriented leadership skills. The goal of this phase is to design and implement the specific intervention strategy and tasks.

It is also during this phase that the community organization is broadened and maintained, and outside support is used and developed. Indigenous leadership is likewise developed within the community. Evaluation is ongoing, and tasks are revised as needed. Tasks need to be evaluated and chosen according to the specified time limits. If the most appropriate task is too time-consuming, then the committee will need to reevaluate the goal or the time frame.

Toseland and Rivas (1987) state that the middle phase is characterized by repetition and diversity. The repetition occurs within the structure of the meetings: the opening portion for a warm-up and socialization, the middle portion for the tasks at hand, and the final portion for summarizing and closing. The diversity is evidenced in the variety of tasks, procedures, and assignments used during this phase in order to design and implement the change effort.

Checklists for Meetings   To Do Before the Meeting:

- Do any special arrangements need to be made?
- Are any materials needed?
- Have people been reminded of their responsibilities?
- Have agenda items been received in advance?
- Do any reports or materials need to be distributed for discussion at the meeting?

Meeting Agenda

- Opening Remarks and welcome
- Review of previous minutes
- Announcements
- Reports from subcommittees
  __ Distribute handouts
  __ Report on assignments
  __ Specify new assignments with target dates
- Items for "discussion only"
- Summary and closing remarks
- Scheduling of next meeting (date, time, and place)

To Do During the Meeting

- Ensure that everyone has had an opportunity to give input
- Introduce new members
- Use *Robert's Rules of Order*
- Remain on task
- Be a model of respect, interest, and patience
- Give praise for accomplishments

To Do After the Meeting

- Send "Thank You" notes to special speakers
- Follow up on assignments
- Type and distribute minutes of the meeting

The effective use of meetings becomes crucial during the middle phase. Various tools—such as agendas, record keeping, and work between meetings—have been designed in an effort to make meetings efficient and on task. A sample meeting agenda is included in the above checklists. Although the tools may be altered to fit the needs of the individual worker and the organization, to neglect them altogether is to "court failure" (Ephross and Vassil 1988:141).

15.4.1.0 TASK PLANNING AND IMPLEMENTATION SEQUENCE

During this phase of organizing, tasks are selected, developed, finalized, implemented, and evaluated. The tasks are developed so as to lead the organization to the fulfillment of its goal(s). Tasks are specific actions taken both within committee meetings and outside the meetings.

The TPIS incorporates constant evaluation and feedback. This information is used to assess the tasks and their relationship to the main goals specified. Throughout the TPIS, tasks may be altered, deleted, or added. The TPIS is an ongoing process. Seldom is one task selected, completed, and evaluated before another task is developed. Usually several tasks are being developed concurrently, which may be at different developmental levels in the planning process.

A case illustration will facilitate the description of the TPIS process in community organization.

A social worker providing family therapy decided mid-way through the treatment process to facilitate a family in organizing neighbors living in their townhouse complex. The family, Mr. and Mrs. Stevens and their three children (all three under the age of seven), was a low-income family living in the W.V. housing cooperative. The W.V. co-op consisted of three hundred townhouses and apartments for singles and families. As part of the co-op, the Stevens family paid a one-time membership fee that made them part-owners in the co-op. The co-op was managed by a board of directors made up of volunteer members of the W.V. co-op.

Mr. and Mrs. Stevens had complained about one of the board members being unethical and treating his position as an opportunity to gain influence and power over the co-op. The social worker saw this as an opportunity to facilitate the family in organizing the membership of the W.V. co-op, as well as helping the couple in working conjointly on a project that interested them both. While other family issues were still being pursued in family therapy, the social worker took on a facilitator/trainer position in helping the Stevens family organize the membership at W.V. co-op. This role made sense in terms of the family's goals to develop better communication skills and to develop joint interests.

Mr. Stevens took on the task of gathering information concerning the bylaws and various means with which to deal with the board member in question, Mr. Andrews. Mrs. Stevens became involved in surveying interest among other members and their willingness to help. She discovered that at no time in the history of the W.V. co-op had the members ever been organized around a particular issue. Board members regularly complained about the seeming apathy among the general membership. Mrs. Stevens was able to find thirty other families interested in trying to remove Mr. Andrews from the board of directors. Mr. Stevens talked with the other board members to gather information and support for their organizing efforts.

15.4.1.1 GENERATING TASK ALTERNATIVES AND SELECTING A TASK

The initial step in the TPIS is to generate a list of task alternatives (see section 4.1.1). This will mean at least one meeting devoted to brainstorming activity. During this activity, tasks are listed without judgment. The tasks will be related to the defined goal.

Tasks may be directed toward developing programs, services, or resources; promoting education and consciousness raising; or promoting policy or procedural changes. The tasks and strategies developed will depend on the nature of the relationship among the various groups involved.

Once a list of tasks is generated, the committee must then select those tasks to be used to meet the goals. Long-term and short-term tasks need to be differentiated with time frames established. A common problem at this stage is that a committee either selects tasks that are too difficult or tasks that underestimate the committee's potential. It is the community organizer's responsibility to help the committee remain realistic in its objectives, as well as to explore individual resistance to more appropriate activities and tasks.

In the W.V. co-op illustration, Mr. and Mrs. Stevens held a meeting of the thirty interested members. They discussed a general membership meeting coming up in six weeks in which elections were to be held. Several members were concerned about a recent flyer that Mr. Andrews had sent out announcing that he had released the other four board members and was appointing his own people during the interim period before the general membership meeting. Mr. and Mrs. Stevens both shared their concerns and explained their goal of trying to encourage enough members to attend the general membership meeting in order to vote Mr. Andrews out. Everyone agreed with this goal, although several additional goals were also suggested. Mr. Stevens was able to maintain interest in the project while focusing on only one goal at a time. Mrs. Stevens then outlined the tasks she saw as necessary in order to be ready for the upcoming meeting. From this list of tasks, she was able to arrive at a consensus in the prioritization of tasks. The first task was to generate a one-page flyer explaining the actions of Mr. Andrews and that the general membership needed to be present at the meeting in order to pass various proposals.

In more complicated structures like SGU, some tasks are generated by subcommittees. The subcommittees included public relations, recruitment (of athletes), fund-raising, and games. The nucleus committee generated tasks for other aspects of the effort, including awards, the hospitality tent, opening and closing ceremonies, and assessment of the project.

15.4.1.2 ELICITING AGREEMENT TO PERFORM TASKS

The commitment to task implementation can take the form of a written or verbal contract. The contract formalizes the tasks and prepares the group for the next phase in the sequence.

Written contracts are best in those cases involving financial accountability. Those individuals who will be contracted for services will need a written agreement. Furthermore, policies and procedures concerning the budget for the task and procedures for any reimbursement can be specified.

Agreement should also be established as to who will be responsible for further planning and implementation of the tasks. If subcommittees are to be used, then these should also be formed with an agreement of participation by the members.

In our co-op example, Mr. Stevens explained the task and asked for a commitment from everyone present to pair up and canvass the co-op, personally distributing flyers and talking to members. When others began adding other tasks, he acknowledged the suggestions and then referred back to the original goal, to remove Mr. Andrews from the board. Directly from that meeting, every person volunteered to go out in groups of two, knocking on doors to explain what was happening within the board of directors and to solicit support to attend the general membership meeting.

15.4.1.3 PLANNING DETAILS OF TASK IMPLEMENTATION

Before implementing the tasks, the details need to be determined. This includes specifying who, what, where, when, and how. This activity is developed in concert with the activity "Anticipating Obstacles to Task Performance" (section 15.4.1.6). The more prepared the organization, the greater the likelihood of success.

Once agreement has been reached to perform the tasks, the group is prepared to work out the details for implementation (see section 4.1.3). The use of subcommittees is helpful in dividing up components of the task.

In the W.V. co-op example, Mr. Stevens divided the flyer distribution task into its various components. First, all the current information was gathered during the organizational meeting. Those facts that seemed the most appropriate were compiled for inclusion on the flyer. While the flyer was being typed and copied, Mr. Stevens discussed what the residents were to be told.

15.4.1.4 ESTABLISHING RATIONALE AND INCENTIVES

Incentives can be of two sorts. Some consist of adding something pleasant to the environment. These are called positive reinforcers, such as adding programs, resources, policies, or increased community esteem. Other incentives include the removal of something unpleasant, or negative reinforcers (Skinner 1953). In the W.V. co-op example, the incentive is a negative reinforcer. In other words, the incentive is the avoidance of the negative consequences of having Mr. Andrews on the board of directors.

The social worker used this incentive to develop a strategy to motivate the general membership to become involved. Mrs. Stevens discovered that a quorum (50 percent of the membership) was required at the general membership meeting in order to enact proposals. Getting the necessary number of members for a quorum to a general membership meeting had never been done before. Mr. and Mrs. Stevens outlined some of the negative consequences of having Mr. Andrews on the board. They discussed that having him on the board would affect public relations with the community and could eventually affect their investment in the co-op. In fact, as the volunteers began talking to the co-op members, the threat of losing their investment indeed angered them to the point of making a commitment to become involved and to participate in the upcoming meeting. When the general membership meeting was held, a quorum was present.

15.4.1.5 SIMULATING THE TASK

Simulating the task can be helpful to ensure that everyone understands his or her role, as well as to discover any obstacles to implementation. Rehearsals can be helpful in preparing for such tasks as marches or parades, debates, live interviews, town meetings, lobbying, and skits or plays, as well as in testifying before a board, court, or government body. Any time the task appears complex and individuals are unsure of the expectations, role play and rehearsal can be quite helpful.

During this phase it may be discovered that more planning is needed, or that consulting an expert is required. Further, unanticipated obstacles may also be encountered that will need to be addressed. For example, in the W.V. co-op case above, as the details of the flyer distribution were discussed, several volunteers expressed a fear of talking to people. The social worker had explained to Mrs. Stevens that some role playing may be useful. During the role play it was discovered that attention had not been given to identifying an alternative candidate to replace Mr. Andrews. This became another goal that a smaller task group was assigned to explore.

15.4.1.6 ANTICIPATING OBSTACLES TO TASK PERFORMANCE

Sometimes the difference between an effective and ineffective community organizer rests on his or her ability to anticipate obstacles. Four kinds of obstacles can be encountered: those that lie within individual committee members; those that lie within the organizer; those posed by individuals who are against the organization; and those dealing with basic logistics required for the task.

Obstacles posed by individual committee members or the community can either be a result of lack of skills and knowledge necessary to perform the task or of resistance to some aspect of the task or organization. In the event that individuals require added skills and knowledge, the organizer will need to assess how best to approach the problem. If the obstacle is the result of some form of resistance, then care should be taken to address this issue and to try to resolve differences.

The community organizer needs to examine equally his or her own role for possible obstacles in the organizing process. Obstacles may include lack of skill or a mismatch of leadership styles; for example, one might get too bogged down with processing relationships and neglect the task functions of organizing. Social workers need to be aware of their leadership styles and their weaknesses, as well as strive for a balance among the styles. Another obstacle may manifest itself in the form of unconscious processes within the organizer. Similar to the micro-level clinician, Burghardt (1982) states that self-awareness is vital for the organizer.

The experienced organizer has learned to anticipate the opposition that the organization will receive and to respect those opposing groups. Often those who oppose the goals of a community organization wield much formal or informal power and influence. Therefore the organizer will need to consider the tasks carefully in light of the opposition they may generate.

Obstacles may also come in the form of basic logistics problems, such as the inability to secure media coverage for the planned event, inclement weather during a march, or unforeseen withdrawal of financial resources. Often a rehearsal of the task can help expose possible obstacles before actual implementation. This was the case for the SGU group that discovered some omissions in their planning when they walked through each step of the Games. The organizer plays an important role as a troubleshooter by modeling for the community organization good problem-solving skills when the unforeseen is encountered.

In our W.V. co-op illustration, during the simulation of the flyer distribution task, members raised some possible obstacles: What if an insufficient number of members show up at the membership meeting? What is Mr. Andrews's legal standing, since he is talking about getting an attorney? Should the police be notified to be on hand at the meeting, in the event of a confrontation? Mr. Andrews is promising to make some popular changes to the bylaws; how should we respond to this? All these issues were discussed, and, where appropriate, tasks were accepted by individuals or groups to address them.

15.4.1.7 SUMMARIZING TASKS

At the conclusion of each organization meeting, tasks need to be summarized. Once the task has been designed, everyone should understand who is responsible for its implementation, as well as who will help in its implementation. If possible, the location(s), date(s), and time(s) should be specified. Naturally a clear, brief description of the task should also be reviewed. The individual responsible for taking notes of the meetings will need to record the specifics of the tasks and review this at the next meeting.

The community organizer may want to consider developing some form of telephoning committee to call and remind individuals of their task responsibilities or to review their progress. Organizers may assume that their project is the single most important event in the lives of the committee and community. However, a realistic understanding of individuals' many other pressing activities should remind the organizer to be patient when responsibilities are forgotten or incomplete. Keeping on top of this through frequent contact with committee members will prevent some of those inevitable sleepless nights.

Another advantage of task summaries is to get renewed commitments from those involved in implementing the task. By verbally committing themselves to the task, committee members are more likely to follow through with their commitments.

As the community organization progresses, the social worker needs to focus on developing indigenous leadership from within the community. Even if this is an ad hoc task group, the organizer can use this opportunity to train future leaders and organizers. This will mean, among other things, assigning more and more responsibility to the community members for task implementation and evaluation.

From our case illustration, Mrs. Stevens had each subgroup summarize what their assignments were and when these were to be accomplished. One of the members did not realize that it was her responsibility to contact one of the other board members to ask about the co-op attorney. Summarizing the tasks caught this important misunderstanding.

15.4.1.8 REVIEWING TASK PROGRESS

The initial portion of the committee meetings should be devoted, in part, to a review of the progress to date of the tasks and assignments. This generally comes in the form of subcommittee reports. Information gathered from these reports will aid in evaluating progress, and may call attention to some changes that might need to be made in the task or in task assignments. The committee can then decide to continue, modify, or discontinue the task. Furthermore, additional tasks may be generated as a result of this review process.

It is not uncommon, once tasks are implemented, for committee members to begin generating additional tasks. This, in part, is the result of seeing a plan developed and implemented with some success. Care must be given not to overload the committee with tasks and assignments. The experienced organizer knows not to be taken in by the initial enthusiasm of the group to the point of overplanning, and consequently causing the committee to feel burned out. Moderation is the key in maintaining balanced optimism.

The review process allows individuals to make an accounting of their assignments. When progress is being made on the task, praise needs to be given. Praise tends to be most effective when working with groups of people if individual contributions are recognized as well as those of the subcommittee or group as a whole. This helps to generate a sense of teamwork and group pride.

In situations where little progress has been made, a careful examination is needed to assess the nature of the problem. The social worker should ask questions in a nonjudgmental manner. Individuals should not be challenged or made defensive during the meeting. If the social worker believes confrontation is needed, then this should take place privately.

In the W.V. co-op example, the subcommittee in charge of reviewing the bylaws and exploring the legal options for removing Mr. Andrews met to review the progress. The members were discouraged as it looked as though removing him was not possible. Part of the task of distributing flyers was asking co-op members to sign a form and return it to the management office officially requesting a general membership meeting to hold elections. Another member was disappointed because only sixty out of the three hundred members responded to this request. Mr. Stevens, a member of this subcommittee, worked to boost morale and reviewed the progress that had been made to date. In this case, the review process was used as a way to maintain interest in the project.

15.4.1.9 Reviewing Target Problems

Periodically the target problem needs to be reviewed and an evaluation made concerning progress in alleviating or ameliorating the specified problem. This helps the group to remain focused on the organization's goals and objectives. Too often, groups take on a life of their own as the goals expand beyond the parameters originally specified. The review provides feedback on the success of the tasks, as well as uncovering areas that need attention.

The problem review includes referring to the problem specifications developed previously. Sometimes during the course of community organizing the problems are altered, either because of the community's involvement or because of other outside factors. Therefore reevaluating the specified problems and any changes that may have occurred is helpful.

Usually organizations find that additional tasks are needed to bring about the changes in the environment that were originally sought. The TPIS is an ongoing process of task development and evaluation. The committee needs to evaluate its mission and objectives periodically to ensure that its aims can be met within the bounds of the time frames established.

The importance of the review process can be seen in the case example. During one of the planning meetings, the social worker had suggested to Mrs. Stevens that she review the target problem to see if its definition still made sense. While everyone still agreed that Mr. Andrews was the problem, the group discovered that no one had yet adequately addressed the need for viable candidates for whom they could vote. A total of three vacancies had to be filled. It was decided that three candidates running together as a group would appear too blatant an opposition to Mr. Andrews and might therefore generate sympathy for him. Instead, the three candidates decided to run individually rather than as a slate. This, in fact, turned out to be a good decision: The three individual candidates appeared neutral and stood in marked contrast to Mr. Andrews and his slate of candidates.

15.4.2.0 REVISING UNSUCCESSFUL TASKS

As mentioned above, many obstacles may arise that prevent successful environmental changes. Before completely revising goals and tasks, an evaluation of why the task is unsuccessful needs to be done. For example, did the task fail to produce the desired effect? Did the task produce the desired change but have other unanticipated effects as well?

Was the failure the result of tasks not being performed? These kinds of questions will help the organization assess the failure and learn from it. After a thorough evaluation of the tasks, the organizer can proceed to revise tasks, including target dates for their completion.

Sometimes tasks are unsuccessful when the problem has not been clearly specified or its significance has not been understood by the community. Another problem might be unreasonable or overambitious goals. Unsuccessful tasks may have to be dropped altogether or revised in light of new information. The progress toward the goal of a community organization depends on the successful completion of tasks by various subcommittees. Thus dropping or revising tasks will have to be done after careful analysis of the nature of the problem.

In the experience of one of the authors who worked for a Community Action Program (CAP) agency in the 1970s, failure to complete tasks on time was owing to several factors, including (1) overly ambitious goals; (2) lack of clarity in the tasks; (3) lack of delegation of clear authority to responsible persons; (4) lack of communication among members assigned to the task; and (5) lack of time limits for task completion.

When tasks are unsuccessful, a careful evaluation is needed to examine possible reasons for the lack of success. The review process will provide feedback as to whether the lack of success is the result of conflict at some level or of the ineffectiveness of the task.

In the W.V. co-op illustration, the subcommittee in charge of reviewing bylaws had tried to make significant changes in the bylaws, which were more than twenty-five years old and quite outdated. However, in six short weeks the group could not possibly tackle this awesome responsibility. The task was therefore revised. The subcommittee decided to compile a list of recommendations for the future board of directors to consider. This subcommittee, in fact, became the task force assigned by the new board to review these same issues.

15.4.5.0 USE OF TIME LIMITS

Unlike the locality development model, in which the goal is more relationship focused, in the task-centered approach time is of the essence. In many cases, the success of community organization depends on the successful completion of many tasks within given time frames. Tasks, which are the basis for subsequent steps in the community organization process, must be completed on time.

Management of time is all the more important in the task-centered model because of the communities' vertical ties to external governmental and private agencies who set schedules over which local communities have little or no control. Bringing out a program brochure on time for a fund-raising activity not only leads to a sense of accomplishment and achievement but also ensures future contributions from donors. Similarly an organization devoted to developing shelters for the homeless must act quickly in order to have the shelters in place before the winter months. Groups working to generate needed resources for AIDS patients are often working against a time frame that is not in their control.

The organizer needs to keep in mind that managing time can also be difficult. Local community members, who all volunteer their services for the cause, have limited time, usually only in the evenings and on weekends. Their organization, on the other hand, has to deal with agencies and other organizations during daily working hours. Thus a careful selection of who can do what, where, how, and when is vital.

Referring to the W.V. co-op example, Mr. and Mrs. Stevens were successful in having Mr. Andrews removed from the board. The candidates whom their organization supported won the elections, and vast changes were implemented. Much of the group's success was, in fact, the result of its time-limited nature. Many of the volunteers were extremely busy and unwilling to work on the project if it went on too long. Also the task, which was to prepare for a general membership meeting, had an inherent time limit since the meeting was scheduled for a certain date, and the group was forced to meet that deadline.

15.4.6.0 CHECKLIST FOR THE MIDDLE PHASE

___ 1. Am I providing sufficient leadership to the committee and subcommittees in the development and implementation of tasks?

___ 2. Am I monitoring the work of the subcommittees?

___ 3. Are time lines being met?

___ 4. Are meetings effective and efficient? Are minutes typed and distributed in a timely fashion?

___ 5. Am I maintaining relationships both inside and outside the nucleus?

___ 6. How am I evaluating progress?

___ 7. What am I doing to develop indigenous leaders?

15.5.0.0 COMPONENTS OF TERMINATION

The termination or final phase begins after the tasks have been implemented and reviewed. Generally, the length of this phase tends to be
fairly brief depending on the number of tasks completed and the size of
the organization. If tasks were numerous, some time may be spent during this phase evaluating and planning for the future. The termination
phase is more than just marking the end of intervention. It consists of
(1) a final problem review; (2) future plans; and (3) reactive discussion.
Termination in task-centered community organization does not necessarily indicate the termination of a working relationship with committee members. Often, members will continue to work together, albeit in
a different capacity or as part of a new task group.

Termination tends to be a difficult issue for all social workers, including those who are intervening at the macrolevel. It seems sometimes that organizations never die, they just focus on new problems.
This is partly because social problems never seem to go away. In task-
centered intervention, termination is discussed from the initial meeting.
The goal is not that the committee become a new agency or bureaucracy but rather to focus on and resolve specific target problems. Perhaps an agency or program is developed out of the efforts of a community organization, but once this goal is met the community
organization terminates and leaves that program or agency to become
a self-governing entity.

During this phase the community organizer begins to use more
process and maintenance skills. The tasks have been completed and
now the organization needs to feel a sense of closure to the process. Parties, socials, and dances are an integral part of the organizing process,
thus giving importance to the socio-emotional leadership style. Such an
activity at the termination stage recognizes and rewards the heroes and

heroines, creating a sense of pride in the community. It is essential that everyone who participated in the organizing effort is recognized. Awarding certificates of appreciation during the closing banquet is usually met with much appreciation.

One of the authors had the chance to work for the Economic Opportunity Agency in Little Rock, Arkansas, during 1973 and 1974. One of the projects undertaken by this agency was the creation of a center for mentally challenged children which was to be run and operated by the local community. One of the project's main goals was to develop a sense of community among the group and develop indigenous leadership. The main task included organizing a talent show in order to raise money for the project. The agency enlisted the help of between two hundred and three hundred community members to assist in this project. The talent show was a success, giving a big start to the retardation center. Because so many people were involved, an awards banquet was organized to honor them. The banquet included dinner, a speaker, and certificates of appreciation. This important termination ceremony also acted to maintain the sense of community among the participants which the agency had sought to instill. As the community organizers learned, even the termination phase requires careful planning and preparation. At the end of the ceremony, it was discovered that one of the key actors in the organizing effort had been overlooked and had not received a certificate of appreciation. Much talking and apologizing was needed to mend this oversight and to ensure that this mistake did not permanently alienate this individual from future involvement in the center.

15.5.1.0 THE FINAL PROBLEM REVIEW AND FUTURE PLANS

In the case of individuals, life goes on after termination. The successful outcome gives individuals a sense of accomplishment, a new perception of the problem, and confidence in their ability to handle future problems. This is not necessarily so in the case of community organizing. Demographic changes or the departure of local leadership creates a vacuum. In many cases, the process of community organizing may have to begin again from scratch. The SGU group averted this problem by locating a local agency that was willing to sponsor the Games as an on-going, annual event. The final review enables the organization leadership to obtain a relatively accurate evaluation of the progress made. A careful charting of where "we were" to where "we are" provides an impetus to "what else" and "where we can go" feelings.

A major advantage of the task-centered community organization approach is the visibility of the task achieved, no matter how small. Thus this final review serves as the basis for realistic praise and rewards for those involved in the organizing effort. "The intent is to bring about positive feelings of achievement" (Fortune 1985:24).

Even though the accomplishment of specific tasks within a specified time frame may be the goal of task-centered community organization, such organizing efforts have long-term consequences. The final review and evaluation will never provide us with a complete picture of the life of an individual, group, or community.

For example, the program Head Start, when evaluated at the beginning, did not show positive results. However, evaluation of children in this program a few years later showed the improvements that were made by "late spurts" children. Research suggests that Head Start children had fewer delinquent tendencies, were more likely to finish high school, and were more likely to hold after-school jobs (Di Netto 2000). Yet there remains controversy over evaluations of Head Start and other programs, making evaluation important, controversial, political, and never final.

Similarly evaluation of Community Action Programs soon after implementation indicated dismal results. No dent was made in the poverty figures at the time. Yet the long-term effects have shown that the creation of jobs, participation of the poor in their neighborhood activities, and so on, has had a profound effect on the children who have gone on to do better than their parents. Therefore social workers need to keep in mind the long-term picture of the effects of intervention. This calls for evaluation of programs and social welfare projects long after the organizing effort, including short-term, long-term, direct, and indirect effects.

Once the evaluation process is completed, future plans need to be outlined. They can include procedures for monitoring and stabilizing the situation, as well as future reassessments.

Finally, time needs to be allowed for feedback and reactions. During this period, the community organizer uses interpersonal skills to bring closure to the group. Accomplishments, individual growth, and personal efforts during the project need to be recognized. Any successful community project has required much effort and planning, and all those involved need to feel appreciated for their work.

15.5.2.2 CHECKLIST FOR THE FINAL PHASE

___ 1. Have I documented the task-planning process for future reference?
___ 2. Are plans for maintenance of accomplishments in place?
___ 3. Are leaders identified to carry on the work?
___ 4. Have the efforts of all participants been recognized?
___ 5. Have we celebrated our accomplishments?

15.5.6.0 CASE ILLUSTRATION

Youth Excelling and Succeeding (YES) Project

The seventy-fourth Texas State legislature in 1996 set aside competitive grants for eleven neighborhoods with high rates of juvenile delinquency. The purpose of these grants was to improve the quality of life of the young people and the living conditions in the communities. The intent of the policy makers was to empower the neighborhoods so that they could deal with the problem of juvenile delinquency locally. In order to compete for funding, it was necessary to build a neighborhood organization for the purpose of identifying community needs, developing proposals, and demonstrating commitment to the project. It was also necessary that the organization include representation from the diverse ethnic groups, local agencies and churches, and the youth who resided in the neighborhood.

University-affiliated social workers decided to lead an effort to compete for funding for one of the targeted neighborhoods. The neighborhood chosen was economically deprived and had a high rate of juvenile delinquency. The population was predominantly white (60 percent) with sizable numbers of African-American and Hispanic residents and a small number of Asian-Americans.

The organizers met initially with representatives from a local foundation who had experience organizing within the community. They were able to secure the foundation's commitment as a partner in the project. The organizing group was expanded by inviting representatives from local social service agencies, high schools, and a bank to a meeting. The purpose of this meeting was to plan neighborhood forums that they would lead. In addition to teaching facilitation skills, organizers led the group in developing tasks necessary to arrange a place and program for the forums, secure publicity, write letters of invitation, and make phone calls. Incentives for participation included the lure of almost one million dollars in grant money and the opportunity to rebut the neighborhood's negative reputation for juvenile crime and to lessen residents' concerns about living conditions.

Two neighborhood forums were held and were attended by more than two hundred people. During the first forum, procedures for applying for the grant and for developing a viable organization were shared. State officials explained the procedures for the grant, including the seven-week time limit. The organizers described the selection of a steering committee and the nature of future meetings. During the second forum, the residents in attendance were divided into eight groups of about twenty-five people each. The groups were asked to brainstorm about community problems and strategies for solving them. By the end of the second meeting several things were accomplished: (1) residents came to know one another better; (2) everyone had an opportunity to provide input; (3) the opinions of youth were sought and rapport built; (4) residents better understood the problems and possible strategies; and (5) a plan of action with specific tasks was developed.

Having engaged a large number of interested residents, the organizers were now in a position to formalize a steering committee that would be truly representative of the community's ethnic and demographic composition. To do so, elections were held to fill the available fifteen seats. The initial meeting of the steering committee was facilitated by the social worker. Duties and responsibilities were discussed as well as the concepts of empowerment and respect for the dignity of all. Members were charged to gain "a vision for their community." The steering committee identified the lack of representation of whites, Asian-Americans, and Hispanics as a problem. The group decided to include the two Asian-Americans who had received the most votes and increase Hispanics and whites by including more representatives from social agencies. The final composition of the steering committed consisted of twenty-seven diverse members.

The steering committee wisely elected a very able chairperson. He was an experienced leader who was committed to accomplishing the goal and the principles of empowerment. He was able to engage the youth, who came up with the name YES (Youth Excelling and Succeeding).

After careful consideration of the comments and suggestions residents made during the forums, the steering committee identified three target problems: (1) lack of supervised recreational facilities and activities for young people; (2) lack of a mentoring program for school children; and (3) lack of employment opportunities within the community for young people. The committee advertised meetings for six focus groups (youth, parents, clergy, service providers, school system, and businesses) to discuss the target problems in relation to areas of concern identified in the grant guidelines. With the input from the focus groups, the steering committee decided to develop programs in three areas: (1) five activity centers; (2) mentoring programs within the high school; and (3) employment and training opportunities. A subcommittee was appointed for each of the program areas. The subcommittees were asked to outline the components of the program, determine the program's feasibility, identify sites and sponsors for program activities, and project an actual budget.

The results of the subcommittees' work were discussed by the steering committee, which voted on the proposed programs. The final grant proposal included the following programs: (1) four activity centers with a budget of $227,632; (2) mentoring with a budget of $210,508; and (3) a year-round employment program, including job training and GED training and certification, with a budget of $693,428. The proposal was funded one month after submission for an amount of $900,000 to be spent over seventeen months.

The organizers not only had the satisfaction of helping a community attain resources it needed to address conditions in the community, but they knew that they left behind a viable group of indigenous leaders. The effort could not have succeeded without an emphasis on time limits and careful delineation of tasks.

PART FIVE *Diversity and Conclusions*

16

TASK-CENTERED WORK WITH CULTURALLY DIVERSE CLIENTS

Blanca Ramos and Charles Garvin

16.2.0.0 INTRODUCTION

Social workers are increasingly providing services to clients whose cultural backgrounds are different from their own. To work effectively with these diverse clients, task-centered practitioners should consider a variety of social and cultural factors. Although members of all cultural groups have similar basic needs, the ways that they conceive, perceive, and respond to them may show considerable cross-cultural variability. A client's worldview, values, beliefs, and help-seeking practices can greatly influence the treatment process and outcome. In this respect, social work practice models that incorporate values commonly held across cultures and/or the flexibility to accommodate cultural variation can be especially helpful.

The task-centered approach offers a clearly viable alternative for social work practice with culturally diverse clients (Devore and Schlesinger 1999; Lum 1996; Reid 1996). Several components of the TC model and their implicit underlying values are consistent with those of various cultural groups. Further, other components can readily be adapted in order to achieve cross-cultural applicability.

The purpose of this chapter is to discuss task-centered work with clients from different cultural groups. First, we identify the characteristics and principles of the TC model that are cross-culturally congruent, providing a rationale as to why TC is applicable. Second, we indicate required adaptations to the TC model in order to attain cultural relevance when working with culturally diverse clients. The remainder of the chapter describes the adaptations for culturally diverse practice that are pertinent to pretreatment, initial phase, middle phase, and termination. This content builds on all the preceding chapters of this book in which reference is made to adaptations of task-centered practice to work with different cultural groups. We have not repeated this material here. Illustrations are provided throughout this chapter with reference to specific cultural groups, such as African-Americans, Native Americans, Latinos(as), Asian-Americans, Russians, and Middle Easterners. This work must also be sensitive to gender and culture issues but these will be subsumed under discussion of cultures rather than separate sections of the chapter.

Here, we view culture as a fluid, dynamic entity while maintaining a flexible attitude toward its role in the treatment process. Clients' cultural and personal backgrounds are also shaped by their unique individual characteristics, experiences within their own culture, and interactions with the majority or dominant society. Task-centered workers should expect that cultural characteristics will vary among members of the same cultural group as a result of acculturation, generation, gender, and socioeconomic status. Similarly, oppression stemming from gender, racial, and ethnic differences can influence a client's worldview, values, beliefs, and attitudes (Aponte and Johnson 2000). A number of investigations have been conducted of adaptations of the task-centered model for work with various ethnic groups. Among these are the work of Brown and Lewis (1979) related to Native Americans, Chou (1992) related to Chinese families in Taiwan, Nofz (1988) also related to Native Americans, and Nguyen (1999) related to Vietnamese families.

Appropriateness for Culturally Diverse Populations TC is generally consistent with values commonly held across cultures. The following TC characteristics make it particularly applicable with culturally diverse clients: (1) use of a variety of intervention strategies; (2) the notion of task accomplishment; (3) provision of short-term services; (4) the existence of individual, group, and family models; (5) respect for client-defined problems; (6) work with collaterals; (7) consideration of environmental contexts; and (8) a focus on change of oppressive environments.

Practitioners can employ a wide range of intervention strategies allowing them to consider those that are most compatible with each client's own cultural context. TC not only offers an array of intervention strategies but also encourages workers to seek others advocated in a variety of practice approaches. Thus the most culturally appropriate tasks can be devised through borrowing from both mainstream and culture-specific approaches to practice.

The notion of task accomplishment is applicable cross-culturally. The experience of successful task completion becomes even more significant when working with clients who often feel overpowered by their environments, such as members of oppressed ethnic groups and recently arrived immigrants (Miley, O'Melia, and DuBois 2001). According to Lum (2000), two necessary ingredients for changing a problem situation are task mastery and a sense of accomplishment. As we shall discuss later in this chapter, however, the word *task* has cultural meanings that must be understood.

The short-term nature of service is completely consistent with the expectations and cultural beliefs of clients from many cultures and is more affordable than long-term approaches, since it requires far fewer resources. This preference for brief, short-term helping methods is generally shared cross-culturally. For example, these short-term methods have been found to be acceptable to cultural expectations among clients of African, Asian, and Latino descent (Organista and Dwyer 1996; Berg and Miller 1992). In some cultural groups, natural healers, who have been traditionally called on to intervene in life problems, are also expected to provide quick resolutions (Atkinson et al. 1998; Herrera 1996).

Similarly some writers suggest that long-term approaches are uneconomical, which severely limits their availability among culturally diverse disenfranchised clients (Sharf 2000). As noted in preceding chapters, short-term approaches are also likely to benefit clients who drop out of treatment, since this generally occurs in the early stages and most of the treatment benefits occur in a relatively brief time. Providing clients with the most relief in the shortest period of time is particularly appropriate in work with clients from some groups such as African-Americans, Native Americans, and Asian-Americans, who tend to have higher drop-out rates (Davis and Proctor 1989). We shall further consider cultural implications of short-term work later in this chapter.

The group and family models can be used effectively with clients for whom individual work may not be optimal because of their cultural preferences. Task-centered treatment offers the flexibility to select the group or family as the primary system of work, while taking into account cultural factors that may facilitate problem solution. For example, a worker may choose to compose groups with clients solely from the same ethnic background since they are most likely to share similar life experiences, concerns, and cultural characteristics, such as styles of communication and patterns of self-disclosure.

Target problems are client-determined, which allows for cross-cultural differences in problem definitions. Problem definitions are directly influenced by the worldview held by a particular cultural group, and these will differ depending on the client's values and beliefs (Fong and Furuto 2001; Kim, Snyder, and Lai-BitkEr 1996). TC focuses on solving problems as clients perceive them. Clients are asked what they would like to be different in their lives, thus minimizing the influence of the social worker's own cultural biases on defining, prioritizing, and solving targeted problems. Further, although social workers will offer suggestions, the client has the final word. For culturally different clients, this gesture may signify respect not only for their choices but also for their underlying cultural beliefs. The term *problem* also has cultural meanings that we shall comment on later in this chapter.

In task-centered practice we work with all the systems (what workers sometimes refer to as collateral contacts) that are needed for successful problem resolution. When working with culturally diverse groups, one should consider representatives of the client's natural support systems, which is compatible with the values and beliefs of many cultural groups. Natural supports are primary group networks that function as a first tier of coping survival behaviors and may include family, friends, church, and natural healers. For example, the church has historically been a major source of social support for African-Americans, providing fellowship and activities that are essential in nurturing and developing a positive sense of self (Edwards 1996; Westbrooks and Starks 2001). As is typical among most Native American groups, the Lakota's extended kinship network functions as an extensive social support system (Brave Heart 2001). In some Latino communities, natural healers have traditionally served a critical function by providing practical advice and assistance with everyday problems (Herrera 1996).

TC considers problems within their environmental contexts, which helps identify potential contingencies stemming from racism, prejudice, and poverty typically associated with oppressed and vulnerable cultural groups. Historically in the United States, African-American, Native American, Latino, and some Asian-American groups have experienced unequal treatment and limited access to resources. For example, African-Americans have undergone chronic unemployment. Frameworks specifically developed for cross-cultural practice emphasize the need to recognize potential links between problems and environmental factors (Browne and Mills 2001; Devore and Schlesinger 1999; Lum 2000). In TC, problems are part of a larger context and may include environmental contingencies, which is an important dimension of individual functioning. This implies that some tasks may deal with changing oppressive environments or mitigating their negative effects, and this topic will be expanded on later in this chapter.

Clients from extremely vulnerable cultural groups can be enabled to change their oppressive environments through tasks, while workers can seek to remove environmental conditions through tasks and advocacy. Oppressive environments, which provide only limited opportunity for meeting needs and aspirations, are common to many cultural groups (Browne and Mills 2001). Work with oppressed clients should help them both to overcome systemic barriers and to incorporate environmental changes (Atkinson, Morten, and Sue 1998; Davis and Proctor 1989; Devore and Schlesinger 1999). In TC, clients can be helped to formulate tasks that seek to change their environmental conditions. Analogously, and to supplement the clients' efforts, as we have stated, the worker can help change their social environment through tasks and advocacy at the individual and system levels.

Adaptations of the Task-Centered Model for Work with Culturally Diverse Clients   While TC has several characteristics that render it culturally relevant, some adaptations to the model's strategies and procedures may be deemed necessary to strengthen its cross-cultural applicability.

These include allowing flexibility to its highly structured format, as well as incorporating a heightened sensitivity to cultural variations with regard to the concepts of time and problem solving.

In some cases, it may be necessary to modify the model's highly structured procedural format to accommodate cultural variation. For example, additional time and effort may be needed to address the client's cultural nuances. Among some Middle Eastern groups, problem definition may take longer as they tend to describe their problems within the context of a number of external events (Jalali 1996). In work with Latinos, spending extra time to build the client-worker relationship by gradually earning the client's trust is an essential first step toward task achievements (Weaver and Wodarski 1996).

TC must be applied with a heightened sensitivity to cultural differences regarding the concept of time. For some Native Americans and Latinos who tend to be present-oriented, "things take more or less as long as they do." Thus they may be less likely to be organized by clocks and calendars and less preoccupied with trying to control the future by planning ahead and being on time (Sutton and Broken Nose 1996; Weaver and Wodarski 1996). TC workers should be flexible and tolerant with clients, who, as a result of their time orientation, may arrive late for appointments and may not respond well to fixed, rigid schedules.

Applying the notion of problem solving requires an understanding of its various meanings cross-culturally. An underlying assumption in TC is that the individual has control over life situations and personal problems are solvable. In some societies, however, problems are believed to be fated to occur, and life situations are directed by external forces (Falicov 1998; Fuller 1995). Thus the assumption that an individual has control over life situations and that problems are solvable may not be applicable in certain societies. In many Middle Eastern cultures, for example, individuals believe that problems are not only fated to occur, but they also gracefully accept their outcomes (Jalali 1996). A similar worldview is found among many Latinos and Native Americans. Some Russian clients may not always accept the beliefs that life's problems have a rational solution or the values that emphasize maintaining a positive mental attitude (Althausen 1996). Beyond culturally specific fatalistic beliefs, for clients from historically marginalized groups, the notion of problem solving as a function of an individual's control over situations does not reflect their experiences in oppressive environments. In these cases, TC workers are encouraged to help clients empower themselves by drawing on their energy, strengths, and resources to change their environments or, when appropriate, to leave them. We shall supply more details on how to respond to cultural meanings of the term *problem* later in this chapter.

When working with culturally diverse clients, workers should first determine the level of congruency between the cultural values of the client and the assumptions underlying TC. TC workers should become familiar with the client's cultural background while, at the same time, recognizing the individuality of each client in order to avoid making stereotypical assumptions. A number of interrelated factors must be considered, including the client's ethnic group membership, acculturation level, immigration history, generation, and socioeconomic background. Cultural factors should also be considered in the selection of system level, the selection of action system, and the client's expectations regarding the worker's role.

16.2.5.0 WORKER-CLIENT RELATIONSHIPS IN DIFFERENT CULTURES

Culture influences a client's expectations regarding the worker's role in the treatment process. Assuming a collaborative, egalitarian role may be more appropriate for some cultural groups than others. Clients from more authoritarian societies often prefer a more directive communication style, expecting the worker to function as a teacher who tells them what to do (Sharf 2000). For example, some Asian-American clients prefer the worker to assume the role of an expert who provides concrete, tangible advice while maintaining formality and conversational distance (Lee 1996). Similarly many Latinos perceive practitioners as authority figures, with knowledge and skills not available to everyone, who should be treated with deferential behaviors. When appropriate, practitioners can help empower clients by encouraging them to become more active participants in the treatment process.

TC workers can be especially helpful to less acculturated clients, in their roles as cultural brokers, by addressing culturally based issues that may directly interfere with the treatment. For example, when clients are experiencing pressures from two cultures as a polarity, the practitioner can help to bring these differences to a greater awareness by employing a nonjudgmental, respectful approach. Among Soviet Jewish immigrants, who originally come from a social and economic system that fosters dependency on the government, the worker may be viewed largely as a bureaucrat who bears responsibility for their needs. Additional functions useful in work with culturally diverse clients include those of mediator, educator, and advocate.

16.2.6.0 THE APPROPRIATE SYSTEMS FOR WORK

When selecting a system level, it is of the utmost importance to explore the influences of the client's community and social milieu in causing or maintaining targeted problems. For example, African-American clients are often affected by a number of systems, including the extended family, church, schools, welfare, courts, and public housing. Among clients from disadvantaged, disenfranchised groups, oppression, which is structurally based, directly affects both the individuals and their communities. In acknowledging the systemic source of problems, issues of racism, discrimination, and powerlessness can be addressed. Consistent with empowerment practice, TC workers must consider the various system levels in order to mobilize resources, advocate for clients, and work with collaterals.

When selecting the system for work, it is important to take into account the client's cultural norms and expectations regarding treatment. While a decision to work with the individual may be the most appropriate with clients from some cultural groups, for others it may be inconsistent with their life experiences and cultural values. For example, some Native Americans, whose personal experiences have been primarily as members of a larger group (i.e., the tribe), may not be comfortable in one-to-one, client-worker interactions that stress the value of individualism (Earle 1999). Many Asians and African-Americans place less emphasis on self-reliance and prefer to rely on the support of family and community, promoting interdependence rather than independence (Sapp 1996).

Among some Asian and Latino groups, where the family system lies at the immediate center of their cultural milieu (Lum 1996; Paniagua 1994; Paulino and Burgos-Servido 1997), the family may be a more appropriate system for work (Atkinson, Morten, and Sue 1998; Lee 1996). Further, when working with the family system to resolve targeted problems, one must be especially attuned to the cultural norms of family interactions. For instance, in many Asian groups, their long-standing traditions of respect and authority make interactions among family members both limited and prescribed (Sharf 2000). Similarly it is crucial to recognize the leadership role of elders, who are accorded deference and respect in recognition of their lifelong accomplishments and contributions to the family and community (Weaver and Wodarski 1996). Yet selecting the family as the primary system may require total family involvement and flexibility, as well as sensitivity to cultural and individual variation. For example, among some African-Americans, a focus on the family may heighten feelings of responsibility and guilt (Hines and Boyd-Franklin 1996). TC workers can draw on culturally relevant collaterals who may act as contributors to the problems or resources in effecting their solution.

The idea of getting help from others in a group with respect to one's problems has different meanings in different cultures. In some cultures, it is regarded as unacceptable to tell people outside the family about problems that might reflect negatively on the family, and this is often found with respect to clients from many Asian backgrounds. In contrast, many Native Americans have experienced personal problems that are dealt with in tribal conclaves and might see the group in this light if all other members have the same tribal background. This issue should be discussed with clients in pregroup interviews, and, depending on how strong the individual's feelings are on the subject, this may militate against using a group modality unless or until the issue is resolved.

16.3.0.0 COMPONENTS OF THE INITIAL PHASE

Several initial-phase activities will be modified when working with clients so as to take cultural diversity into consideration. Those that are discussed in the following sections include explanation of procedures, time limits, obtaining necessary information, targeting problems, and problem specification.

16.3.1.0 CULTURALLY RELEVANT WAYS OF EXPLAINING PROCEDURES

Task-centered work should be easy to explain to persons from many different cultural backgrounds because of the nontechnical implications of the word *task*. People from all cultures undertake activities (tasks) to accomplish their purposes or to attain their goals. It behooves the practitioner, however, to investigate the meaning of the word *task* to people from different milieus.

This discussion of culturally relevant ways of explaining these procedures does not assume that, based on clients' cultures, they will have vastly different ways of understanding this word. This depends on individual experience and level of acculturation to the larger society. To avoid stereotyping, the practitioner must always individualize the client and avoid assumptions that all people from a particular cultural background use terms in the same way and that this way differs substantially from the way others from different cultures use the terms. This may or may not be true.

Having said this, we assert that if the client's primary language is not English, the practitioner should investigate what the translation of *task* is in the client's native language and what the implications of the use of that word are. Are these implications pleasant or unpleasant, and are there any other emotional implications in the use of that word. Even if clients' primary language is English, they may attach some meanings to the word *task* that will either enhance the process or impede it. *Task* may mean something imposed by authority figures, for example, rather than something the client chooses.

In the task-centered group work situation, the practitioner must be aware of the group processes surrounding any of these culturally oriented discussions. Even when the members have a similar cultural background, they still may attach different cultural meanings to a term. This is because of individual personality and family differences as well as different acculturation experiences. Thus raising an issue about the cultural acceptability of a procedure may result in an intense discussion that concludes with a new consensus about the procedure or an agreement to disagree or may serve as the basis of ongoing tensions in the group. In the latter case, these tensions may impede the process, and the worker should continue to seek some resolution in the group, perhaps after consultation with a person who is familiar with the culture in question.

Many procedures and terms used in task-centered practice will have cultural meanings, and these should be assessed with the clients, usually in the initial phase of treatment. Cultural meanings of task-centered procedures and modifications to these procedures are described in the sections that follow.

16.3.2.0 TIME-LIMITED PRACTICE

Cultures vary in their views of time. In the United States a strong emphasis is placed on being on time, on specifying the time a task should take to complete, and on accomplishing a task efficiently, which means within the shortest possible time span. These values are embedded in our capitalist economy, which seeks to create products efficiently and to minimize production costs. The philosophy of pragmatism is also pervasive in American society, a philosophy that is described as "stressing practical consequences as constituting the essential criterion in determining truth or value."* The idea of practical consequences has strong implications for emphasizing outcomes and efficiency.

Other cultures have values that contrast with the above. These set a higher priority on satisfying the needs of individuals or the groups or families in which they hold membership rather than producing outcomes expeditiously. Some cultures do not have the same sense of organizing activities in terms of time frames but organize them in terms of situational circumstances and needs that may take the participants along paths that are indirect. Practitioners who seek to be culturally sensitive should seek to understand the time frames of clients and to take these into consideration in task-centered work.

[*The Random House Dictionary 1978. (New York: Ballentine Books, 1978), p. 688.]

An example of this was work with a Puerto Rican client. She sought help with obtaining the medical services she needed that were not forthcoming because of a variety of bureaucratic requirements. The practitioner initially wanted to help her agree to carry out tasks to meet these requirements. The practitioner saw this as the quickest way to secure the services. The client wished first to consult a spiritualist practitioner and then to discuss the results of this consultation with her family. She was clearly more concerned with carrying out these "tasks" than the tasks that might quickly satisfy her medical needs. In one sense, her wishes might be understood as her right to determine which tasks she wished to undertake; but, in another sense, these wishes can be understood as her idea of priorities, determined by her culture, that viewed the use of time in a culturally determined way.

16.3.3.0 Obtaining Necessary Information
about Ethnicity

In other chapters we discuss the kinds of information the practitioner will obtain in task-centered work. There are additional types of information that should be obtained with respect to the client's ethnicity. We have already indicated that the practitioner should secure data about how the client's culture views such concepts as tasks, problems, and goals (or comparable terms in the client's native language). We also indicated that this will differ for clients even when they come from the same culture, based on the clients' unique acculturation experiences.

Acculturation can be assessed by securing the following information:

1. How many generations has the client's family been in the United States if their origin was from outside the United States, how long has the client lived in his or her current community, and is this community predominantly composed of persons of the client's ethnicity? This information is relevant based on the assumption that each generation is more likely than the previous one to be exposed to the values of the larger culture. In the case of Mexican-American clients, there will be differences based on what part of the United States the family has lived in, as some parts (e.g., Texas, California, New Mexico) have large numbers of people of Mexican origin and strong Mexican traditions.

Other sections (e.g., the Northeast) have smaller proportions of people of Mexican origin.

A number of states in the Southwest have citizens of Mexican backgrounds because these territories were acquired through conquest and this has strong implications for Mexican-American citizens' views of American society. People from Puerto Rico have a different type of history, and the acculturation issue relates to such things as the ties the individual maintains to Puerto Rico and to the large Puerto Rican communities in the continental United States, such as those in New York City. Cuban-Americans, in contrast, have often come to the United States because of their opposition to the political situation in Cuba. Their degree of socialization relates to the extent to which they maintain ties to Cuba and to Cuban-American communities.

With Native Americans, for obvious reasons, the issue is not how many generations the client's family has been in the United States but what the client's relationship is to the tribal community, such as that found in reservations. If the clients live in an urban community, the question is what their relationship is to the tribal community. If there is little relationship, the question of the number of generations of separation is relevant.

For African-Americans, there is a high probability that the client's family is descended from people forcibly brought to the United States as slaves, and the clients' views of this history of oppression are salient. Nevertheless many African-Americans have families that, at one point, lived in other countries such as those in the Caribbean, and these have their own traditions and have left unique cultural imprints.

2. What acculturation experiences have the clients had related to the larger American culture? These include the educational institutions they have attended, the work environments to which they have been exposed, and the peer groups with which they have affiliated. These also include the religious institutions with which they are or have been affiliated. Some religious organizations strongly reinforce the values of the clients' cultural group, such as churches in the black communities, Catholic churches in Latino communities, and religious institutions associated with each Asian-American group. On the other hand, the client may have chosen to affiliate with a church that is not part of his or her ethnic heritage.

16.3.4.0 TARGETING PROBLEMS AND
DETERMINING PROBLEM PRIORITIES

These words have idiosyncratic meanings that may affect their use in task-centered work. Some people do not like to think of themselves as having "problems" but may find it acceptable to have "challenges" or "difficulties." A number of other terms exist in every culture to identify life's vicissitudes, and the practitioner should examine this issue, again with the help of good informants from the culture, including the clients themselves.

In other places in this volume we discuss various ways of helping clients to prioritize problems. Here, regarding this aspect, we will discuss the influence of culture on establishing problem priorities. In this process, it will be helpful to the worker to consult with the client and other cultural informants for answers to the following questions:

1. How serious does the culture regard this problem?

2. What are the consequences from cultural forces for the client who does not pay attention to this problem?

3. What does the culture mandate that its members do with reference to the problem, and what are the consequences of not doing this?

For example, a Korean-American woman, Mrs. K., was in a task-centered group for adults who were caretakers for the elderly. She selected two problems for her work in the group. One was difficulty in arranging caretaking for her mother, who was in the early stages of Alzheimer's disease, while Mrs. K. went to work. The other was dealing with her mother's opposition to her health professionals because they were not Korean, and she thought they were prejudiced against her. With reference to the first problem, Mrs. K. informed the group that her particular Korean community, centered around her church, placed care for elderly relatives as a very high obligation. Koreans who do not take this injunction seriously are severely criticized and sometimes ostracized. Members of the culture, especially women, are expected to care for these relatives personally. These facts placed this problem at a very high priority, probably higher than the second problem, so Mrs. K. concluded that she should think of goals and then tasks with reference to the first problem before she worked on the second one.

16.3.6.0 DEVELOPING THE PROBLEM SPECIFICATION
IN CULTURALLY RELEVANT WAYS

As we have indicated in this book, the process of problem specification is to determine how the problem displays or reveals itself. We shall not repeat what we have said elsewhere in this book in sections devoted to individuals, families, groups, and so forth, but rather comment here on understanding the influence of culture on how a problem displays or reveals itself.

First, in different cultures people are socialized to describe unmet needs and wants (i.e., "problems") in different ways (Lum 2000:180–209). It is also important to realize that the problems of clients from many ethnic groups are highly related to the racism and other forms of oppression that these clients experience (Sue 1981).

For example, some cultures lead people to "somaticize" discomfort, which means to describe it in terms of unpleasant bodily sensations such as a headache or backache. Other cultures lead people to refer to the negative impact of spiritual forces and to view themselves as being punished or acting under the influence of these forces or suffering for reasons that are beyond their understanding (such as the sufferings of Job in the Bible). Still other cultures emphasize that discomfort is a manifestation of some discord between themselves and others or between themselves and the environment. In this line of analysis, one can even understand the psychoanalytic view that problems are related to one's unconscious conflicts as equally a cultural manifestation.

What we have just said still requires the worker to raise the kinds of questions about the problem that we present in the other chapters. This includes whether the client sees the problem in terms of its frequency, intensity, location in one's life space, or manifested more in one behavioral sphere (i.e., affect, cognition, action) than another. In addition, we suggest here that the influence of culture on this subjective view of the client be examined. This will have an impact on the tasks selected and the evaluation of effectiveness.

For example, Sue, a second-generation Chinese-American client, was seen in her university's counseling service during her first semester at the university. She was sent there by the health service where she went because of a number of physical complaints. The staff of the health service could find no physical basis for her complaints, as all the tests indicated that she was in good health. Sue could not understand why she was sent to the counseling service for treatment of her physical symptoms, but she respected the authority of the health professionals and followed through on their referral.

At the counseling service she complied with the request of the social worker to explain her personal situation. She spoke with some hesitation of her sense of loneliness. She was attending college far from her family and friends and knew few others of her ethnic background in the university community. She also indicated that her family would not understand why she went to a counseling service and spoke about her situation with reference to her family. She also explained that she was excluded from some of the friendship groups forming in her dorm.

The worker spent several sessions acknowledging Sue's physical complaints and her reluctance to come to the counseling center. Her concerns about her family's reactions were also acknowledged. Only then could she discuss her social situation and her wish to work on it. Ultimately a task-centered approach was helpful to her, and she developed tasks related to connecting with other Asian-American students, explaining her situation to her family, and forming relationships with students in her dorm who came from other backgrounds but shared her interests, such as her love of music.

16.3.7.0 GOALS.

People from some cultures are likely to think in terms of long-term goals when solving problems, whereas those from other cultures may be less future-oriented and may primarily think of the immediate reasons for an activity or even prefer to act in a spontaneous manner. Thus some clients may either reject the determination of goals or remain uninvolved in this process. The practitioner should find out how the client views setting future objectives. If there is opposition to this process, the practitioner has several courses of action available. One is to explain the reasons for setting goals to see if this makes the process acceptable to the client. A second course is to work within a task-centered framework based on short-term goals.

For example, one Native American client sought employment. He did not accept the long-term goal of obtaining more education but accepted the short-term one of learning about career options.

The solution-based approach discussed in chapter 1 asks clients to think in terms of future scenarios of what their life would be like if current difficulties were absent. This concept may be more acceptable and meaningful to clients from a variety of cultures, especially those that view life as a series of stories and metaphors. Using this concept rather than the more abstract one of goals should not interfere with the basic procedures of task-centered work. A series of research investigations should be conducted to explore this issue, as well as many others, in culturally relevant ways.

16.4.0.0 COMPONENTS OF THE MIDDLE PHASE

Throughout this book we have given basic information on the procedures to be utilized during the middle phase. The purpose of the following discussion is to indicate how cultural diversity impacts on these procedures.

16.4.1.0 TASK PLANNING AND IMPLEMENTATION SEQUENCE

We indicated earlier in this chapter that all the terms used in task-centered practice must be assessed for the ways they might be viewed under varying cultural conditions. This is certainly true with reference to the most central term *task* as it even gives this model its name. We actually know little in social work about the cultural meanings attached to most of our terms, although we can guess at the cultural meanings attached to those that are generally used by nonprofessionals, such as *problem*. This is certainly an area ripe for research. Our suggestion, therefore, rather than guessing, is to question the clients about how they view a term. The following is an example of a discussion with a client with reference to discussing the idea of a "task."

Robert, an American citizen with a Latino background, was being interviewed for a task-centered group for clients of an alcohol treatment center. The worker indicated to him that the group was one that helped members to accomplish tasks that will enable them to reach their goals. The worker asked Robert what he thought of when he heard the term *task*. He replied that it reminded him of the homework assignments he was given in school. He added that he hated homework. The worker indicated that this was not what she wanted to imply, and she asked Robert if there were things he did when he wanted to accomplish something. He said "sure," and the worker asked for a recent example. Robert said he wanted to buy a car to get to work, as his old car had broken down and would cost too much to repair. He asked several friends if they knew anyone who had a used car for sale. The worker said that this was a good example of what she meant by *task*, namely, something he did to get something he wanted. She wondered whether Robert had a better term to use for this kind of thing, and he said he would call this simply "a thing to do." The worker suggested that, in this group, the worker and Robert could suggest that members be asked if they want to use the phrase "things to do" in place of the term *task*.

16.4.1.1 GENERATING TASKS IN CULTURALLY RELEVANT WAYS

The following are approaches to incorporating cultural issues into the selection of tasks:

- In group situations in which other group members share the same culture, they can be very helpful in suggesting tasks that take the culture into consideration. We also believe that the use of task-centered group work may be especially appropriate for this reason as opposed to individual work.
- Workers may wish to use the idea of The Task Planner (Reid 2000) in generating their own task planners for problems frequently en-

countered in ethnic groups they serve. They can create focus groups to do this or use informants from the cultures in question to help with this. It may even be appropriate to have such lists of tasks in the languages of the clients when their primary languages are not English (e.g., Spanish, Korean).

- Tasks should also draw on, wherever appropriate, resources and institutions found in the ethnic community, such as its mutual aid organizations, churches, businesses, mass media, and community leaders. For example, one African-American client who was new to the community chose the task of searching for a job in the local African-American newspaper and visiting several black ministers to ask their help in locating work.

- The worker should be sensitive to helping the client construct tasks that "fit" with the culture in terms of its time sense, values regarding appropriate activities, and views as to who should be involved in tasks. It is also important to inquire of the client about the ways that members of the client's community seek and receive help to accomplish tasks. In some ethnic communities, there is a strong sense of the community's responsibility for its members. In other ethnic communities, the family members will go to great lengths to help one another and will expect to be called on. Certain family members, such as the grandmother in the African-American community, play this role.

The following are some items to consider in finding culturally relevant resources to help clients with their tasks:

- Resources within the client's ethnic community that may help clients with their tasks, such as religious figures, community-based self-help groups, ethnically oriented social service organizations, ethnically based employment and training organizations, education professionals sharing the client's ethnicity, and indigenous healers

- Indigenous helpers, such as shamans in the Native-American community, Curanderos in the Mexican-American community, and spiritualists in the Puerto-Rican community

- The extended family is often a resource, and persons may be considered kin who are not viewed as "family" in the worker's community. Neighbors in the client's ethnic community may also be so viewed.

16.4.1.6 ANTICIPATING OBSTACLES TO TASK PERFORMANCE RELATED TO ETHNIC OPPRESSION

The worker should be sensitive to obstacles to task performance posed by various forms of ethnic oppression. The following are examples of such obstacles that are frequently found:

1. Clients may be denied access to resources because of institutional racism, defined by Lum as "educational, economic, social, and political organizations that intentionally or unintentionally perpetuate racial inequality" (2000:194). He goes on to state that "institutionally racist practices relate to employment, housing, education, and inadequacies in program services." Thus clients who undertake tasks related to securing housing or schooling may be impeded by racism. The implication of this is that the client may wish to take on additional tasks either to change the racist practices or to circumvent them. An example is an African-American client, a high school student, who originally defined his task as enrolling in college preparatory classes. A school counselor repeatedly sought to steer him to vocational classes, such as those training students to be cooks. The student thought that nothing could be done to alter the counselor's attitudes, so he chose the task of petitioning for another counselor who had the reputation of encouraging black students.

2. Clients may be denied access to resources because of the racist attitudes of an individual that are unrelated to that individual's position in a system. This can occur in interpersonal encounters required by the client's task. An example was a Latino teen-age client who sought help in making friends. She chose the task of approaching another student in her school to ask her to go out for a soft drink at the local teen hangout. This invitation was met with a hostile rejection, and the student was later told by another Latino student that the student in question only socialized with "Anglos." In discussing this with her worker, the student was helped to see that this rejection might not be experienced from all other "Anglo" students but that she could observe the student first to see how that student interacted with Latinos before making a friendly gesture.

3. Lum also refers to "cultural racism," which he defines as "the beliefs, feelings, and behaviors of members of a cultural group who assert

the superiority of the group's accomplishments, achievements, and creativity and attribute this claimed cultural superiority to genetic composition" (p. 194). This can pose several kinds of problems to clients that will affect this task-oriented treatment process. On the one hand, cultural racism can fuel the interpersonal and institutional racist phenomena we have just discussed. On the other hand, clients may internalize cultural racism, which means that they, without fully realizing it, view themselves as inferior. This will affect the goals they work toward and the tasks they choose to reach these goals. Workers can respond to this by challenging the client's feelings of inferiority

An example of this was Bob, a Native-American client, who was in a program to help recovering alcoholics. He needed more education in order to hold a good job. However, he voiced many concerns about enrolling in an educational program, citing his poor academic record. The worker helped him to see that the worker himself, as a resident of Bob's particular reservation, had not been offered good schooling or encouragement to succeed in school. The worker also pointed out that, when members of his tribe had taught him various skills, he learned quickly. In the light of this discussion, Bob chose tasks related to obtaining more education.

16.5.0.0 COMPONENTS OF TERMINATION

In many cultures, relationships that have a great deal of importance and meaning to individuals are not meant to be terminated in an abrupt fashion, if at all. This may even include relationships with professionals. The worker, in these circumstances, will be expected to offer the possibility of continuing or resuming the relationship. Under these circumstances, and where agency circumstances allow, we recommend that the worker hold out the possibility of being available again if the need arises. This is also true of task-centered work that occurs in a group setting when the members may also expect that the relationships will be broken off in an abrupt fashion.

In addition, in many cultures the end of a process is marked by a ceremony. It would behoove the worker to inquire of persons familiar with the culture whether this is true and, if so, what the nature of such ceremonies is likely to be. In any case, the client can be asked whether he or she wishes to suggest a "ritual" that marks the end of this phase of work. This may include a moment of silence, a prayer (offered by the client), a song, a poem, or a reading of a passage in a book. The worker will have to consider what the limits of his or her participation are in terms of ethical and boundary issues.

16.5.1.0 CULTURAL ISSUES IN THE FINAL PROBLEM REVIEW

We indicated in section 5.1.0 that a final review relates to examining the nature of changes in targeted problems. In addition, cultural issues that might be reviewed include the following:

1. Did efforts to reduce or remove the problem lead to changes in racist or other socially oppressive circumstances?
2. How were other members of the client's ethnic group affected by the changes that were made?
3. How was the client's sense of his or her own ethnic identity affected by the changes in the problem? For example, did the client have an improved respect for himself or herself as a member of an ethnic group? How was the client's ethnic identity affected by the task-centered process?

16.5.3.0 FUTURE PLANS RELATED TO OPPORTUNITIES PRESENT IN THE CULTURE

As we have stated in many places in this chapter, the worker should become familiar with resources in the client's cultural community, such as self-help groups, mutual aid organizations, and ethnically based services. When these do not exist, the worker in a community organization role may work with others to create such resources or help the client to do the same. In any case, we believe that the client should be helped to connect to, and make use of, such resources whenever this is appropriate.

15.5.5.0 REACTIVE DISCUSSION

Within each culture, there are ways that individuals have been social-ized to deal with "endings." Individuals may be encouraged or discour-aged from expressing sorrow. They may or may not be offered solace within their ethnic interactions for possible loss of relationships. They may or may not be encouraged to experience a sense of elation when they have accomplished something, as, in some cultures, this may be seen as expressing too much pride in oneself. It again behooves the worker to seek to understand these feelings about endings with regard to how cultural norms and experiences affect them.

17

CONCLUSION: WRAPPING IT UP

Generalist practice has been described as a "perspective in search of a conceptual framework" (Schatz, Jenkins, and Sheafor 1990:217). When the first edition of this book was written, we believed that the integration of the generalist perspective with TC would provide the generalist with a practice technology and the task-centered practitioner with a perspective. While we encountered no insurmountable obstacles nor mutually exclusive concepts or constructs in marrying these two robust orientations, we were uncertain as to whether this integration would be viable. Since that time, the integrated model has been applied successfully by countless students. In addition, it has been accepted by the academic community. Gorey, Thyer, and Pawluck (1998) categorized TC as a generalist approach in their meta-analysis. Lehmann and Coady (2001), in their thoughtful compilation of approaches for generalist-eclectic practice, indicate that TC can be "construed as part of our generalist-eclectic approach" (412). Furthermore, they note that of all the approaches reviewed, "only TC and feminist theories devote considerable attention to broad social issues" like poverty (414). Of course, some questions remain and there is much data to be gathered.

In this chapter we review the concepts that are critical to the integration of the approaches. We examine consistencies and variations in the use of TC concepts in work across various systems. We begin to address one of the most important questions that remains, which concerns movement among and between various systems. Finally, we address the work that remains to be done.

17.1.0 The Concepts That Unite Us

The concepts that unite TC and generalist practice include target problems, collaterals, and context. They are examined below, respectively.

Critical to the integration of the approaches is the movement of the problem to the center of attention. This act enables us to be clear about that which is to be changed, to avoid assuming that a particular system must be changed, and to avoid focusing on one system when, in fact, several systems might be implicated. When we place the individual (or any other system) in the "bull's eye," it suggests that this system is to be altered in some way. This practice runs the risk of "blaming the victim." When we place the problem in the center of the target and engage in a systemic analysis of the problem with the participation of the primary system, we not only avoid blaming the system but make it possible to engage in a power analysis—a component of empowerment practice. Furthermore, the shift from system to problem enables us to identify all the systems involved. This is important for social workers because we regularly encounter complex social problems that are multidetermined.

Focusing on the problem has one additional advantage. This concerns knowledge generation. Developing effective strategies to resolve specific problems is easier than changing human systems because the way a problem manifests itself has less variability than human systems have.

The concept of collaterals provides another means to unite a problem-solving approach to generalist practice. Collaterals are the representatives of other systems. Our work with them allows us to engage other systems in solving problems. The emphasis on confidentiality has probably interfered with our ability to include or even think about including other systems in change efforts. This does not mean that the confidentiality of the primary system should be abridged. Rather, it means that more effort must be made to help members of the primary system understand the importance of obtaining the help and cooperation of others. Engaging the primary system in a systemic problem analysis is likely to promote this understanding.

Finally, the concept of context enables us to examine the system in which the problem is located somewhat more closely. Contextual information is often guided by theories of human behavior as it manifests itself in individuals, families, groups, organizations, and communities. Unfortunately our knowledge base is not sufficiently robust to allow us to identify the important dimensions of the context with much certainty. Nevertheless, including this concept enables us to examine the larger environment of the problem without losing sight of the smaller one. It is as though we alternate between telescopic lenses and those more suitable for close-ups.

17.2.0 VARIATION AND CONSISTENCY IN WORK ACROSS SYSTEMS

As we trace the use of TC concepts across work with various systems, it becomes apparent that the concepts unite work at different levels but, also, that they are used somewhat differently with diverse systems. The concepts to be examined are target problems, collaboration, tasks and the TPIS, context, and time limits.

17.2.1 TARGET PROBLEMS

The concept of target problems and how they are defined is the most important one within TC. Target problems are either something onerous, and thus to be eliminated, or something desirable, and thus to be attained. Work with different systems is similar in that target problems are always the focus of attention. It is also similar in that target problems are always defined, or at least accepted, by the primary system. As a result, the ability to locate and identify target problems is critical to work with all systems.

As primary systems increase in size, however, we observe variation in the degree of concern about the target problem among the various participants, as well as differences in the source of concern. Teenagers might define the target problem as an extension of curfew. Parents might be uninterested in extending curfew but might see it as a means to secure cooperation in other areas, like improving grades. Some members of the staff in an organization might be experiencing less burnout than others but might be willing to work to resolve the problem because they realize that they are likely to need the cooperation of their colleagues about other matters in the future. Among participants in community groups, the nature of the motivation can vary widely. Those representing profit-making enterprises, for example, might work to resolve a community problem because they anticipate an increase in sales, whereas other participants might have more altruistic motives.

This variation in degree and source of motivation to resolve target problems points to another essential skill: the ability to involve those with differing interests. This skill entails identifying the vested interests of participants and using these interests to secure cooperation.

17.2.2 COLLABORATION

Just as target problems are important to securing cooperation, collaboration is vital to maintaining it. A concern about collaboration is seen in work with all primary systems. However, more differentiation exists among participants with respect to the amount of collaboration as the number of them increases and as the roles between social worker and participants change.

In both individual and group work, collaboration is ongoing between the social worker and the individual or the group. In work with families, however, the collaboration with a particular family member varies with the target problem. The collaboration of children is not usually important when the problem concerns the marital system, for example. This phenomenon also occurs in work with organizations and communities. In organizations, some problems, like budgeting, will fall almost exclusively into the administrator's domain while others will involve the entire staff. In community work, some members will be exclusively involved in particular aspects of problem resolution, for example, in printing announcements. In working with families, organizations, and communities, therefore, decisions need to be made about the amount and type of collaboration that is required with each member in order to resolve a target problem.

In work with organizations, we see another important shift with respect to collaboration. This shift occurs because of the administrator's authority. This authority allows the administrator to demand cooperation. Even without such a demand, cooperation is more likely to be secured because the administrator controls matters that are important to staff, such as salary. However, the frequent neglect of collaborating or the misuse of power is likely to result in staff alienation or, at least, limited problem solving. The community worker is probably at the other end of the continuum from the administrator with respect to the need to collaborate. Because almost all the participants are likely to be volunteers who have other important commitments, maintaining their cooperation is critical and is the community worker's ongoing responsibility.

17.2.3 TASKS AND THE TPIS

In practice at all levels, emphasis is on taking action to resolve target problems. In TC, action is conceptualized as tasks and the use of the various task activities that are a part of the TPIS. It is in the use of the TPIS that differences across systems are revealed. Some of these differences are the result of time limitations. For example, in working with groups, using all the activities with all members of the group is often not possible. As a result, the practitioner must decide which activities to omit. Some differences in the use of TPIS are the result of the nature of the participants. Simulating task performance may not be necessary with a competent community member, for example. Finally, some differences probably result from variations in knowledge development. The TPIS has been used less frequently with the larger systems, and its value has not been investigated. Increased experience and more research may identify other activities that should be incorporated when working with these systems.

17.2.4 CONTEXT

The greatest conceptual differences across systems concern the context of the problem. This is because our ability to examine context is determined, to a large extent, by theories that explain how individuals, families, groups, organizations, and communities function, and various theories are needed to understand the functioning of each level of system.

Context, it will be recalled, refers to the biopsychosocial and historical factors that surround the target problems. When the primary system is an individual, common dimensions of context include health and physical and intellectual functioning, information and knowledge, resources, stage of development, roles, cognition, self-concept, environmental contingencies, skills, stress, and social support. When the primary system is a family, additional dimensions need to be considered; for example, communication and the management of power. When the primary system is a group, we are also interested in characteristics like the developmental stage of the group and its cohesiveness. Organizations require consideration of the degree of structure of the organization and the organizational goals, among other concerns. Resolving problems in communities requires that we consider the various subsystems within the community and their interaction. (Other dimensions to consider for each system are identified in the sections labeled, "Theoretical Base," in the preceding chapters.)

The notion of context is the most recent conceptual development within TC. As yet, little is known about the impact of the various dimensions of context on problem solving. It is our expectation that this concept will be central in curriculums of advanced generalist practice. We also expect that, as knowledge develops, more will be learned about which dimensions are important and how they impact the effort to resolve problems.

17.2.5 Time Limits

Time limits are used in work across the various systems. In addition, they are used for the same purpose: to mobilize effort. Similarities in their use can be seen within microsystems (individual, family, and group) and within macrosystems (organizations and communities). In work with microsystems, time limits tend to be set early, somewhat arbitrarily, only once, and rarely exceed twelve sessions. In work with macrosystems time limits are often set for particular tasks, and thus many may be set and new ones established throughout the course of work. They are often based on a real phenomena, such as voting on legislation or opening a new service. Thus they are less arbitrary, and work may occur for much longer than twelve weeks.

In summary, TC across the systems is more similar than it is different. All the important concepts are employed in working with each system. Thus the skill necessary to implement a concept when working with one system, like targeting problems, is likely to be transferable to work with other systems. However, the transferred skill is also likely to need shaping or refining to fit the circumstances of other systems.

17.3.0 MOVEMENT AMONG SYSTEMS

The issue of moving among systems is really at the heart of generalist practice, since the generalist practitioner is defined as one who works with a variety of systems. How, then, does the practitioner decide when to work with one particular system? Since virtually nothing is known about this crucial question, a useful beginning might be to propose a "typology of movement." This typology can then provide a means to investigate what actually occurs, and hence begin to generate some useful information about the question. Our typology includes the following: (1) consistent primary systems with referral; (2) incremental movement, same problem; (3) incremental movement, different problems; (4) simultaneous movement, same problem; (5) different primary systems, specialized practice area; and (6) different primary systems, multiple practice areas. Each of these kinds of movement is described and illustrated below. They are presented in the order of least-to-most generalist.

17.3.1 CONSISTENT PRIMARY SYSTEMS WITH REFERRAL

Consistent primary systems describes the way most traditional social workers practice. They specialize in work with one system—*either* individual or families or groups or organizations or communities. The danger in this kind of practice is that problems that do not fit the practice are often not even heard, let alone resolved. For example, an individual client complains about the danger of the neighborhood to a social worker who works with individuals. Because the social worker is unprepared to deal with the problem, it might pass unheard or with a simple expression of sympathy. A more problem-oriented, individual worker might go so far as to help the client plan ways to cope with the danger. But neither would be likely to do anything to lessen the danger. A better option is to refer the client and the problem to a community organizer while the social worker continues to work with the client on other problems. In this pattern, individual workers would not be generalists but several of them, each of whom specializes in work with a different system, could comprise a generalist system of service.

While increased use of referrals might not be the ideal form of generalist practice, it is a useful possibility for two reasons. First, it would enhance the quality of service available to clients even when the practitioners' skills are limited. Second, it is inappropriate under certain circumstances for generalists to take on a particular system, even though they might have the skill to do so. For example, in most situations it would be inappropriate for the social worker-administrator to treat the family or marital problems of a staff member.

17.3.2 INCREMENTAL MOVEMENT, SAME PROBLEM

The *incremental movement, same problem* path is one of the most common ways in which movement occurs. Movement, in this pattern, is motivated by failure: Social workers proceed to engage different systems one by one as they learn that each system cannot or will not resolve the problem. A case was cited in part 1 of this book where a social worker first engaged the family, then the school principal, and finally legal aide in an effort to resolve the problem of a student who was prohibited from graduating.

17.3.3 INCREMENTAL MOVEMENT, DIFFERENT PROBLEMS

Movement, in this pattern, is motivated by learning about the existence of other problems in related systems. In this pattern, the practitioner begins work with one system but, in the course of work, learns that a related system is also having difficulty. The problems of the second system are not the same as the target problems in the first system, however. This pattern is illustrated by a case in which the school social worker received a referral for a child who needed eyeglasses. The social worker met with the mother to begin to resolve the problem, but the mother shared the fact that the family was about to be evicted and requested help. As a result, there was movement among systems and an additional target problem. It should be noted that, in this pattern, the practitioner might continue to work with the original primary system to resolve the original target problem, as well as working with the new system and new problem.

17.3.4 SIMULTANEOUS MOVEMENT, SAME PROBLEM

This pattern is seen less often than the incremental ones. In this pattern, the social worker engages several systems at one time for the purpose of resolving one problem. This pattern is illustrated by the case of Mrs. Carter, the woman whose target problem was that her children had been removed by a child welfare agency. The practitioner simultaneously engaged the woman, the court system, public assistance, the child welfare agency, and a housing agency in order to secure the children's return.

17.3.5 DIFFERENT PRIMARY SYSTEMS, SPECIALIZED PRACTICE AREA

This pattern describes the social worker who specializes in one problem area, for example, work for and with battered women. Such a practitioner might council the women as individuals or in groups and work with their families. He or she might raise funds, provide education to community groups, organize interest groups to promote legislation, and provide consultation to law enforcement agencies. This pattern might also be called "generalist-specialist" practice.

17.3.6 Different Primary Systems, Multiple Practice Areas

This pattern describes the social worker who decides which type of system to engage on a problem-by-problem basis. This is the epitome of generalist practice in that the practitioner works with a variety of populations, problems, and systems. This is the pattern that requires the most investigation. How does the worker decide which systems to involve? The pattern is probably most frequently seen in rural or semi-rural locales where the paucity of social workers makes generalist practice a necessity. It is expected that the development of task-centered generalist practice (TCG) will enable more social workers to practice with this degree of flexibility and this pattern of practice.

17.4.0 Remaining Issues

After decades of practice and research with TC, we know a great deal about its implementation. We know far less about task-centered generalist practice. The questions that must be systematically addressed in order to develop the generalist aspect of TC (or any other approach) include the following: Which systems were engaged? In what role? How extensively were they engaged? What was the pattern of movement among systems? As we accumulate this kind of information about work with particular problems, we will be in a better position to suggest which systems are important to the resolution of certain problems. Obtaining this kind of data will also move us toward addressing the fundamental question of whether the generalist perspective contributes to the effectiveness of practice.

Finally, we will end this book by identifying a problem that besets the profession of social work and by making a plea for its resolution. The problem is that we have no consensus about approaches to practice. This is a relatively recent phenomena. For most of the profession's history, only two approaches were employed—psychosocial or functional. In 1957 Perlman articulated the problem-solving approach. Since that time, the number of approaches has proliferated. Unfortunately little attention has been paid to the effectiveness of most of them. This splintering of effort impedes our ability to develop robust methods of helping and a substantive knowledge base for the profession. Our plea, then, is for cooperation among those conducting research. Specifically we urge more comparative research and, in particular, investigations that test the effectiveness of TC against other approaches to practice. The results of such studies would strengthen all the approaches tested and provide information that would enhance our ability to choose the preferred method for particular client-problem-situation configurations.

REFERENCES

Acosta, F. X., and J. Yamamoto. 1984. "The Utility of Group Work Practice for Hispanic Americans." *Social Work with Groups* 7:63–73.

Acosta, F. X., J. Yamamoto, L. A. Evans, and W. M. Skilbeck. 1983. "Preparing Low-Income Hispanic, Black, and White Patients for Psychotherapy: Evaluation of a New Orientation Program." *Journal of Clinical Psychology* 39:872–77.

Althausen, L. 1996. "Russian Families." In M. McGoldrick, J. Giordano, and J. K. Pierce, eds., *Psychological Intervention and Treatment of Ethnic Populations*, 680–87. New York: Guilford.

Amey, C. H., and S. L. Albrecht. 1998. "Race and Ethnic Differences in Adolescent Drug Use: The Impact of Family Structure and the Quantity and Quality of Parental Interaction." *Journal of Drug Issues* 28:283–98.

Anderson, J. D. 1982. "Generic and Generalist Practice and the BSW Curriculum." *Journal of Education for Social Work* 18:37–45.

Aponte, H. J., and J. M. Van Deusen. 1981. "Structural Family Therapy." In A. S. Gurman and D. P. Kniskern, eds., *Handbook of Family Therapy*, 310–60. New York: Brunner/Mazel.

Aponte, J. F., and L. R. Johnson. 2000. "The Impact of Culture on the Intervention and Treatment of Ethnic Populations." In J. F. Aponte and J. Wohl, eds., *Psychological Intervention and Cultural Diversity*, 18–39. Boston: Allyn and Bacon.

Atkinson, D., G. Morten, and D. Sue. 1998. *Counseling American Minorities*, 5th ed. Boston: McGraw-Hill.

Austin, D. M. 1989. "The Human Service Executive." *Administration in Social Work* 13:13–36.

Bailey-Dempsey, C. 1991. "Students At-Risk of Failure: A Task-Centered Management Approach." Ph.D. dissertation proposal, State University of New York at Albany.

Bailey-Dempsey, C., and W. J. Reid. 1996. "Intervention Design and Development: A Case Study." *Research on Social Work Practice* 6(2):208–28.

Bales, R. F. 1950. *Interaction Group Process.* Reading, Mass.: Addison-Wesley.

Balgopal, P. R., and T. V. Vassil. 1983. *Groups in Social Work: An Ecological Perspective.* New York: Macmillan.

Bandura, A. 1986. *Social Foundations of Thought and Action: A Social Cognitive Theory.* Englewood Cliffs, N.J.: Prentice-Hall.

Barker, R. L. 1995. *The Social Work Dictionary,* 3rd ed. Washington, D.C.: National Association of Social Workers.

Bartlett, H. M. 1970. *The Common Base of Social Work Practice.* Washington, D.C.: National Association of Social Workers.

Baum, B. H., and B. Parihar. 1984. "Toward a New Model for the Evaluation of Human Service Systems." *Social Development Issues* 8:62–72.

Bayes, M. 1972. "Behavioral Cues of Interpersonal Warmth." *Journal of Counseling Psychology* 39:333–39.

Beck, A. T. 1976. *Cognitive Therapy and the Emotional Disorders.* New York: International Universities Press.

Bednar, R. L., and T. J. Kaul. 1994. "Experiential Group Research: Can the Canon Fire?" In A. E. Bergin and S. L. Garfield, eds., *Handbook of Psychotherapy and Behavioral Change: An Empirical Analysis*, 2nd ed., 631–63. New York: Wiley.

Bennis, W. G. 1966. *Changing Organizations.* New York: McGraw-Hill.

Berg, I. 1997. *Family-Based Services: A Solution-Focused Approach.* New York: Norton.

Berg, I. K., and S. D. Miller. 1992. "Working with Asian American Clients: One Person at a Time." *Families in Society* 73(6):356–63.

Berg-Cross, L. 1997. *Couples Therapy.* Thousand Oaks, Calif.: Sage.

Berk, L. E. 1998. *Development Through the Lifespan.* Needham Heights, Mass.: Allyn and Bacon.

Bertcher, H. 1994. *Group Participation: Techniques for Leaders and Members.* 2nd ed. Thousand Oaks, Calif.: Sage.

Beutler, L. E., P. P. Machado, and S. A. Neufeldt. 1994. "Therapist Variables." In A. E. Bergin and S. L. Garfield, eds., *Handbook of Psychotherapy and Behavioral Change*, 4th ed., 229–69. New York: Wiley.

Biklen, D. P. 1983. *Community Organizing: Theory and Practice.* Englewood Cliffs, N.J.: Prentice-Hall.

Birchler, G. R., and S. H. Spinks. 1981. "Behavioral-Systems Marital and Family Therapy: Integration and Clinical Application." *The American Journal of Family Therapy* 8:6–28.

Bisno, H. 1987. "Interpersonal Transactions in Community Practice." In F. M. Cox, J. Erlich, J. Rothman, and J. Tropman, eds., *Strategies of Community Organization*, 4th ed., 143–49. Itasca, Ill.: F. E. Peacock.

Blake, R. R., and J. S. Mouton. 1985. *The Management Grid III*. Houston: Gulf.

Bloom, M. 1969. "The Selection of Knowledge from Behavioral Sciences and Its Integration in the Social Work Curriculum." *Journal of Education for Social Work* 5(1):15–28.

Bloomquist, M. L. 1996. *Skills Training for Youth with Behavioral Disorders: A Parent and Therapist Guidebook*. New York: Guilford.

Blundo, R. 2001. "Learning Strengths-Based Practice: Challenging Our Personal and Professional Frames." *Families in Society: The Journal of Contemporary Human Services* 82:296–304.

Bohart, A. C., and L. S. Greenberg. 1997. *Empathy Reconsidered: New Dimensions in Psychotherapy*. Washington, D.C.: American Psychological Association.

Boszormenyi-Nagy, I., and D. N. Ulrich. 1981. "Contextual Family Therapy." In A. S. Gurman and D. P. Kniskern, eds., *Handbook of Family Therapy*. New York: Brunner/Mazel.

Bowen, M. 1978. *Family Therapy in Clinical Practice*. New York: Aronson.

Boyd-Franklin, N., and B. Bry. 2000. *Reaching Out in Family Therapy: Home-Based, School, and Community Interventions*. New York: Guilford.

Brager, G., and H. Specht. 1973. *Community Organizing*. New York: Columbia University Press.

Brave Heart, M. 2001. "Culturally and Historically Congruent Social Work with Native Clients." In R. Fong and S. Furuto, eds., *Culturally Competent Practice*, 285–98. Boston: Allyn and Bacon.

Briar, S. 1977. "Social Work Practice: Contemporary Issues." *Encyclopedia of Social Work* 2(17):1529–34. Washington, D.C.: National Association of Social Workers.

Briar, S., and H. Miller. 1971. *Problems and Issues in Social Casework*. New York: Columbia University Press.

Briesmeister, J. M., and C. E. Schaefer, eds. 1998. *Handbook of Parent Training: Parents as Co-Therapists for Children's Behavior Problems*. 2nd ed. New York: Wiley.

Brilliant, E. L. 1986. "Social Work Leadership: A Missing Ingredient." *Social Work* 31:325–31.

Brower, A. M. 1989. "The Group Work Research Dilemma." *Journal of Social Service Research* 13:1–7.

Brown, L. 1991. *Groups for Growth and Change*. New York: Longman.

Brown, L. B., and R. Lewis. 1979. "The Task-Centered Model in Work with American Indians." In The Social Welfare Reform Forum, *Proceedings of the 106th Annual Forum*, National Conference on Social Welfare, Philadelphia, 13–17. New York: Columbia University Press.

Browne, C., and C. Mills. 2001. "Theoretical Frameworks: Ecological Model, Strengths Perspective, and Empowerment Theory." In R. Fong and S. Furuto, eds., *Culturally Competent Practice*, 10–32. Boston: Allyn and Bacon.

Bundy-Fazioli, K. 2001. *Strengthening Team Collaborations in Foster Care*. Albany, N.Y.: School of Social Welfare, University at Albany, State University of New York.

Burghardt, S. 1979. "The Tactical Use of Group Structure and Process in Community Organization." In F. M. Cox, J. Erlich, J. Rothman, and J. Tropman, eds., *Strategies of Community Organization*, 3rd ed., 113–30. Itasca, Ill.: F. E. Peacock.

Burghardt, S. 1982. *Organizing for Community Action*. Beverly Hills: Sage.

Caracena, P. F., and J. R. Vicory. 1969. "Correlates of Phenomenological and Judged Empathy." *Journal of Counseling Psychology* 16:510–15.

Caspi, J., and W. J. Reid. 1998. "The Task-Centered Model for Field Instruction: An Innovative Approach." *Journal of Social Work Education* 34:55–70.

Caspi, J., and W. J. Reid. In press. *Educational Supervision in Social Work: A Task-Centered Model for Field Instruction and Staff Development*. New York: Columbia University Press.

Cawley, R. 1996. "The Incomplete Revolution: The Development of Community Work in Quebec CLSCs." *Community Development Journal* 31:54–56.

Chambliss, C. H. 2000. *Psychotherapy and Managed Care*. Boston: Allyn and Bacon.

Chatterjee, B. 1962. "Some Issues in Urban Community Development." *International Review of Community Development* 9:114.

Cherbosque, J. 1987. "Differential Effects of Counselor Self-Disclosure Statements on Perception of the Counselor and Willingness to Disclose: A Cross-Cultural Study." *Psychotherapy* 24:434–37.

Chou, Y. C. 1992. *Developing and Testing an Intervention Program for Assisting Families in Taiwan Who Have a Member with Developmental Disabilities*. Ph.D. dissertation, University of Minnesota.

Christensen, D. N., J. Todahl, and W. C. Barrett. 1999. *Solution-Based Casework: An Introduction to Clinical and Case Management Skills in Casework Practice*. New York: Aldine De Gruyter.

Chu, J., and S. Sue, 1984 "Asian/Pacific Americans and Group Practice." *Social Work with Groups* 7:23–36.

Churchill, S. R. 1966. "State of Second Treatment Contract." Unpublished ms. Ann Arbor: University of Michigan, School of Social Work.

Cnaan, R. A., and J. Rothman. 1986. "Conceptualizing Community Intervention: An Empirical Test of Three Models of Community Organization." *Administration in Social Work* 10:41–56.

Compton, B., and B. Galaway. 1989. *Social Work Processes*. Homewood, Ill.: Dorsey.

Corcoran, K., and J. Fischer. 2000. *Measures for Clinical Practice: A Source Book*. New York: Free Press.

Coulton, C. J. 1991. "Developing and Implementing Quality Assurance Programs." In R. L. Edwards and J. A. Yankey, eds., *Skills for Effective Human Service Management*, 251–66. Silver Springs, Md.: National Association of Social Workers.

Cox, E., and R. J. Parsons. 2000. "Empowerment-Oriented Practice: From Practice Value to Practical Model." In P. Meares and C. Garvin, eds., *The Handbook of Social Work Direct Practice*, 113–29. Thousand Oaks, Calif.: Sage.

Croxton, T. A. 1974. "The Therapeutic Contract In Social Treatment." In P. Glasser, R. Sarri, and R. Vinter, eds., *Individual Change Through Small Groups*, 169–85. New York: Free Press.

Crozier, M. 1964. *The Bureaucratic Phenomenon*. Chicago: University of Chicago Press.

Crump, B., J. Alonzo, S. Horst, J. Jacobs, and B. Lasher. 2000. *Special Games Unlimited*. Unpublished manuscript, School of Social Work, West Texas A&M University, Canyon, Texas.

Cunningham, P. B., and S. W. Henggeler. 1999. "Engaging Multiproblem Families in Treatment: Lessons Learned throughout the Development of Multisystemic Therapy." *Family Process* 38(3):264–81.

D'Augelli, A. R. 1974. "Nonverbal Behavior of Helpers in Initial Helping Interaction." *Journal of Counseling Psychology* 21:360–63.

Dattilio, F. M. 1998. "Cognitive Behavioral Therapy." In F. M. Dattilio, ed., *Case Studies in Couple and Family Therapy: Systemic and Cognitive Perspectives*, 62–82. New York: Guilford.

Davis, L. 1984. "Essential Components of Group Work with Black Americans." *Social Work with Groups* 7:97–109.

Davis, L. 1996. "Role Theory." In F. Turner, ed., *Social Work Treatment*, 4th ed., 581–600. New York:Free Press.

Davis, L. E., and E. K. Proctor. 1989. *Race, Gender, and Class: Guidelines for Practice with Individuals, Families, and Groups*. Englewood Cliffs, N.J.: Prentice-Hall.

Denzin, N. K. 1992. *Symbolic Interactionism and Cultural Studies: The Politics of Interpretation*. Cambridge, Mass.: Blockwell.

De Jong, P., and I. K. Berg. 1998. *Interviewing for Solutions*. Pacific Grove, Calif.: Brooks/Cole.

Department of Commerce, Bureau of the Census. 2000. *Statistical Abstract of the United States: The National Data Book*. Springfield, Va.: National Technical Information Service.

de Shazer, S. 1982. *Patterns of Brief Family Therapy*. New York: Guilford.

de Shazer, S. 1988. *Clues: Investigation Solutions in Brief Therapy*. New York: Norton.

Devore, W., and E. Schlesinger. 1999. *Ethnic-Sensitive Social Work Practice*. 5th ed. Boston: Allyn and Bacon.

Dewey, J. 1933. *How We Think*. Boston: D. C. Heath.

Di Netto, D. M. 2000. *Social Welfare: Politics and Public Policy*. 5th ed. Boston: Allyn and Bacon.

Doel, M., and P. Marsh. 1991. *Task-Centered Social Work*. United Kingdom: Wildwood House.

Doherty, W. J. 1981a. "Cognitive Processes in Intimate Conflict: Extending Attribution Theory." *American Journal of Family Therapy* 9:3–12.

Doherty, W. J. 1981b. "Cognitive Processes in Intimate Conflict: Efficacy and Learned Helplessness." *American Journal of Family Therapy* 9:35–44.

Donahue, K. M. 1996. *Developing a Task-Centered Mediation Model*. Doctoral dissertation, State University of New York at Albany.

Dunham, A. 1963. "Some Principles of Community Development." *International Review of Community Development* 11:141–51.

D'Zurilla, T. J. 1988. "Problem-Solving Therapies." In K. S. Dobson, ed., *Handbook of Cognitive-Behavioral Therapies*, pp. 85–13. New York: Guilford.

D'Zurilla, T., and M. Goldfried. 1971. "Problem Solving and Behavior Modification." *Journal of Abnormal Psychology* 78:107–26.

Earle, K. A. 1999. "Cultural Diversity and Mental Health." In P. L. Ewalt, ed., *Multicultural Issues in Social Work*, 423–38. Washington, D.C.: National Association of Social Workers.

Early, T. J., and L. F. Glenmaye. 2000. "Valuing Families: Social Work Practice with Families from a Strengths Perspective." *Social Work* 45:118–30.

Edwards, V. 1996. "Clinical Case Management with Severely Mentally Ill African Americans." In P. Manoleas, ed., *The Cross-Cultural Practice of Clinical Case Management in Mental Health*. New York: Haworth.

Eli, K. 1984. "Social Networks, Social Support, and Health Status: A Review." *Social Service Review* 57:133–49.

Ellis, A. 1962. *Reason and Emotion in Psychotherapy*. New York: Lyle Stuart.

Ellis, A., and W. Dryden. 1987. *The Practice of Rational-Emotive Therapy (RET)*. New York: Springer.

Emery, R. E., K. M. Kitzmann, and M. Waldron. 1999. "Psychological Interventions for Separated and Divorced Families." *Coping with Divorce, Single Parenting, and Remarriage*. Mahwah, N.J.: Erlbaum.

Ephross, P., and T. Vassil. 1988. *Groups That Work: Structure and Process*. New York: Columbia University Press.

Epstein, L. 1988. *Helping People: The Task-Centered Approach*. Louis, Mo.: Mosby.

Epstein, L., and D. S. Bishop. 1981. "Problem-Centered Systems Therapy of the Family." In A. S. Gurman and D. P. Kniskern, eds., *Handbook of Family Therapy*, 444–82. New York: Brunner/Mazel.

Epstein, N., and D. H. Baucom. 1998. "Cognitive-Behavioral Couple Therapy." In F. M. Dattilio, *Case Studies in Couple and Family Therapy: Systemic and Cognitive Perspectives*, pp. 22–38. New York: Guilford.

Epstein, N., L. M. Baldwin, and D. S. Bishop. 1983. "The McMaster Family Assessment Device." *Journal of Marital and Family Therapy* 9:171–80.

Erikson, E. 1950. *Childhood and Society*. New York: Norton.

Everett, C. A., S. Nichols-Volgy, and W. C. Nichols. 2000. "Single Parent Families: Dynamics and Treatment Issues." In M. A. Pace-Nichols, ed., *Handbook of Family Development and Intervention*. New York: Wiley.

Ewalt, P. L. 1977. "A Psychoanalytically Oriented Child Guidance Setting." In W. J. Reid and L. Epstein, eds., *Task-Centered Practice*, 27–49. New York: Columbia University Press.

Fahrion, S. L., and P. A. Norris. 1990. "Self-Regulation of Anxiety." *Bulletin of the Menninger Clinic* 54(2):217–31.

Falicov, C. 1998. *Latino Families in Therapy: A Guide to Multicultural Practice*. New York: Guilford.

Fanjoux-Cohen, L., A. Bandini, P. D. Werner, and R. J. Green. 1998. "Rethinking Marital Enmeshment: Distinguishing Intrusiveness from Closeness-Caregiving among French Couples." *European Psychiatry* 13(1):46–51.

Feitel, B. 1968. "Feeling Understood as a Function of a Variety of Therapist Activities." Ph.D. dissertation, Teachers College, Columbia University.

Feldman, S. 1980. "The Middle Management Muddle." *Administration in Mental Health* 8:3–11.

Festinger, L. 1950. "Informal Social Communication." *Psychological Review* 57:271–82.

Fischer, J. 1973. "Is Casework Effective? A Review." *Social Work* 18:5–20.

Flexner, A. 1915. "Is Social Work a Profession?" *National Conference of Charities and Corrections Proceedings*, 579–90. Chicago: Hildman.

Fong, R., and S. Furuto. 2001. *Culturally Competent Practice*. Boston: Allyn and Bacon.

Foreyt, J. P., and G. K. Goodrick. 1984. "Cognitive Behavior Therapy." In R. J. Corsini, ed., *Encyclopedia of Psychology*, 231–34. New York: Wiley.

Forsyth, D. R. 1990. *Group Dynamics*. 2nd ed. Pacific Grove, Calif.: Brooks/Cole.

Fortune, A. E. 1981. "Communication Processes in Social Work Practice." *Social Services Review* 55:93–128.

Fortune, A. E., ed. 1985. *Task-Centered Practice with Families and Groups*. New York: Springer.

Fortune, A. E. 2002. "Terminating with Clients." In A. R. Roberts and G. J. Greene, eds., *Social Workers—Desk Reference,* 458–63. New York: Oxford University Press.

Fortune, A. E., B. Pearlingi, and C. D. Rochelle. 1992. "Reactions to Termination of Individual Treatment." *Social Work* 37(2):171–78.

Foster, S. L., R. J. Prinz, and K. D. O'Leary. 1983. "Impact of Problem-Solving Communication Training and Generalization Procedures on Family Conflict." *Child and Family Behavior Therapy* 5:1–23.

Fraser, N. 1989. *Unruly Practices.* Minneapolis: University of Minnesota Press.

Fraser, N., and L. Nicholson. 1988. "Social Criticism Without Philosophy: An Encounter Between Feminism and Postmodernism." In M. Featherstone, ed., *Postmodernism,* 373–94. Beverly Hills, Calif.: Sage.

Freedman, J., and G. Combs. 1996. *Narrative Therapy.* New York: Norton.

Freud, S. 1930. *Civilization and Its Discontents.* Translated and edited by J. Strachey. New York: Norton.

Fuller, J. 1995. "Getting in Touch with Your Heritage." In N. Vacc, S. De Vaney, and J. Wittmer, eds., *Experiencing and Counseling Multicultural and Diverse Populations.* 3rd ed. Bristol: Accelerated Development.

Garbarino, J. 1982. *Children and Families in the Social Environment.* New York: Aldine.

Garfield, S. L. 1994. "Research on Client Variables in Psychotherapy," 190–228. In A. E. Bergin and S. L. Garfield, eds., *Handbook of Psychotherapy and Behavioral Change,* 4th ed., 190–228. New York: Wiley.

Garfield, S. L., and A. E. Bergin. 1994. "Introduction and Historical Overview." In A. E. Bergin and S. L. Garfield, eds., *Handbook of Psychotherapy and Behavioral Change,* 4th ed., 3–18. New York: Wiley.

Garvin, C. 1974. "Task-Centered Group Work." *Social Service Review* 48:494–507.

Garvin, C. 1986. "Developmental Research for Task-Centered Group Work with Chronic Mental Patients." *Social Work with Groups* 9:31–42.

Garvin, C. 1987. "Group Theory and Research." In A. Minahan, ed., *Encyclopedia of Social Work,* 18th ed., 682–96. Silver Springs, Md.: National Association of Social Workers.

Garvin, C. 1990. "Short-Term Group Therapy." In R. A. Wells and V. J. Giannetti, eds., *Handbook of the Brief Psychotherapies,* 513–36. New York: Plenum.

Garvin, C. 1997. *Contemporary Group Work.* 3rd ed. Boston: Allyn and Bacon.

Garvin, C., W. J. Reid, and L. Epstein. 1976. "A Task-Centered Approach." In R. Roberts and H. Northen, eds., *Theories of Social Work with Groups,* 238–67. New York: Columbia University Press.

Geertjens, L., and O. Waaldijk. 1998. "Client-Centered Therapy for Adolescents: An Interactional Point of View." In B. Thorne, ed., *Person-Centered Therapy: A European Perspective.* London: Sage.

Geismar, L. L., and M. A. LaSorte. 1964. *Understanding the Multiproblem Family: A Conceptual Analysis and Exploration in Early Identification.* New York: Associated Press.

Germain, C. 1985. "The Place of Community Work within an Ecological Approach to Social Work Practice." In S. Taylor and R. W. Roberts, eds., *Theory and Practice of Community Social Work,* 30–55. New York: Columbia University Press.

Germain, C. B., and A. Gitterman. 1996. *The Life Model of Social Work Practice.* 2nd ed. New York: Columbia University Press.

Gibbons, J., I. Bow, and J. Butler. 1985. "Task-Centered Social Work after Parasuicide." In E. M. Goldberg, J. Gibbons, and I. Sinclair, eds., *Problems, Tasks, and Outcomes: The Evaluation of Task-Centered Casework in Three Settings,* 169–257. Boston: Allen and Unwin.

Gibbons, J. S., J. Butler, P. Urwin, and J. L. Gibbons. 1979. "Evaluation of a Social Work Service for Self-Poisoning Parents." *British Journal of Psychiatry* 133:111–18.

Gibson, J., J. Ivancevich, and J. Donnelly. 1982. *Organizations: Behavior, Structure, Process.* Plano, Tex.: Business.

Ginsberg, L. H., H. L. Gochros, R. P. Porter, V. L. Schneider, and L. G. Schultz. 1972. "An Experiment in Overseas Field Instruction." *Journal of Education for Social Work* 8:16–24.

Glassman, U., and L. Kates. 1990. *Group Work: A Humanistic Approach.* Newbury Park, Calif.: Sage.

Glassman, U., and L. Kates. N.d. "The Technical Development of the Democratic, Humanistic Norms of the Social Work Group." New York: Adelphi University School of Social Work.

Glueck, S., and E. Glueck. 1950. *Unraveling Juvenile Delinquency.* Cambridge, Mass.: Harvard University Press.

Goldstein, H. 1973. *Social Work Practice: A Unitary Approach.* Columbia: University of South Carolina Press.

Gordon, T. 1970. *Parent Effectiveness Training.* New York: Peter H. Wyden.

Gorey, K. M., B. A. Thyer, and D. E. Pawluck. 1998. "Differential Effectiveness of Prevalent Social Work Practice Models: A Meta-Analysis." *Social Work* 43:269–78.

Gottman, J. 1994. *Why Marriages Succeed or Fail.* New York: Simon and Schuster.

Gottman, J., et al. 1976. *A Couple's Guide to Communication.* Champaign, Ill.: Research Press.

Granvold, D. K. 1995. "Cognitive Treatment." In R. Edwards, ed., *Encyclopedia of Social Work,* vol. 1, 19th ed., 525–38. Washington, D.C.: National Association of Social Workers.

Green, J. W. 1982. *Cultural Awareness in the Human Services.* Englewood Cliffs, N.J.: Prentice-Hall.

Green, R. J., and P. D. Werner. 1996. "Intrusiveness and Closeness-Caregiving: Rethinking the Concept of Family 'Enmeshment.'" *Family Process* 35(2):115–35.

Greenberg, L. S., R. K. Elliott, and G. Lietaer. 1994. "Research on Experiential Psychotherapies." In A. E. Bergin and S. L. Garfield, eds., *Handbook of Psychotherapy and Behavioral Change*, 4th ed., 509–42. New York: Wiley.

Grinnell, R. M., Jr. 1973. "Environmental Modification: Casework's Concern or Casework's Neglect?" *Social Service Review* 47:208–20.

Gross, E. 1968. "Universities as Organizations: A Research Approach." *American Sociological Review* 33:518–44.

Guerney, B. 1982. "Relationship Enhancement." In E. K. Marshall and P. D. Kurtz, eds., *Interpersonal Helping Skills*. San Francisco: Jossey-Bass.

Gulati, P., and G. Guest. 1990. "The Community-Centered Model: A Garden-Variety Approach or a Radical Transformation of Community Practice?" *Social Work* 35(1):63–68.

Gutierrez, L. M. 1990. "Working with Women of Color: An Empowerment Perspective." *Social Work* 35:149–53.

Haase, R., and D. Tepper. 1972. "Nonverbal Components of Empathic Communication." *Journal of Counseling Psychology* 19:417–24.

Hackney, H., and L. Cormier. 1994. *Counseling Strategies and Objectives*, 4th ed. Needham Heights, Mass.: Allyn and Bacon.

Hall, A. D., and R. E. Fagen. 1956. "Definition of System." In L. V. Bertalanffy and A. Rapoport, eds., *General Systems*, vol. 1, 18–28. Ann Arbor: University of Michigan.

Hall, R. H. 1977. *Organizations: Structure and Process*. Englewood Cliffs, N.J.: Prentice-Hall.

Halloway, S. 1980. "Up the Hierarchy: From Clinician to Administrator." *Administration in Social Work* 4:1–14.

Hampson, R. B., and W. R. Beavers. 1996. "Family Therapy and Outcome: Relationships between Therapist and Family Styles." *Contemporary Family Therapy* 18:345–70.

Hardcastle, D., S. Wenocur, and P. R. Powers. 1997. *Community Practice: Theory and Skills for Social Workers*. New York: Oxford University Press.

Hargrove, D. S. 1974. "Verbal Interaction Analysis of Empathic and Nonempathic Responses of Therapists." *Journal of Consulting Clinical Psychology* 42:305.

Harrold, M., J. R. Lutzker, R. V. Campbell, and P. E. Touchette. 1992. "Improving Parent-Child Interactions for Families of Children with Developmental Disabilities." *Behavior Therapy and Experimental Psychiatry* 23(2):89–100.

Hart, A. F. 1984. "Clinical Social Work and Social Administration: Bridging the Culture Gap." *Administration in Social Work* 8:71–78.

Hartford, M. 1971. *Groups in Social Work*. New York: Columbia University Press.

Hartman, A., and J. Laird. 1978. "Diagrammatic Assessment of Family Relationships." *Social Casework* 59:465–76.

Hartman, A., and J. Laird. 1983. *Family-Centered Social Work Practice*. New York: Free Press.

Hasenfeld, Y. 1983. *Human Service Organizations*. Englewood Cliffs, N.J.: Prentice-Hall.

Havassy, H. M. 1990. "Effective Second-Story Bureaucrats: Mastering the Paradox of Diversity." *Social Work* 35:103–09.

Havighurst, R. J. 1972. *Developmental Tasks and Education*. New York: McKay.

Henry, W. P., H. H. Strupp, T. E. Schacht, and L. Gaston. 1994. "Psychodynamic Approaches." In A. E. Bergin and S. L. Garfield, eds., *Handbook of Psychotherapy and Behavioral Change*, 4th ed., 467–508. New York: Wiley.

Herrera, R. 1996. "Crisis Intervention: An Essential Component of Culturally Competent Case Management." In P. Manoleas, ed., *The Cross-Cultural Practice of Clinical Case Management in Mental Health*, 99–118. New York: Haworth.

Hersey, P., and K. Blanchard. 1982. *Management of Organizational Behavior*. Englewood Cliffs, N.J.: Prentice-Hall.

Hines, P., and Boyd-Franklin. 1996. "African-American Families." In M. McGoldrick, J. Giordano, and J. Pearce, eds., *Ethnicity and Family Therapy*, 2nd ed., 347–63. New York: Guilford.

Ho, M. K. 1984. "Social Group Work with Asian/Pacific-Americans." *Social Work with Groups* 7:49–61.

Hodge, B. J., W. P. Anthony, and L. M. Gales. 1996. *Organizational Theory: A Strategic Approach*, 5th ed. Upper Saddle River, N.J.: Prentice-Hall.

Hodge, D. R. 2001. "Spiritual Assessment: A Review of Major Qualitative Methods and a New Framework for Assessing Spirituality." *Social Work* 46:203–14.

Holland, T. P. 1995. "Organizations: Context for Social Services Delivery." In R. L. Edwards, ed., *Encyclopedia for Social Work*, 19th ed., vol. 2, 1787–94. Washington D.C.: National Association of Social Workers.

Holland, T. P., and Petchers, M. K. 1987. "Organizations: Contexts for Social Delivery." In A. Minahan, ed., *Encyclopedia of Social Work*, 18th ed., vol. 2, 729–36. Silver Spring, Md.: National Association of Social Work.

Holmes, T. H., and R. H. Rahe. 1967. "The Social Readjustment Rating Scale." *Journal of Psychosomatic Research* 11:213–18.

House, R. J. 1971. "A Path-Goal Theory of Leader Effectiveness." *Administrative Science Quarterly* 16:321–38.

Hudson, W. W. 1982. *The Clinical Measurement Package: A Field Manual*. Homewood, Ill.: Dorsey.

Hudson, W. W. 1990. "Computer-Based Clinical Practice: Present Status and Future Possibilities." In L. Videka-Sherman and W. J. Reid, eds., *Advances in Clinical Social Work Research,* 105–17. Washington, D.C.: National Association of Social Workers.

Huh, N. S. 2000. " A Task-Centered Approach for the Elderly in the Community." *Korean Journal of Social Welfare,* Vol. 11, pp. 23–32.

Ivey, A. E., and J. Authier. 1978. *Microcounseling.* Springfield, Ill.: Charles C. Thomas.

Jackson, D. D. 1965. "Family Rules: The Marital Quid Pro Quo." *Archives of General Psychiatry* 12:589–94.

Jacobs, D. E., E. Charles, T. Jacobs, H. Weinstein, and D. Mann. 1972. "Preparation for Treatment of the Disadvantaged Patient: Effects on Disposition and Outcome." *American Journal of Orthopsychiatry* 42:666–74.

Jacobson, N. S., and A. Christensen. 1996. *Integrative Couple Therapy: Promoting Acceptance and Change.* New York: Norton.

Jacobson, N. S., and G. Margolin. 1979. *Marital Therapy: Strategies Based on Social Learning and Behavior Exchange Principles.* New York: Brunner/Mazel.

Jalali, B. 1996. "Iranian Families." In M. McGoldrick, J. Giordano, and J. K. Pierce, eds., *Psychological Intervention and Treatment of Ethnic Populations,* 347–63. New York: Guilford.

Janzen, C., and O. Harris. 1986. *Family Treatment in Social Work Practice.* 2nd ed. Itasca, Ill.: Peacock.

Janzen, C., and O. Harris. 1997. *Family Treatment in Social Work Practice.* 3rd ed. Itasca, Ill.: Peacock.

Johns, G. 1996. *Organizational Behavior: Understanding and Managing Life at Work,* 6th ed. New York: Harper Collins.

Johnson, D. H., and C. J. Gelso. 1980. "The Effectiveness of Time Limits in Counseling and Psychotherapy: A Critical Review." *Counseling Psychologist* 9:70–83.

Johnson, D. J. 1971. "The Effect of Confrontation in Counseling." *Dissertation Abstracts International* 32:180A.

Johnson, D. W. 1997. *Reaching Out: Interpersonal Effectiveness and Self-Actualization,* 3rd ed. Boston: Allyn and Bacon.

Johnson, D. W., and F. P. Johnson. 1996. *Joining Together: Group Theory and Group Skills.* 6th ed. Boston: Allyn and Bacon.

Johnson, D. W., and R. Matross. 1977. "Interpersonal Influence in Psychotherapy: A Social Psychological View." In A. S. Gurman and A. M. Razin, eds., *Effective Psychotherapy,* 395–432. Oxford: Pergamon.

Jones, J., A. Christiansen, and N. Jacobson. 2000. *Integrative Behavioral Couple Therapy: Comparative Treatments for Relationship Dysfunction.* New York: Springer.

Jones, J. F., and A. Kumssa. 1996. Distance Training in Local Social Development, and the Emerging Technologies. *Social Development Issues* 18:1–11.

Kagan, R., and S. Schlosberg. 1989. *Families in Perpetual Crisis*. New York: Norton.

Kagan, R., and W. J. Reid. 1984. "Critical Factors in the Adoption of Emotionally Disturbed Youth." *Child Welfare* 56:63–73.

Kane, D. n.d. "Ronnie Paige: Case Recording Guides," unpublished.

Katz, D. 1981. Notes on Teaching Task-Centered Casework. New Brunswick, N.J.: School of Social Work, Rutgers University.

Kaul, M. L. 1976. "Delhi Urban Community Development: A Case Study in Community Organization Effort." *International Review of Community Development* 35–36:162.

Kaul, M. L. 1988. "Developing Neighborhood Organizations as Social Structures for Peace." *International Social Work* 31(1):45–52.

Kelly, M. I. 1990. *School-Home Notes: Promoting Children's Classroom Success*. New York: Guilford.

Kemp, S. P., J. K. Whittaker, and E. M. Tracy. 1997. *Person-Environment Practice*. New York: Aldine De Gruyter.

Kerr, M. E. 1981. "Family Systems Theory and Therapy." In A. S. Gurman and D. P. Kniskern, eds., *Handbook of Family Therapy*, 226–64. New York: Brunner/Mazel.

Kettner, P. M., J. M. Daley, and A. W. Nichols. 1985. *Initiating Change in Organizations and Communities: A Macro Practice Model*. Monterey, Calif.: Brooks/Cole.

Khinduka, S. K. 1987. "Community Development: Potentials and Limitations." In F. M. Cox, J. Erlich, J. Rothman, and J. Tropman, eds., *Strategies of Community Organization*, 4th ed., 353–62. Itasca, Ill.: Peacock.

Kilgore, D. K. 1995. *Task-Centered Group Treatment of Sex Offenders: A Developmental Study*. Ph.D. dissertation, State University of New York at Albany.

Kim, Y., B. Snyder, and A. Lai-BitkEr. 1996. "Culturally Responsive Psychiatric Case Management with Southeast Asians." In P. Manoleas, ed., *The Cross-Cultural Practice of Clinical Case Management in Mental Health*. New York: Haworth.

Kimmel, W. 1983. Needs Assessment: A Critical Perspective. In R. M. Kramer and H. Specht, eds., *Readings in Community Organization Practice*, 3rd ed., 289–304. Englewood Cliffs, N.J.: Prentice-Hall.

Kiresuk, T. J., and G. Garwick. 1979. "Basic Goal Attainment Procedures." In R. Compton and B. Galaway, eds., *Social Work Processes*, 2nd ed., 412–21. Homewood, Ill.: Dorsey.

Kirst-Ashman, K. K., and G. H. Hull, Jr. 2001. *Generalist Practice with Organizations and Communities*, 2nd ed. Belmont, Calif.: Wadsworth Thompson Learning.

Kleist, D. M. 1999. "Single-Parent Families: A Difference that Makes a Difference? *The Family Journal: Counseling and Therapy for Couples and Families* 7(4):373–78.

Klier, J., E. Fein, and C. Genero. 1984. "Are Written or Verbal Contracts More Effective in Family Therapy?" *Social Work* 29:298–99.

Knei-Paz, C., and D. S. Ribner. 2000. "A Narrative Perspective on 'Doing' for Multiproblem Families." *Families in Society* 81(5):475–82.

Koontz, H., and C. O'Donnell. 1968. *Principles of Management.* New York: McGraw-Hill.

Koss, M. P., and J. Shiang. 1994. "Research on Brief Psychotherapy." In A. E. Bergin and S. L. Garfield, eds., *Handbook of Psychotherapy and Behavior Change*, 4th ed., 664–700. New York: Wiley.

Kramer, R., and H. Specht, eds. 1983. *Readings in Community Organization Practice.* 3rd ed. Englewood Cliffs, N.J.: Prentice-Hall.

Kuehlwein, K. T. 1998. "The Cognitive Therapy Model." In R. Dorfman, ed., *Paradigms of Clinical Social Work*, 125–148. New York: Brunner/Mazel.

LaFrance, M., and C. Mayo. 1974. "Newsline." *Psychology Today* (May):30.

Larsen, J., and C. Mitchell. 1980. "Task-Centered Strength-Oriented Group Work with Delinquents." *Social Casework* 61:154–63.

Lawrence, E., K. Eldridge, A. Christiansen, and N. Jacobson. 1999. "Integrative Couple Therapy: The Dyadic Relationship of Acceptance and Change." *Short-Term Couple Therapy* 1:1–12.

Lazarus, R. S. 1966. *Psychological Stress and the Coping Process.* New York: McGraw-Hill.

LeCroy, C. W., and C. C. Goodwin. 1988. "New Directions in Teaching Social Work Methods: A Content Analysis of Course Outlines." *Journal of Social Work Education* 24:43–49.

Lee, E. 1996. "Asian American Families: An Overview." In M. McGoldrick, J. Giordano, and J. K. Pierce, eds., *Psychological Intervention and Treatment of Ethnic Populations*, 227–248. New York: Guilford.

Lee, J. A. B. 1996. "The Empowerment Approach to Social Work Practice." In F. J. Turner, ed., *Social Work Treatment*, 4th ed. New York: Free Press.

Lee, P. 1929. "Presidential Address." In *National Conference of Charities and Corrections Proceedings*, 3–20. Chicago: University of Chicago Press.

Lehmann, P., and N. Coady. 2001. *Theoretical Perspectives for Direct Social Work Practice.* New York: Springer.

Lehrer, P. M., and R. L. Woolfolk. 1993. *Principles and Practices of Stress Management.* New York: Guilford.

Levant, R. F. 1984. *Family Therapy: A Comprehensive Overview.* Englewood Cliffs, N.J.: Prentice-Hall.

Levinson, J. F. 1997. *Fostering Therapeutic Alliance Using Therapist Training in Relational Empathy.* Dissertation Abstracts International, 58 (4B) U.S.: University Microfilms International.

Levy, R. L. 1977. "Relationship of an Overt Commitment to Task Compliance in Behavior Therapy." *Journal of Behavior Therapy and Experimental Psychiatry* 8:25–29.

Lewinsohn, M. A., and P. D. Werner. 1997. "Factors in Chinese Marital Process: Relationship to Marital Adjustment." *Family Process* 36(1):43–61.

Lewis, J. M., W. R. Beavers, J. T. Gossett, and V. Austin Phillips. 1976. *No Single Thread: Psychological Health in Family Systems.* New York: Brunner/Mazel.

Liberman, R. P. 1988. "Social Skills Training." In R. P. Liberman, ed., *Psychiatric Rehabilitation of Chronic Mental Patients,* 147–98. Washington, D.C.: American Psychiatric Press.

Lorion, R. P. 1978. "Research on Psychotherapy and Behavior Change with the Disadvantaged: Past, Present, and Future Directions." In S. L. Garfield and A. E. Bergin, eds., *Handbook of Psychotherapy and Behavior Change: An Empirical Analysis,* 903–38. New York: Wiley.

Lorsch, J. W. 1976. "Contingency Theory and Organization Design: A Persona Odyssey." In R. H. Kilman, L. R. Pondy, and D. P. Slevin, eds., *The Management of Organization Design,* vol. 1, 141–65. New York: North-Holland.

Luiselli, J. K. 1998. "Maintenance of Behavioral Interventions." *Mental Health Aspects of Developmental Disabilities* 1(3):69–76.

Lum, D. 2000. *Social Work Practice and People of Color,* 4th ed. Pacific Grove, Calif.: Brooks/Cole.

Manis, F. 1971. "Education for Social Work: Field Work in Developing Nations." *International Social Work* 14:17–20.

Mann, B., and K. C. Murphy. 1975. "Timing of Self-Disclosure, Reciprocity of Self-Disclosure, and Reactions to an Initial Interview." *Journal of Counseling Psychology* 22:304–8.

Martí-Costa, S., and I. Serrano-García. 1987. "Needs Assessment and Community Development: An Ideological Perspective." In F. M. Cox, J. Erlich, Rothman, and J. Tropman, eds., *Strategies of Community Organization,* 4th ed., 362–73. Itasca, Ill.: Peacock.

McGoldrick, M., J. K. Pearce, and J. Giordano. 1982. *Ethnicity and Family Therapy.* New York: Guilford.

McNeil, C. B., and A. D. Herschell. 1998. "Treating Multi-Problem, High Stress Families: Suggested Strategies for Practitioners. *Family Relations* 47(3):259–62.

Meenaghan, T. M., R. O. Washington, and R. M. Ryan. 1982. *Macro Practice in the Human Services.* New York: Free Press.

Mehrabian, A. 1973. "Inference of Attitude from the Posture, Orientation, and Distance of Communicator." In M. Argyle, ed., *Social Encounter.* Chicago, Aldine.

Meichenbaum, D. 1977. *Cognitive Behavior Modification: An Integrated Approach.* New York: Plenum.

Metcoff, J., and C. A. Whitaker. 1982. Family Micro Events: Communication Patterns for Problem Solving." In F. Walsh, ed., *Normal Family Processes,* 251–74. New York: Guilford.

Meyer, C. H. 1970. *Social Work Practice.* New York: Free Press.

Meyer, C., ed. 1983. *Clinical Social Work in the Ecosystems Perspective.* New York: Columbia University Press.

Meyer, C. 1995. "The Ecosystems Perspective: Implications for Practice." In C. Meyer and M. Mattaini, eds., *The Foundations of Social Work Practice,* 16–27. Washington, D.C.: National Association of Social Workers.

Meyer, C., and M. Mattaini. 1995. *The Foundations of Social Work Practice.* Washington, D.C.: National Association of Social Workers.

Middleman, R. R. 1981. *The Non-Verbal Method of Working with Groups.* Hebron, Conn.: Practitioner's Press.

Middleman, R. R., and G. G. Wood. 1989. *The Structural Approach to Direct Practice in Social Work.* New York: Columbia University Press.

Midgley, J., A. Hall, M. Hardiman, and D. Narine. 1986. *Community Participation, Social Development, and the State.* London: Methuen.

Miley, K., M. O'Melia, and B. DuBois. 2001. *Generalist Social Work Practice: An Empowering Approach.* Boston: Allyn and Bacon.

Miller, I. W., N. B. Epstein, D. S. Bishop, and G. I. Keitner. 1985. "The McMaster Family Assessment Device: Reliability and Validity." *Journal of Marital and Family Therapy* 11:345–56.

Minuchin, S. 1974. *Families and Family Therapy.* Cambridge, Mass.: Harvard University Press.

Minuchin, S., B. Montalvo, B. G. Guerney, Jr., B. L. Rosman, and F. Shumer. 1967. *Families of the Slums.* New York: Basic Books.

Mondros, J. B., and S. M. Wilson. 1994. *Organizing for Power and Empowerment.* New York: Columbia University Press.

Moe, E. O. 1959. "Consulting with a Community System: A Case Study." *Journal of Social Issues* 15(2):29.

Moffett, J. 1968. *Concepts in Casework Treatment.* London: Routledge and Kegan Paul.

Monkman, M., and P. Allen-Meares. 1985. "The TIE Framework: A Conceptual Map for Social Work Assessment." *Arete* 10(1):41–49.

Morales, A., and B. Sheafor. 1977. *Social Work: A Profession of Many Faces.* Boston: Allyn and Bacon.

Morrison, N. C. 1995. "Successful Single Parents." *Journal of Divorce and Remarriage* 22:205–19.

Murphy, J. 1987. "Social Workers Fight Nuclear Waste in Texas Panhandle." *National Association of Social Workers Texas Network* 12(8):1.

Myers, L. L., and B. A. Thyer. 1997. "Should Social Work Clients Have the Right to Effective Treatment?" *Social Work* 42:288–98.

Naleppa, M. J., and W. J. Reid. 1998. Task-Centered Case Management for the Elderly: Developing a Practice Model. *Research on Social Work Practice* 8:63–84.

Naleppa, M. J., and W. J. Reid. 2000. "Integrating Case Management and Brief Treatment Strategies: A Hospital Based Geriatric Program." *Health and Social Work* 31:1–23.

National Association of Social Workers. 1996. *National Association of Social Workers Code of Ethics*. Washington, D.C.: National Association of Social Workers.

Naleppa, M. J., and W. J. Reid. In press. *Social Work with the Elderly: A Task-Centered Case Management Approach*. New York: Columbia University Press.

Newcome, K. 1985. "Task-Centered Group Work with the Chronically Mentall Ill in Day Treatment." In Anne E. Fortune, ed., *Task-Centered Practice with Groups and Families*, 78–91. New York: Springer.

Neugarten, B. L. 1979. "Time, Age, and the Life Cycle." *American Journal of Psychiatry* 136:887–94.

Nguyen, W. 1999. "Using a Task-Centered Approach with Vietnamese Families. In K. S. Ng, ed., *Counseling Asian Families from a Systems Perspective*, 55–62. Alexandria, Va.: American Counseling Association.

Nichols, M. P., and R. C. Schwartz. 2001. *Family Therapy*, 5th ed. Needham Heights, Mass.: Allyn and Bacon.

Nofz, M. P. 1988. "Alcohol Abuse and Culturally Marginal Indians." *Social Casework* 69:67–73.

Norlin, J. M., and W. A. Chess. 1997. *Human Behavior and the Social Environment: Social Systems Theory*. Boston: Allyn and Bacon.

Northen, H. 1988. *Social Work with Groups*. 2nd ed. New York: Columbia University Press.

Nugent, W. 1992. "The Affective Impact of a Clinical Social Worker's Interviewing Style: A Series of Single-Case Experiments." *Research on Social Work Practice* 2:6–27.

Nurius, P., and S. Berlin. 1995. "Cognition and Social Cognitive Theory." In R. Edwards, ed., *Encyclopedia of Social Work*, vol. 1, 19th ed, 513–24. Washington, D.C.: National Association of Social Workers Press.

Olson, D. H., H. I. McCubbin, and Associates. 1983. *Families: What Makes Them Work*. Newbury Park, Calif.: Sage.

Organista, K., and E. V. Dwyer. 1996. "Clinical Case Management and Cognitive-Behavioral Therapy: Integrated Psychosocial Services for Depressed Latino Primary Care Patients." In P. Manoleas, ed., *The Cross-Cultural Practice of Clinical Case Management in Mental Health*. New York: Haworth.

Orlinsky, D. E., K. Grawe, and B. K. Parks. 1994. "Process and Outcome in Psychotherapy—Noch Einmal." In A. E. Bergin and S. L. Garfield, eds., *Handbook of Psychotherapy and Behavior Change*, 4th ed, 270–378. New York: Wiley.

Osborn, A. F. 1963. *Applied Imagination*. New York: Scribners.

Paniagua, F. A. 1994. *Assessing and Treating Culturally Diverse Clients*. Thousand Oaks, Calif.: Sage.

Panzetta, A. 1983. "The Concept of Community: The Short Circuit of the Mental Health Movement." In R. M. Kramer and H. Specht, eds., *Readings in Community Organization Practice*, 3rd ed., 36–46. Englewood Cliffs, N.J.: Prentice-Hall.

Parihar, B. 1984. *Task-Centered Management in Human Services*. Springfield, Ill.: Charles C. Thomas.

Parks, C. D., and L. J. Sanna. 1999. *Group Performance and Interaction*. Boulder, Colo.: Westview.

Parsons, T. 1957. "The Mental Hospital as a Type of Organization." In M. Greenblatt, D. J. Levinson, and R. H. Williams, eds., *The Patient and the Mental Hospital*, 108–29. Glencoe, Ill.: Free Press.

Parsons, T. 1960. *Structure and Process in Modern Societies*. New York: Free Press.

Patterson, C. H. 1985. *The Therapeutic Relationship: Foundations for an Eclectic Psychotherapy*. Pacific Grove, Calif.: Brooks/Cole.

Patti, R. J. 1983. *Social Welfare Administration*. Englewood Cliffs, N.J.: Prentice-Hall.

Patti, R. J. 2000. "Landscape of Social Welfare Administration." In R. J. Patti, ed., *Handbook of Social Welfare Management*. Thousand Oaks, Calif.: Sage.

Paulino, A., and J. Burgos-Servedio. 1997. "Working with Immigrant Families in Transition." In E. Congress, ed., *Multicultural Perspectives in Working with Families*, 125–41. New York: Springer.

Payne, M. 2000. *Teamwork in Multi Professional Care*. Chicago: Lyceum.

Peller, J., and J. L. Walter. 1995. "Solution-Focused Brief Therapy." In R. A. Dorfman, ed., *Paradigms of Clinical Social Work*, 71–92. New York: Brunner/Mazel.

Perlman, H. H. 1957. *Casework: A Problem-Solving Process*. Chicago: University of Chicago Press.

Perlmutter, F. D. 1983. "Caught In-Between: The Middle Management Bind." *Administration in Social Work* 7:147–61.

Perlmutter, F. D. 1990. *Changing Hats: From Social Work Practice to Administration*. Silver Springs. Md.: National Association of Social Workers.

Perrow, C. 1961. "The Analysis of Goals in Complex Organizations." *American Sociological Review* 26:856–66.

Perrow, C. 1967. "A Framework for the Comparative Analysis of Organizations." *American Sociological Review.* 32:194–208.

Perrow, C. 1970. *Organizational Analysis: A Sociological View.* Belmont, Calif.: Brooks/Cole.

Pett, M. G. 1982. "Predictors of Satisfactory Social Adjustments of Divorce Single Parents." *Journal of Divorce* 5:1–17.

Piaget, J. 1952. *The Origins of Intelligence in Children.* New York: International University Press.

Pierce, W. D. 1971. "Anxiety about the Act of Communication and Perceived Empathy." *Psychotherapy: Theory, Research, Practice* 11:63–65.

Pierce, W. D., and D. L. Mosher. 1967. "Perceived Empathy, Interviewer Behavior, and Interviewee Anxiety." *Journal of Consulting Psychology* 31:101.

Pincus, A., and A. Minahan. 1973. *Social Work Practice: Model and Method.* Itasca, Ill.: Peacock.

Plant, R. 1970. *Social and Moral Theory in Casework.* London: Routledge and Kegan Paul.

Pomeroy, E. C., A. Rubin, and R. J. Walker. 1995. "Effectiveness of a Psychoeducational and Task-Centered Group Intervention for Family Members of People with AIDS." *Social Work Research* 19:129–52.

Pope, B. 1979. *The Mental Health Interview.* New York: Pergamon.

Pope, B., S. Nudler, M. R. Von Korff, and J. P. McGee. 1974. "The Experienced Professional Interviewer Versus the Complete Novice." *Journal of Consulting and Clinical Psychology* 42:680–90.

Poppen, R. 1998. *Behavioral Relaxation Training and Assessment.* 2nd ed. Thousand Oaks, Calif.: Sage.

Ramakrishnan, K. R., P. R. Balgopal, and M. A. Patchner. 1990. "Gandhian Ideology of Nonviolence and Peace: A Parallel to Social Work Practice." In D. S. Sanders and J. K. Matsuoka, eds., *Peace and Development: An Interdisciplinary Perspective,* 207–21. Honolulu: University of Hawaii Press.

Raushi, T. M. 1994. *A Task-Centered Model for Group Work with Single Mothers in the College Setting.* Ph.D. dissertation, State University of New York at Albany.

Reid, W. J. 1975. "A Test of the Task-Centered Approach." *Social Work* 20:3–9.

Reid, W. J. 1977. "Process and Outcome in the Treatment of Family Problems." In W. J. Reid and L. Epstein, eds., *Task-Centered Practice.* New York: Columbia University Press.

Reid, W. J. 1978. *The Task-Centered System.* New York: Columbia University Press.

Reid, W. J. 1979. "The Model Development Dissertation." *Journal of Social Service Research* 3:215–25.

Reid, W. J. 1985. *Family Problem-Solving*. New York: Columbia University Press.

Reid, W. J. 1987 "Task-Centered Approach." In Ann Minahan, ed., *Encyclopedia of Social Work*, 18th ed., 757–63. New York: National Association of Social Workers.

Reid, W. J. 1992. *Task Strategies: An Empirical Approach to Social Work*. New York: Columbia University Press.

Reid, W. J. 1994. "Field Testing and Data Gathering on Innovative Practice Interventions in Early Development." In J. Rothman and E. J. Thomas, eds., *Intervention Research*, 245–60. New York: Haworth.

Reid, W. J. 1996. "Task-Centered Social Work. In F. J. Turner, ed., *Social Treatment*, 4th ed. New York: Free Press.

Reid, W. J. 1997. "Research on Task-Centered Practice." *Social Work* 21:132–37.

Reid, W. J. 2000. *The Task Planner: An Intervention Resource for Human Service Professionals*. New York: Columbia University Press.

Reid, W. J. 2002. "Knowledge for Direct Social Work Practice: An Analysis of Trends. *Social Service Review*, 76: 6–33.

Reid, W. J., and C. Bailey-Dempsey. 1994. "Content Analysis in Design and Development." *Research on Social Work Practice* 4:101–14.

Reid, W. J., C. Bailey-Dempsey, E. Cain, T. Cook, and J. D. Burchard. 1994. "Cash Incentives versus Case Management: Can Money Replace Services in Preventing School Failure?" *Social Work Research and Abstracts* 18:227–38.

Reid, W. J., and C. Bailey-Dempsey. 1995. "The Effects of Monetary Incentives on School Performance." *Families in Society* 76:331–40.

Reid, W. J., and K. DuFresne. 1985. "The Single Mother Family." In W. J. Reid, ed., *Family Problem Solving*, 261–83. New York: Columbia University Press.

Reid, W. J., and T. Donovan. 1990. Treating Sibling Violence. *Family Therapy* 71:49–59.

Reid, W. J., and L. Epstein. 1972. *Task-Centered Casework*. New York: Columbia University Press.

Reid, W. J., L. Epstein, L. B. Brown, E. R. Tolson, and R. H. Rooney. 1980. "Task-Centered School Social Work." *Social Work in Education* 2:7–24.

Reid, W. J., and A. E. Fortune. In press. "The Task-Centered Model." In A. R. Roberts and G. Green, eds., *Social Workers' Desk Reference*. New York: Oxford University Press.

Reid, W. J., and B. Kenaley. 2000. "Task-Centered for TANF Families." Document prepared for the Profession Development Program, University at Albany, State University of New York.

Reid, W. J., L. Rotering, and A. E. Fortune. 1989. "Family Problem Solving and Therapy: A New Look." *Family Therapy* 16:197–206.

Richardson, C., S. Kairys, T. LaManna, and H. Krell. 1983. Locality Development: A Case Study. *Social Development Issues* 7(2):31–41.

Robin, A. L., M. Bedway, and M. Gilroy. 1994. "Problem-Solving Communication Training." In C. W. LeCroy, ed., *Handbook of Child and Adolescent Treatment Manuals*, 92–125. New York: Lexington.

Rogers, C. R. 1957. "The Necessary and Sufficient Conditions of Therapeutic Personality Changes." *Journal of Consulting Psychology* 21:95–103.

Rogers, E. M., and F. F. Shoemaker. 1971. *Communication of Innovations: A Cross-Cultural Approach.* New York: Free Press.

Rooney, R. H. 1978. "Separation Through Foster Care: Toward a Problem-Oriented Practice Model Based on Task-Centered Casework." Ph.D. dissertation, University of Chicago.

Rooney. R. H. 1980. "Task-Centered School Social Work." *Social Work in Education* 2:7–24.

Rooney, R. H. 1981. "A Task-Centered Reunification Model for Foster Care." In A. A. Malluccio and P. Sinanoglu, eds., *Working with Biological Parents of Children in Foster Care.* New York: Child Welfare League of America.

Rooney, R. H. 1988. "Socialization Strategies for Involuntary Clients." *Social Casework* 69:131–39.

Rooney, R. H. 1992. *Strategies for Work with Involuntary Clients.* New York: Columbia University Press.

Rooney, R. H. n.d. "Return from Foster Care" and "Narrative Supplement to Return from Foster Care: Videotape Introduction."

Rooney, R. H., and M. Wanless. 1985. "A Model for Caseload Management Based on Task-Centered Casework." In A. E. Fortune, ed., *Task-Centered Practice with Families and Groups*, 187–99. New York: Springer.

Rose, S. 1977. *Group Therapy: A Behavioral Approach.* Englewood Cliffs, N.J.: Prentice-Hall.

Rossi, A. S. 1975. "Transition to Parenthood." In W. Sze, ed., *The Human Life Cycle*, 505–40. New York: Jason Aronson.

Rothman, J. 1980. *Social R&D Research and Development in the Human Services.* Englewood Cliffs, N.J.: Prentice-Hall.

Rothman, J. 1996. "The Interweaving of Community Intervention Approaches." *Journal of Community Practice*, 33:69–99.

Rothman, J., and J. Tropman. 1987. Models of Community Organization and Macro Practice Perspectives: Their Mixing and Phasing. In F. M. Cox, J. Erlich, J. Rothman, and J. Tropman, eds., *Strategies of Community Organization*, 4th ed., 3–26. Itasca, Ill.: Peacock.

Ruben, D. H. 1998. "Social Exchange Theory: Dynamics of a System Governing the Dysfunctional Family and Guide to Assessment." *Journal of Contemporary Pschotherapy* 8(3):307–25.

Rzepnicki, T. L. 1985. "Task-Centered Intervention in Foster Care Services: Working with Families Who Have Children in Placement." In

A. E. Fortune, ed., *Task-Centered Practice with Families and Groups*, 172–84. New York: Springer.

Saleebey, D. 1997. *The Strengths Perspective in Social Work Practice*. 2nd ed. New York: Longman.

Sapp, M. 1996. "Irrational Beliefs that Can Lead to Academic Failure for African American Students Who Are at Risk." *Journal of Rational-Emotive and Cognitive Behavioral Therapists* 14:123–34.

Sattler, J. M. 1977. "The Effects of Therapist-Client Racial Similarity." In A. S. Gurman and A. M. Razin, eds., *Effective Psychotherapy*, 252–90. Oxford: Pergamon.

Scharlach, A. E. 1985. "Social Group Work with Institutionalized Elders: A Task-Centered Approach." *Social Work with Groups* 8:33–48.

Schatz, M. S., L. E. Jenkins, and B. W. Sheafor. 1990. "Milford Redefined: Model of Generalist and Advanced Generalist Social Work." *Journal of Social Work Education* 26:217–31.

Schein, E. H. 1970. *Organizational Psychology*. Englewood Cliffs, N.J.: Prentice-Hall.

Schulman, E. D. 1978. *Intervention in Human Services*. 2nd ed. St. Louis, Mo.: Mosby.

Shamasundar, C. 1999. "Understanding Empathy and Related Phenomena." *American Journal of Psychotherapy* 53:232–45.

Sharf, R. S. 2000. *Theories in Psychotherapy and Counseling*. 2nd ed. Australia: Brooks/Cole.

Sharlin, S. A., and M. Shamai. 2000. *From Distress to Hope: Therapeutic Intervention with Poor Unorganized Families*. New York: Haworth.

Sheafor, B. W., C. R. Horejsi, and G. A. Horejsi. 2000. *Techniques and Guidelines for Social Work Practice*. 5th ed. Boston: Allyn and Bacon.

Sheafor, B. W., and P. S. Landon. 1987. "Generalist Perspective." In A. Minahan et al., eds., *Encyclopedia of Social Work*, 18th ed., 660–69. Silver Spring, Md.: National Association of Social Workers.

Shimkunas, A. 1972. "Demand for Intimate Self-Disclosure and Pathological Verbalization in Schizophrenia." *Journal of Abnormal Psychology* 80:197–205.

Siporin, M. 1975. *Introduction to Social Work Practice*. New York: MacMillan.

Skinner, B. F. 1953. *Science and Human Behavior*. New York: Free Press.

Sloane, R. B., A. H. Cristol, M. C. Pepernik, and F. R. Stapels. 1970. "Role Preparation and Expectation of Improvement in Psychotherapy." *Journal of Nervous and Mental Disease* 150:18–26.

Sloane, R. B., F. R. Staples, A. H. Cristol, N. J. Yorkston, and K. Whipple. 1975. *Psychotherapy Versus Behavior Therapy*. Cambridge, Mass.: Harvard University Press.

Smith, G. B., and Schwebel, A. I. 1995. "Using a Cognitive-Behavioral Family Model in Conjunction with Systems and Behavioral Family Therapy Models. *The American Journal of Family Therapy* 23(3):203–13.

Smith, J. C. 2001. *Advances in ABC Relaxation: Applications and Inventories*. New York: Springer.

Solomon, B. B. 1976. *Black Empowerment: Social Work in Oppressed Communities*. New York: Columbia University Press.

Spanier, G. B. 1976. "Measuring Dyadic Adjustment: New Scales for Assessing the Quality of Marriage and Similar Dyads." *Journal of Marriage and the Family* 38:15–28.

Spiegal, J. P. 1981. "An Ecological Model with an Emphasis on Ethnic Families." In E. R. Tolson and W. J. Reid, eds., *Models of Family Treatment*. New York: Columbia University Press.

Spivack, G., J. J. Platt, and M. B. Shure. 1976. *The Problem-Solving Approach to Adjustment*. San Francisco: Jossey-Bass.

Staples, F. R., and R. B. Sloane. 1976. "Truax Factors, Speech Characteristics, and Therapeutic Outcome." *Journal of Nervous and Mental Disease* 163:135–40.

Staples, L. 1984. *Roots to Power: A Manual for Grassroots Organizing*. New York: Praeger.

Steiner, D., and M. Mark. 1985. "The Impact of a Community Action Group: An Illustration of the Potential of Time Series Analysis for the Study of Community Groups." *American Journal of Community Psychology* 13(1):13–30.

Stierlin, H. 1972. *Separating Parents and Adolescents*. New York: Quadrangle.

Strupp, H. H., and M. S. Wallach. 1965. "A Further Study of Psychiatrists' Responses in Quasi-Therapy Situations." *Behavioral Science* 10:113–34.

Strupp, H. H., R. E. Fox, and K. Lesser. 1969. *Patients View Their Psychotherapy*. Baltimore, Md.: The Johns Hopkins University Press.

Stuart, R. B. 1980. *Helping Couples Change: A Social Learning Approach to Marital Therapy*. New York: Guilford.

Sue, D. W. 1981. *Counseling the Culturally Different: Theory and Practice*. New York: Wiley.

Sutton, C., and M. Broken Nose. 1996. "American Indian Families: An Overview." In M. McGoldrick, J. Giordano, and J. K. Pierce, eds., *Ethnicity and Family Therapy*, 2nd ed., 31–44. New York: Guilford.

Tannenbaum, R. 1987. *Leadership and Organization*. New York: Garland.

Tepper, D. T. 1973. Communication of Counselor Empathy, Respect, and Genuineness Through Verbal and Non-Verbal Channels." *Dissertation Abstract International* 33 (9-A):4858.

Thomas, D. 1977. *Marital Communication and Decision-Making—Analysis, Assessment, and Change*. New York: Free Press.

Thomas, D. 1980. Research and Community Work. *Community Development Journal* 15(1):30–40.

Thomas, E. J. 1978. "Mousetraps, Developmental Research, and Social Work." *Social Service Review* 52:468–83.

Thomas, E. J. 1984. *Designing Interventions for the Helping Professions*. Newbury Park, Calif.: Sage.

Tolson, E. R. 1977. "Alleviating Marital Communication Problems." In W. J. Reid and L. Epstein, eds., *Task-Centered Practice*, 100–12. New York: Columbia University Press.

Tolson, E. R. 1988. *The Metamodel and Clinical Social Work*. New York: Columbia University Press.

Tolson, E. R. 2001. "The Task-Centered Model." In P. Lehmann and N. Coady, eds., *Theoretical Perspectives for Direct Social Work Practice: A Generalist-Eclectic Approach*, 203–223. New York: Springer.

Tolson, E. R., and L. Brown. 1981. "Client Drop-Out Rate and Students' Practice Skills in Task-Centered Casework." *Social Casework* 62:308–13.

Torczyner, J. 1983. "Dynamics of Strategic Relationships." In R. M. Kramer and H. Specht, eds., *Readings in Community Organization Practice*, 168–80. Englewood Cliffs, N.J.: Prentice-Hall.

Toseland, R. W., and M. Coppola. 1985. "A Task-Centered Approach to Group Work with Older Persons." In Anne E. Fortune, ed., *Task-Centered Practice with Families and Groups*, 101–14. New York: Springer.

Toseland, R. W., and R. F. Rivas. 1984. *An Introduction to Group Work Practice*. New York: Macmillan.

Toseland, R. W., and R. F. Rivas. 1987. "Working with Task Groups: The Middle Phase." In F. M. Cox, J. Erlich, J. Rothman, and J. Tropman, eds., *Strategies of Community Organization*, 4th ed., 114–42. Itasca, Ill.: Peacock.

Toseland, R. W., and R. F. Rivas. 2001. *An Introduction to Group Work Practice*. Boston: Allyn and Bacon.

Tovian, S. M. 1977. "Patient Experiences and Psychotherapy Outcome." Ph.D. dissertation, Northwestern University, Evanston, Illinois.

Truax, C. B. 1970. "Length of Therapist Response, Accurate Empathy, and Patient Improvement." *Journal of Clinical Psychology* 26:539–41.

Truax, C. B., and R. R. Carkhuff. 1967. *Toward Effective Counseling*. Chicago: Aldine.

Truax, C. B., J. Wittmer, and D. G. Wargo. 1971. "Effects of the Therapeutic Conditions of Accurate Empathy, Non-Possessive Warmth, and Genuineness in Hospitalized Mental Patients During Group Therapy." *Journal of Clinical Psychology* 27:137–42.

Tsui, P., and G. L. Schultz. 1985. Failure of Rapport: Why Psychotherapeutic Engagement Fails in the Treatment of Asian Clients." *American Journal of Orthopsychiatry* 55:561–69.

Verderber, K. S., and R. F. Verderber. 2001. *Inter-Act: Interpersonal Communication Concepts, Skills, and Contexts*, 9th ed. Belmont, Calif.: Wadsworth.

Viggiani, P., W. J. Reid, and C. Bailey-Dempsey. In press. "Social Worker-Teacher Collaboration in the Classroom: Help for Elementary Students." *Research on Social Work Practice*.

Vinter, R. D. 1963. "Analysis of Treatment Organizations." *Social Work* 8:3–15.

Vosler, N. R. 1990. "Assessing Family Access to Basic Resources: An Essential Component of Social Work Practice." *Social Work* 35:434–41.

Vuchinich, S., and J. Angelelli. 1995. "Family Interaction During Problem-Solving." In M. A. Fitzpatrick and A. L. Vangelisti, eds., *Explaining Family Interactions*, 177–205. Thousand Oaks, Calif.: Sage.

Walsh, F. 1998. *Strengthening Family Resilience*. New York: Guilford.

Walz, T., S. Sharma, and C. Birnbaum. 1990. *Gandhian Thought as Theory Base for Social Work*. Occasional Paper Series, No. 1. Urbana: University of Illinois at Urbana-Champaign, School of Social Work, Program for International and Cross-Cultural Social Welfare.

Warren, R. 1983a. "The Community Model." In R. M. Kramer and H. Specht, eds., *Readings in Community Organization Practice*, 3rd ed., 28–36. Englewood Cliffs, N.J.: Prentice-Hall.

Warren, R. 1983b. "The Good Community: What Would It Be?" In R. Warren and L. Lyon, eds., *New Perspectives on the American Community*, 393–401. Homewood, Ill.: Dorsey.

Watzlawick, P., J. H. Beavin, and D. D. Jackson. 1967. *Pragmatics of Human Communication*. New York: Norton.

Weaver, H., and J. Wodarski. 1996. "Social Work Practice with Latinos." In D. Harrison, B. Thyer, and J. Wodarski, eds., *Cultural Diversity and Social Work Practice*. Springfield, Ill.: Charles C. Thomas.

Weil, M. 1982. "Community Organization Curriculum Development in Services for Families and Children: Bridging the Micro-Macro Practice Gap." *Social Development Issues* 6(3):40–54.

Weil, M. 2000. "Social Work in the Social Environment: Integrated Practice—An Empowerment/Structural Approach." In P. Allen-Meares and C. Garvin, *The Handbook of Social Work Direct Practice*, 373–410. Thousand Oaks, Calif.: Sage.

Weiner, M. E. 1990. *Human Service Management: Analysis and Applications*. Belmont, Calif.: Wadsworth.

Weiss, R. L., G. R. Birchler, and J. Vincent. 1974. "Contractual Models for Negotiation Training in Marital Dyads." *Journal of Marriage and the Family* 36:321–30.

Westbrooks, K. L., and S. H. Starks. 2001. "Strengths Perspective Inherent in Cultural Empowerment: A Tool for Assessment with African American

Individuals and Families." In R. Fong and S. Furuto, eds., *Culturally Competent Practice*, 101–18. Boston: Allyn and Bacon.

Wheelan, S. A. 1994. *Group Processes: A Developmental Perspective.* Boston: Allyn and Bacon.

Wiener, M. F. 1978. *Therapist Disclosure: The Use of Self in Psychotherapy.* Boston: Butterworths.

Wodarski, J. S., M. Saffir, and M. Frazier. 1982. "Using Research to Evaluate the Effectiveness of Task-Centered Casework." *Journal of Applied Social Sciences* 7:70–82.

Wolk, J. L., I. F. Way, and M. Bleeke. 1982. "Human Service Management: The Art of Interpersonal Relationships." *Administration in Social Work* 6:1–10.

Wood, K. M., and L. L. Geismar. 1989. *Families at Risk.* New York: Human Sciences Press.

Wylie, R. C. 1979. *The Self-Concept.* Vol. 2: *Theory and Research on Selected Topics.* Lincoln: University of Nebraska Press.

Wylie, R. C. 1984. "Self-Concept." In R. J. Corsini, ed., *Encyclopedia of Psychology*, 282–85. New York: Wiley.

Yalom, Irvin. 1975. *The Theory and Practice of Group Psychotherapy.* 2nd ed. New York: Basic Books.

Zander, A. 1990. *Effective Social Action by Community Groups.* San Francisco: Jossey-Bass.

Zastrow, C. 1982. *Introduction to Social Welfare Institutions.* Homewood, Ill.: Dorsey.

Zuk, G. H. 1978. "Values and Family Therapy." *Psychotherapy: Theory, Research, and Practice* 15:48–55.

Zwick, R., and C. C. Attkisson. 1984. "The Use of Reception Checks in Client Pretherapy Orientation Research." *Journal of Clinical Psychology* 40:446–52.

AUTHOR INDEX

SUBJECT INDEX